HARDWARE/SOFTWARE
DESIGN OF DIGITAL SYSTEMS

HARDWARE/SOFTWARE DESIGN OF DIGITAL SYSTEMS

R. E. H. BYWATER
University of Surrey

Prentice/Hall PHI International

ENGLEWOOD CLIFFS, NEW JERSEY   LONDON   NEW DELHI

SINGAPORE   SYDNEY   TOKYO   TORONTO   WELLINGTON

Library of Congress Cataloging in Publication Data

BYWATER, R E H   1943–
    Hardware/software design of digital systems.

    Bibliography: p.
    Includes index.
    1. Electronic digital computers—Design and construction.
    I. Title.
    TK7888.3.B94   621.3819'58   80-14876
ISBN 0-13-383950-8

British Library Cataloguing in Publication Data

BYWATER, R E H
    Hardware/software design of digital systems.
    1. Computer architecture.
    I. Title.
    001.6'4044   QA76.9.A73
ISBN 0-13-383950-8

ISBN 0-13-383950-8

PRENTICE-HALL INTERNATIONAL, INC., *London*
PRENTICE-HALL OF AUSTRALIA PTY., LTD., *Sydney*
PRENTICE-HALL OF CANADA, LTD., *Toronto*
PRENTICE-HALL OF INDIA PRIVATE LIMITED, *New Delhi*
PRENTICE-HALL OF JAPAN, INC., *Tokyo*
PRENTICE-HALL OF SOUTHEAST ASIA PTE., LTD., *Singapore*
PRENTICE-HALL, INC., *Englewood Cliffs, New Jersey*
WHITEHALL BOOKS LIMITED, *Wellington, New Zealand*

Printed in the United States of America

81 82 83 84 85 5 4 3 2 1

To Valerie, David and Kay

CONTENTS

PREFACE

This book has been written as a second-level text on computer engineering. It is designed for students who already possess some elementary knowledge of digital computers and some familiarity with computer programming. It has also been prepared with practising digital system engineers in mind and provides a reference for design approaches.

Although partitioned into the major sub-system groups found in a normal computer, the techniques described are quite general—referring equally well to the logical design of most digital equipment. The now legion applications of the microprocessor have brought computer-like structures, techniques and programming to a wide variety of low-cost applications not obviously calling for the use of a computer. These include digital instruments, toys, wristwatches and a host of other, frequently consumer, products.

It is assumed that the reader is familiar with electronic logic design and is, at least, mindful of the approaches to writing a computer program. The book therefore does not dwell on all the mapping, tabular and sequential logic-design procedures, nor does it provide a primer in any language. However references are given to back-up material at the end of each chapter.

Chapter 1 briefly explores the historical background to digital computing and illustrates the exponential-like growth of computer power, complexity and applications. It shows how the computer has grown from near non-existence in the 1940s to a multibillion dollar industry. The digital computer is also shown against a general background of computing including its less prominent relations, the analog and hybrid computers. Finally the technological side of computers is introduced to illustrate some of the elementary building blocks that are used and the drawing standards that appear in later chapters.

Most of us are, by now, familiar with the essentially binary nature of digital computers. However, many extensions to binary are normally in evidence in order to achieve more compact, convenient representations of values or to create negative, as well as positive, quantities. Chapter 2 initially treats number systems in terms of arbitrarily chosen radices (bases) but goes on to examine the more popular methods and techniques in common use.

Processors are treated, in Chapter 3, from a hierarchical viewpoint—making little early distinction between hardware and software forms. This concept is maintained through to hardware processor architecture—the major theme of this chapter. By adhering to hierarchy as the important aspect, it has been found quite easy to show the connections and relationships between software, firmware, registers, register-transfer languages and binary logic.

Until the early 1970s, the provision of memory adequately distinguished the digital computer from any other "calculating" device. Memory still forms the one resource around which all processing revolves, but now it is available so very compactly, conveniently and at low cost in semiconductor forms that it is found in many noncomputer products as well. Chapter 4 examines a number of memories, starting with those fabricated from gates (and representing the fastest available), through to the various slow, but capacious, electromechanical forms. In addition, read-only and non-addressed memories are described, together with their applications.

Although some digital applications make little apparent use of fast arithmetic as such and therefore don't demand their high arithmetic speeds or exotic functions be provided, there are many that do. Also, many so-called "non-numerical" applications, such as pattern recognition, word processing, and file management are, in fact, implemented by numerical techniques. They may use fast arithmetic to gain rapid access to non-numerical records, or to supply complex address information for file retrieval. "Number crunching" is still used, but is often very disguised. Chapter 5 outlines the various arithmetic techniques currently used in micros, minis and mainframe computers. Attention is focused on methods used in commercial machines and therefore ones complement, end-around-carry and negabinary methods, to mention but a few, are given only scant reference. Particular emphasis is laid on parallel arithmetic, speed-up methods and floating point. This reflects how falling hardware costs have made complex, high-performance arithmetic possible at a reasonable cost.

Chapter 6 is concerned with "tying the ends together". After the "grand design" of processors, data flow logic and all the other "broad-bush" processor activities, the timing and control of these functions is described. This is an area which frequently contains "irregular" logic—devoid of pattern and symmetry. It is the area in which most design errors are made in terms of logic, electronics and time tolerancing. This chapter looks at several popular approaches to design both for computers and more generalized digital systems.

Although students come into early contact with many computer peripherial devices such as Teletypes, visual-display units (VDUs) and the like, there is usually only a vague notion of how they are connected to the computer. Chapter 7 shows how this interfacing is done, how the computer distinguishes between the devices and how it arbitrates between several such devices all demanding service at the same time.

In many respects, microcomputers are similar to traditional machines. However, technological differences exist, the application areas are usually dissimilar and the designer, be he hardware or software orientated, finds constraints which are unique to the microcomputer. Chapter 8 is devoted solely to this topic, although the reader is urged to note similarities, as well as differences, between microcomputers and others, from the design view-point.

For most computers, software and firmware are usually far more expensive than the hardware. The investment in development time, maintenance and enhancement can be enormous. Chapter 9 looks briefly at the general structure of the programs and routines that are needed to convert the computer hardware into a usable system. It considers the users, software writers and hardware designers' points of view and shows how the complex software structure, as we know it today, has evolved. The hardware material from previous chapters is linked through to the user requirements to produce an edifice of facilities, involving a mix of technology, firmware and software techniques. Specifically, assembly and machine-independent languages are descibed, together with methods for translating programs written in these languages into machine-executable form. In addition, an outline is given of simple operating systems which are necessary for the overall control of computer activites. The chapter ends with a consideration of how the hardware/software edifice will evolve as a consequence of expected technological and other improvements.

Chapter 10 attempts to bring together the many design techniques described earlier in the book. It is impossible to invoke them all, but it is hoped that the use of a real design example will, at least, bring reality and insight to the total design process.

Hardware/Software Design of Digital Systems, having been written as a course text, develops ideas from simple concepts through to detailed design. There is therefore some dependence on understanding early chapters in order to appreciate the systems described in later ones. However, all chapters have cross references and may be read in isolation.

The following are the main points of dependence:

Chapter 5   depends on Chapter 2.

Chapter 6   depends on Chapter 3 for an appreciation of the problems in processor design.

Chapter 7   depends on Chapter 3 for the processor end of the peripheral device-to-computer interface.

Chapter 8   depends on most of the preceding chapters in order that it be read to greatest advantage.

Chapter 9   requires little in-depth knowledge of the content of any preceding chapters but a slight familiarity with them would certainly help.

Chapter 10 depends on a knowledge of the material of most of the previous chapters for the full implications of its content to be understood.

I would like to take this opportunity to thank Dr R. G. Bennetts, Dr M. G. Hartley, Mr Giles Wright and Mr Alan Whittle for their valuable comments and suggestions, Professor W. F. Lovering for initiating the project and Professor J. D. E. Beynon and the late Professor D. R. Chick for their help and facilities. I am also indebted to Dr F. G. A. Coupe for his assistance with the preparation and proofreading of Chapter 10.

In particular, I would like to thank my wife, Valerie, for her constant support and encouragement.

R. E. H. BYWATER

Haslemere, Surrey, England

HARDWARE/SOFTWARE
DESIGN OF DIGITAL SYSTEMS

1 INTRODUCTION

This introductory chapter is intended to indicate the scope of this book and present the *basic concepts* in close order before they are enlarged in succeeding chapters. Paramount amongst these concepts is that of a computing hierarchy, i.e. that the computer is a multilevel system ranging from individual components, transistors, etc. at the lowest level to programs, jobs and operating systems at the highest level. In this chapter *concepts of detail* such as memory, processing and technology are also briefly explored so that, by the time later, more detailed chapters are read, the aims of the text as a whole are understood.

Most of the book is concerned with systems, taken from the hardware viewpoint. However, it is quite impossible to consider hardware in isolation and frequent references are therefore made to computer programs, software and algorithms. Without these, the "customer" end of the business, the reasons for designing hardware in the manners described would be completely lost.

Hardware/Software Design of Digital Systems explores the systems architecture of all the major types of digital computer—and a number of more general digital structures as well. Most of the concepts and designs described and analyzed are applicable to all digital systems. Many have close relationships with programming techniques as well.

1.1 HISTORY

Computers process information. There are several major types which go about the job in different ways. In simple terms, the range of computers can be shown by a spectrum (Fig. 1.1), with digital computers at one end and analog computers (Scott, 1970) at the other.

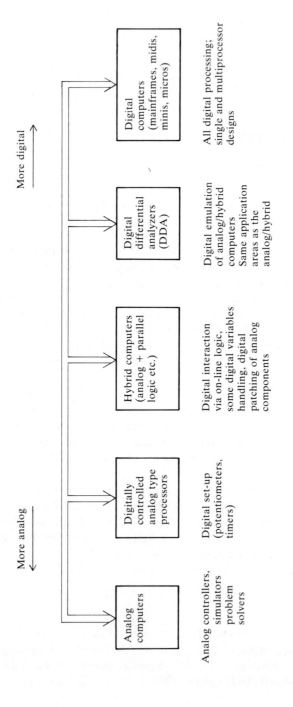

Fig. 1.1. Simplistic spectrum of computer processing from analog to digital.

Digital computers are presented with information—and process it—in discrete form; that is, variables can be represented by a limited set of codes, each one of which stands for a precise value. If the value to be represented is not exactly one of those offered in the computer's list, the nearest one must be used. This means that every variable is misquoted by some amount; this is known as the round-off error (Salazar, 1977). By the use of a sufficiently high number of codes in the digital computer's repertoire, the error can be made as small as desired. It cannot be eliminated (Chapter 2).

On the other hand, the analog computer substitutes some electrical variable, usually voltage, to represent a physical variable, i.e. it makes an electrical "analog" of the quantity. As voltage is, for all practical purposes, continuous (as are most real-life variables), no round-off problem exists. However, the processing of this voltage analog is fraught with sources of error and, generally, the final accuracy of results produced by an analog computer is far inferior to those of the digital computer.

Another fundamental difference between these two extreme members of the computing spectrum is that not only are variable amplitudes discrete in the digital computer but so is their representation on the time axis (Fig. 1.2). This can lead to further errors when time-dependent processing is carried out (so called "sampled systems"—Connors, 1972). Again, the analog computer does not suffer from this shortcoming, although its own built-in weaknesses will more than offset this advantage. The reader is advised to refer to Bekey and Karplus (1968) and Mandl (1967) for a fuller treatment of analog computers.

Alternatives which attempt to bring together the advantages of the analog and digital computer are the *hybrid computer* (Bekey and Karplus, 1968) and the *digital differential analyzer* (Sizer, 1968; Bywater, 1973; Wilkins, 1970).

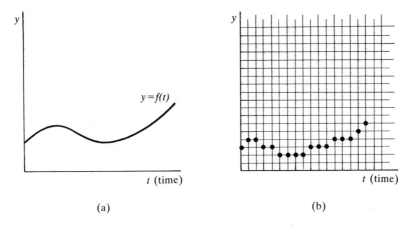

(a)   (b)

Fig. 1.2 (a) A continuous (analog) wave form; (b) the same waveform subject to time and amplitude quantization.

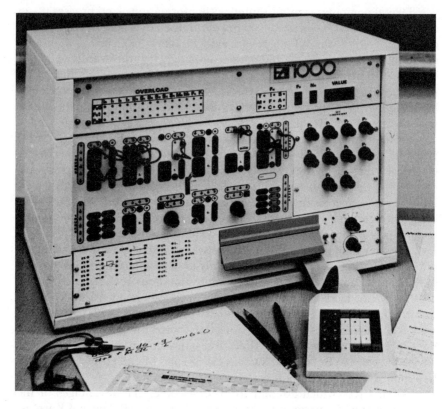

A small desktop analog computer for solving differential equations and simulating simple physical systems. (Courtesy Electronics Associates Inc., West Long Branch, New Jersey).

The hybrid computer is essentially an analog computer with additional parallel logic and other digital facilities. As with the analog, it represents each part of the problem it is solving with a separate piece of electronics—an integrator or multiplier or function generator. All these units work in parallel and continuously and the solution is obtained virtually instantaneously. The addition of digital components gives the machine flexibility by giving it the ability to make decisions as solutions evolve. However, most of these machines, which are normally used for physical system simulation, are very complex, expensive and subject to considerable maintenance overheads. They are nothing like as widely used as the admittedly slower digital computer.

The digital differential analyzer has received a limited amount of attention since the middle 1950s—virtually as long as the digital computer. A modern DDA attempts to overcome the slow performance of the digital computer (when solving simulation and control problems) by using a multiplicity of special purpose computing elements, all working in parallel. In other words, it is a digitized version of the parallel analog computer, having digital integrators, multipliers etc. If it were not for the limited number of applications, which center largely on plant control, simulation and navigation, it might be a more important member of the "processing" family.

Since time unrecorded, man has used his fingers and sticks to indicate quantities, to keep records of property and to do simple arithmetic. This is a form of digital computing, since the numbers are discrete. The first mechanical calculating device in widespread use was the Abacus. Its origins also lie in prehistory and it is still used widely in some Oriental countries.

The earliest proposals for mechanical calculators, of the type that might be recognized today, date from the seventeenth century and are generally attributed to Leibniz and Pascal. Charles Babbage was particularly interested in the use of mechanical calculators to replace human labor in the preparation of logarithmic and trigonometric tables, and in the early 1820s made a proposal for a so-called "difference engine" (Morrison and Morrison, 1961). He followed this with a proposal for an "analytical engine" in the 1830s, which used Jacquard cards. These semi-stiff cards were joined together to form a rather cumbersome version of modern paper tape. They contained, in the form of punched holes, data (the numbers on which the engine was to operate) and instructions (the operations to be carried out on the data). Both engines executed instructions in a sequence like the modern computer, but neither could alter the order of execution of instructions, and neither was completed!

An *electromechanical* (relay) version of the Babbage analytical engine was proposed by Aiken (1965) of Harvard University in 1937. It was completed in 1944 and was known as MARK 1. Relays, like electronic logic, can be given the ability to make logical decisions, to perform binary arithmetic and to store information in binary. Like the Babbage engines, MARK 1 was incapable of altering the order of execution of the instructions presented to it—"branching", as we know it.

The first *thermionic* computer was ENIAC, but it was really only another version of the original fixed-sequence machine. In England, the PILOT ACE and English Electric DEUCE machines were being developed but appeared somewhat later.

Around 1945, John von Neumann made proposals for a digital computer structure which still holds sway today. His proposals included the storage of instructions in the computer rather than on cards or paper tape and the concepts of having a machine consisting of:

1. processor;
2. memory;
3. control and timing unit;
4. input/output media.

The first commercial machine, which incorporated these concepts and which is largely attributable to Eckert and Mauchly, was UNIVAC 1. It appeared commercially from 1951 onwards (Chapter 3).

Amongst the many problems encountered with early computers was the provision of more than a trivial amount of memory (McDermott, 1976). Various schemes were tried with varying degrees of success. F. C. Williams in the UK developed a system based on charge storage on a CRT screen. This must have been one of the earliest dynamic memories—the charge gradually leaked away and had to be replenished by successive scans of the tube. In 1953, the first ferrite core memory appeared (Chapter 4). It was developed at MIT and had, at that time, the advantage of a speed in keeping with the requirements of the computer's arithmetic unit for the retrieval and depositing of numbers. In addition, because it holds information in the form of magnetization induced in a magnetic material, no electrical power is required to retain the information, once recorded. This kind of memory is known as "non-volatile". Ferrite memories are still in use today in a few specialized applications, such as those requiring resistance to radiation hazards. However, semiconductor memories, which gave the promise of cheap mass storage, did not appear until the late 1960s.

The transistor was invented in 1948. This was a point-contact device and was quickly superseded by the junction transistor in the 1950s. The first transistor computers began to appear in the 1950s and showed promise of both better performance and, more important, far greater reliability than vacuum tubes. Solid-state physics and semiconductor fabrication techniques led, via epitaxy and the planar process, to the ability to manufacture complete circuits of transistors, diodes, resistors and even small capacitors on a single wafer of silicon. Such devices are known as integrated circuits and first appeared, in commercial form, in the early 1960s. Typical commercial bipolar units had two gates on a 1.25 mm (0.05 in) square die. The density rose above 30 gates by 1966 and above 500 by 1971.

Metal-oxide semiconductor (MOS) logic circuits came into prominence in the middle 1960s, offering high gate densities, low power, fewer manufacturing procedures but slower operation and interfacing difficulties. However, MOS technology was the first to realize an integrated circuit so complex that a complete computer processor could be formed on it. This is called a microprocessor and appeared in 1971 in limited quantities. Since then, microprocessor and support components, such as memory chips, have risen in complexity to over 60 000 gates on a 6 mm (0.25 in) square chip and contain MOS gates incurring only 2 ns delay. Some support components, particularly memory, having a more regular structure, waste less chip area and can achieve over 10^6 active components per square inch. The relative costs of hardware based on such developments is difficult to gauge, but allowing for inflation, the cost per unit of storage is about \$8 per decimal digit stored using valves and less than $\frac{1}{2}$ cent using integrated circuits. This is the component cost (only) in both cases.

A consequence of greater computing power and falling hardware costs has been a curious double turnabout since the early days of MARK 1 and ENIAC. Those machines used large numbers of concurrently operating (parallel) arithmetic elements, under the control of a single timing mechanism, to obtain a reasonable calculating speed. The introduction of electronics around 1950 made serial structures, with their smaller number of components, much more attractive. In any case, there was such an increase in speed derived from the use of vacuum tubes, instead of electromechanical relays, that it was, at the time, considered unlikely that the power offered by parallel electronic systems was ever going to be required. Serial calculation brings down the number of devices very profoundly with a consequent increase in reliability—a commodity in very short supply with the use of vacuum tubes and relays.

The demand for greater computing power has continued, unabated, for 30 years, and the use of transistors and integrated circuits has increased reliability to the point whereby complex parallel structures, using vast numbers of devices, are quite practical. We now enjoy both parallelism and distributed computing using many processors, each of which has one or more parallel arithmetic units, each of which handles large quantities of data concurrently. Each processor may be sited at the place it is needed rather than just next door to the other processor in the network. As an example of this, a local processor could be placed in each bank and used for the preparation and formatting of transactions and records, data reduction, etc. A central installation for the group of banks, possibly consisting of more than one large machine, would then form a focus of activity to which all the satellite processors could communicate. This "networking" has several advantages, one of which is that the failure of one or more processors need not lead to total system shutdown. It need only mean a reduction of services (response, facilities) whilst repairs are being carried out. This resistance to catastrophic failure results in what is known as "graceful degradation".

Networks also offer the possibility of cross checking processing through the use of several processors in voting or other situations in which either the number of processors in agreement or even the track record of good processing of individual processors is used as a measure of the validity of computing carried out. Each processor will carry out the same task and results will be compared. This means a degree of redundancy has been introduced, as clearly more processing could be completed if each processor were given a separate task. However, the increased confidence obtained in the results produced is often considered worth the cost.

Applications for modern digital systems are almost without limit. However, certain types of computer architecture and technology are more suitable and cost effective for some applications than others.

Large machines (mainframes), possibly networked, are applied to large-scale operations, often involving large amounts of processing (number crunching) for scientific applications or the handling of vast numbers of transactions. Examples of the latter are public utilities and accounting, airline reservations, telephone exchanges, image processing, public records, national security, data banks and management information systems or the keeping of huge records (financial transactions, banking, inventory, equipment and component movements, logistics).

Medium-size machines, "midi" and "mini" computers, have far more processing power than even the most powerful early machines, so that their names can be somewhat misleading. Even mini computers can handle upward of a dozen simultaneous users, operate at speeds of several million arithmetic instructions per second and can handle records of more than 10^9 decimal digits or letters by direct access. However, they are sufficiently compact and competitively priced that individual medium-size companies can afford them and house them in ordinary premises without (necessarily) needing special clean-rooms or air conditioning, etc. They can be used for any applications from scientific computing to data base (management information) systems to highly sophisticated process controllers, manufacturing process controllers and monitors. They can be operated in distributed, parallel or networked form and can communicate with other digital equipment such as microcomputers, other minis or centralized mainframes. They can communicate via telephone lines, private communications channels or microwave links. In addition, they can support a wide variety of peripheral devices from teletypes to high-speed printers and VDUs to mass-storage media.

Microcomputers are operationally characterized by being of low (hardware) cost, often simple to use, of low power but quite flexible in operation. They are usually much less powerful than minicomputers, can often support only one user at a time and are frequently configured so that they perform only one basic function, e.g. gasoline station pump monitoring. As these applications use fixed programs (software), retention of the instructions needed to carry out their tasks is easily provided in a memory form whose contents are fixed at manufacture. Such memories, unlike those which can be written to, are easily manufactured in a non-volatile form. This is the so-called read-only memory or ROM. Use of ROM can eliminate the cost of peripheral memories to hold programs.

Micros, not surprisingly, find applications in a wide variety of areas from calculators, digital watches, TV games, process monitoring (e.g. telephone exchanges), point-of-sale terminals, traffic-signal control, certain areas of signal processing and conditioning, word processing and as slave processors to mini and mainframe computers.

1.2 PROCESSING

Processing is the work carried out in a computer. The computer is basically a system which can perform a number of operations in a sequential manner. Even so-called parallel machines can be decomposed into a collection of units each one of which works, internally, sequentially. Parallel machines are merely those having a number of units which operate concurrently.

The task carried out by a computer is known as a job and, initially, will almost certainly be defined in a way which is not suitable for direct entry to the machine. The task, as originally defined, will use terms and require facilities which are at much higher level than the computer—which can only accept a string of suitably coded instructions. The original task will be a statement in plain language (English) or expressed in algebraic or suchlike notation. The first action is upon the user of the computer and is to redefine the task into an ordered set of procedures, which are executable by the computer. This form is known as an *algorithm*.

In order to reduce the human labor involved and to reduce the number of different occasions that such "translation" has to occur, high-level languages such ALGOL, FORTRAN, COBOL and PL/1 have been developed. They allow procedures or algorithms to be presented to the computer in a quasi-English, quasi-mathematical form. Such languages define an unambiguous protocol, semantics and syntax between the user and the machine, so that each part of the algorithm can be translated into the correct machine-executable form.

A program known as a *compiler*, and itself written in machine-executable code, possibly by the manufacturers of the computer, accepts the user's job and compiles it into machine code. In effect, it treats the user's program as if it were data to the compiler. The data output of the compiler is the machine code. An important property of high-level languages is their "machine independence". That is, a program, once written in FORTRAN, can be compiled and run on any computer, provided a FORTRAN compiler is available for the computer in question. (This statement needs some qualification because some compilers have a restricted set of facilities and sometimes the hardware they are written for has limited capabilities.) Clearly, the compiler will be particular to a certain computer, as it will have been written in that machine's language. The machine language calls on the unique patterns of binary 0s and 1s which define each instruction to be obeyed by the computer's hardware.

Most computers also have a language written for them which is intermediate between a high-level one and machine code. It is *machine dependent* but uses mnemonics (in the form of easily remembered letter groups such as JMP for JUMP to transfer control) and labels rather than absolute memory addresses. This takes much of the drudgery out of programming at the machine level, makes relocation possible, editing of programs easy and is often the "target" to which high-level languages are compiled rather than straight machine code. This permits relocation (see p.352) and other properties which give flexibility to be retained until the last moment. Such a language is known as an *assembly language*, so called because the machine-code version is assembled from the mnemonics (see p.346) and macros (see p.361) contained in the assembly program. Roughly speaking, there is a one-to-one correspondence between each assembly-language statement and each one of the machine-code instructions in the computer's "menu".

At this point, a hierarchy of processing is beginning to emerge, starting at the top with the user and ending at the machine level (Anon., 1974). We can continue this process into the computer itself, by noting that each machine instruction is executed by a sequence of *micro-instructions* of a very elementary nature. Each micro-instruction in the *microprogram* may be no more complex than moving data from one part of the computer to another or adding two numbers together. The microprogram is only a set of tasks which, if carried out in the right order, will correctly interpret and execute the instructions. In its simplest form, the microprogram consists of a set of sequences, one for each instruction in the machine-code "menu".

The microprogram, as it clearly defines the hardware by defining its instruction repertoire, is normally fixed. It is either stored as a pattern of 1s and 0s in an inviolable memory (ROM) in the processor or as a unique set of (hard-wired) interconnections. If the former, alteration of the instruction set *can* be made possible by simply altering the pattern of bits in the ROM. This allows *emulation* of one processor by another, that is, one processor can have the same instruction set as another and yet contain different hardware. Such a processor is known as *microprogrammable* (Chu, 1972).

A microprogram written to define the "appearance" of a machine to the outside world is known as its *firmware*. This is a term suggesting that this information is intermediate between the information implicit in the fixed-for-all-time hardware of the processor and the readily altered software which can be stored in alterable memories (RAM).

Finally, each register, adder and logic network in the processor is fabricated from gates, each of which is a collection of transistors and other electronics. A slightly fanciful hierarchy starting from the user and ending with the electronics of a digital system is shown in Fig. 1.3.

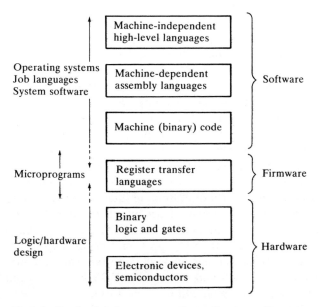

Fig 1.3 Simple digital computer software/hardware hierarchy.

1.3 CONCEPTS OF INSTRUCTIONS

Having seen that an initial task must be redefined in algorithmic or sequence form, we must now consider what steps this involves and to what level this redefinition must be taken.

A very simple example of a task might be to ask a computer to find the square root of a quantity (X). Not only do no computers have hardware for evaluating a square root but the symbol is not even defined in 1s and 0s for entry to a computer. A typical high-level language way to represent this task would be SQRT(X), the "SQRT" standing for square root. The use of parentheses serves the dual purpose of separating the variable from the function and indicating that "SQRT" is a function rather than say, the name of a variable (like X). The compiler would recognize this function and proceed to substitute a set of machine-executable instructions for the function. (These instructions would have been implanted by the compiler writer into the compiler and would be based on a suitable algorithm for evaluating a square root.) A simple algorithm is Newton's, based upon the formula

$$x_{n+1} = \tfrac{1}{2}\left(x_n + \frac{X}{x_n}\right),$$

where x_n is the guess at iteration n. This merely requires repeated application of the formula to converge (home in) on the root. It only demands add, subtract, multiply, and divide instructions, which are all normally offered in the computer's instruction repertoire (machine-code set). Such an algorithm would work for all positive numbers presented to it, converge rapidly on the answer to make as little work for the processor as possible and only demand an initial "guesstimate" x_0 of the root to get started. The machine code output from the compiler, which substitutes for the initial function, is a series of elementary machine-code instructions.

There are one or two important points to note about the resulting machine-code program. Apart from arithmetic operations, there must be an instruction which will have to determine when the estimate achieved at any time is "good enough". The process is a converging one and does not guarantee to find the exact root. Often the square root of a number cannot be expressed to a finite number of binary bits. Therefore, the program must be "put out of its misery" sometime. For this particular program, to note that the *change* of estimate has fallen below some specified value will be quite suitable. This is decision making and is an important concept, introduced by von Neumann in the 1940s and first used in EDVAC. The second point is that the same sequence (evaluation of the formula) is carried out many times—and not necessarily a fixed number for all X. To be able to store this program in the computer's memory rather than to have to supply the sequence of instructions from outside the machine, greatly speeds up processing and relieves the burden on input devices. This is known as the *stored program concept*. Not only is the program normally stored in the computer (in machine code), the memory form is often unalterable once initially loaded. This is a frequent practice in microcomputer systems, for the need to store programs externally to the machine in, say, expensive magnetic memories, is eliminated. A typical example is to be found in a simple calculator, which would have a fixed program to correctly interpret the meaning of each key pressed and to initiate a (fixed) program sequence for that key. There is never any need to reprogram the calculator, as the meaning of each key is fixed for all time. However, many micros and all other computers have at least some read/write memory so they can be used for many different and unrelated tasks, as the user wishes.

At this point it will be useful to look at the "menu" of instructions made available in the different styles of computers and to compare them with the functions made available in the various languages, calculations and the like. At the lowest level, a typical microcomputer would have the instruction menu shown in Table 1.1.

Minicomputers offer all the above together with more exotic addressing facilities which make data retrieval and handling much easier. They also have, in most cases, built-in fast multipliers/dividers. Binary-coded decimal

	Machine-code instruction	Remarks
Arithmetic	Add	
	Subract	Not all micros offer this
	Increment/decrement	
	Clear accumulator	Not all micros offer this
	Multiply/divide	Only the big 16-bit micros
	Floating point	None offer this on the microprocessor chip
	Binary-coded decimal	Some 8-bit and most 16-bit units (but see multiply/divide)
	Compare (register with accumulator)	
Logical	AND, OR,	Most offer a selection
	NOT, EX-OR	Most—but only a 1-place
	Shift/rotate	shift per execution of the instruction
Transfer control	Branch, jump, subroutine call	Conditional and unconditional made available (sometimes a nesting limit is imposed on subroutines)

Table 1.1

(BCD) and floating-point arithmetic (add, subract, multiply and divide) are sometimes "bolt-on" hardware extras, sometimes standard items.

Mainframe machines have all the above facilities as standard. However, note that instructions more complex than multiply/divide are not generally offered. Therefore, software must be used to evaluate roots, trigonometric functions and algebraic expressions. A calculator having such functions on its keypad has the functions stored as procedures in fixed memory, the procedures being based on the machine-code set. It is therefore not surprising that trigonometric and other functions can take between 0.1 and 2 s to evaluate on a low-cost calculator. In a minicomputer, such calculations take from hundreds to tens of thousands of microseconds (μs).

1.4 FUNCTIONAL PARTS OF A DIGITAL COMPUTER (Mano, 1976)

John von Neumann introduced the concept of a digital computer based on five distinct parts: input and output devices, a processor, memory and timing/control. This concept has survived for over 30 years and greatly influences most current computer architecture.

Input and output can handle both programs (instructions) and operands (data). Similarly, memory can hold (store) both instructions and data. This has three major benefits:

1. If two memories were used, one for data (operands) and one for instructions, the size of each would have to be defined. Some applications require considerable data memory, e.g. transactions, archives, message switching, utilities; whereas others require relatively little in comparison with instruction storage, e.g. large scientific and control problems. Use of a single memory means that the user can aportion memory space as he wishes.

2. A single memory reduces the number of data paths (highways and buses) needed to route data from one part of the computer to another. There is a hardware and cost saving.

3. Instructions can become the data for other instructions and be modified by them—another von Neumann concept. The result is that the same instruction can be used for a slightly different purpose each time it is used (as an instruction). Between times, it may have its address or modifier bits altered so that, for instance, it points to a different element in an array or executes a subtly different task. By having instructions and data occupying a single memory space, it is simple to specify the address of an instruction as if it were the operand for another instruction. It then becomes modified (*instruction modification*).

For most computers, memory forms the "focus" of activity and the input and output ports and the processor all refer to it as an exchange for information.

1.5 TECHNOLOGY

Relays, valves, transistors and even fluidic devices, because of the ease with which two states (logic 0 and 1) can be defined, can be used as logic devices. In all cases, the causal sequence of input – delay – output response is applicable. However, the speed of response of the various technologies spans several orders of magnitude. The relays used in early computers could be rarely activated in much less than 10^{-2} s, and valves could not switch in much less than about 2×10^{-7} s, but modern integrated transistor logic gates can change state in as little as 0.1–0.2 ns. More commonly, gates with propagation delays between 1 and 10 ns are used.

Some of the functions performed by a computer, such as arithmetic, decision making and logical operations, are essentially combinational. That is, the result of such an operation is not a function of any previous calculations and can therefore, theoretically, be implemented in combinational logic. In fact, even with the low hardware costs enjoyed today, only addition and subtraction are normally implemented fully combinationally; multiplication sometimes is—division very rarely. For the more complex operations, those aspects which are repetitive are committed to the time domain so that the same logic can be reused in an iterative process. This greatly reduces the logic requirements but naturally increases the execution time. The time domain can either be invoked by hardware loops (to reuse logic) or by software.

Some computer functions are clearly sequential, i.e. by nature time dependent. Such functions are performed by flip-flops (to hold data and status information) or by more general logic, which has feedback connections from gate outputs to inputs. Any form of processing which has an element of sequence about it, including the allocation of time to activities, arranging that microprogram steps are carried out in the right order, etc., is sequential. There are well-documented design and minimization procedures and the reader is recommended to refer to these if he is not already familiar with such techniques (Marcus, 1975).

1.6 GATING AND LOGIC SYSTEMS (Boole, 1954; Nagle, 1975; Marcus, 1975)

The advantages of the use of two-state (binary) operation in mechanized computation are well known. A large number of devices, both electrical and non-electrical, have two well-defined states which can be identified and associated with a logical 1 and 0. Relays have energized and non-energized states; vacuum tubes and transistors have cut-off (non-conduction) and saturation. The assignment of logic states to physical states is quite arbitrary, so that logic 0 can mean cut-off and logic 1 saturation, or vice versa. For arithmetic assignments, the same arbitrariness exists so that either cut-off or saturation can mean value 1. However, very frequently, logic 1 and binary 1 correspond to the same physical state. In order that these assignments do not cause confusion to the logic designer (or anybody else who has to understand his drawings), a system of logic conventions is widely used, which reflects the logic designer's intentions. This is preferable to the slavish use of the same symbols to represent the same physical device.

The convention adopted here is that of the American Standards Association (ASA-MIL). The idea is to use a gate symbol according to function, say

AND or OR. Thus, although De Morgan's Laws (Marcus, 1975) show a duality between AND and OR functions such that AND gates can perform the OR function (and vice versa), the logic symbol reflects the *use* to which the designer intends to put the gate. This makes the "reading" of logic much easier. The only non-arbitrary attributes of a gate are the voltages applied to it and derived from its outputs. After that, the relationships between voltages and logic states and binary values is not fixed. A short list of devices is shown in Fig. 1.4.

In order to use logic gates to build subsystems, some knowledge of their operation is required together with an awareness of the variety of complex-function integrated-circuits available (Mano, 1979).

Of the operating characteristics other than speed, probably the noise margin of a gate is most important. A gate input has only to discriminate between a logic 0 and 1, i.e. between two voltages. An ideal gate would be able to make this discrimination "fine" without limitation, so that, for instance, if logic 0 and 1 were defined as 0 V and 5 V respectively, then any input to the gate below/above 2.5 V would be correctly interpreted as logic 0/1. This is an unreasonable expectation as it would require the gate to have an infinite gain. A band of uncertainty must exist in which correct discrimination cannot be guaranteed or a correct output obtained. For transistor–transistor logic (TTL) this band lies between about 0.8 V and 2.0 V. In order that TTL misses this band—with some to spare—the guaranteed gate output voltages have to be outside 0.8–2.0 V. The additional margin can be eroded by operating temperature, noise voltages induced on interconnections and variations in gate supply voltage. The extra band is called the gate *noise margin* and does not have to be the same for both logic levels. However, it generally is. For TTL, the worst-case loadings and other conditions should leave noise margins of 0.4 V in both logic levels, that is, the guaranteed minimum/maximum gate output voltages are 2.4 V/0.4 V for logic 1/0. For most logic families, the noise margin tends to be very much the same, gauged as a percentage of the logic swing. For TTL this is 0.4/2.0=20%. So families with smaller logic swings tend to have smaller noise margins, e.g. emitter-coupled logic (ECL) has typical margins of about 150 mV for an 800 mV logic swing.

Modern semiconductor technology has made a wide variety of very useful and often complex logic functions available on single chips. The quintessence of this is the microprocessor. However, even on a smaller scale, logic subsystems can be fabricated with relatively few packages and, mercifully, often with little knowledge, on the user's part, of the internal structure and electronics of the devices. It must be clear from this that the *external* specification of the chip is of paramount importance—that it should be rigorously and unambiguously defined.

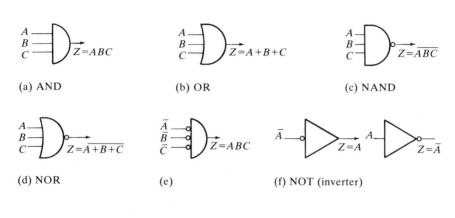

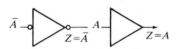

(a) AND

(b) OR

(c) NAND

(d) NOR

(e)

(f) NOT (inverter)

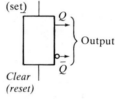

(g) Buffer (non-inverting amplifier)

(h) S–R flip-flop

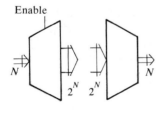

(i) Data flip-flop (D type)
(edge-triggered)

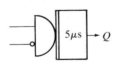

(j) Decoder/encoder

(k) Monostable with positive
and negative triggering

Fig. 1.4 Selection of logic symbols used in this text (based on the ASA MIL standard).

Small-scale integrated (SSI) chips offered in the early 1960s consisted of only 1 or 2 gates per package. The term SSI is still used for such devices although the gate count can be up to 10 or 20. Typical functions offered are all varieties of simple gates, simple flip-flops and counter/divider functions, bus drivers, monostables, etc.

Medium-scale integrated (MSI) circuits started to appear around 1967 and can provide complete subsystem functions on a single die. The gate count is higher but the most important point is the aim of providing whole functions such as RAM, ROM, multibit counters, register files, arithmetic/logic units (ALU), etc. (see Chapters 4, 5). Many of the devices are designed so they may be joined to make longer words, e.g. 4-bit units joined to form 8-, 12-, 16-bit systems.

(Very) large-scale integrated [(V)LSI] circuits appeared around 1970 and consisted largely of microprocessors and their support chips such as memory, input/output interfaces, system controllers and the like. However, other chips appeared which help considerably with general logic design, such as programmable logic arrays (PLA) and uncommitted logic arrays (ULA). A PLA is a synthesis of the classical multi-output AND–OR construct of Quine and McCluskey.

By the use of two-connection matrices, both the intermediate products and the output assignments can be made by the user. Invertor gates at the inputs and outputs further generalize the device. ULAs are chips in which the die area is divided into cells, which may be interconnected, as specified by the user. (These connections are usually committed at manufacture.) Each cell can be one of a variety of user-definable logic elements, from a manufacturer's menu. Each cell may be anything from a simple gate, through simple compound gate functions, up to a flip-flop or counter.

Having now briefly encountered the constituent parts of a typical digital system and recognized some of the more obvious attributes required of these parts, the detailed exploration of a representative system can be undertaken. Using von Neumann's partitioning, Chapters 2 and 5 are concerned with computer arithmetic, Chapters 3 and 8 with processors/microprocessors, Chapter 4 with memory, Chapter 6 with control/timing and Chapter 7 with input/output. Chapter 9 considers the software design of a digital system and Chapter 10 takes a complete design example to show how all the constituents can be brought together to form an effective whole.

A modern desktop computer system—the Hewlett-Packard Series 9800 System 45—having high-level language facilities, large memory capacity, graphics and hard (paper) copy output, all in one unit. (Courtesy The Hewlett-Packard Co., Santa Clara, California). →

A modern microprocessor contains tens of thousands of active devices and yet is only a fraction of an inch square. This chip is the 16-bit Ferranti military bipolar F100L microprocessor shown in the eye of a darning needle. (Courtesy Ferranti (UK) Ltd., Bracknell, Berks, UK).

EXERCISES

1.1 To what accuracy can quantities be represented in a digital computer using (a) 8, (b) 12 and (c) 16 bits?

1.2 A digital computer issues a series of numbers, each of n bits, to a digital–analog converter (DAC), to generate a waveform. What is the RMS noise present in the waveform, assuming the numbers have been derived from an ADC which has been sampling a source analog signal? Express your answer in terms of the number of bits to which the digital system operates.

1.3 Compare the gate densities that have been obtained in a sample of computers from the last 30 years. Note also the power required per gate and the speed of operation of each device.

1.4 Compare the instruction menus and general facilities of a number of mainframe, mini and microcomputers. Tabulate and compare the relative costs and performances of these machines, where they are known.

1.5 Write programs for any computer which evaluates square roots, reciprocals etc., but using only the *instructions* available in the machine code (or assembly language)—not the full facilities of a high-level language.

1.6 Take an ordinary four-function calculator and calculate square roots on it using Newton's method. Attempt to devise a simple system for obtaining a reasonable initial guesstimate, with a view to minimizing the number of iterations needed for a prescribed accuracy.

1.7 Compare the performance, power consumption, noise margins of a variety of modern logic families. Your list should include MOS, CMOS, TTL, ECL and any other significant families you choose.

REFERENCES

Aiken, H. H. (1965), "Proposed automatic calculating machine," *IEEE Spectrum*, **1**, 62–69.

Anon (1974), "Computer hardware description languages," *Computer*, **7** (12).

Bekey, G. A. and Karplus, W. J. (1968), *Hybrid Computation*, Wiley, New York.

Boole, G. (1954), *An Investigation of the Laws of Thought*, Dover Publications, New York.

Bywater, R. E. H. (1973), *Systems Organisation of Incremental Computers*, Ph.D. Thesis, University of Surrey, UK.

Chu, Y. (1972), *Computer Organization and Microprogramming*, Prentice-Hall, Englewood Cliffs, N.J.

Connors, F. R. (1972), *Signals—S.I. Units*, Edward Arnold, London.

McDermott, J. (1976), "Semi-conductor memories," *Electronic Design*, **24** (12) 78–82.

Mandl, M. (1967), *Fundamentals of Electronic Computers—Digital and Analog*, Prentice-Hall, Englewood Cliffs, New Jersey.

Mano, M. (1976), *Computer System Architecture*, Prentice-Hall, Englewood Cliffs, N.J.

Mano, M. (1979), *Digital Logic and Computer Design*, Prentice-Hall, Englewood Cliffs, N.J.

Marcus, P. (1975), *Switching Circuits for Engineers*, 3rd. edn, Prentice-Hall, Englewood Cliffs, N.J.

Morrison, P. and Morrison, E. (1961), *Charles Babbage and his Calculating Engines*, Dover, New York.

Nagle, H. T., Carrol, B. D. and Irwin, J. D. (1975), *An Introduction to Computer Logic*, Prentice-Hall, Englewood Cliffs, N.J.

Salazar, A. C. (ed.) (1977), *Digital Signal Computers and Processors*, IEEE Press, 1977. (Distributed by Wiley, New York.)

Schmid, H. (1970), *Electronic Analog-Digital Conversions*, Van Nostrand Reinhold, New York.

Scott, N. R. (1970), *Electronic Computer Technology*, McGraw-Hill, New York.

Sizer, T. R. H. (ed.) (1968), *The Digital Differential Analyser*, Chapman & Hall, London.

Wilkins, B. R. (1970), *Analog and Iterative Methods*, Chapman & Hall, London, 1970.

2 NUMBER SYSTEMS AND ARITHMETIC FUNDAMENTALS

2.1 RADIX AND CODING (Flores, 1963; Lewin, 1972; Phistor, 1958; Peterson, 1961).

When representing quantities and performing arithmetic calculations, most people automatically use the decimal system. This almost certainly arises from the fact that we have 10 fingers. However, for some purposes, people frequently use other radices. Examples are base 12 for inches (as a submetric of a foot) and even today base 60 is used for seconds and minutes in the measure of time. All of these nondecimal radices are represented and manipulated in *decimal-coded* form, i.e. a multidecimal digit number is used to represent values of these measures which are 10 or greater.

Example: 59 seconds.

For automatic computing purposes, it is evident from consideration of the comments put forward in previous chapters that a binary system of coding is to be preferred. However, it is not infrequent to find *binary coding* methods in computers which are used to represent higher radices. *Binary-coded decimal* (BCD) is often used for base 10 arithmetic using base 2 logic just as we use base 10 to represent base 60 minutes and seconds. Much less often, the hardware in computers is used for bases other than 10.

A group of digits can represent a quantity by having (usually) an unique coding of these digits for each value of the quantity. In decimal, if we wish to represent 1000 different values, then $\log_{10}1000$, i.e. 3, digits are necessary. The values to be represented need not be equally spaced from each other by value (but they usually are) and the assignment of the 1000 codes to the 1000 values may be arbitrarily chosen (but it is usually not). The coding is most often assigned such that each of the (3) digits may be given a "weight" (value) according to its position in the codeword, and these weights are usually arranged to follow a geometric progression through the digit positions. This latter point is important when considering, for instance, BCD, for it greatly affects the implementation of arithmetic schemes in logic. The above assignments are so universally assumed for hand calculations that any alternative possibilities are either ignored or just not appreciated.

Whatever is true for one radix, in terms of coding and arithmetic laws, is true for another radix—merely the representation of values and the number of digits required alter.

2.2 RADIX CONVERSION

If the weight of each digit follows a geometric progression through the digit positions in a codeword, an integer quantity may be conveniently represented in a "nested" form:

$$\text{Quantity to be represented} = x$$
$$\text{Radix} = r.$$

Digit positions starting at the right-hand-side: $0, 1, 2, \ldots, n-1$. Then any digit may have any integer value from 0 to $r-1$ and

$$x = a_{n-1}r^{n-1} + a_{n-2}r^{n-2} + \cdots + a_0 r^0$$
$$= a_0 + r[a_1 + r[a_2 + \cdots + a_{n-1}]]] \qquad (1.1)$$

The nested representation gives the clue for conversion of a quantity from one radix to another and is therefore, not surprisingly, the basis for mechanized conversion as well.

If x is to be converted from radix r (as in eq. (1.1)) to radix t, then (1.1) can be divided a number of times by t to yield the corresponding digits, radix t.

This follows from translation of eq. (1.1) to a form radix t, i.e.

$$x = b_0 + t(b_1 + t(b_2 + \cdots + b_{m-1})))))))), \qquad (1.2)$$

where b_0, b_1, etc., lie in the range 0 through $t-1$. If x (radix r) is divided by t, an integer quotient and remainder will be formed thus (from (1.2)):

$$\frac{x}{t} = Q + R,$$

where $Q = b_1 + t(b_2 + \cdots + b_{m-1}))))))$ and $R = b_0$. Further division of the quotients formed will yield b_1, b_2, etc as the remainders.

Example   Convert 355 (radix 10) to binary (radix 2).

Here $r=2$ and $t=10$.

$$
\begin{array}{r}
2)\ \underline{355} \\
2)\underline{177} \quad \text{Rem}=1 \quad b_0 \\
2)\ \underline{88} \quad \text{Rem}=1 \quad b_1 \\
2)\underline{44} \quad \text{Rem}=0 \quad b_2 \\
2)\underline{22} \quad \text{Rem}=0 \quad b_3 \\
2)\underline{11} \quad \text{Rem}=0 \quad b_4 \\
2)\underline{5} \quad \text{Rem}=1 \quad b_5 \\
2)\underline{2} \quad \text{Rem}=1 \quad b_6 \\
2)\underline{1} \quad \text{Rem}=0 \quad b_7 \\
0 \quad \text{Rem}=1 \quad b_8
\end{array}
$$

Answer in binary is

$$b_8 b_7 b_6 ... b_0 = 101100011.$$

The bits b_0, b_1 etc. have weights 2^0, 2^1, etc., so that the value of the binary representation is

$(1\times 2^0)+(1\times 2^1)+(0\times 2^2)+ \cdots =1+2+32+64+256=355$ in decimal.

Notice that in this procedure we:

1. divide by the object (desired) radix;

2. perform the arithmetic in the source radix (or, in a computer, in binary-coded radix r);

3. obtain the answer from the least significant (ls) digit first.

If we attempt to convert from a radix (r) with which we are not familiar, the need for radix r arithmetic makes the calculation slow (and very error prone)—in fact, to have a mind like a cash register would be a distinct advantage!

Example   Convert 134 (radix 9) to radix 7.

Before proceeding, it should be pointed out that the *decimal* value of this number is

$$(4\times 9^0)+(3\times 9^1)+(1\times 9^2)=4+27+81=112_{10}.$$

Using the division algorithm (base 9):

$$7 \overline{)1^13^54}$$
$$7 \overline{)1^17} \quad \text{Rem}=0$$
$$7 \overline{)2} \quad \text{Rem}=2$$
$$0 \quad \text{Rem}=2.$$

Answer: 220_7

Check: $220_7 = (0 \times 7^0) + (2 \times 7^1) + (2 \times 7^2)$
$$= \quad 0 \quad + \quad 14 \quad + \quad 98 \quad = 112_{10}.$$

So far, only integers have been considered. Insofar that radix conversion is a process whereby a quantity is *subdivided* so as to reveal object radix digits of weight t^0, the conversion of fractions is a process which forms *multiples* of the original quantity to reveal object digits of weight t^0. This creates an integer of n bits whose most significant bit is the first bit to emerge from the doubling operation. To return this integer to fractional form it is simply necessary to shift it n places to the right. This effectively negates all the doubling that has been performed on the original decimal fraction.

Example   Convert decimal 0.656 to binary:

$$.656 \times$$
$$2$$
$$\text{digit} \times 2^0 \rightarrow 1 \overline{)\,.312 \times}$$
$$2$$
$$0 \overline{)\,.624 \times}$$
$$2$$
$$1 \overline{)\,.248 \times}$$
$$2$$
$$0 \overline{)\,.496}$$
$$\vdots$$
$$\vdots$$

Answer: $0.1010 \ldots$ (radix 2).

Just as for integer conversion, each integer digit formed is taken away and used as a result digit—it does not take part in any subsequent calculations. However, although for any *integer* (radix r) there is an exact representation (radix t) [because all radices can be made to cover all integer values], the same does not apply to *fractions*. The example above has no exact representation to a finite number of bits. This is obvious, as the 1s digit in the calculations above will never become zero—it will just keep cycling 6, 2, 4, 8,

6.... Hence, there will always be a residue from the multiplications. In fact, even quite "simple" decimal fractions have no *exact* binary counterpart.

Example 0.1_{10} (i.e. $\frac{1}{10}$)$=0.0001100110011\ldots$

$$=0.0\dot{0}01\dot{1} \text{ in binary.}$$

Therefore, whenever a decimal to binary fraction conversion is carried out, an uncertainty will exist in the last bit position. For the method above, conversion to n binary places leaves an error ϵ in the range $0 \leq \epsilon < 2^{-n}$. This error range is particularly unfortunate as it is *biased*, so that if many conversions are carried out on decimal data and the calculations performed in binary are such that conversion errors aggregate, a considerable and cumulative loss of accuracy will be experienced.

Example   If 100 decimal fractions are converted to binary and added, the expected error will be

$100 \times$ (expected error from each conversion)$=100 \times (\frac{1}{2} \times 2^{-n})$
$=50 \times 2^{-n}$ with a variance of 8.33×2^{-n}.

A better approach is to attempt to make the conversion error distribution symmetrical about zero for uniformly distributed (statistically independent) quantities. This is conveniently done by performing the conversion to $n+1$ bits and then rounding the answer to the nearest n bits. A suitable rounding algorithm consists of dropping the $(n+1)$th bit if it is zero and adding $2^{-(n+1)}$ to the answer if the $(n+1)$th bit is 1.

Example   Convert 0.467 to 3 binary places (a) unrounded and (b) rounded.

(a)   Unrounded: 0.467×
$$\frac{2}{}$$
0) .934×
$$\frac{2}{}$$
1) .868×
$$\frac{2}{}$$
1) .736

Answer: 0.011 (i.e. 0.375_{10}); $\epsilon=0.467-0.375=0.092$.

(b)   Rounded (continuing 1 further step):

$$1) \ .736\times$$
$$\underline{2}$$
$$1) \ .472$$

Answer to 4 places (unrounded): 0.0111.
The ls bit $=1$ so add 2^{-4}

$$0.0111$$
$$\underline{1}$$
$$0.1000$$

Answer rounded to 3 places:
0.100 (i.e. 0.5); $\epsilon=-0.033$.

Rounding has two advantages:

1.   The error bound is now $-2^{-(n+1)}\leqslant\epsilon<2^{-(n+1)}$, which means the maximum error is halved, but more importantly,
2.   the error distribution is symmetrical about zero, which means that errors will not accumulate *pro rata* but according to a square-root law:

Example   Add 100 quantities with an uniform error distribution

$$-2^{-(n+1)}\leqslant\epsilon<2^{-(n+1)}.$$

The error bound for the sum is $\pm25\times2^{-n}$, with a mean of zero. So the error distribution is symmetrical about zero with a variance of 8.33×2^{-n}.

2.3   UNSIGNED BINARY AND DECIMAL CODES

Most automatic computation is carried out using one of the simpler binary codes. The considerations as to which code should be chosen depend on

1.   whether both positive and negative (signed) quantities are to be handled or just positive (unsigned) ones;
2.   the effect of the code on the speed and cost of arithmetic—bearing in mind that a compromise decision may be necessary involving consideration of the types of arithmetic instructions and their mix (frequency with which each instruction type occurs);
3.   the codes used and the devices and equipment which are to be connected to the system.

Most frequently, simple binary-weighted codes are used because of the cheapness and availability of suitable integrated circuits (IC) for the purpose.

Unsigned binary

The most straightforward code is the one in which the bits are weighted
1,2,4,8,...from the right-hand end of the codeword. It is convenient to
identify the bits from the right-hand end with subscripts 0,1,2,3,...which
correspond to the power to which 2 is raised to give the weight of each bit
(Fig. 2.1). In this notation, it is possible to incorporate integer, fraction or
even mixed integer/fraction representations. There is no indication of the
position of a radix point, so just as in the use of a slide rule, the position must
be remembered by the user (programmer). This has the advantage of allowing any value of scale factor (radix point position) to be invoked but can be
dangerous if different parts of an equipment or calculation have the point in
different positions in the computer word.

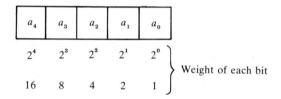

Fig. 2.1   Unsigned binary

If the arrangement in Fig. 2.1 has k bits (or cells), the range of numbers
that can be represented (x) is:

$$0 \leqslant x < 2^{k-1},$$

assuming the radix point is to the immediate right of a_0 for ordinary integers
or

$$0 \leqslant x < 1$$

in steps of 2^{-k} if the radix point is to the left of a_k for ordinary fractions. There
is no objection to assuming that the radix point is

1. somewhere between a_k and a_0 if mixed numbers are to be used, or
2. further left than a_k if only small fractions ($\leqslant 1$) are required, or
3. further right than a_0 for large integers. Note that in this case, the steps
    between unit changes of x will no longer be in units but some larger
    amount 2^l, where l is the number of implied cells between a_0 and the
    radix point.

Binary numbers tend to use large numbers of bits. This is inconvenient
when programming a computer or displaying binary results. Very often, bits
are grouped for display purposes into threes or fours. Essentially, this is

binary-coded base 8 or 16, respectively. It does not alter the inner workings of machinery in any way but is very convenient to use. Grouping bits into threes and fours is usually known as *octal* and *hexadecimal*, respectively. Groups of 3 bits can take any value from 0 to 7 and can therefore allow expression of $3n$-bit computer words by n digits. Groups of 4 bits present a slight difficulty because there are 16 combinations for a 4-bit group. A part decimal, part letter set is used to express values: $0,1,2,\ldots,8,9,A,B,\ldots,F$ to correspond to $0000,0001,0010,\ldots,1000,1001,1010,1011,\ldots,1111$.

Example Express binary 001011110110 in octal and hexadecimal.

Forming groups of 3 gives $(001)(011)(110)(110)=1366_{(8)}$.
Forming groups of 4 gives $(0010)(1111)(0110)=2F6_{(16)}$.

A useful property of binary numbers is that they may be doubled or halved by shifting 1 place left or right, respectively. This corresponds to multiplying or dividing a decimal number by 10 if it is shifted 1 place left or right.

Example Shifting 0011110 (30) left gives
                       0111100 (60) and left again gives
                       1111000 (120).
However, a further left shift gives 1110000, causing the loss of a bit from the top of the register and hence loss of accuracy. This is called *overflow* and must usually be guarded against. If the same original number is right shifted, it becomes
                       0001111 (15),
but shifting again gives
                       0000111 (7)
through loss of a bit—this time from the ls bit position. This is a far less disastrous loss than in the previous case, but may still cause problems in certain calculations.

Because binary numbers are represented to a finite number of bits, only a finite range of values is available. If the contents of a binary register are successively *incremented*, eventually a maximum possible value will be reached (2^k-1 for unsigned binary). An attempt to reach the next value will make the register return to zero (just like the mileometer of an automobile at 99 999 miles). This anomalous condition is also called overflow. Similarly, if an attempt is made to decrement a register below zero, 2^k-1 will be recorded. This is known as *underflow*. Both overflow and underflow must be trapped in a digital system as they can produce gross errors in calculations.

2.4 UNSIGNED BINARY-CODED DECIMAL (BCD)

Binary-coded decimal (BCD) has already been mentioned in this chapter as a way of representing radix 10 using radix 2 machinery. In principle, the cell layout for BCD is a simple variation of that for binary (Fig. 2.2). However, each cell now has 10 possible values—0 through 9. This makes *at least* 4 bits necessary to code each digit. Four bits gives $2^4 = 16$ combinations of available code, which is adequate. Codes involving more than 4 bits are occasionally employed because of their error-resilient properties (Marcus, 1975).

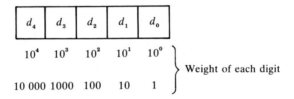

Fig. 2.2 Unsigned BCD

Binary code	Decimal value
0000	0
0001	1
0010	2
0011	3
0100	4
0101	5
0110	6
0111	7
1000	8
1001	9

Table 2.1 8421 BCD

The simplest arrangement for BCD is to use the 4 bits as if coding the binary equivalent of each digit (Table 2.1). Because a weighted binary code is used for each digit, this system is named after the weight values, i.e. "8421 BCD". The codes for 10–15, i.e. 1010,1011,1100,1101,1110,1111, are not used and are invalid. The system is therefore moderately redundant insofar that only 10/16, i.e. 62.5%, of the binary combinations for each digit are used. A measure for the redundancy when representing multidigit quantities can be made as follows:

Assume that we are dealing with large numbers in order to avoid the quantizing effects of small ones.

To represent a number x in binary requires n bits, where

$$n > \log_2 x.$$

Let us therefore say that $n = \log_2 x$ for this analysis.

To represent a number in BCD requires m *digits*, where

$$m > \log_{10} x.$$

If 4 bits are needed for each digit, then $d = 4 \log_{10} x$ *bits* are required for BCD.

$$\therefore \frac{d}{n} = \frac{4 \log_{10} x}{\log_2 x} = 4 \log_{10} 2 \approx 1.2.$$

That is, about 20% more bits are required for BCD compared with binary.

The use of only 10 out of the 16 possible combinations of 4 bits to represent each decimal digit raises

$$\frac{16!}{10!6!} = 8008$$

code combinations, including a majority of unweighted ones, i.e. those for which it is not possible to assign a weight to each bit.

One of these codes which is unweighted (but nonetheless very useful) is called *excess-3 BCD*. Although the bits are strictly unweighted, they may be treated as weighted if we are prepared to accept that the sum of weighted "1" bits is 3 more than the decimal digit value. Hence the name. The code is shown in Table 2.2. In effect, instead of the first 10 codes out of the 16

Binary code	8421 *code binary value*	Decimal value
0011	3	0
0100	4	1
0101	5	2
0110	6	3
0111	7	4
1000	8	5
1001	9	6
1010	10	7
1011	11	8
1100	12	9

Table 2.2   Excess-3 BCD

possible for 4-bit codewords being used, the *middle* 10 are used. The effect of this is to give a *reflecting* code. Pairs of codewords equidistant from the line in Table 2.2 are exact 1s complements of each other, i.e. decimals 3 and 6 are 0110 and 1001. In general, decimals n and $9-n$ are 1s complements of each other, so that the 9s complement (useful for decimal subtraction) of an excess-3 coded decimal number n may be obtained by inverting each bit of n. This allows excess-3 subtraction to be carried out using an excess-3 adder (which will probably be available already).

Example   9 subtract 4 in excess-3 is

$$1100 \text{ subtract } 0111$$

Invert each bit of the 4 to form the 9s complement=1000.
Add 1 to this complement to convert it to 10s complement=1001.
Add 9 and (-4):

$$1100+1001=0101 \quad (5).$$

An excess-3 adder will treat 1001 as if it were 6, thus $9+6=5$ (carry 1).

The carry is ignored (it always turns up if the result is positive) and the 5 used as the result. (To re-establish the result in excess-3 notation, 3 (0011) would have to be added, giving 1000.)

2.5 SIGNED BINARY CODES

Frequently, both positive and negative quantities must be handled in a digital system. If a single bit is added to an existing n-bit number, its range doubles from

$$0 \leqslant x < 2^n - 1 \quad \text{to} \quad 0 \leqslant x < 2^{n+1} - 1.$$

If, instead of adding to the positive range of a number, we add an equal negative range, the extra bit can act as a sign. This does not mean, necessarily, that it is a sign bit in the generally accepted sense of the word, but in almost all cases, the extra bit assumes one logic state whenever quantities are positive and the other state when they are negative.

The obvious way of signing numbers is to add a bit to an n-bit word without otherwise affecting the word or the magnitude being represented by the original n bits. For example, if $+7$ is coded $00\ldots0111$, then -7 can be coded $10\ldots0111$. The sign bit is in front of the n-bit magnitude. This is the method we normally use in everyday paper-and-pencil calculations. The sign bit, unlike the other n bits, has no value or weight—it is just a non-numeric indicator of sign. This signing method is known as *sign and modulus* or *sign and magnitude*. Although often used in computer systems, it carries two difficulties which preclude its wider use:

1. There is no unique zero. (Is there a difference between $+0$ and -0?) In sign and modulus, $+0$ and -0 are represented by $0\ 000\ldots0000$ and $1\ 000\ldots0000$ respectively.
2. Addition and subtraction mechanization is difficult because of the multiplicity of time-consuming decisions that must be made as a calculation proceeds.

Example (-5) subtract (-7).

A pencil-and-paper approach would start by having to decide whether, in effect, addition or subtraction were needed.

It might proceed algorithmically as follows:

> Subtract (-7) really amounts to addition of $+7$.

Rearranging the problem: (-5) add $(+7)$. We still have a minus, so subtraction is required. Subtract the smaller from the larger operand to avoid a negative result. Decide on the sign of the result.

Sign and modulus is quite suitable for multiplication and division because the sign of the result is determined solely by the laws of algebra and is not dependent on the magnitudes of the operands. (Minus zero, however, must always be treated with respect!) The laws of algebra state that if two operands are multiplied or divided, then, if they are of like sign, the result is always positive; else negative. When two operands must be added or subtracted, it is not uncommon to convert them to one of the other signing schemes described below to avoid the "decisions problem". When the result is obtained, it is converted back to sign and modulus.

Offset codes

These go under various names including offset binary, unipolar and excess-N. The idea is that, if signed numbers are a problem, then just add a positive bias to all numbers so that they stay positive (except under anomalous conditions such as arithmetic underflow or overflow).

First, the most negative allowable excursion of operands must be decided. For binary offset systems, this is usually a power of 2, and because numbers are usually assigned equal positive and negative ranges, it is -2^{n-1} for n-bit integers. Thus, an integer x can lie in the range

$$-2^{n-1} \leqslant x < 2^{n-1}$$

which means that, of the 2^n combinations of n-bit numbers available, 2^{n-1} are negative, i.e. -1 through -2^{n-1}, and 2^{n-1} are positive, i.e. 0 through $2^{n-1}-1$.

This system has certain attractions because it eliminates the "decision making" of the sign and modulus system and is the system of coding frequently found in analog–digital and digital–analog converters (ADC and DAC). This latter point should not be surprising as most ADCs and DACs are basically unipolar in terms of their design and are made bipolar by an electronic bias (or offset). Sometimes, the code used is in 1s complement form and is then known as complementary offset binary (COB).

The coding method, including the effect of the offset, therefore makes $0000\ldots00000$ the most negative value, $1000\ldots0000$ the representation of zero and $1111\ldots1111$ the most positive value. In effect, a positive binary range of 0 to "full-scale" ($000\ldots0000$ to $111\ldots111$) has been "stretched" to cover negative values as well. This means that the "half way mark" in binary coding, i.e. $1000\ldots000$, is now "zero value". A codelist for 4-bit integers is given in Table 2.3 along with the equivalent sign and modulus and COB codes.

Value	Unipolar (offset) code	COB	Sign and modulus code
+7	1111	0000	0111
+6	1110	0001	0110
+5	1101	0010	0101
+4	1100	0011	0100
+3	1011	0100	0011
+2	1010	0101	0010
+1	1001	0110	0001
+0	1000	0111	0000
−0	1000	0111	1000
−1	0111	1000	1001
−2	0110	1001	1010
−3	0101	1010	1011
−4	0100	1011	1100
−5	0011	1100	1101
−6	0010	1101	1110
−7	0001	1110	1111
−8	0000	1111	No code for this value

Table 2.3   Offset versus sign and modulus codes.

Note that this system gives an unique zero. Arithmetic using this system is not completely free from problems because of this bias that has been introduced.

Example   Add two numbers a and b.

a and b will be represented by $a+N$ and $b+N$, where $N=2^{n-1}$ (n is the number of bits in each number, i.e. 4 for Table 2.3).
The correct result (including offset) should thus be $a+b+N$.

This requires addition of the operands to give $a+b+2N$ followed by a subtraction of N.

If N is an integer power of 2, it is easy to subtract N as only the most significant (ms) bit of the sum $(a+b+2N)$ is involved. It is just inverted.

Numerical example   If $a=3$, $b=-4$, then using Table 2.3,

$$a=1011 \quad \text{and} \quad b=0100.$$

Adding, as if the operands are unsigned, we get

$$
\begin{array}{r}
1011 \\
\underline{0100} \\
1111
\end{array}
$$

Subtracting N by inverting the ms bit gives 0111 which is -1 in Table 2.3.

Subtraction example   To subtract two numbers a and b. The problem is similar to that for addition except:

As a and b are represented by $a+N$ and $b+N$, subtraction yields:

$$(a+N)-(b+N)=a-b.$$

This is *not* the right answer in *unipolar* coding—the offset N must be reinstated to give $a-b+N$. Inversion of the ms bit of $a-b$ will do this. If

$$a=-3 \quad \text{and} \quad b=+2,$$

then from Table 2.3, $a=0101$ and $b=1010$. Subtraction gives

$$
\begin{array}{r}
0101 \\
\underline{1010} \\
1011
\end{array}
$$

Inversion of the ms bit of $a-b$ gives 0011, which is -5 (from Table 2.3).

Multiplication and division cannot be carried out directly in unipolar coding. To multiply a and b (represented by $a+N$ and $b+N$) to give $a*b+N$ (in unipolar) would require several operations in addition to the multiplication *per se*.

To divide a by b to give $a/b+N$ from operands coded as $a+N$ and $b+N$ would be almost impossible. For multiplication and division, the operands could be converted to, say, sign and modulus, and converted back afterwards. (Sign handling and arithmetic for multiplication/division in sign and modulus is particularly easy.)

Complement notation

The most popular signing method uses complementation, because it avoids the problems of both the sign and modulus and unipolar methods by giving the "sign bit" a weight. Of the complementation methods available, by far the most popular is the so-called "2s complement" notation. Its name comes from its early widespread use in the representation of fractions whereby negative fractions $(-a)$ were represented by the positive complement $(2-a)$. As with ordinary binary integers, zero is coded as $000\ldots000$ and the most positive value as $0111\ldots1111$. This uses up 2^{n-1}, or half, of the 2^n combinations of n-bit codewords. Counting down from zero, modulo 2^n, gives -1 as $111,\ldots,1111$ etc. A list of 4-bit 2s complement notation integers is given in Table 2.4 (with unipolar shown for comparison).

2s complement notation	Unipolar code	Value
0111	1111	+7
0110	1110	+6
0101	1101	+5
0100	1100	+4
0011	1011	+3
0010	1010	+2
0001	1001	+1
0000	1000	0
1111	0111	-1
1110	0110	-2
1101	0101	-3
1100	0100	-4
1011	0011	-5
1010	0010	-6
1001	0001	-7
1000	0000	-8

Table 2.4   2s complement and unipolar notations.

Inspection of Table 2.4 will show that 2s complement may be called a weighted code if the ms bit is assigned the weight -2^{n-1}, where n is the number of bits in the codeword. *All* the other $n-1$ bits have normal, positive weights.

There are some interesting properties of 2s complement notation:

1. If we think modulo 2^n, then there is no discontinuity at zero as with sign and modulus, so decision-free arithmetic is possible.

Example (-5) subtract (-7) is 1011
$$\begin{array}{r} 1001 \\ \hline 0010 \end{array} = +2.$$

2. The code is *reflecting* about an imaginary axis at value $=-\frac{1}{2}$ (for integers). Thus, values x and $-x-1$ have 2s complement notation codes which are the 1s complement of each other.

Example Table 2.4 shows $+2$ and -3 have codes 0010 and 1101 respectively.

This reflection is very useful for the determination of the magnitudes of negative numbers.

Example The magnitude of 111001 based on the weights of bits (starting from the 1s end) is $|1+8+16-32|=7$. Alternatively, using the reflecting principle, we can complement the code, determine the value of its reflection and add 1. Thus, the 1s complement of 111001 is 000110. This is 6. Add 1 and we get 7.

This same principle yields a system for determining $-x$ given x (regardless of the sign of x). To find $-x$, 1s complement the code and add 1. If $x=111011$ ($=1+2+8+16-32=-5$), then $-x=000100+1=000101=+5$. This method for negating x provides the basis of subtraction by addition. See Chapter 5.

3. In decimal, we are used to the occurrence of nonsignificant digits, particularly leading zeros in integers i.e. $0099=099=99$, etc. Less obvious is the occurrence of nonsignificant leading 9s in negative numbers. For instance, a new automobile driven backwards 3 miles will indicate 99,997 on its mileometer (odometer) or 9997, 997 or 97 if it has only 4,3 or 2 dials. The nines are, again, nonsignificant. The same happens in 2s complement binary except that it is leading 1s that are nonsignificant.

Examples $011=0011=00011$ ($=$three)
$\qquad\qquad\quad 101=1101=11101$ ($=$ minus three).

In some calculations, it is necessary to be able to test a 2s complement notation number with a view to expressing it to fewer bits. Excessive compaction of a number is obviously going to lead to loss of significant bits. A simple algorithm for making such a decision is: The top bit of a 2s complement notation number may be removed (i.e. is nonsignificant) if it is equal to the next bit. This is obviously reasonable for positive quantities which have leading zero(s), i.e. $00011\rightarrow0011\rightarrow011$. The time to stop is when we run out of zeros as a further iteration would make the quantity suddenly appear negative. For negative numbers of n bits, the top two bits (if both 1s) have weights -2^{n-1} and $+2^{n-2}$ respectively ($=-2^{n-2}$). Removal of the top bit will now make the $n-2$ bit have a negative weight (as it is *now* the leftmost one). Its weight will thus be -2^{n-2}. Therefore we may proceed, for example,

$11101 \rightarrow 1101 \rightarrow 101$, but no further. (The number will suddenly change sign if we proceed further.)

Conversion between notations for signed numbers

Referring to Tables 2.3 and 2.4, by inspection we can derive the simple relations that exist between the coding methods for sign and modulus, unipolar, COB and 2s complement notations. However, it should be noted that certain exceptions exist if the conversion involves the same word length for both the source and object notations: e.g., sign and modulus cannot represent -2^{n-1} but unipolar and 2s complement can.

	Conversion from	to	Relation	
Positive numbers	Unipolar	SM	Invert ms bit	
	Unipolar	2s C	Invert ms bit	SM = sign and modulus
	Unipolar	COB	Invert all bits	2s C = 2s complement
	SM	2s C	No change	
	SM	COB	Invert all bits (bar ms)	
Negative numbers	Unipolar	SM	2^n–unipolar	
	Unipolar	2s C	Invert ms bit	
	Unipolar	COB	Invert all bits	
	SM	2s C	$\left\{ \begin{array}{c} 2^{n-1} - (\text{SM}) \\ (\text{modulo } 2^n) \end{array} \right\}$	

Table 2.5

2.6   SIGNED BINARY-CODED DECIMAL (BCD)

Two commonly used methods exist:

1. complement method (10s complement);
2. sign and modulus.

The complement method is a BCD version of 2s complement notation and for a $4n$-bit number x the value range is

$$-5 \times 10^{n-1} \leq x < +5 \times 10^{n-1}.$$

Thus, an example of a 10s complement notation BCD subtraction would be:

$$(-39) \text{ subtract } (-42).$$
-39 and -42 would be coded as $100 - 39 = 61$
and $100 - 42 = 58$.
$$61 - 58 = 3.$$

Using binary bits, this would be

$$(-39) \quad \boxed{0110}\boxed{0001}$$
$$\text{subtract}$$
$$(-42) \quad \boxed{0101}\boxed{1000}$$
$$\boxed{0000}\boxed{0011}$$
$$\leftarrow \text{borrow}$$

Note: the subtractions are carried out modulo 10.

The sign and modulus method is also commonly used because the arithmetic decision-making time is a negligible proportion of the total arithmetic time. In addition, the display of negative results does not require any additional operations. This is important in calculators.

In order to maintain the "4-bit slice" form of the numerical part of such operands, it is quite common for a full 4 bits to be used for the sign. The + and − signs are then arranged to be chosen from the "invalid" combinations (10 through 15) of 4 bits.

Example The Extended Binary-Coded-Decimal Interchange Code (EBCDIC) uses 1100 and 1101 to represent + and −.

2.7 FLOATING-POINT REPRESENTATION AND ARITHMETIC (Garner, 1976)

A major disadvantage of ordinary binary (or BCD) is the need for the programmer/operator to remember the scale factors of the operands and to adjust them before arithmetic operations, in order to align the implied radix points. This is very inconvenient and not in the "spirit" of "automatic" computation.

The system of floating-point operation (which is associated with *real* operations in ALGOL, FORTRAN, etc.) uses two fields rather than one to represent a quantity. The format for a quantity x is

$$x = F \times 2^E,$$

where F is known as the fraction (or mantissa) and E the exponent (or characteristic). (Two of the terms are reminiscent of Napier's logarithms—there is certainly a connection.)

It is usually assumed that F is a signed fractional value lying in the approximate range $-1 < F < +1$, and that E is a signed integer. There are some options:

1. As with fixed point (ordinary representation), the radix point associated with F *could* conceivably be anywhere the user desires but the enormous range of values yielded by quite a moderate word length for E usually makes such an option redundant.

2. If the system is to work in octal, hexadecimal or BCD (the latter for calculators using scientific notation) the corresponding formats would be $F\times8^{E}$, $F\times16^{E}$, and $F\times10^{E}$.

Because two variables are involved in the determination of the value of any one operand, a large number of versions of the same quantity can be formed.

Example Assuming 2s complement notation is used for F and E, then 7.25 could be represented as in Fig. 2.3. The relationship between the many versions is that the overall value of the operand can be held constant if, for every 1 place that F is right-shifted, the value of E is increased by 1 (incremented).

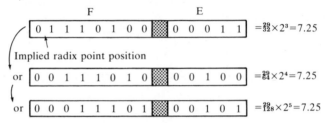

Fig. 2.3 Floating point representation of +7.25

If F is shifted sufficiently far to the right, bits will be lost and accuracy impaired, so that there is a case for keeping F as far to the left as possible. It follows that this maximizes the precision to which any operand can be held. However, there is a limit to how far left F can be shifted without abrogating the inequality $|F|<1$. When F is shifted as far to the left as possible, it is said to be *normalized*, and the process of doing this is called *normalization*. The top box in Fig. 2.3 is normalized according to the rules of 2s complement notation, as a further left shift would cause F to appear negative.

In general, for 2s complement, a sufficient test of normalization is to check for equality of the two leftmost bits of F. If they are equivalent, then further left-shifting of F is possible. This also works for negative numbers.

Example F E

$$\boxed{11101000}\boxed{00100}\ =-\tfrac{3}{16}\times2^{4}=-3$$

∴ Shift F left 1 place and decrement E

$$\boxed{11010000}\boxed{00011}\ =-\tfrac{3}{8}\times2^{3}=-3$$

Again

$$\boxed{10100000}\boxed{00010}\ =-\tfrac{3}{4}\times2^{2}=-3$$

A further left shift would make F appear positive. Thus, if 2s complement is used, the *normalized* range for F is:

1. F positive $\frac{1}{2} \leqslant F < 1$, where $01000 \ldots 000 = F_{min} = \frac{1}{2}$
    and $01111 \ldots 111 = F_{max}$.
2. F negative $-\frac{1}{2} > F \geqslant -1$, where $10111 \ldots 111 = F_{min}$.
    $10000 \ldots 000 = F_{max} = -1$.

It should be noted that normalization of an operand requires E to be decremented at each step. Clearly, this can, under extreme circumstances, cause E to underflow. For the above example, the permissible range for E is $-2^4 \leqslant E < 2^4$. If E is -2^4 and F needs normalization, E will underflow. Under these circumstances, the whole operand is cleared to zero—as the implication is a *very* small operand value. This condition is known as *exponent underflow* and its occurrence is often symptomatic of poor programming strategy. Many computers set a flag (flip-flop) when exponent underflow occurs to act as a programmer warning.

Floating-point arithmetic (strategy)

(a) Addition/subtraction

Before two operands may be added/subtracted, their implied radix points must be aligned, that is, the operands must acquire equal characteristics (exponents) before addition/subtraction can commence. Suppose the operands are

$$\text{operand } 1 = F_1 \times 2^{E_1},$$
$$\text{operand } 2 = F_2 \times 2^{E_2},$$

where $E_1 \geqslant E_2$ (for argument's sake). To align the radix points, either operand 1 can have F_1 shifted to the left and E_1 correspondingly decremented until $E_1 = E_2$ or operand 2 can have F_2 right shifted and E_2 incremented until $E_1 = E_2$. Clearly, the first choice could cause F_1 to overflow (particularly if it were already normalized). The only option is to *denormalize* operand 2. This process is known as *scaling*.

Example Add 4.5 and 1.5.

$$F_1 \times 2^{E_1} \quad \boxed{0.1001000} \boxed{00011} = \tfrac{9}{16} \times 2^3 = 4.5$$

$$F_2 \times 2^{E_2} \quad \boxed{0.1100000} \boxed{00001} = \tfrac{3}{4} \times 2^1 = 1.5$$

Denormalizing operand 2 gives

$$\boxed{0.0110000} \boxed{00010} = \tfrac{3}{8} \times 2^2 = 1.5$$

then

$$\boxed{0.0011000} \boxed{00011} = \tfrac{3}{16} \times 2^3 = 1.5$$

At this point, the two characteristics are equal and addition may take place. The result characteristic is equal to the common characteristic, i.e. 3. The result is

$$\boxed{0.1100000\,|\,00011} = \tfrac{3}{4} \times 2^3 = 6.$$

In this example, the result was already in normalized form. This need not be the case, and *post-normalization* of the result may be necessary. Several eventualities are possible during computation:

(a)   The addition/subtraction of the operands may cause *fractional overflow*.

Example $0.75 \times 2^0 + 0.625 \times 2^0$ (no scaling necessary).
Addition of the mantissae gives 1.375×2^0. The result mantissa is no longer fractional. However, the result can be normalized by right-shifting the mantissa and incrementing the characteristic. In binary:

$$\boxed{01100000\,|\,00000} \quad \tfrac{3}{4}$$

$$\boxed{01010000\,|\,00000} \quad \tfrac{5}{8}$$

$$\overset{*\;\dagger}{\boxed{0\,|\,10110000\,|\,00000}} \quad \tfrac{11}{8} \times 2^0$$

Normalizing:

$$\boxed{01011000\,|\,00001} \quad \tfrac{11}{16} \times 2^1$$

It is clear that the mantissa adder/subtractor must have an extra bit to prevent loss of the additional ms bit. The same basic mechanism is usually employed for normalization (involving right- as well as left-shifting). It may also be tied in with the scaling logic.

Negative-result mantissae can also be generated. In 2s complement it is easy to test for mantissa overflow by inspecting bits $*$ and $\dagger$ above. If they are non-equivalent, then *fractional underflow* has occurred.

(b)   If the result mantissa does overflow or underflow, the normalization process involves incrementation of E. This may cause E to overflow. A disastrous loss of accuracy can result from this condition known as *exponent overflow*. Frequently, computation is abandoned and a warning flag set.

(c)   Another anomalous result can occur when operands of unlike sign are added or operands of like sign subtracted.

Example $\tfrac{3}{4}$ subtract $\tfrac{3}{4}$.

$$F_1 \times 2^{E_1} \quad \boxed{01100000\,|\,00000} \quad \tfrac{3}{4} \times 2^0$$

$$F_2 \times 2^{E_2} \quad \boxed{01100000\,|\,00000} \quad \tfrac{3}{4} \times 2^0$$

Subtraction causes a zero result mantissa. An unchecked attempt at normalization of the result would cause an inescapable loop to be entered. Thus, detection of a zero result mantissa must be incorporated to prevent post-normalization under such circumstances. There is a more subtle point—the fact that both operands were the same (as represented) is very dubious. If we assume we are doing "real" computing with "real" measured quantities rather than arithmetic on discrete numbers, then two identical measured values seem *very* unlikely. For the format above, a difference of measured values as large as 2^{-8} may have caused the 8-bit mantissae fields to hold the measurements as identical quantized values, viz. $\frac{3}{4}$. The finite lengths of the F fields may be implied to have made discrimination between two similar (but not exactly equal) measurements to *appear* identical. A situation exists in which lack of *significant bits* in the F field has caused failure of *discrimination*. A difference of 2^{-8} could be *easily* recorded in the above floating-point format

$$\boxed{01000000}\boxed{11001}$$

so the error is due to lack of bits to represent F. If a zero F field results from such a calculation, a zero result has to be recorded (there is no option), but many computers also set a *significance-error* flag. Again, poor programming strategy is *often* the cause of such a situation.

Multiplication and division (Tocker, 1958)

These are executed in floating point using the connectives:

$$(\text{operand } 1)\times(\text{operand } 2)=(F_1\times2^{E_1})*(F_2\times2^{E_2})$$
$$=(F_1*F_2)\times2^{[E_1+E_2]}$$

and

$$(\text{operand } 1)\div(\text{operand } 2)=(F_1\times2^{E_1})/(F_2\times2^{E_2})$$
$$=(F_1/F_2)\times2^{[E_1-E_2]}.$$

The processes of multiplication/division of the mantissae follow the same pattern as for integer arithmetic as do addition/subtraction of the exponents.

It should be noted that exponent overflow and underflow are both possible with both operators and that zero operands must be trapped, particularly zero divisors.

It is normal for the incoming operands to be in normalized form, or if not, for them to be normalized prior to multiplication/division. Because of this, very little post-normalization is necessary and maximum precision is maintained.

Example Multiplication if F_1 and F_2 are normalized (sign and modulus mantissae assumed).

Then

$$\tfrac{1}{2} \leqslant |F_1|, |F_2| < 1.$$

Therefore

$$\tfrac{1}{4} \leqslant |F_1 * F_2| < 1.$$

The result mantissa will often require no post-normalization and, at most, a single-place post-normalization.

Example Division if F_1 and F_2 are normalized such that

$$\tfrac{1}{2} \leqslant |F_1|, |F_2| < 1$$

then

$$\tfrac{1}{2} < |F_1 / F_2| < 2.$$

Left-shifting post-normalization of the result will never be necessary, but *one place right-shifting* post-normalization may.

EXERCISES

2.1 Convert the following decimal quantities to (a) binary (8 significant bits); (b) BCD; (c) hexadecimal (6 significant digits):

$$35.00, \quad 0.77, \quad 18.35.$$

What are the conversion errors (in per cent) if the results are (i) truncated to the required number of places or (ii) rounded to the nearest digit/bit?

2.2 How many binary bits are needed to represent the following:

(a) integers x; x in the range $0 \leqslant x \leqslant +999\ 999$

(b) integers y; y in the range $-99\ 999 \leqslant y \leqslant +99\ 999$

(c) fractions f; f in the range $-1 < f < +1$ to a precision of $\pm 0.005\%$?

2.3 Develop code tables to represent decimal digits 0–9 for the following BCD codes: (a) 8421; (b) 5421; (c) 7421; (d) $74\overline{2}\overline{1}$; (e) 2421; (f) 51111; (g) 2-out-of-5 (see note (ii) below), identifying which are reflecting codes.

Notes: (i) $\overline{2}$ and $\overline{1}$ have weights of -2 and -1 respectively.

  (ii) 2-out-of-5 means that each codeword has only two 1s (and hence three 0s).

2.4 What are the values of the following if assumed to be coded (a) in 2s complement notation; (b) unipolar; (c) sign and modulus:

$$101111, \quad 011101, \quad 111111, \quad 000000?$$

2.5 Develop combinational logic networks using iterative cells of the form shown in Fig. 2.4 to convert signed integers (a) from sign and modulus to 2s complement; (b) from 2s complement to unipolar.

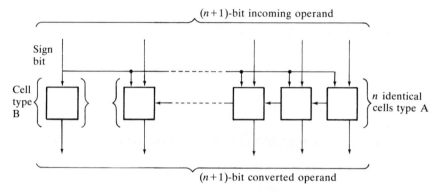

Fig. 2.4

2.6 If floating-point operands are contained in 6-bit, 2s complement notation, mantissae and 4-bit unipolar code characteristics, what is the range of positive and negative values that can be represented if the mantissae are (a) always normalized (b) not necessarily normalized?

REFERENCES

Flores, I. (1963), *The Logic of Computer Arithmetic*, Prentice-Hall, Englewood Cliffs, New Jersey.

Garner, H. L. (1976), "A survey of some recent contributions to Computer Arithmetic," *Trans IEEE Comp*, **C-25** (12), 1277–82.

Lewin, D. W. (1972), *Theory and Design of Digital Computers*, Nelson, London.

Marcus, M. P. (1975), *Switching Circuits for Engineers*, 3rd edn, Prentice-Hall, Englewood Cliffs, N.J.

Peterson, W. W. (1961), *Error Correcting Codes*, Wiley, New York.

Phistor, M. (1958), *Logical Design of Digital Computers*, Wiley, New York.

Tocker, T. D. (1958), "Techniques of multiplication and division for automatic binary computers," *Q. J. Mech. Appl. Math.* **11**, 364–84.

3   ASPECTS OF PROCESSOR DESIGN

3.1   INTRODUCTION: ALGORITHM COMPUTATION AND THE PROCESSOR

A processor can be a piece of hardware or equipment, a suite of software or a combination of the two. However, in this chapter, we are going to consider the hardware processor — a collection of registers, logic and arithmetic units which, together with a memory medium, is capable of carrying out computational tasks.

An important attribute of a processor is its "menu" of instructions, i.e. those jobs it can carry out by itself from a single command or instruction. Such *instructions* can be carried without the processor having to be told how to do them. Instructions are merely listed in a *program* and *executed* in turn by the processor without any adscititious agency being necessary.

In the vast majority of circumstances in which a processor is used, the job (process) to be carried out is so complex, it must be defined by a series of instructions. As the complexity of tasks rises, so too does the number of combinations of such tasks. For economy's sake, it is preferable to have a limited number of instructions which can be used as building blocks rather than an enormous repertoire of complex ones. Thus, a typical process is defined by a series of instructions which *are* executable by the processor, the instructions and the order of execution being defined by the manner in which the process may be carried out.

Example   A process consists of finding the square root of a number. The processor's "menu" of instructions does not include the extraction of a square root, but does include the more fundamental instructions ADD, SUBTRACT, MULTIPLY and DIVIDE. An *algorithm* can be described which, by an *iterative* (repeated) procedure, will converge on the square root of a number from some initial guess.

46

A suitable algorithm is

$$x_{n+1} = \tfrac{1}{2}\left[x_n + \frac{A}{x_n}\right],$$

where A is the number whose root is sought and x_n is the best estimate at the step n. The process is started with some initial guess x_0 and the formula used repeatedly until the required degree of accuracy is obtained. It will be noted that only simple instructions are needed to evaluate the formula and that, as is typical of such processes, the same *loop* of instructions is used a large number of times (Fig 3.1).

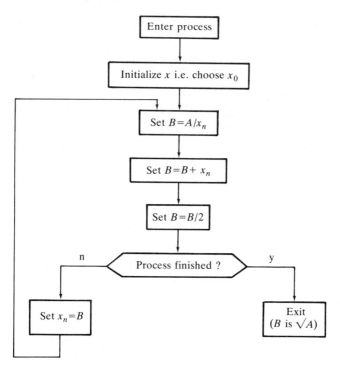

Fig. 3.1 Evaluation of a square root

The quantities x_n and B are contained in memory locations (addresses) in the system's main memory or, more likely, in registers in the processor. Note that the use of the "=" sign in Fig 3.1 is not used in the conventional manner as in "equivalence" but as the symbol for "becomes", as in FORTRAN programming. Thus $B=B+x_n$ should be read as "B becomes equal to its original value plus x_n." The new value of B, $[B+x_n]$, replaces the original value of B. The original value of B is thus lost unless copied elsewhere prior to execution of this instruction. This is a form of arithmetic which is related to the subtotals that are formed in a "point of sale" terminal (cash point) in a supermarket. This approach is very useful for computational purposes and is very frequently employed.

3.2 PROCESSING HIERARCHY

Having established that the processor is a "device" for executing processes and algorithms by a series of instructions it offers on a "menu", it is possible to show a processor as a hierarchy, with the process as the highest level and the transistors and gates which form the hardware as the lowest level (Fig. 3.2).

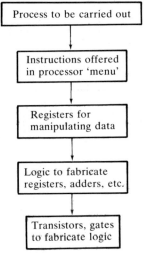

Fig. 3.2 Schematic of process hierarchy

As we proceed from the highest to the lowest level, it will be noticed that the individual "units" and "concepts" get progressively simpler but a corresponding expansion takes place both in the space and time domains. In the square-root example, a complex process could be replaced by a series of simple ADD and other instructions. However, both the number of instructions and the number of times each has to be executed is quite large. In order to execute any *one* instruction, several processor registers will be involved and repeatedly used. Each register is fabricated from a large number of logic gates. Expansion in the space domain therefore comes about from the large number of memory locations, registers and logic needed—expansion in the time domain arises because of replacement of single (complex) processes by repeated application of simple processes.

If we consider Fig. 3.2 from the point of view of general computer systems, then only the top level is being used to represent the whole software realm. We can subdivide this level into another set of levels with high-level languages and process definitions occupying the very top position, through operating systems, job-control languages, system-implementation languages, assemblers to machine languages at the lowest level.

Although not self evident until later in this chapter, it is worth pointing out, even at this stage, that there is not a rigidly defined, time invariant, breakpoint between software and hardware. In fact a third level, called *firmware*, can be identified which forms an interface between the two. Roughly speaking, software (and hence software processes and processors) is such that alteration of its form is easily carried out—software is held in a readily updated medium, i.e. a computer's memory or on punched cards, magnetic tape, etc. Hardware is rigidly and unalterably defined as its form is palpable equipment, i.e. logic and registers. On the other hand, firmware is a form of software held in a type of memory which can have its contents altered, if required. As firmware is usually used, in conjunction with hardware, to define the instructions "menu" offered by a processor, it is not altered very frequently. To alter firmware is to alter the "appearance" of a machine, which is never done lightly. Firmware makes possible the *emulation* of one machine by another by making possible the execution of the instructions of a *target* machine by a *host* (with suitably written firmware). This concept is discussed more fully in Section 3.7.

3.3 INSTRUCTION FORMATS

Turning to the details of a hardware processor and considering the "specification" of each instruction, the following information is needed. (It will be assumed that the main memory is used both to hold instructions and data (operands) as in Fig. 3.3.)

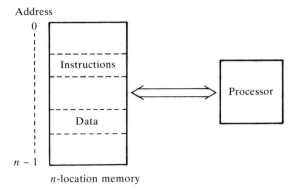

Fig. 3.3 Processor memory connection

1.   Which of the "menu" of instructions is to be used (called the operation code or "op-code" for short)? It might be an ADD or JUMP (BRANCH) instruction or any one of 40 to 200 normally available. Each operation can be given an unique, fixed, binary code to identify it. For 40–200 instructions, up to 8 code bits ($2^8 = 256$) may be required.

2 & 3.   If we assume that most arithmetic operations need up to two operands (variables x and y) on which to operate, (e.g. ADD requires two) then the memory locations of these must be given. If an n-location memory is used and either operand can be *anywhere* in this memory, then *each* can be accessed by an address code with $\log_2 n$ bits. If $n = 16$K (i.e. 2^{14}, or 16 384), then 14 bits are needed for each address code.

4.   Arithmetic operations generally produce a single result variable, so an address with $\log_2 n$ bits is needed for the result destination in memory.

5.   Upon completion of the instruction, the memory location of the next instruction is needed. This demands another code with $\log_2 n$ bits.

An instruction which gives parts 1–5 explicitly would need a total of 64 bits (Fig. 3.4). For a system with a larger memory, even more bits would be required.

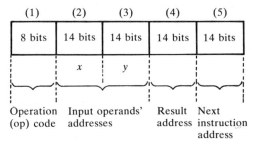

Fig. 3.4   Explicit 5-part instruction

In practice, this number of bits and the choice of instructions it offers is quite excessive.

(a)   The cost of memory rises with the number of bits per location. In the interests of economy, the number of bits per instruction should be minimized.

(b)   The flexibility that "free" operand and result addressing gives is rarely of importance. More important, savings can be made if at least one operand comes from a fixed location. (If a location is fixed, it needs no address bits.) The fixed location is usually, but not always, a flip-flop register called the *accumulator*, and is lodged in the processor. Two important variations are to be found:

(i) The accumulator may be a fixed main-memory location (say, location 0) which would still need no address code as the address would be implicit, or

(ii) many processors use more than one accumulator and so a *few* bits may be needed to address the desired one. For a processor with 8 accumulators, 3 bits are required ($2^3 = 8$)—this is still a great deal less than before.

(c) If an accumulator is used as the source of one incoming operand, it can also serve as the destination for arithmetic results. This will eliminate a complete address field (unless more than one accumulator is used and the accumulator-derived input operand address is different from the result destination address). The use of an accumulator gives very much the same sort of action as the subtotalling mechanism in a point-of-sale terminal–that is, the total in the accumulator before the instruction is executed is *replaced* by its new value after execution.

(d) There is little to be gained by allowing instructions to be placed in memory other than in a manner such that the next instruction to be executed is in the next main-memory location. That is, if the order of execution of instructions $a,b,c,d,\ldots$ is $a,b,c,d,\ldots$, then they should be lodged in memory locations $n, n+1, n+2, \ldots$. By so doing, it is not necessary to have an explicit "next instruction address" portion in each instruction, i.e. part 5. Instead, the processor can keep a record of the memory location of the current instruction being executed and thereby provide the memory address to retrieve each instruction as it is to be used. The next instruction address field in Fig 3.4 can be eliminated and a single binary counter with $\log_2 n$ bits used to keep this record in the processor. This is known as a program counter (PC) and is incremented each time an instruction is executed. The $\log_2 n$ bits are supplied to the main memory from PC each time an instruction is to be fetched.

The instruction format can now be reduced to a minimum. This is called a single-address instruction format (Fig. 3.5).

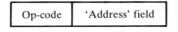

Fig. 3.5 Simple single address instruction format

For arithmetic instructions, the address field refers to the main-memory location of one operand—the other being, by implication, in the accumulator. The result is returned to the accumulator.

For single-operand instructions, such as "negate x" or "shift y", the accumulator can be the operand source. This leaves the address field free to condition what happens to the accumulator contents. For example, it might define the direction and number of places the accumulator's contents are to be shifted (rotated). That the "address" field is not used for an operand access is made known to the processor when the operation code is examined (decoded). (A shift instruction would naturally have a different operation code from, say, an ADD instruction.)

For branching (JUMP) instructions, the address field can hold the destination address, i.e. the memory location of the next instruction to be executed. Again, the operation code implies the use to which the "address" field is to be put.

3.4   REGISTER STRUCTURE AND INSTRUCTION EXECUTION

We are now in a position to define some of the components of a processor, bearing in mind that considerable variations will exist, particularly according to the number of parts in Fig. 3.4 which are made implicit. Figure 3.6 shows a typical processor for use with simple instructions. To execute an instruction, the contents of the program counter are routed to the memory address port (MAP) via a data selector. This latter device is needed to select the source of the memory address. On this occasion, the contents of PC are required to fetch an instruction—later, the contents of a register holding the operand address will be selected. A data selector is similar to a set of "railroad points" in operation. If "select" is in one logic state, bits are selected from one source; if "select" is in the other logic state, the other source is selected (Fig. 3.7).

The output from the memory is the instruction to be executed which is deposited in an instruction register (IR) in the processor. The IR releases the main memory for other tasks and gives a resting place for the instruction (from which the operation code and address part can be drawn).

The contents of the operation code portion of IR are passed to a decoder to ascertain which instruction on the "menu" is to be processed. In the simplest scheme, the decoder takes the instruction, in its encoded form, and issues a set of logic signals each of which is associated with a separate instruction. If the processor has a "menu" of 8 ($=2^3$) instructions, the decoder has 3 inputs and 8 outputs. For each of the 8 three-bit codes, only one output is a logic 1. By inspecting individual decoder outputs, it is therefore possible to identify the instruction and thereby determine the necessary processor activity to correctly execute the instruction (Fig. 3.8).

The other part of the IR in Fig. 3.6 contains an "address" portion. In the event of the instruction being arithmetic (as determined by the operation code), the address is that of an operand in memory. This address is now sent,

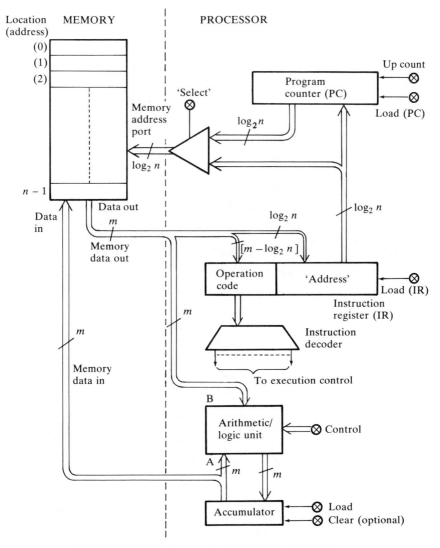

Fig. 3.6 Simple processor for single-address instructions

via the data selector, to the memory address port. The "select" control for the data selector will have been switched in readiness.

The output from the memory on this second occasion is an operand which is passed to the arithmetic/logic unit (ALU) for processing. After processing, the arithmetic result is lodged in the accumulator. PC is incremented so that it now points to the next instruction.

Summarizing the actions for, say, a simple arithmetic instruction, we have:

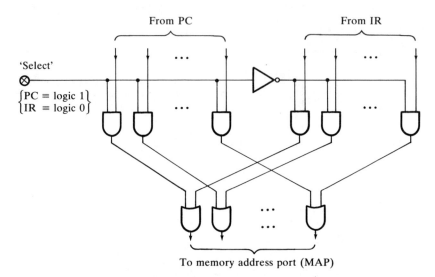

Fig. 3.7 Two-input data selector

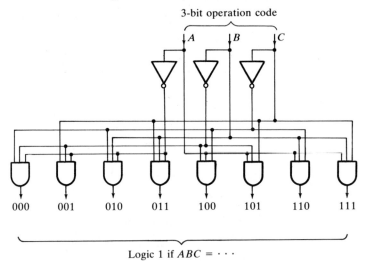

Fig. 3.8 3-input : 8-output decoder

1. PC→MAP
2. READ MEMORY
3. MEMORY→IR (instruction)
4. IR (address portion)→MAP
5. READ MEMORY
6. MEMORY→ALU: ACCUMULATOR→ALU
7. PROCESS ARITHMETIC
8. RESULT→ACCUMULATOR

where MAP, ALU ; nd ACC stand for memory address port, arithmetic/logic unit and accumulator, respectively. It should be noted that incrementing (up-counting) the PC can take place any time between steps 4 and the end of the instruction, without detriment. In many processors, it is incremented at the earliest opportunity so that PC spends most of its time pointing to the *next* instruction! The data selector's select control has only to be at certain logic levels at specific times, i.e. logic 1 on step 1 and logic 0 on step 4. On other occasions, its logic state is immaterial. In logic parlance, this is usually known as a "don't care" situation for which either logic state will allow correct operation of the system. The ALU, in its simplest form, might only consist of a programmable adder/subtractor as described in Chapter 5. In this instance, it would only require a single control input to determine its operation at any time. Such a control wire can derive its information directly from the instruction decoder—from that output corresponding to the SUBTRACT instruction. It will be seen that a SUBTRACT instruction is identical to ADD except for step 7 above. The difference in operation code changes the control input to the adder/subtractor and thereby changes the instruction.

In a practical processor, several other instructions would have to be included on the "menu" to make even a low-cost system worthwhile. Amongst these are:

1. *Conditional and Unconditional BRANCH*

The sequence for this is:

1. PC→MAP ⎫
2. READ MEMORY ⎬ as above
3. MEMORY→IR (instruction) ⎭
4. IF CONDITION MET* THEN IR (ADDRESS)→PC;
   ELSE PC+1

*If the BRANCH is unconditional (i.e. GO TO), then the branch always takes place and there is no condition to be met. If the branch is conditional, it only takes place if the condition is met. Otherwise, nothing happens except that PC is incremented in readiness to fetch the next instruction from memory.

Examples of conditions that might be tested are:

(a) State of the accumulator
    That is, is it zero?
        has it just overflowed?
        has the last instruction produced a negative result? etc.
(b) Conditions external to the processor
    That is, what are the states of sense wires entering the processor from peripheral devices?
        Examples might be whether an analog–digital converter (ADC) is ready with new data for the processor or that a "mains-fail" indicator

has operated. In this event, the processor must quickly suspend operations and dump information from power-dependent (volatile) memory,
such as flip-flop registers, into non-volatile memory such as a ferrite-
core memory.

(c)   Many other possibilities.

Which condition is to be tested by the conditional-branch instruction can be
determined in several ways. One of the most popular is to have a separate
operation code for each condition. Therefore, many different instructions
may be called "conditional branch" but each will make reference to a
different condition. The condition(s) chosen is ANDed with the instruction
decoder output (Fig. 3.9).

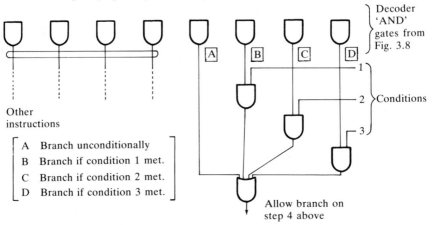

Fig. **3.9**   Operation codes define branch conditions to be met

2. *Subroutine Calls*

Many processes in a computer, be they arithmetic or logical, can be partitioned into a hierarchy of subprocesses of lesser complexity. For instance, if
decimal multiplication is required on a system only capable of performing
binary add and subtract, the decimal multiplication can be reduced to a
series of decimal additions and subtractions which can be called as required
by the multiplication program. As the multiplication proceeds, each multiplier bit is inspected and an addition or subtraction (multibyte in either case)
instituted. However, in order to carry out decimal addition and subtraction,
a routine could be called from time to time which was capable of decimal
addition/subtraction on a *per digit* basis. This is a "nest" of subroutines, i.e.
the original program calls a subroutine, which in turn calls a second one, and
so on (Fig. 3.10). In order that a subroutine is called and returned from
properly, certain information is needed. The SUBROUTINE CALL
instruction needs to know where the subroutine is in memory—this can be

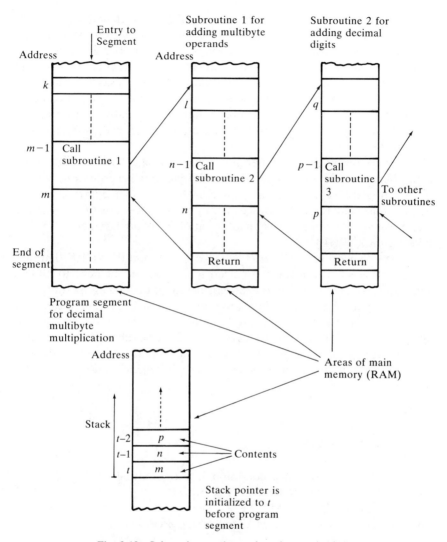

Fig. 3.10 Subroutine nesting and stack organization

provided by the address field of the call instruction in a similar manner to a BRANCH instruction. However, the idea of a subroutine is that, once computed, control should return to the original (calling) program as if the subroutine occupied memory locations between the calling instruction and the *actual* instruction in the next memory location. Therefore, a return address must be retained somewhere. Part of memory can be used for this or some hardware in the processor. In both cases, the need to be able to nest subroutines means that more than one address must be retained and that the return addresses are loaded back into the PC in the right order. For the example of Fig. 3.10, the order of storing addresses needs to be m,n,p and the order of reloading them to PC is p,n,m. Clearly a LIFO is required (see Sect. 4.7). If the LIFO is in the processor (Intel 4004), there is a severe limit to the depth that can be economically attained. (Often this is 5 or less.) If the LIFO is in main memory (Intel 8080/5, Motorola 6800, etc.), it can be of almost unlimited depth but requires a hardware pointer to indicate the current stacking point. Both systems are used in microprocessors and conventional computers.

The address register is generally known as a "stack pointer" and is of n bits, where the main memory capacity is 2^n bytes. Such a pointer requires to be able to avail itself of (at least) some of the more elementary arithmetic instructions available in the processor. In particular, it must be possible to increment and decrement it when information is put on the stack (PUSH) or taken from it (POP).

The two instructions SUBROUTINE CALL and RETURN therefore work in concert: the former is placed in a program segment to allow a subroutine to take place and the latter is placed at the end of the subroutine to return control to the calling program. This arrangement means that subroutines can be made available to many programs and can be called at any point in a program. Sometimes it is possible for a subroutine to be called directly from a main program or sometimes from another subroutine.

Summarizing the microactions for these instructions, we have the following:

SUBROUTINE CALL
1. PC→MAP
2. READ MEMORY
3. MEMORY→IR
   (If the call or return is conditional, test condition here)
4. STACK POINTER REGISTER→MAP
5. WRITE PC TO MEMORY
6. IR (Address)→PC. UPDATE STACK POINTER

RETURN
1. PC→MAP
2. READ MEMORY
3. MEMORY→IR
   (If the return is conditional, test condition here)
4. DOWNDATE STACK POINTER
5. STACK POINTER→MAP
6. READ MEMORY
7. MEMORY→PC

3.5 PROCESSOR DESIGN CONSIDERATIONS

The simple processor style so far described has attributes which can be found in most processors for micro, mini and mainframe computers. The major attribute is the sequencing of events into roughly:

1. acquisition of instructions from memory (instruction fetching);
2. acquisition of any data from memory (operand fetching);
3. arithmetic/logical processing (arithmetic execution);
4. depositing of results in memory and finish.

However, practical processors may differ widely in the manner in which they carry out this sequence, the variations showing the various design compromises that had to be made to yield a cost effective system, capable of wide application.

Accumulators and scratch-pads

Amongst the more important considerations in obtaining high performance (fast instruction throughput) is the proportion of time taken in each activity concerned with any instruction. If we had opted for the most generalized form of instruction which made memory accesses for both operands and wrote arithmetic results back to memory, a total of four memory accesses would have been made–one for the instruction, two for reading operands and one to write away the result. For a simple processor, the likely proportions of time for the ADD instruction might be 500 ns for each memory operation and 100 ns for arithmetic. A five-part ADD instruction would therefore need $(4 \times 500 + 100) = 2100$ ns. Already we have seen that use of the accumulator removes two memory accesses by making it the source of one operand and the destination for results. As the accumulator is a flip-flop memory, it requires an almost negligible time for reading and writing. Use of the accumulator will therefore reduce the instruction time to two memory operations plus arithmetic, say $2 \times 500 + 100 = 1100$ ns. Of course, more sophisticated instructions, such as multiply, will not show such a vast improvement, but then the proportion of multiplications in most programs is small compared with additions.

For multiplication, we might expect the arithmetic time to be 1000 ns, compared with 100 ns for addition. The comparative instruction times with and without an accumulator are 3000 and 2000 ns, respectively.

It is still apparent from inspection of these execution times that the highest proportion of time is spent in memory accesses. A further, significant, improvement can be made if the memory accesses are further reduced. If a scratch-pad system or multiple accumulator array is used, it is possible to arrange that the majority of instructions call *both* operands from the scratch-pad (see Chapter 4). The scratch-pad will be almost as fast as the accumulator so that add and multiply arithmetic times would probably be 150 and 1050 ns respectively. Main memory will now be used only to fetch the instruction. Instruction times for ADD and MULTIPLY will now be 500+150=650 ns and 500+1050=1550 ns, respectively.

It is common for all types of processor (micro, mini, etc.) to use at least one accumulator or a scratch-pad. In order to define which scratch-pad registers are to be used, the instruction must contain a scratch-pad address (Fig 3.11). One operand will come from scratch-pad register 1 and the result will be deposited in the same location. The address field for operand 2 can refer to a main-memory location (as before) or just a few bits can be used to define a scratch-pad location. The manner in which this second field is used can be defined by the operation code. If the scratch-pad has a bank of 16 registers (locations), then 4 ($= \log_2 16$) address bits will be needed.

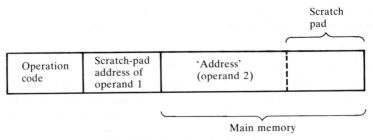

Fig. 3.11   Scratch-pad addressing

Variable-length instructions and operands

A second, very important, consideration in processor optimization is word length. This is nowhere more important than in the microcomputer, where economy is of paramount importance and the volume of memory a prime factor. Clearly, instructions can vary widely in the number of bits needed to define them. Some examples for a simple processor are:

1. Simple accumulator shift operation—only an operation code needed, say,

8 bits.

2. Add operation involving a 16 register scratch-pad—8 bits operation code plus 4 bits for each operand address.

Total,   16 bits.

3. Add operation involving a 64K main memory for one operand. Single accumulator processor structure—8 bits operation code plus 16-bit operand address

Total, 24 bits.

It would be very uneconomical to provide 24 bits for *all* instructions and a 24-bit word main-memory system. This is especially the case since it is to be hoped that a high proportion of instructions executed would be short, simple ones.

There is an approach to this problem which is now adopted for most processors from micro to mainframe: variable-length instructions. The instruction format is constrained to be such that a multiple of a certain number of bits is used. Typically, multiples of 8 bits (1 byte) are used and instructions span 1, 2, 3 or 4 bytes to give instruction lengths of 8, 16, 24 and 32 bits. The main-memory addressing is now byte orientated, which is also very convenient for many input/output devices which may be connected to the system. Part use of a byte is obviously less wasteful on average than part use of, say, a 32-bit word. Instructions which span more than one byte are slotted into contiguous locations (Fig. 3.12).

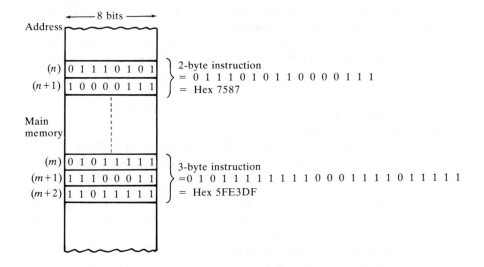

Fig. 3.12   Multibyte instructions

How can the processor, as it fetches instructions from memory, determine the instruction length? As all instructions are at least 1 byte long, clearly the length information must be contained in the first byte. Additional accesses, to build up the complete instruction, then follow. Two basic methods to indicate instruction length are in common use.

(a)   *A special byte length field*
The first part of an instruction is usually the operation code. If this is restricted to 6 bits (giving 64 instruction options), 2 bits then remain to

indicate instruction length. This technique is used on a variety of processors of varying sophistication. On large machines the 2-bit code may refer to a ½ word (16-bit unit) or word (32-bit unit) instruction.

(b)   *Composite operation code and instruction length indicator*

This is only a trivial variation of (a) and relies on the fact that the outputs of the instruction decoder which refer to similar instruction lengths can simply be ORed together. The OR gates generate signals which can initiate further fetches, as required.

Whichever method is used, care must be exercised in the choice of and form of instructions. It has already been stated that the number of main-memory accesses often dominates instruction time. Clearly increasing the number of accesses by the use of multibyte instructions can only worsen the situation. It is therefore important to arrange that the commonly executed instructions make the minimum of memory accesses. Fortunately, this comes about naturally, to some extent.

As operands occupy memory as well as instructions, consideration must be given to word length in this context. Operands are used in a number of formats: (see Chapter 2):

integer arithmetic;
floating-point arithmetic;
patterns of bits (logical);
strings of alphanumeric characters (i.e., mixtures of alphabetic and
   numeric characters, and in practice other characters found on a normal
   keyboard).

Integer arithmetic, in many cases, can invoke as few as 8 bits in counting type processes. If multiplication and division (in particular) are involved, the number can rise to 24 or more.

Floating-point arithmetic frequently operates to 8 or more *digits* precision with exponents in the range $10^{\pm 50}$, or more. Upwards of 32 bits are needed for this.

Decimal arithmetic involves quartets or "nibbles" of bits, i.e. 4 per digit. Precision of up to 16 digits is sometimes required.

Alphanumeric characters usually use 8 bits per character. There is no limit to the number of characters involved in a single "string".

It is clearly quite impossible to choose a computer word length which will meet all the requirements above. However, there is a natural partition on 8 bits insofar that it is usually convenient to partition operands and characters into whole bytes. Integers and floating-point numbers can be readily configured to be of 1, 2, 3 or more whole bytes. Decimal digits can be packed 2 to a byte and alphanumeric characters can use 1 byte each. It is therefore not surprising that most microcomputers are based on the 8-bit word, that minicomputers use word lengths of 16, 24 and 32 bits, and that mainframe computers use 32, 48 and 64 bits. In all cases, this makes byte-orientated addressing possible.

3.6 ADDRESSING MODES

The manner in which operand addresses and branch destinations have been defined so far is what is known as *absolute* or *direct*. The *actual* address is given as part of the instruction and is therefore fixed. This means that:

1. in order to work properly, a computer program and its data must be loaded to a certain place in memory which cannot be altered without modifying the addresses written as part of the program;
2. in a computer with a large memory, every address must be laboriously written down. Each address could be up to 6 digits or 20 bits.

If a computer is to handle several programs at the same time (multi-programming), that is have more than one program resident in memory at any one time, it must be possible to move these programs around. By so doing, the best use can be made of the memory available for any given combinations of programs occupying the memory. This is called *dynamic relocation*. It should be noted that, although programs are moved around, they are either moved in one piece or in carefully sliced blocks. Therefore, in general, the position of one instruction or operand *relative* to another is unchanged. As an example, instructions A and B could occupy memory locations m and $m+k$ before being moved and then occupy locations n and $n+k$ after being moved. They are still separated by k locations.

Taking the above points into consideration, a number of addressing modes have to be built into computer systems both to give flexibility, programmer convenience and economy of memory.

A few such modes are:

(a) *Top-of-memory addressing*

Top-of-memory addressing is also variously known as *direct* and *page-zero addressing*. This method is a simple variation on absolute addressing which economizes on the memory space needed for the operand address by only providing some of the least significant bits. The most significant bits are implicitly zero. A typical microprocessor version of this method is shown in Fig 3.13. A normal 16-bit operand address would give access to 2^{16} ($=64K$) bytes of memory. The top-of-memory address would give access to only the first 2^8 ($=256$). A small version of a computer system can often confine most of its program to this area of memory and thereby reduce both the number of

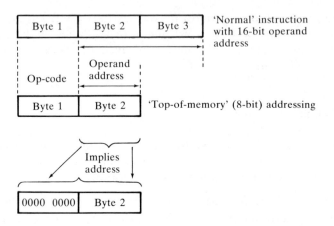

Fig. 3.13 "Top-of-memory" addressing

bytes per instruction from 3 to 2 and reduce the instruction execution time by reducing the number of main-memory accesses. Figure 3.13 is a typical arrangement as used in a microprocessor. Mini and mainframe systems often use similar techniques, although the reason for so doing may be to gain access to a small non-relocatable program at the top of memory which may have some supervisory or system initialization role.

(b) *Base addressing*

A readily implemented method for program relocation without having to change data and jump destinations invokes a register each time an instruction is executed. The contents of this register can be set, say, by the computer's operating system when allocating main memory space for a program. If every operand address and jump destination has the contents of this register added to it, then all parts of a program can be shifted bodily to another part of memory–this shift equalling the value set in this (base) register.

   If the user writes a program as if he has sole occupancy of memory, then the addresses he uses can be on the assumption that his program is located at the top of memory (location 0). If, subsequently, the operating system requires to move his program such that it starts at location 2000, then 2000 must be loaded to the base register for *that* program (Fig. 3.14).

   In order to avoid increasing computer execution time through having to add B to all jump destinations and (main-memory) operand accesses, the base register contents must be available in a flip-flop register or some other bipolar memory. A hardware adder is used to add the base-register contents to the user-supplied address. The adjusted address can then be used as the programmer originally intended. There are several design points:

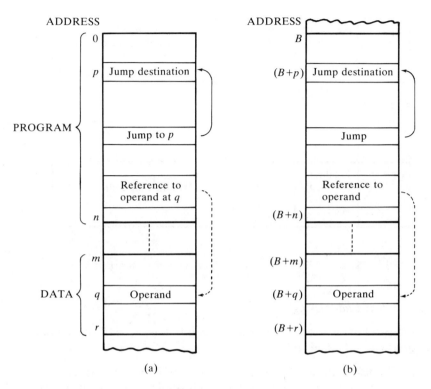

Fig. 3.14 User's program (a) as written original program: (no reference to base register), (b) relocated in memory (base register contains B)

1. The base, being a fast register, is very much like an accumulator in its realization. In fact, as arithmetic normally has to be performed on it to establish a base address, the base register is frequently just a particular register (location) in a scratch-pad memory. Its use, under these circumstances, must be restricted to providing a base. It is not generally available for computation.

2. Use of a scratch-pad location instead of a flip-flop register gives great flexibility because as many or as few locations can be assigned as bases or for general computation, as required. A typical instruction format, involving use of a 16-location scratch-pad for both bases and arithmetic registers is shown in Fig 3.15. Not infrequently, it is assumed that the user's program will use only a small fraction of the main memory available. Therefore, the scratch-pad, and hence the base register, may be, say, 24 bits, whilst the user's address is only of 16 bits. The 8 most significant bits not available in the user's address are assumed to be zeros when added to the 24-bit base-register's contents.

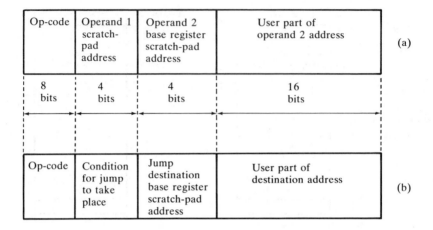

Fig. 3.15 Use of base register in a relocation system for (a) arithmetic and (b) jump instructions

(c)   *Indexed addressing*

In the event of the user requiring more than 16 bits, i.e. 64K of memory, two options can be taken up:

1.   The user's program is segmented into 64K blocks and treated separately by the operating system. This allows adjustment of the base register value when a block boundary is crossed during the execution of a program.

2.   More frequently, the user's program can make up addresses consisting of more than one part. To the 16-bit portion can be added the contents of yet another 24-bit register. This is often known as an *index register*. As with the base register, it can either be a special flip-flop register or a scratch-pad location. If the former, like the base register, the system must provide for arithmetic to be performed on it in order that it may be initialized and modified. If the latter, then it enjoys all the arithmetic flexibility of any other arithmetic scratch-pad location. However, this is a location for user, rather than operating system, use. A memory address is now the sum of the base and index values plus the user's address field in the instruction. To invoke a particular scratch-pad location to be used as an index, instructions must necessarily contain yet another 4-bit field, making the instruction length in Fig. 3.15 total 36 bits.

In many microprocessors, the index is a single flip-flop register. The range of arithmetic that may be performed on it is generally restricted to

LOAD, STORE (move the contents of the index register to a specified memory location), INCREMENT and DECREMENT.

Examples of the use of an index register abound, but generally, it is invoked when the user would otherwise have to repeatedly write similar segments of code differing only in the operand addresses used. Such examples appear in array, string, table-orientated and multibyte operations.

Example If the contents of a table are to be totalled, the alternative to writing a separate instruction for accesses to each table entry is to increment the index register's contents each time. On successive executions of the ADD instruction, the effective address will be one greater (Fig 3.16).

Although some administration is necessary to use the system of Fig. 3.16, e.g. keeping a count of the table entries accessed and thus determining

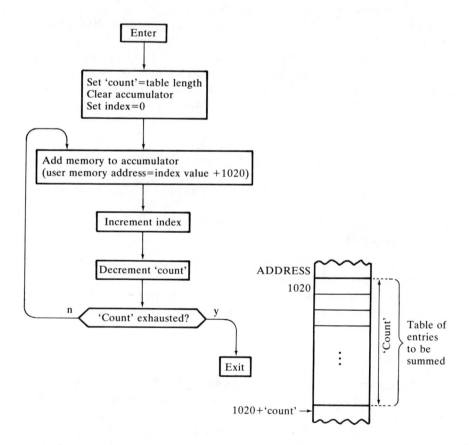

Fig. 3.16 Use of index register in summation of a table's contents

when the task is completed, the amount of code needed is usually much less than if separate "add-to-accumulator" instructions are used. If the facilities for index-register arithmetic exist, the index register can keep its own tally of table entries accessed. This can be done by initializing the index register with the table length, accessing the table from the bottom up (by *decrementing* the index register) and exiting when the index becomes zero. This saves both the use of a separate counter, some code and some execution time.

(d)   *Indirect addressing*

Use of an index register is one example of what is known as *indirect addressing*, i.e. the user supplies not an address (direct) but the address (scratch-pad location) *of* an address. A few micro and mainframe systems exist which employ *doubly indirect addressing*. As the name implies, the user supplies the address of an address which contains the operand address. Its applications are very similar to that of the index approach although it is, through its flexibility, somewhat more difficult to use. In microcomputer systems, doubly indirect addressing is used to get round the disparity between address and data-field lengths. A typical 8-bit microcomputer system may use 16-bit (2-byte) addressing to gain access to a reasonably large memory. If an 8-bit RAM (scratch-pad) forms the first part of a doubly indirect system, a method for translating from 8- to 16-bit working is made possible.

Step 1:   The user address invokes one 8-bit field in the scratch-pad.
Step 2:   This 8-bit field is capable of addressing any one of 256 double-byte locations in main memory, i.e. double bytes at locations 0 and 1, 2 and 3, ...,510 and 511.
Step 3:   The double-byte location contains the 16-bit operand address required.

Use of single indirect addressing to the double-byte memory location can alter the memory contents to provide an indexing facility. Change of user address to the scratch-pad or change of scratch-pad contents gives the flexibility of being able to set up a large number of indexed systems which can be called at will.

(e)   *Relative addressing*

As the programmer's currently used segment of code may only represent a small fraction of the main memory available, it is clearly unreasonable for him to have to use addresses whose bit length reflects the memory and not *his* program size. For example, he may only be using 8K bytes of a 1 megabyte memory. His program only requires 13 bits ($2^{13}=8192$) to give unlimited addressing. However, 20 bits ($2^{20} = 1\ 048\ 576$) are needed to access any part of memory. It is assumed that the program segment may be located anywhere in the available memory. Uneconomical use of addressing fields gives rise to excessive use of memory for such fields, and may also increase instruction execution time if instructions become multiword as a consequence.

In many circumstances, a relative addressing system, particularly for branch (jump) instructions, appears preferable to an "absolute" one. For a branch instruction, the user address indicates how *far* the destination is from the current instruction. This can be a positive or negative quantity depending on whether the branch is forwards, i.e. to a higher memory address, or backwards. In effect, the program counter (PC) is being used as the "base" register to which the signed user offset is added. Typically 2s complement notation is used to "sign" the user's offset. The "base" is frequently taken from the instruction *following* the current one so that a user (relative) address of zero would merely cause the destination to be next instruction in memory. This would be equivalent to a no branch, no operation, instruction. (Earlier in this chapter it was pointed out that the program counter is usually incremented as soon as it has fetched the current instruction. It is therefore only necessary to add the user offset to this value to compute the absolute destination address.)

The relative system of addressing is particularly useful where relocation is used in multi-access or multiprogramming situations, because no base address is required. The base will have already been established as part of the program-counter contents when this block of code was relocated and execution started. Therefore, a base register does not have to figure as part of a branch instruction. Instruction length and execution time are thus both saved. The base register, is, regrettably, not made completely redundant as it is still required for operand accesses. (Relative addressing is not always used in this manner as it sets a fixed addressing relationship between program and data areas, which is sometimes undesirable.).

(f) *Other addressing methods*

Many other, less often used, addressing methods exist. Some have specialized uses such as those which increment or decrement a register used for indirect addressing after each time it is used. Others are just slight variations on those already described. Yet others are just the same in operation as those described but have other names! As an example, if an address field is not required explicitly in an instruction, e.g. for the accumulator in a single-accumulator processor, the address mode may be called "accumulator", "implied", "inherent" or "non-addressed".

3.7 FIRMWARE

Although the implementation of processor timing and control logic is considered in more detail in Chapter 6, at least the requirements and options will be outlined at this point.

Let us refer to the elementary sequences which were detailed earlier in this chapter to realize some of the instructions which are normally made available on a processor's menu. A clear parallel can be drawn between programming at machine level to realize a complex function such as extraction of a square root, and a sequence of elementary steps to realize a machine instruction. For most processors, it is unreasonable to assume that machine instructions are directly implementable in combinational logic. Therefore, a layer of "programming" usually exists between the machine-instruction level and the logic level in the processing hierarchy. The essential difference between machine-level programming and this lower level (microprogramming) lies in the simplicity of the *microsteps*, which involve little more than the transfer of the contents of one register to another or from a register to an adder, etc. However, it is the combination of the registers, adders and other logic in the processor, together with the microprogram, which gives the processor its "identity" at the machine-code level. In effect, if the layout and size of the registers, etc., is changed, we have a different machine—if the microprogram is changed we have what "appears" to be a different machine.

If the microprogram is an element of the processor which can be reasonably easily changed, the possibility of using one processor to "emulate" another becomes a reality. Manifestly, both hardware and microprogram need to be altered to emulate another processor to best effect—but then we would have essentially built the "target" machine. A compromise lies in altering the microprogram only—the easiest part. In practice, the performance of this hybrid will fall far short of the real machine, for a given technology. However, such an approach has considerable benefits. If a manufacturer introduces a new range of improved machines to supplant an older range, existing customers will be encouraged to purchase the new range if the software they developed (at great expense over a long period) can be run on the new equipment. This can happen if the new computers, although of differing architecture, can emulate the old ones by a change of microprogram. (Under these circumstances, it is to be hoped that the new range will be of such improved performance that even taking into account the degrading effect of emulation, the new range will still be attractive to owners of existing equipment.)

The execution rate of microsteps must necessarily be fast compared with that of machine instructions, as it may take up to several dozen or more microsteps to complete the execution of one instruction. Therefore, microprogram memory must be very fast. In the past such memory has been realized in hardwired logic to maximize speed. However, currently, the use of various semiconductor electrically erasable and reprogrammable read-only memories (EPROM) has brought together both high speed and ready reprogrammability of microprograms.

3.8 MULTIPROCESSOR CONFIGURATIONS

If all reasonable means have been used to enhance the performance of a computer system both in terms of memory speed, input/output transfer rates and processing, it is tempting to consider the use of pluralities of subsystems to secure a desired performance. We have already discussed enhancements to memory systems through parallelism. The use of large numbers of fast peripheral devices such as magnetic disk memories can yield improvements too. So far, we have not considered the effects of or methods for using more than one processor.

Conceptually, the simplest way in which more than one processor can be used is by having several independent computer systems working in parallel, each with its own processor. Certainly, this is the easy way of approaching the problem and it is frequently applied when a large number of *independent* tasks have to be executed.

In many instances, interaction between the systems is essential, be it for sharing data files and records or for task sharing (aportionment). A number of processors may be used in some optimal way on fragments of a total task. According to the attributes of the several processors, the possibility of optimization exists. However, interaction involves questions of intra-system communications, the combinations of data transfers that are allowable and the avoidance of clashes of interest.

Here, just processor and memory subsystems are considered, but input/output and other subsystems could be involved too. In order to avoid each subsystem having to possess more than one interface port (i.e., a means for transferring data into or out of a subsystem), the concept of busing is introduced. A bus is usually a data highway to allow communication between a large number of components, subsystems or even computers

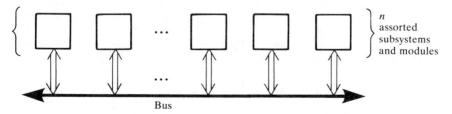

Fig. 3.17 Elementary bus system.

(Fig. 3.17). It is usually arranged to have as many wires as bits in the words to be transmitted, i.e. transmission is bit-parallel. Typical buses have 4-, 8- or 16-bit capacity.

At any one time, only one transaction can take place on the bus, that is, only one subsystem may be "active" and deposit data on the bus. Any combination of the remaining $n-1$ subsystems may be "listeners", although usually only one listens at a time. Control can be exercised either by some external logic and software or by one of the subsystems connected to the bus.

The controller, using control lines other than the bus, can determine which subsystems shall be active (talk) and which shall listen. In some instances, a controller subsystem can relinquish its role and nominate another subsystem as controller.

Earlier, we have already seen situations in which bus implementation of data routing would have been possible.

Example Multiplexure of PC and IR to the memory address port (MAP) in Section 3.4. Here, the processor's microprogram unit is a permanently appointed controller, PC and IR are permanent talkers, which are active alternately, and MAP is a permanent listener. The logic of Fig. 3.7 can be modified to bus form by tying pairs of AND gates together rather than using the OR gates (Fig. 3.18). In effect, the bus performs the OR function, known variously as wired-OR, tie-OR or phantom-OR. The AND gates must be such that their operation is not impaired by being tied together. This largely electrical consideration is discussed more fully in the appendix at the end of this chapter. Applications are also described in Chapters 8 and 10.

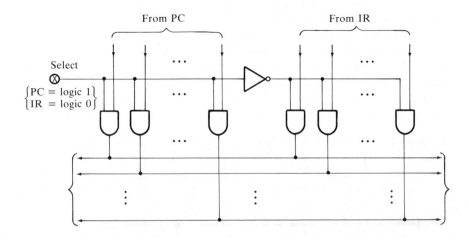

Fig. 3.18 Bus version of Fig. 3.7

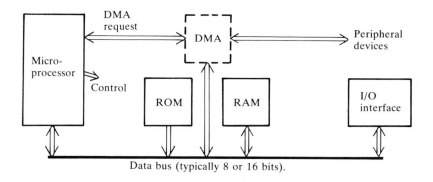

Data bus (typically 8 or 16 bits).

Fig. 3.19 Typical microcomputer data bus

Example Figure 3.19 shows a typical example of busing at the subsystem level. This is a computer system with the microprocessor acting as controller. The listeners can be the microprocessor, ROM,RAM or input/output (I/O) interface. Talkers can be the microprocessor, RAM or I/O interface. Again, only one transaction can take place at a time. In this example, all transactions involve only one talker and one listener at a time. The microprocessor always assumes one of the roles and is therefore never left out of a transaction. An exception to the configuration of Fig. 3.19 occurs when a direct-memory-access unit (DMA) is added to the microcomputer. (This is a device for quickly and autonomously transferring data between RAM and a peripheral device without involving the microprocessor.) Here, the DMA unit sends a request to the microprocessor to temporarily wrest control from it. The microprocessor also ceases to be a participant in bus transactions. When the DMA unit has finished, it returns control to the microprocessor.

In the examples cited so far, there has been no problem over control (and hence timing) because a simple control hierarchy exists in which only one subsystem is used to handle transfers. Even the DMA system of Fig. 3.19 presents no problems as the DMA unit has to *request* the microprocessor for bus control. However, if we have a system consisting of several units of equal status, say processors, no obvious hierarchy exists and each processor will have to compete with the others for control of the bus. Logic will have to be developed to *arbitrate* between requests for control—a situation similar to that described in Chapter 7 in which subsystems compete for access to a common resource. In effect, the bus is a common resource as it can only handle one transaction at a time.

It is clear that buses, although providing a simple and economical communications medium, can degrade the performance of individual subsystems because of request queues forming at the bus. Generally speaking, the provision of multiple-bus systems which connect subsystems having a multiplicity of ports do not help much either as the individual ports will have to queue to obtain service from *within* the subsystem. In other words, multiported subsystems merely move the queuing problem to within the subsystem rather than between subsystems. This argument is not valid if substantial differences exist in the performances of subsystems connected to a bus, for it is likely that the faster subsystems will be able to support several ports to every one associated with a slower subsystem.

3.9 PROCESSOR PIPELINING

Each microstep executed in a processor can be implemented by some combinational logic plus a register to hold results pending the next micro-step. For economy's sake, as much of this hardware as possible is shared amongst a number of processes. As an example, in floating-point arithmetic, the same shift register can be used to pre-normalize operands, scale operands (prior to addition) and post-normalize them. The same register may be used to hold each sub-product during a multiplication instruction (Section 5.8). Such a sharing arrangement generally precludes the execution of more than one instruction at a time. However, if the logic for each microstep has its own combinational section and temporary registers, a pipeline process can be realized. This allows several instructions to be processed at a time with each at a different stage of completion (Fig. 3.20). The rate of instruction execution can therefore be up to n times the rate for a "one instruction at a time" processor if the pipeline contains n sections.

There are a number of difficulties associated with this sort of processing:

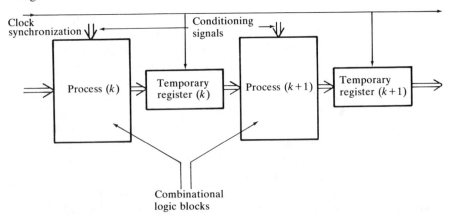

Fig. 3.20   Schematic of pipeline processing

1. Usually a large number of separate pipelines are needed to cater for each type of instruction. In the limit, one pipeline would be required per instruction! However, the use of conditioning signals can make it possible for instructions which need a similar number of pipeline sections to be processed in the same pipe. The instructions which share a pipe would also have to be reasonably similar in "form", e.g. floating-point ADD, SUBTRACT and COMPARE would be a case in point. Conditioning signals include the operation code to differentiate between instructions. By passing the conditioning signals along a shift register pipeline concurrently with the instructions, different instructions can follow each other.

2. Each process in a pipe must take about the same time. The rate of shifting down the pipe is then at a rate tied to the slowest process section. Unless considerable care is exercised, time can be wasted in the faster processes.

3. A pipeline process has to be stopped (halted) periodically because a JUMP (BRANCH, SUBROUTINE CALL) has been encountered and the results of an instruction are needed to determine whether the (conditional) JUMP should be taken or ignored. This empties the pipe and creates a delay before the pipe can be refilled. This is undesirable since the pipeline only gains over the "one instruction at a time processor" if the pipe is full.

4. The high instruction rate of the pipeline processor (sometimes as little as 10 ns per instruction) makes enormous demands on the computer's memory. Unless the memory can match the instruction fetch and operand access rates required, the system will "bottleneck". The use of buffer memories and interleaved memory techniques is very common in these circumstances.

The pipeline processor is particularly useful if the processor has a very small instruction "menu", as happens in some specialized applications such as real-time simulation and signal processing. It represents an interesting contrast with multiprocessor configurations—the latter processing many instructions concurrently but only one instruction in any one processor at a time.

3.10 MAN/PROCESSOR INTERFACES

Manual access to the various parts of a computer system is most readily provided via the processor. The processor has many registers and flags which will require inspection during maintenance, low-level software development and system modification and reconfiguration. Through the processor, it is possible to impinge manually on all parts of the computer system, be it memory, peripheral devices or telecommunications lines. The major forms of access are by an engineer's control panel/visual display mounted directly on and interfaced directly to the processor or by a console typewriter (operator's Teletype). This latter is just an ordinary Teletype but specifically used for maintenance and operator protocol. The engineer's panel can allow, via a suitable keyboard and displays, inspection of any processor register, memory location, flag condition or microprogram step. It would also permit manual operation of the processor, i.e. setting of registers and flags to any value, making the processor run (execute), halt or perform single instructions or, indeed, single microsteps. This approach gives the complete flexibility needed by the development and maintenance engineers. Regrettably, such a facility is expensive and poorly utilized, except as adumbrated.

The console Teletype is a much less expensive and better utilized alternative. However, it requires resident software in the processor to effect the appropriate protocol—a monitor ROM, perhaps. The other disadvantage is that to operate properly, it requires a certain proportion of the computer to be operational. In the early stages of development or for a variety of faults, this cannot be assumed.

Different approaches to the man/machine interface are adopted according to the system. A large mini, midi or mainframe system will almost certainly have both a comprehensive engineer's panel and a console Teletype. The two together form a short hierarchy for fault diagnosis, according to the severity of the fault.

Microprocessor systems have so few components in a minimal system that it is sufficient to use a teletype (or VDU or keypad/display) plus a monitor ROM to give sufficient access. Such a ROM can be used not only for fault diagnosis but also to effect program entry, peripheral control and program editing and debug. Small mini systems may either follow microcomputer practice or provide a minimal keyset/display as well.

The provision of reliable keypads and bright, unambiguous displays, plus the logic in the man/machine interface can be as expensive as a small processor. Indeed, in larger machines, it may be a processor in its own right. Clearly, great care must be exercised in interface design if the correct balance between economics and usefulness is to be achieved.

3.11   APPENDIX: TIE-ORING OF GATES FOR BUS OPERATION

Several methods are in common use but they all have characteristics which are shared, i.e., it must be possible for the controller subsystem to disable all potential talkers apart from the chosen one. Disabling in this context means that a gate connected to the bus will not influence the operation of the bus

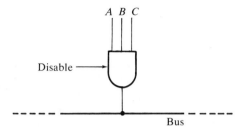

Fig. 3.21 Schematic of a bus-connectable AND gate.

whatever the input logic levels applied to it. An AND gate with a "disable" input is shown in Fig. 3.21.

"Disable" may be triggered by either a logic 0 or 1, depending on the gate electronics. As "talking" refers to the injection of current to the bus, the disable operation is essentially one of preventing transistors, connected to the bus, from coming into conduction.

For transistor–transistor logic (TTL), two output forms exist and therefore two approaches to disabling are used (Fig. 3.22).

In Fig. 3.22(a) only one active transistor T_1 is connected to the bus. Disabling is simply effected by applying a logic 0 at D. This cuts off the transistor T_1 in the same way as a logic 0 at A, B or C. All talkers share a common load resistor R_L which pulls the bus to a logic 1 when all talker transistors are cut off.

For the "totem-pole" arrangement in Fig. 3.22(b), both transistors T_2 and T_3 must be cut off when the talker is disabled. A logic 1 at the disable input diverts current into the base of the multi-collector transistor and brings the bases of transistors T_2 and T_3 to near ground potential. Whatever the states of A, B and C under these circumstances, the talker is inactive. There are many ways in which a totem pole may be disabled—this form has been shown as simple illustration and does not represent common practice. Gates of the type described are variously referred to as "tri-state", and "three state"—which describes their three outputs—logic 0, logic 1 or inactive (high impedance).

For TTL, it will be noticed that logic 1 ($\nleqslant 2.4$ V) is achieved either by the active talker issuing a logic 1 or by disabling *all* talkers. Hence, the active state, i.e. when a talker is passing current, is logic 0. This is what is known as an "active logic-0" system and is effectively a negative logic configuration. Other logic families may be logic 0 or logic 1 active. As an example ECL (for which logic 0 and 1 may be -1.6 V and -0.8 V respectively) is logic 1 active. If the talker transistor, which is an emitter follower, is cut off by the disable signal, the more negative logic level will be achieved (logic 0). (The output transistor for many ECL gates is in conduction for both logic 0 and logic 1 outputs. Disable for such gates then means that the transistor is in a lesser

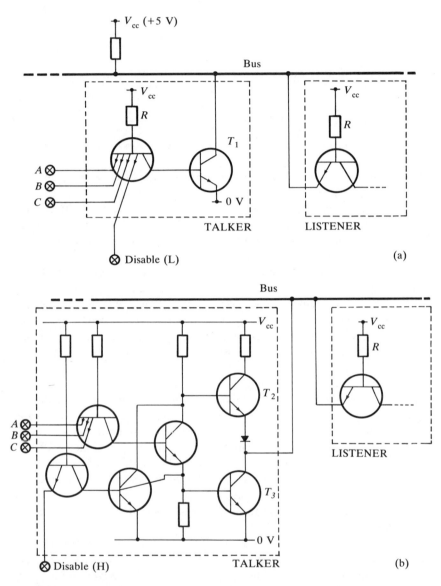

Fig. 3.22 TTL bus implementation for (a) open-collector and (b) 'totem-pole' talkers.

state of conduction, i.e. not being able to pass sufficient current to achieve a logic 1.) For some technologies, particularly those using long bus lines, twin balanced-wire techniques must be used to minimize both the sending and receiving of interference. Such buses also need to be terminated at both ends to prevent signal reflections.

EXERCISES

3.1 Take typical microprocessors, mini and mainframe computers and compare their instruction sets, paying particular attention to the number of *essentially* different types and the number of minor variations on each type. Notice how the operation codes relate to the different instruction types and their variations.

3.2 Write program segments for the square-root routine of Section 3.1, using machine-code instructions from the processors in Exercise 3.1. Compare the times to complete one loop.

3.3 From curves of the form $y = f(x) - A$, derive algorithms and write programs for the extraction of cube and fifth roots of x.

3.4 If the processor of Fig. 3.6 is to work with a main memory of 8K words and have 32 instructions in its menu, how many locations should each memory location have and how many bits are needed for PC and IR?

3.5 Develop the logic for a 4-way, 2-bit data selector using only AND, OR and NOT gates.

3.6 Develop the logic of Fig. 3.6, so that the processor is capable of operating with instructions having a two-address format. (The instructions can be assumed to be of the one-word, fixed-length variety.)

3.7 A hypothetical single-address processor having a one word per instruction format has a menu of four instructions: ADD, SUBTRACT, BRANCH UNCONDITIONALLY and BRANCH IF ACCUMULATOR NEGATIVE. Develop a block diagram of such a processor and its arithmetic unit. Decide on a set of operation codes to suit the instruction set and design the logic for instruction decoding and conditions processing. Minimize the amount of logic used.

3.8 Write a combined flowchart for the instructions of the previous question and condense them as much as possible by sharing similar tracts of microsequence. (*Hint:* use the output from the instruction decoder to provide branching information after shared tracts.)

3.9 Modify your processor design of Exercises 3.7 and 3.8 so that the branch instructions become "relative" ones.

3.10 Design the logic for an arithmetic unit for use in a single-address processor. (One operand will come from the accumulator and one from memory.) The unit should be able to add, subtract and multiply in 2s complement notation and share a common, parallel, adder array. (Only the most significant product word should be returned to the accumulator after multiplication.)

3.11 A program segment has to be written to memory for evaluating square roots of 3-byte binary numbers using Newton's algorithm. The processor can add, subtract and shift (rotate). Subroutines should be used as follows:

Subroutine 1   forms a quotient using the formula in Section 5.9 calling subroutine 2 for forming products.

Subroutine 2   forms the product of 3-byte operands calling subroutine 3 to form 2-byte products of 1-byte operands.

Subroutine 3   forms 2-byte products from 1-byte operands using add, subtract and rotate (through carry) instructions.

The software is to be allocated memory space as follows:

The main segment starts at 0100 and finishes at 0180 (decimal)
Subroutine 1 starts at 0200 and finishes at 0280 (decimal)
Subroutine 2 starts at 0300 and finishes at 0380 (decimal)
Subroutine 3 starts at 0400 and finishes at 0480 (decimal)
Stack pointer initialized to 0500.

Draw up an *outline* flowchart of the software sufficient to ascertain which subroutines are called and when. Determine the contents of the stack throughout the run time of the program segment.

3.12 Given that processor activity can be partitioned into just two sections, namely memory cycles (fetching and writing) and instruction execution (the remainder), compare the performances of the following systems for ADD, BRANCH (unconditionally), MULTIPLY and STORE (transfer the contents of the accumulator to memory—the address is given in the address field):

(a) Single-address processor, ferrite core memory (access and cycle times of 0.5 μs and 1.0 μs); (data are available from memory after 0.5 μs and can be used by the processor during the write-back part of the memory cycle).

(b) As for (a) but a MOSRAM replaces the ferrite-core memory having equal read and write times of 1.0 μs.

(c) As for (b) but using a 0.5 μs MOSRAM.

(d) Repeat (a)–(c) but for a *two*-address system with no accumulator and the STORE instruction replaced with a MOVE (transfer contents of one location to another).

Notes: 1. The *execution* times for the instructions are: ADD (0.3 μs), BRANCH (0.1 μs), MULTIPLY (2.0 μs) and STORE (0.1 μs).

2. All instructions use one memory word regardless of instruction format.

3.13 What is the effect on your results of Exercise 3.12 if the instructions used in part (a) are two words long?

3.14 How many bytes are needed to represent variables to about 0.01% precision in a multibyte system?

3.15 By inspecting the instruction set of the Motorola M6800 microprocessor and arranging it in a matrix form, determine which bits of the operation code are used to determine instruction type (i.e. addressing mode, etc.). Identify the instructions which do not follow this pattern.

3.16 Write program segments for the Motorola M6800 and Intel 8080 microprocessors for adding two *n*-byte unsigned operands. Compare the program space required and the execution times when *n* is large. (*Hint*: make use of indexed addressing and memory pointers, where possible.)

3.17 Write notes on the various addressing modes made available in the following microprocessors: Intel 8080, Motorola M6800, Fairchild F-8, Texas Instruments TMS9900.

3.18 Examine the internal register and bus structure of a number of microprocessors by reference to the manufacturer's literature and determine (in outline) the data movements necessary to execute each instruction offered. Take note of the manner in which the internal busing is organized.

3.19 Write a merged flowchart for floating-point addition, subtraction and comparison. Outline the logic needed for each stage. Subdivide each stage so that it only needs about 30 gate delays to process and thereby develop a pipeline processor for these instructions. (*Note*: assume the mantissae are of 56 bits.)

REFERENCES

Hill, F. J. and Peterson, G. R. (1978), *Digital Systems : Hardware Organization and Design*, Wiley International, New York.

Lewin, D. W. (1972) *Theory and Design of Digital Computers*, Nelson, London, Chapters 2 and 9.

Peatman, J. B. (1978), *Microcomputer-based Design*, McGraw-Hill, New York.

User's manuals for Intel 8080, Motorola M6800, Fairchild F-8 and T.I. TMS9900.

4 MEMORY SYSTEMS

4.1 INTRODUCTION

Memory is the key component which distinguishes the computer from any other digital system. It is the memory that allows the storage of program material and thereby makes the sequence of operations to be carried out readily available for the processor. Anyone who has had the opportunity to carry out some complex operation on both programmable and nonprogrammable calculators must be aware of the advantage of program storage. (A programmable calculator is therefore, in many respects, a computer in the terms discussed here.) A computer would normally hold data as well as program material in memory for the same reason.

Having established the desirability of storing such information in the computer, it is now possible to define some attributes of a memory and to compare the currently available memory forms with this ideal. Without being too concerned at this point with the finer points of organization but concentrating purely on the "spirit" of defining some medium for holding large numbers of binary patterns, the following characteristics would appear ideal:

1. unlimited capacity;
2. negligible writing and access times;
3. negligible energy demand to operate;
4. nonvolatility (no loss of information due to failure of the power supplies);
5. low cost per unit of memory (bit);
6. high reliability and immunity to environmental factors.

With this large number of factors to consider, it is not surprising that a wide variety of memory forms, involving different physical principles of information retention, have been developed over the years. Some of these varieties have been developed hand in hand as other computer components have evolved—in particular, semiconductor memories (discussed later in this chapter). However, also not surprisingly, no single memory has been developed so far which enjoys all the above attributes—development would have come to a halt in such an event! Nonetheless, many memories are characterized by possessing combinations of these attributes, and the manner in which these memories are used in systems reflects their advantages in such applications.

Principally, this chapter is going to consider memory used in conventional current micro, mini and mainframe computer situations—in particular, the difficult question of how different types of memories should be used in concert to best effect will be answered. A mixed system is known as a memory *hierarchy*. In addition, less common situations will also be considered such as those of interest to the military and certain manufacturing and industrial plant where the environment may be hostile due to radiation or mechanical or thermal stress.

The chapter is organized into a series of sections starting with a description of simple memories. Thereafter, memories will be considered in terms of decreasing speed and cost. The final sections will be concerned with memory hierarchies and the manner in which differing memories are interfaced.

4.2 READ/WRITE MEMORIES FABRICATED FROM LOGIC MODULES

Whatever developments take place in logic systems to increase speed, either by increasing the speed of individual gates or by design techniques involving parallelism or pipelining (see Section 3.9), there is a corresponding pressure on the memory designer to match them. (There is no point in being able to process information at high speed if the data cannot be obtained (accessed) at a speed suitable for the processor or disposed of after the processing has taken place.) Fortunately, the same logic elements that do the processing can always be used to provide memory at the highest level, so at least individual gate speeds and fastest memory operation times go hand in hand. Furthermore, parallelism in a processor's operation can be matched by parallelism in memory operation. That is, the storage and access of information can be done on a bit-parallel, or even a word-parallel basis. There is thus no intrinsic reason why an improvement in gate performance should not precipitate a corresponding memory development.

Flip-flops (Marcus, 1972; Millman and Halkias, 1972)

The most basic semiconductor storage element is the flip-flop. This is a
device which can hold just one bit of information and must therefore have
two stable states. In order to be "settable" to either state, it must have two
inputs—one to *set* it (logic 1) and one to *reset* it (logic 0). Figure 4.1 shows
how a basic two-state device, the fed-back non-inverting buffer, can be
developed into the two-input flip-flop. In (a) we have a gate whose output
will stay at logic 1 if so set but which will also stay at logic 0 if initially set to 0.
However, there is no way in which its state, once set, can be altered.
Replacement of the gate by an OR gives an extra input which will allow the

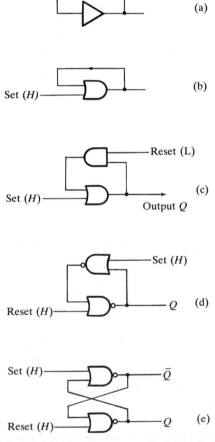

Fig. 4.1 Development of the flip-flop: (a) two-state device; (b)
"set" (mechanism to change output from 0 to 1); (c) "reset"
(mechanism to break feedback loop); (d) flip-flop using two identical
gates; (e) conventional schematic.

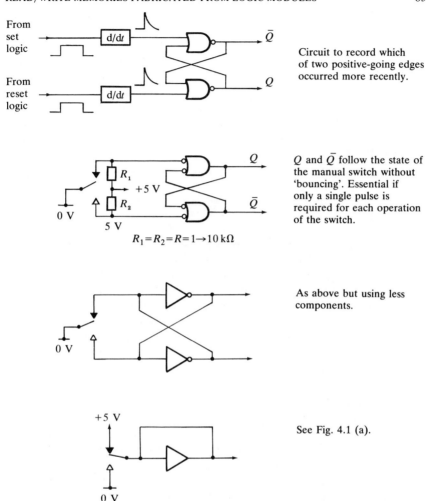

From set logic

Circuit to record which of two positive-going edges occurred more recently.

From reset logic

Q and $\bar{Q}$ follow the state of the manual switch without 'bouncing'. Essential if only a single pulse is required for each operation of the switch.

$R_1 = R_2 = R = 1 \rightarrow 10 \, \text{k}\Omega$

As above but using less components.

See Fig. 4.1 (a).

Fig. 4.2 Two applications of the flip-flop: (a) pulsed operation; (b) switch interface for "bounce-free" operation. (Choice depends gate technology used, e.g. TTL, CMOS, etc.)

output to be set, when required. However, such an arrangement, once set, cannot be reset. The feedback "loop" can be broken by an AND gate which, when its free input is 0, forces the OR output back to the reset (0) state (Fig. 4.1(c)). More conventional versions of the basic arrangement of (c) are shown in (d) and (e).

This device is often known as the R–S or S–R flip-flop because of the two inputs "S" (set) and "R" (reset). The two outputs are complementary, i.e. they assume opposite logic levels (states) at any time. Operation is as follows for the NOR implemented version shown in Fig. 4.1:

In its quiescent state, both the set and reset inputs are at logic 0. Under these conditions, the inputs exert no influence on the flip-flop. If we assume that one of the outputs is at logic 0, then it is clear that the other will be at logic 1 by inversion through the remaining NOR gate. This is a stable situation since the latter NOR gate's logic 0 output ensures that the (assumed) logic 1 on the first output is maintained. If the gate whose output is a logic 1 now has a logic 1 applied to its free input, the state of the device changes, i.e. the gate to which the input was applied will now have a logic 0 output and the other gate a logic 1. By noticing the symmetry of the flip-flop, it is easy to deduce the effect of applying a logic 1 to the remaining free input (whilst the other input is logic 0).

Although used in a variety of applications (Fig. 4.2), the flip-flop has two serious drawbacks:

1. Normally, it must be protected against inadvertant simultaneous application of set and reset commands, for it ceases to be a memory element under such circumstances. If the set and reset commands are *removed* simultaneously, the resulting state of the device is indeterminate. Whilst "set" and "reset" are both asserted, i.e. active, the two flip-flop states (outputs) cease to be complementary.

2. The flip-flop is, at *all* times, vulnerable to the states of the set and reset inputs. Frequently, processing involves *loops* of operations whose hardware counterpart is *feedback*. The feedback frequently only involves the use of combinational logic so that some mechanism is needed to break the loop and prevent oscillation (Fig. 4.3). A typical situation represented by Fig. 4.3 is that of an accumulator. Each bit of an accumulator consists of an adder mechanism—which is combinational, and a flip-flop for holding one bit of a running total. The input allows fresh numbers to be entered and totalized. If there were no mechanism to break the loop, an incoming number could be added to the running total many times over, as it would merely circulate round the loop indefinitely. One convenient form of protection consists of logic for gating the set and reset inputs with a control signal (called CLOCK or STROBE). A NOR gate representation is shown in Fig. 4.4.

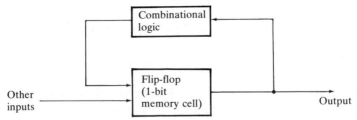

Fig. 4.3   Use of a flip-flop in a hardware loop.

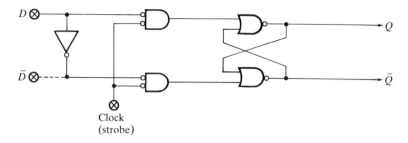

Fig. 4.4 Latch (or gated) flip-flop.

When CLOCK is at logic 1, both SET and RESET inputs to the basic flip-flop are at logic 0 and therefore ineffective. Hence the flip-flop is immune to changes in the state of the D (data) input. The flip-flop will respond to changes in D at all times that CLOCK is at logic 0. In this device, known as a LATCH or GATED FLIP-FLOP, it is common for the $\bar{D}$ input to be derived from D (using an inverter), rather than separately. This both reduces the number of connections to the latch and eliminates the possibility of both SET and RESET being simultaneously applied to the flip-flop.

The circuit of Fig. 4.4 is only a *slight* improvement on the basic S–R flip-flop because it is still not really a device which would be ideal for use in Fig. 4.3. In practice, it is usually not possible to arrange that CLOCK opens the latch gates for a sufficiently short time to prevent an oscillatory loop. (It is not unusual for flip-flops to have their outputs directly connected to their own inputs—so the loop delay can be very short.) Therefore, the *latch* is most frequently used in situations in which gates are needed to protect the flip-flop but where *no electrical feedback* is involved. Figure 4.5 shows latches applied to a display system.

It is assumed that the data to be displayed are available only at certain specified times at the processor's output port. At other times, the data line can contain garbage (from the display's viewpoint). So it is necessary to open the latch gates only when the data are valid—they are kept closed at other

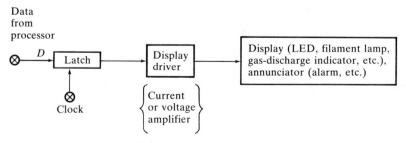

Fig. 4.5 Latch application.

times. If the latch of Fig. 4.4 is used in this application, CLOCK would be at logic 0 only when the data are valid.

To overcome the difficulties of having to provide unreasonably short clock pulses to operate the latch of Fig. 4.4, the circuit of Fig. 4.3 can be enhanced by using two latches in tandem. The system is not unlike that of a two-gate canal lock in which water from the higher level is prevented from flowing into the lower level by arranging that one gate (at least) is always closed. The same can be done with latches by arranging that one is operated by CLOCK and the other by $\overline{\text{CLOCK}}$ (Fig. 4.6). This flip-flop is known as a *master–slave* type.

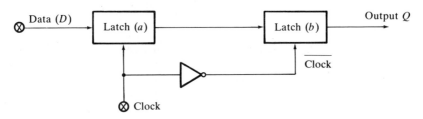

Fig. 4.6   Development of master-slave flip-flop from two latches.

Whatever the state of CLOCK, *one* of the latches must have its gates closed and therefore there is never direct feedthrough from data (D) to output (Q) (or $\bar{Q}$). The operation is summarized in Fig. 4.7, where it may be seen that *effectively* the configuration samples D on the logic 0 to 1 transition of CLOCK. The transition, being fast, can be reasonably approximated to an *instant* of time rather than a *duration*—which would be a necessary attribute of a practical pulse.

Inspection of Fig. 4.7 shows that provided the propagation time exceeds the data hold time, then the extreme form of feedback, i.e. direct connection of Q or $\bar{Q}$ to D, is permissible. This is usually the case. Figure 4.7 can be readily redrawn for the logic 1 to 0 transition of the output which, of course, also uses the rising edge of CLOCK.

Other flip-flops (Marcus, 1972)

(a) *J–K flip-flop*

This flip-flop can be developed from any basic edge-triggered flip-flop and is simply a form which allows any of the four possible binary events to take place when the flip-flop is clocked. The four possibilities are:

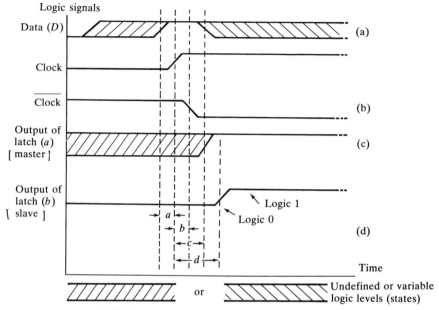

Fig. 4.7 Setting of master-slave flip-flop from the reset state: a=set-up time—the time during which data must be valid before rising edge of clock (typically 10 ns for TTL); b=internal clock inverter propagation delay; c=hold time—the time during which data must continue to be valid after rising edge of clock; d=propagation time—the delay from rising edge of clock to output of flip-flop.

no change of state;
always set the flip-flop;   } Regardless of
always reset the flip-flop;   } its state before
always change the state of the flip-flop. } clocking.

These four possibilities can be encoded onto two control bits for the flip-flop which are applied, as levels, immediately prior to the application of CLOCK. A common encoding form and its corresponding state diagram are shown in Fig. 4.8.

Comment	J	K	Q_{n+1}
No change	0	0	Q_n
Always set	1	0	1
Always reset	0	1	0
Always change	1	1	$\bar{Q}_n$

Fig. 4.8 Transition table for $J - K$ flip-flop.

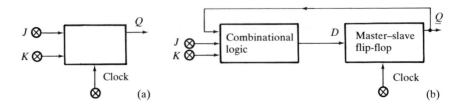

Fig. 4.9 Master–slave (MS) flip-flop: (a) conceptual; (b) master–slave implementation.

The flip-flop, in conceptual and master–slave form, is shown in Fig. 4.9. As the J and K inputs are controls, they must be established before clocking with a suitable set-up time margin (Fig. 4.10).

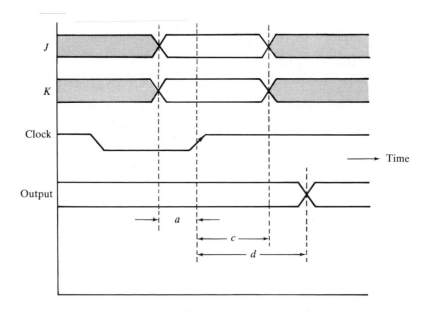

Fig. 4.10 J–K flip-flop timing (*Note: a—d* have the same meanings as in Fig. 4.7.).

If a master–slave (M–S) implementation for the J–K flip-flop is used, the necessary combinational logic can be derived by remembering that Q_{n+1} corresponds to the state of D at the time of the $(n+1)$th clock pulse (Fig. 4.11).

Figure 4.11 shows that

$$D=\bar{J}\bar{K}Q_n+J\bar{K}\bar{Q}_n+J\bar{K}Q_n+JK\bar{Q}_n=J\bar{Q}_n+\bar{K}Q_n.$$

J	K	Q_n	Q_{n+1}	D
0	0	0	0	0
0	0	1	1	1
0	1	0	0	0
0	1	1	0	0
1	0	0	1	1
1	0	1	1	1
1	1	0	1	1
1	1	1	0	0

Fig. 4.11 State table for master–slave J–K flip-flop.

The Karnaugh map for this system is shown in Fig. 4.12. The existence of a static hazard shown dotted in Fig. 4.12 is of no consequence as this is, of course, a clocked (synchronous) system.

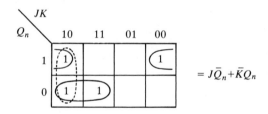

$$= J\bar{Q}_n + \bar{K}Q_n$$

Fig. 4.12 Combinational logic for MS J–K flip-flop.

(b) *D-type flip-flop*

This is also an edge-triggered flip-flop but uses fewer gates than the master–slave type. However, some of its inputs impose a heavier load on circuits driving it. A typical circuit and timing diagram are shown in Fig. 4.13.

Some other types of flip-flop are introduced in the tutorial examples at the end of this chapter and the worked solutions in the *Teachers' Manual*.

Latches, master–slave and D-type flip-flops use ordinary gates and therefore benefit whenever improvements in gate technology take place. For the highest-speed logic families, flip-flops can toggle (switch from 0 to 1 and back) at rates up to around 1 GHz. Regrettably, the very fastest logic families tend to consume the greatest amounts of power and force the use of highly refined fabrication techniques (to keep device dimensions small).

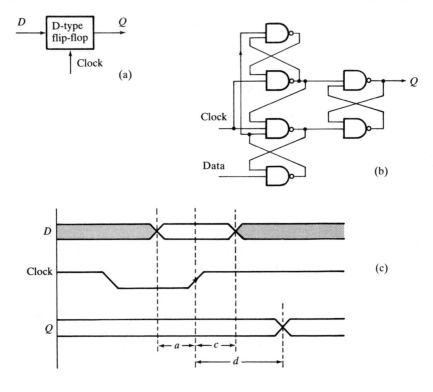

Fig. 4.13 D-type flip-flop: (a) conceptual; (b) typical logic; (c) timing.

Consequently, such flip-flops are very expensive and create problems of heating and power provision. Every effort is therefore made in the provision of memory for a processor to minimize the use of such memory forms without seriously sacrificing overall performance.

If, after taking such factors into account, the data rate of the flip-flops is insufficient, then paralleling techniques may have to be introduced. The parallel register is the most common form and consists of a set of flip-flops arranged with a common clock line. A typical application is in the fabrication of an accumulator incorporating a parallel adder (Fig. 4.14).

Each operand to be accumulated is presented, in sequence, to one side of the parallel adder. The current subtotal, stored in the parallel register, is presented to the other side of the adder. A sufficient time is allowed for the adder to settle and then a clock pulse is applied to all the flip-flops concurrently. The original subtotal in the register is now replaced by the new one. It will be observed that this example is yet another in which the use of latches would be unsuitable as a combinational feedback path exists from every

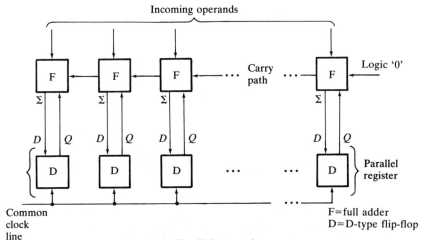

Fig. 4.14 Parallel accumulator.

flip-flop Q output, through an adder back to the flip-flop's D input. The timing for the accumulator of Fig. 4.14 is shown in Fig. 4.15.

Timing periods a, b, c, d represent the adder array settling time, flip-flop data set-up time, flip-flop data hold time and flip-flop propagation times, respectively. It may be seen that the input operand must be static for at least $(a+b)$ ns before clock is applied and for not less than c ns after clock. At all other times, the input operand is ignored and may be altered at will.

The parallel register described is typically used as the accumulator and temporary (one location) memories in various parts of processors and control units in a computer.

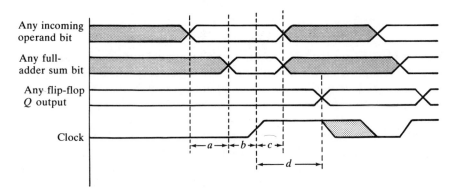

Fig. 4.15 Accumulator timing.

Scratch-pads (Hill and Peterson, 1978, Ch. 18)

Parallel registers, although very fast, are only used in relatively small measure in most systems because:

1. They are not suitable for large-scale integration (LSI) as two leadouts are needed per flip-flop (apart from power, clock and other service lines such as clear, etc.).
2. Being fabricated from 6–10 gates per flip-flop, they use considerable chip area and power.
3. The large number of chips, and hence leadouts, makes for high fabrication costs in terms of printed-circuit cards and inter-card wiring.

An alternative approach is to use matrices of flip-flops where possible. Such a memory is normally organized so that access to any flip-flop takes a fixed time, regardless of the order in which such access takes place. This is known as a random-access memory. The fastest such memories usually employ a bipolar technology. This gives rise to an alternative name to "scratch-pad", viz. bipolar-random-access memory.

Each flip-flop can be made quite simple if the edge-triggering characteristic is omitted. The use of a matrix also means that flip-flops can share the interface to the outside world which both saves on power and simplifies the design of the basic cell.

A typical cell and its equivalent circuit are shown in Fig. 4.16. Each flip-flop consists of a pair of directly coupled cross-connected multi-emitter transistors. If all the emitters are grounded, then the flip-flop operates conventionally, that is, just one transistor is on and one is off at a time. Typically, the saturation conditions for an "on" transistor are $V_{be}=0.7$ V and $V_{ce(sat)}=0.1$–0.4 V. If I_c and I_b are the collector and base "on" currents, then

$$I_c=[V_{cc}-V_{ce(sat)}]/R$$

and

$$I_b=[V_{cc}-V_{be}]/R.$$

h_{FE} must be greater than I_c/I_b, which for all practical purposes is little more than 1. This is easy to achieve. The value of R is chosen to be as high as possible to reduce power consumption, limited only by (a) the difficulties associated with fabricating high-value integrated resistors; (b) the need to charge the inevitable stray circuit capacitances, at a suitably high speed, when switching takes place. A typical cell consumes 0.5–2 mW.

A single current sense and write circuit is shared by all the cells and it is arranged that only one cell can, at any time, draw current through this circuit. The equivalent logic circuit of a single cell is shown in Fig. 4.16(b) and it is seen that the multi-emitter configuration performs the dual function of providing a flip-flop and a cell select gate on each input to the cell. This

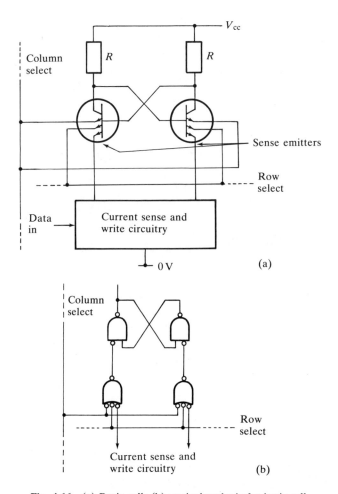

Fig. 4.16 (a) Basic cell; (b) equivalent logic for basic cell.

provides the basis of a two-dimensional selection arrangement. Treating the two dimensions as rows and columns, n address lines can select any one of 2^n cells. Assuming the use of a square matrix, this means that splitting the n address wires into two blocks of $n/2$ gives addressing to a square of side $2^{n/2}$.

The cell design of Fig. 4.16 can be used in a *matrix* by using *row* and *column* select connections to the emitters of *each* cell. Normally, all column and row wires are at logic 0 (approximately 0 V). If any cell has a logic 1 imposed on *either* its column or row select wire, no change takes place as there is still a "ground" connection available for every transistor via one of its emitters. However, if a cell has a logic 1 on *both* column and row select wires, the only ground connection for any transistor is via the current sense circuitry (Fig. 4.16). The state of the selected flip-flop can thus be determined by noting the current difference through the two active emitters. All cells can share the same current sense circuitry as "none-selected" cells will draw their current through the one or two select wires, which are at logic 0.

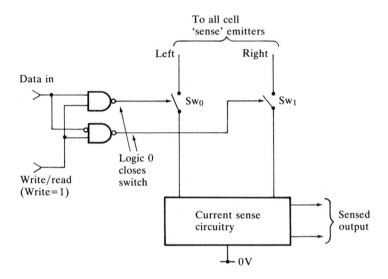

Fig. 4.17 Schematic of the data-writing mechanism for a cell.

Writing to the selected cell can be accomplished by column and row selection (as for reading) accompanied by gating of the current paths through the current sense circuitry (Fig. 4.17). If a logic 0 is to be written, Sw_0 is opened and Sw_1 closed. If the flip-flop of Fig. 4.16(a) is connected to the circuitry of Fig. 4.17, then whatever the previous state of the flip-flop, the left-hand transistor will be forced off as no emitter current can flow. The right-hand transistor will therefore conduct. If a logic 1 is to be written, Sw_0 is closed and Sw_1 opened. The flip-flop is then forced to the opposite state. It can be seen by referring to Figs. 4.16 and 4.17, that the state of the selected cell will be available at the chip output during write as well as read.

The simplicity of the individual cells in the matrix means that the burden of timing is thrown upon external circuitry. (Incorrect sequences of address set up and writing, in particular, will cause misoperation of the device.) A typical sequence for reading and writing is shown in Fig. 4.18.

For Fig. 4.18(a), a is the time for which the address must be "settled" before the correct cell is selected and its contents read; b is a short time

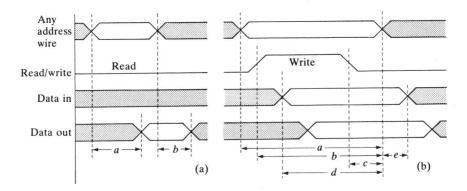

Fig. 4.18 Typical RAM/scratch-pad timing for (a) reading and (b) writing data.

during which the data are still valid after the address has been disturbed. For bipolar memories, a and b are typically 50 ns and 20 ns. For Fig. 4.18(b), the situation is more complex as it is necessary to ensure that writing *only* to the cell selected is accomplished and that the correct data are written. Timing intervals a, b, c and d are therefore very critical.

It can be readily seen that the correct operation of an edge-triggered flip-flop is much easier than for a flip-flop used as a cell in a scratch-pad. In addition, an important difference should be noted in terms of data rate. If 8 flip-flops are used for data storage, then 8 edge-triggered flip-flops will operate at least 8 times as fast as an 8-cell flip-flop matrix. Primarily, this is because the 8 cells in a matrix have their incoming and outgoing data "funnelled" through single-bit ports, whereas each edge-triggered flip-flop has its own port. (The factor is often rather more than 8 because of the need to leave time for cell-selection circuitry to operate before the cell is read. This selection circuitry must be capable of sinking current from all the emitters to which it is tied. The high current drivers needed for this tend to operate slowly.)

A number of integrated circuits, variously known as register files and parallel register arrays, have been developed in order to reduce this unfortunate data "funnelling" effect without resort to ordinary parallel register structures with their high lead-out count. Most are arranged on a word-select basis i.e. a matrix of $m \times n$ flip-flops is used where selection is of any m-bit word selected from n. If n is small, a separate chip lead-out may be made available to select each word. If n is large, an encoded address bus of $\log_2 n$ wires is provided so that each of the n combinations yielded by $\log_2 n$ wires represents an unique memory address. Apart from register files, several bipolar scratch-pads (often known as bipolar random-access (or read/write) memories) are organized such that the matrix is, in effect, 3-dimensional—the third dimension representing bit width. In this way a 64-bit scratch-pad is reorganized from an 8×4 matrix. Such an arrangement yields a memory of 16 locations (4×4) *each* of 4 bits. A fourfold increase in data rate results due to there now being 4 data ports.

Regrettably, particularly for large scratch-pads, three-dimensional arrays have the disadvantage of requiring more power (for driving sense circuitry), but, more importantly, need a greater number of chip leadouts. Table 4.1 shows the lead-out count (for data ports and address lines only) for various scratch-pads. Alternatively, the conclusions from Table 4.1 can be drawn from an information-flow standpoint. If any wire in a system can handle, say, 1 bit per 50 ns, then a high data throughput can only be obtained by having a large number of wires, i.e. wide data buses.

Number of locations	Number of bits per location	Total number of cells	Leadouts required
16	1	16	6
4	4	16	10
64	1	64	8
16	4	64	12
256	1	256	10
64	4	256	14
1024	1	1024	12

Table 4.1

Metal-oxide-semiconductor memories

Bipolar devices, flip-flops, and scratch-pads represent the very fastest end of the memory spectrum. However, they all demand large amounts of power and usually cannot, as a consequence, be fabricated in large-scale integrated (LSI) form.

A technology, of many variants, which allows high packing densities and low power consumption but generally inferior performance, is metal-oxide-semiconductor or MOS. Very simple structures are possible using very few manufacturing processes. Furthermore, if the difficult area of timing/control is delegated to external circuitry, MOS, like bipolar technology, can benefit considerably by further reducing the complexity of individual memory cells. This also greatly increases memory density.

Several basic storage methods using MOS technology exist, each with its own advantages and disadvantages:

1. static RAM;
2. dynamic RAM;
3. shift register arrays;
4. hybrid and other techniques.

(a) *Static metal-oxide-semiconductor RAM (MOSRAM)*

These devices are often just MOS versions of bipolar circuits (scratch-pads). The transistors can be enhancement or depletion types—the supporting logic can be MOS,CMOS (complementary MOS), SOS (silicon on sapphire) or otherwise. The resistors, where needed, can be either integrated resistors or gate-to-drain strapped MOS transistors. It is, from the systems standpoint, of little consequence which technology is used provided the external characteristics of access time, special support circuitry, electrical interface and power requirements are known.

The most important parameter for these memories is the access time, which is a function of the raw speed of individual logic elements. An MOS transistor, when it is switched on, presents a certain resistance between source and drain. This resistance limits the current that charges stray circuit capacitances. The speed of charging is therefore improved if either the resistance or stray capacitance is made smaller. The situation for a CMOS logic gate is illustrated in Fig. 8.6.

The geometry of the transistors and the chip doping levels will largely determine the transistor-on resistance. The geometry and fabrication techniques determine the stray capacitance. The stray capacitances are largely formed between circuit nodes (aluminum tracks and pads and within the transistor element areas) and the substrate. The substrate is usually p-doped silicon and therefore a semiconductor. The equivalent circuit between a circuit node and substrate is a reverse biased p–n junction (diode). Some technologies, notably SOS, eliminate the conductivity of the substrate (and hence one plate of the resultant capacitor) by using an insulator (sapphire) as the substrate material. Stray capacitances are then only inter-node ones and hence far smaller. By so doing, static RAMs can be fabricated with access times approaching that of bipolar devices (less than 100 ns). However, one way in which they lose out, along with many other MOS devices, is in not having electrical characteristics which are very suitable for driving other circuits off the chip. Such external circuitry is very often based on bipolar technology such as TTL. Interface electronics is needed within the chip to couple the internal MOS circuitry to the external bipolar form. This circuitry often requires considerable power which rises with the number of ports provided on the chip. Additionally, because such circuits are in series with incoming and outgoing data lines, they impose signal delays and thereby degrade overall performance.

Typical production static MOSRAMs are limited to about 4K to 8K bits per chip (2^{12} or 2^{13}). This limitation is mainly caused by the chip area needed per bit stored—a function of the number of transistors needed per memory cell. However, cell-selection logic and address-decoding logic also contribute to the chip area required. In comparison with the dynamic MOSRAM (see below), though, the static MOSRAM is easier to use because data, once written, are permanently stored (provided power is made available to the chip). Dynamic MOSRAMs require extra refresh circuitry in order to retain data. Such circuitry is usually "off-chip".

(b) Dynamic MOSRAM

In order to maximize the number of bits that can be memorized in a certain chip area, the basic cell must be as simple as possible. The requirements of a memory cell are usually:

1. to be readily selected, preferably via a two-or more dimensional matrixing arrangement (to minimize address-decoding circuitry);
2. once selected, the cell should be able to accept and retain one bit with a minimum of interference to another cell;
3. the cell's state should be easily read, both with the minimum of interference to other cells and such that the (additional) sense circuitry has the easiest possible task in discriminating between memorized 1s and 0s.

The dynamic MOSRAM generally achieves data retention by placing a charge (logic 1) on a capacitor in each cell. This capacitor may be explicit, i.e. a certain chip area may be assigned to form an integrated capacitor, or it may be implicit, i.e. the natural capacitor existing between one electrode of a MOS transistor and the chip substrate. Use of a capacitor, howsoever formed, has several advantages;

1. the chip area per cell is small relative to the static RAM;
2. the chip can be powered down when not in use (i.e. when not being read, written to or refreshed);
3. cell-matrixing methods are more easily achieved in this (MOS) technology as shown below. This reduces the cell-selection circuitry (address decoding) needed.

An early three-transistor cell is shown in Fig. 4.19.

The capacitor C may have a typical value of 10^{-13} F, i.e. 0.1 pF. A charge (logic 1) can be impressed on the selected cell by applying suitable potentials to the one-row-write wire and column-write wire which the selected cell intersects. These potentials cause T_1 to come into conduction. All other cells will have unsuitable potentials on either or both drain and gate of their

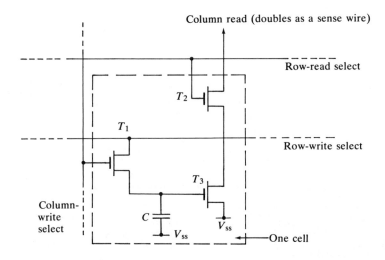

Fig. 4.19 Schematic of a three-transitor dynamic MOSRAM memory cell.

corresponding transistors (T_1). Therefore, only the T_1 of the selected cell will switch on and thereby impress a charge on C. (Meanwhile, all column read and row read wires can have "unsuitable" (deselect) potentials on them.) After writing has taken place, the write wires are returned to the "deselect" potentials so as not to interfere further with the charges on the capacitors.

To read a logic 1 (charge) on a selected capacitor, a 3-input AND gate needs to be formed. The 3 inputs are the charge state of the capacitor and the two read-select wire potentials. The outputs of the AND gates (1 per cell) can be ORed to form the final output. (The AND gate outputs are necessarily mutually exclusive.) In Fig. 4.19, the 3-input AND gate is formed from T_2 and T_3. Only if T_2 and T_3 *both* conduct will a logic sense current flow through the column-read wire. The transistor T_3 can conduct if a suitable potential difference exists between its source and gate—this is determined by the presence or absence of a charge on C. The transistor T_2 will conduct if suitable read-select potentials exist on its gate and drain *AND* if T_3 is in conduction.

The arrangement of Fig. 4.19 clearly reads the selected cell, not as a current flowing along an unique wire, but along one of many column wires. Thus the column-read currents can be ORed to give a single-bit output (single port). These currents, being mutually exclusive, do not cause mutual interference.

A more economical arrangement can use a single transistor in each cell in which read- and write-selection wires are combined, so that just a single column- and row-selection wire passes through each cell (Fig. 4.20). Writing

Poly II Process – poly silicon bit lines

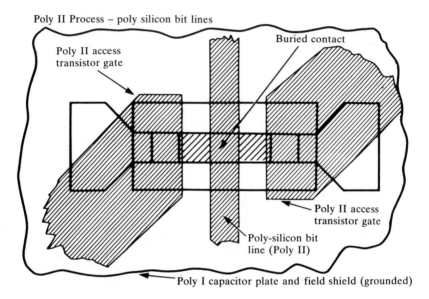

Fig. 4.20 Layout of a single cell for a chip with a 16K-or 64K-bit dynamic memory. The layout is deliberately arranged to be suitable for matrix connection to other cells. (Courtesy MOSTEK Corporation, Carrollton, Texas.)

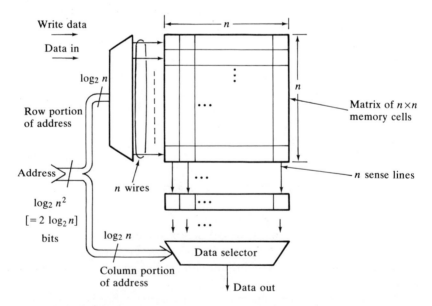

Fig. 4.21 Selection process for dynamic MOSRAM with n^2 bits.

is still much as for the three-transistor cell. Reading is carried out on a per row basis into a parallel register. The read mechanism is often destructive so that a row, once read, must immediately be rewritten from the parallel register back into the selected row (Fig. 4.21).

It will be noted that all n bits from the selected row are read into the parallel register and the whole row rewritten concurrently. Once the row has been deposited in the parallel register, the required bit can be selected for presentation at the chip's output port. An n-bit data selector is used for this purpose and its address is the column address (Fig. 4.22).

A data selector is similar to a decoder but each AND gate includes a data input. The AND gates operate mutually exclusively due to addressing. Only the AND selected will pass its input data to the OR gate. All other AND gates remain inactive regardless of the states of their data-input wires. This mode of operation, using a parallel register, provides a further advantage. The charge on any capacitor can be retained for only 1–2 ms. Every cell in the matrix must be periodically refreshed. (The control/timing for this operation is usually provided by external logic.) The basis of refresh is to read and then write to the same row. All rows must be so treated within the prescribed refresh time. To read each cell individually would take far too long—especially for the larger MOSRAMs. As an example, to read all the memory cells of a 64K bit (2^{16}) MOSRAM with read and write times of 200 ns would take $2^{16} \times 400 = 26$ ms! However, the row-wise organization of

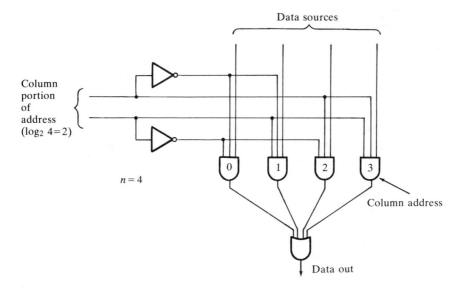

Fig. 4.22   Four-input data selector.

Fig. 4.22 allows n bits to be refreshed at a time. For a 64K-bit RAM, $n=2^8=256$. The refresh time is thereby reduced to 256×400 ns$\cong100$ μs. If refreshing is to be carried out on all bits within 2 ms, then only 5% of each 2 ms will be tied up in refreshing. Row-wise refreshing is simply performed by supplying all possible 256-row addresses and suitable read then write control pulses. The column address portion is either ignored or suppressed. (With many of the larger MOSRAMs, it is normal for the row and column addresses to be entered to the chip via the same port. This saves chip leadouts. For refreshing, the only addresses declared to the chip are therefore row ones.)

In a typical MOSRAM (Hanatek, 1976), several modes of operation are possible. Such modes are especially easy to implement if the system of Fig. 4.22 is adopted. They can be chosen to optimize system performance and some give considerable system flexibility. However, some modes have shorter cycle times than others and this must be taken into account. Some examples are:

1. *Read*—a row address is supplied, followed by a column address. Access time is around 200 ns.
2. *Read–modify–write*—as per read to obtain data followed by a write operation to the same location. In essence, the bit read to the parallel register in the first half of the cycle is replaced by a new bit before the write (second half) of the cycle. Total time is about 400 ns.
3. *Short cycle write*—the read cycle is omitted to reduce the cycle time to around 200 ns. However, the matrix is still written to the parallel register as a consequence of supplying the row address.
4. *Refresh*—a row address is supplied from a $\log_2 n$-bit counter and a read/write cycle executed. The row write to the parallel register is not corrupted before the write cycle.

One of two possible techniques is used to complete a refresh operation in the 1–2 ms available. The refreshing can either be done all in one burst during the last 100 μs of a 2 ms cycle or it can be spread out. The first system is often simpler as it separates normal operation from refresh activity. However, it makes the MOSRAM unavailable for a long unbroken period. For certain real time and other related computing applications, a fast memory response is required and would make this method unacceptable. Alternatively, there are situations in which it is known, a priori, that all *rows* of a MOSRAM are to be read from or written to at intervals of less than the refresh time *at all times*. An example is when a MOSRAM is used to synthesize a shift register in a signal-processing application (see Chapter 10). In such a situation, refreshing takes place by default as part of normal reading and writing. If the shift register is to be operated at various clock speeds, care must be taken to ensure that each row is activated within the refresh time specified for the MOSRAM.

4.3 FERRITE-CORE MEMORIES (Hill and Peterson, 1978, p.60; Nashelsky, 1972)

The use of ferrites as a memory medium spans most of the history of the electronic digital computer. The first practical system was developed at the Massachusetts Institute of Technology (MIT) around 1953. Despite being supplanted by MOSRAM devices in most (particularly commercial) systems, it is still specified for specialized applications such as for rugged military systems, and can be found in large numbers of older, but still operational, equipment.

Ferrites belong to a family of weakly magnetic materials whose magnetization characteristic is distinctly two state and is thus very suitable for the retention of binary data (Fig. 4.23).

As each ferrite core (or "bead") has two states of magnetization, each can hold one bit of information. Thus eight such cores could be used to memorize an 8-bit byte. A considerable volume of material has been written describing ferrite-core memories (Nashelsky, 1972; Lewin, 1980) so that only the essential characteristics will be listed as they affect digital systems design.

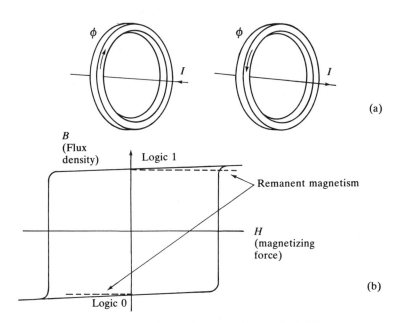

Fig. 4.23 Ferrite-core "bead": (a) magnetising method; (b) magnetic characteristic.

1. The manner of reading from and writing to ferrite memories can vary enormously according to the performance required and size of memory. This, combined with the size of the cores yields read and write times from 0.1 to 5 μs.

2. Reading a core is a destructive process which puts it into the logic 0 state regardless of its state prior to reading. (Reading is based on detecting whether a change of magnetization has taken place as a consequence of doing this.) Therefore reading is normally followed by the equally time-consuming write operation in order to re-establish the data in the location read. The cycle time is defined as the combined read and write times. However, clearly, the data are available for use externally immediately after the read part of the cycle. Regrettably, the memory is not ready for another command until the completion of the remainder of the cycle.

3. As with dynamic MOSRAM memories, read–modify–write cycles are possible by introducing fresh data in time for the write part of the cycle. However, short-cycle writing is not generally possible as writing is organized as the *selective* writing of 1s into the required bit positions. (The system relies on *all* cores being set to logic 0 as the consequence of the preceding read operation—the write operation leaves cores undisturbed which are required to memorize 0s.)

As the information is held in the form of remanent magnetization, no power is needed to retain this information, nor is any refresh operation necessary. Such characteristics make this memory form very attractive as a back-up if a digital system must avoid loss of data when power supplies fail

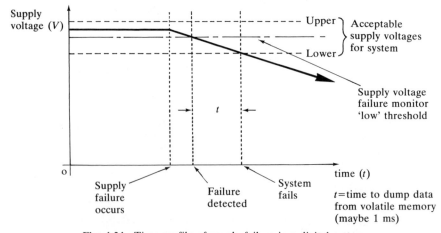

Fig. 4.24 Time profile of supply failure in a digital system.

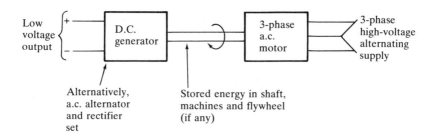

Fig. 4.25 Conversion of high-voltage a.c. to low-voltage d.c. with capability for storage of mechanical energy.

(black out). As ferrite-core memory is quite fast, considerable volumes of data can be dumped to it from volatile memory (registers, scratch-pads, MOSRAMs, etc.) between detection of supply failure and supply-rail voltages falling below their specified levels (Fig. 4.24).

The power-supply system must clearly store a certain amount of electrical energy in order for the system of Fig. 4.24 to operate. This may be by the use of large electrolytic capacitors or in the mechanical energy contained in rotary inverters (Fig. 4.25).

However the energy is stored, it must keep the digital system's supplies within specification for long enough for it to react to the situation. If the current instruction being executed in the processor is complex, and the volume of data to be dumped is high (say, several hundreds of bytes), the supply rails may have to be held within specification for over 1 ms.

An important characteristic of ferrite memory from the military viewpoint is its *relative* immunity to radiation, i.e. neutron bombardment. Most IC memory media are very much more prone to both data loss and even memory-cell destruction under heavy radiation dosage (flux). Particles passing through a memory cell release hole/electron pairs in the semiconductor and effectively discharge memory capacitors. At high fluxes, it is possible to damage semiconductor junctions.

A second important characteristic of ferrites is that, since they have been in use for so long, their failure modes are well known and documented so that their more serious weaknesses have been alleviated. They have therefore been specified for use with growing confidence over a number of years and become highly developed as a consequence. It is therefore not surprising that they have remained a serious contender to more "convenient" memory devices for so long, especially for systems requiring high mean times between failures (MTBF).

Among the more important reasons why ferrites have finally failed to compete with semiconductor memories are:

1. high assembly costs—highly skilled assembly personnel required to thread up to four wires through each core (which may be less than 0.5 mm (0.02 in) in diameter);
2. high volume per bit;
3. complex, high-current-drive electronics required for the matrices;
4. very heavy-duty power supplies needed for large, fast memories;
5. very fast, expensive read amplifiers needed.

Other magnetic memories

Several magnetic memory forms such as plated wire and film memories, were developed during the 1960s. They had several advantages such as higher speed and nondestructive readout but they, too, have largely succumbed to the semiconductor memory and are now used only in isolated applications.

4.4 ELECTROMECHANICAL MAGNETIC MEMORIES (Lewin, 1980, Sections 6.7–6.10)

Ferromagnetic coatings can be applied to a variety of (non-magnetic) bases to give various electromechanical memory forms. The most familiar, both inside and outside the computer industry, is magnetic tape. On this, a very thin film is applied to one side of a mylar (plastic) ribbon. Magnetic tape, as for video and audio recording, can be used in both spool-to-spool and cassette and cartridge form for the bulk storage of binary data. Logic 1s and 0s can be impressed on the tape in several ways. However, regardless of the data format used, the coating is always saturated in one magnetic direction or the other to maximize the flux change encountered by the read head(s) as the tape passes by. Spool-to-spool tapes are usually around 19 mm ($\frac{3}{4}$ in) wide and can accommodate 9 tracks—sufficient for an 8-bit byte (or character) plus a parity bit. A byte can therefore be written or read in a bit-parallel fashion. The longitudinal (byte) density can vary from hundreds to over 2000 per cm (several hundreds to over 5000 per inch). The tape can be run at 4 m/s (160 in/s) or more. This is equivalent to a data rate in excess of 500K bytes per second. A single spool of tape may hold several megabytes of data.

Data are normally organized on the tape in blocks or records in order to aid editing and retrieval. (Each byte does not have an unique address as in fixed semiconductor and ferrite memories.) As tape can only be read whilst it is actually in motion, gaps have to be provided between each record in which the tape can stop. These are typically 19 mm ($\frac{3}{4}$ in) long and may therefore represent several kilobytes of wasted memory space. For this reason, the exact capacity of a spool cannot be specified. The time to access a record depends on the tape position of the record accessed immediately prior to the one in question. It can vary from zero to the time needed to completely wind the tape from beginning to end (maybe 45 s). This is known as serial access and should be compared with "random" access in which the retrieval time is independent of the order of retrieval or the location of the data in memory. From this, it might be inferred that the average access time for a given record on tape is the time to traverse *half* the tape length. In practice it is far less than this because tape is often not fully utilized and the nature of most tasks is such that records are not randomly disposed about the tape.

Cassette and cartridge tape forms usually employ only two tracks (as for audio purposes). Data movement is therefore bit serial. In the simplest system, one track can be used for a clock and the other for data. However, inter-track mechanical skew tolerances from one transport to another cause problems when data are recorded on one transport and read from another. Several schemes to overcome this are used. In one, called *biphase recording*, logic 0s are recorded as pulses (two flux changes) to one track and logic 1s to the other. There is no clock track, for clock can be derived by simply ORing the pulses issued from the two channels. The pulses never overlap because logic 0s and 1s are mutually exclusive, so that head skew problems are largely eliminated (Fig. 4.26). However, it should be noted that whatever recording method is used, it is almost bound to be wasteful of tape because of the introduction of redundant flux changes on the tape. In an ideal system, flux changes (which ultimately limit the physical spacing that can be achieved between adjacent bits) should only occur singly between an adjacent 1 and 0 that have been recorded. The worst case is therefore when 010101...has to be recorded, which imposes 1 flux change per bit. However, if that was the only information recorded, it would be almost impossible and certainly unreliable to determine the number of 0s in a long chain of 0s or 1s in a long chain of 1s. (If the number of similar bits in a chain were unlimited, a perfectly stable transport would be required to "count" the number of bits in a chain.) Thus, in a practical system, flux changes are forced to occur at least once per bit, regardless of the data pattern. In the biphase technique two flux changes per bit are used, so that the bit density is only half the flux density. We might call this a 50% packing-density achievement.

In a typical (84 m—275 ft) cassette, around $\frac{1}{2}$ megabyte of data can be held, but it depends heavily on the bit density achievable and the organization of the data—particularly the use of error-checking methods and the use of space to hold record-indexing (library) information.

Magnetic disk and drum memories work on much the same physical principles as magnetic tape except that the longitudinal (linear) style of the

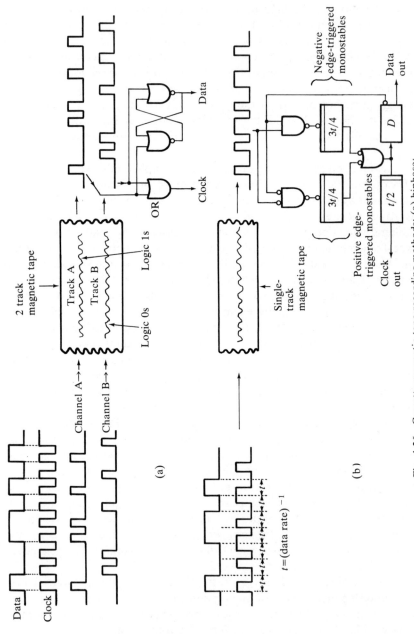

Fig. 4.26 Cassette magnetic-tape recording methods: (a) biphase; (b) phase encoding.

tape ribbon is replaced with an "area"-based substrate. Thus the linear distance between any one memory area and another is greatly reduced. In the case of disk memories, the coating is usually on both sides of a non-magnetic disk of up to 50 cm (20 in) in diameter. For drum memories, the coating is on the cylindrical periphery which may be 15–30 cm (6–12 in) along the axis and around 75 cm (30 in) in circumference.

For both memory forms the memory is organized as a large number of either coaxial (disk) or adjacent (drum) tracks capable of holding several thousands of bits of data. (This is assuming a bit-recording density of 400 or more bits per centimeter—1000 per inch.) Neighboring tracks are on centers of 0.25–0.75 mm (0.01–0.03 in). The individual tracks are about 50–70% of the centers spacing in width. For both systems the option arises as to whether a "one recording/replay head per surface" system is to be employed in which the head must be able to scan from one track to another by physically moving on an arm, or whether a separate head is provided for each track. For the latter, track switching is done electronically—usually by diode selection/address decoding. There are several system-design considerations:

1. Drums are bulky devices and their replacement in a transport by another drum in the manner of magnetic tape spools is not practical. Therefore, drums are what is known as "fixed memory" and, by inference, of finite capacity. The choice of track-selection method is thereby free from the onerous mechanical tolerancing problems that arise from differences of drum diameter and transport dimensions. Both "head-per-track" and "scanning-head systems" are used. However, when the number of tracks is very large, a compromise is possible in which a number of tracks are grouped along the drum axis and "one head per group" is employed. This reduces the amount of mechanical movement necessary to scan all the tracks.

As the recording technique is "out of contact" i.e. the heads *never* touch the recording surface (to obviate wear) a multi-moving-head assembly is very difficult to manufacture. (The head gap is achieved by forcing a thin (approximately 0.025 mm—0.001 in) boundary layer of air between the head and surface by suitable aerodynamic shaping of the head contour.)

In respect of the choice between track-selection systems, two factors which affect data access time should be noted: (a) the time to move heads axially and center them on the required track (virtually eliminated in the head-per-track system), and (b) the time for tangential movement, which depends on the rotation speed of the drum. Time (a) can be around 100 ms for scanning-head systems but only 20 μs for head-per-track ones. Time (b) can be equivalent to one drum rotation time in the worst case, i.e. 60–20 ms for drum speeds of 1000 and 3000 rev/min, respectively. The average wait time is half a revolution; this is termed the *latency time* and is 15–20 ms for current drums. Clearly a head-per-track system combined with a drum with a high rotation speed can cut average access times to around 10 ms. The data rate when the required information is found depends on drum speed, bit density and head organization, but can be up to 5 Mbits per second or over $\frac{1}{2}$ Mbyte per second.

2. The basic comments on track selection and latency time apply equally to disk systems. However, the problems of swapping sets of disks has been overcome (replaceable-disk file) giving a disk transport of unlimited memory capacity. Such systems use the scanning-head technique and retract

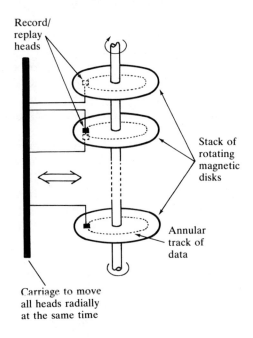

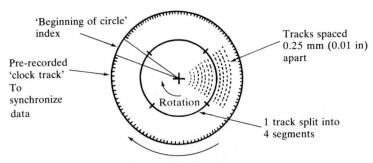

Fig. 4.27 Magnetic disk organization.

the heads when a disk cassette is removed or replaced (Fig. 4.27). Being of the scanning-head type, they cannot achieve the very short access times enjoyed by fixed (head-per-track) disk files.

3. Consideration of track selection and latency times has forced system designers to operate and organize rotating memories in the same manner as magnetic tape—that is not on the basis of a byte at a time, but a *group* of bytes (record, sector). Both disks and drums are naturally sectioned into tracks but, in addition, it is usual for each track to be divided into several segments. A segment may consist of up to several hundreds of bytes and there may be 16 or more (maybe 128) segments per track. A typical access may be for 1 or more segments (Fig. 4.27).

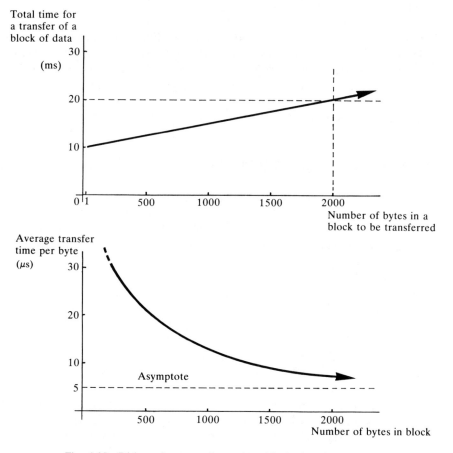

Fig. 4.28 Disk performance for various block sizes based on a latency time of 10 ms and a transfer rate of 200K bytes/s.

Each segment can consist of two fields—the first containing an n-bit pattern which is used as a segment identifier (or label) and the second field to hold the data. A gap usually exists between segments. The time to complete the transfer of a variable number of bytes to or from a rotating memory, including latency, is shown in Fig. 4.28.

As the number of bytes handled in any given transfer rises, the higher is the mean transfer rate. This comes about because the (fixed) latency time becomes a smaller proportion of the total time. However, Fig. 4.28 assumes that all the data transferred are associated with the same track so, clearly, the graph will have upward discontinuities if extrapolated too far. However, the point is clear: there is no point in transferring single bytes to or from a rotating memory—the number should always be several hundred to use the system effectively.

Rotating and some other memory forms are known as semi-random. A random-access memory is one in which the access time is independent of the order in which the data are accessed, e.g. the MOSRAM. In contrast, there is complete dependence in the case of the "sequential" access memory (shift registers, magnetic tape). Rotating memories, particularly those incorporating head-per-track schemes, lie somewhere between the random-access variety and the sequential.

4.5 OTHER READ/WRITE MEMORY FORMS

Semiconductor developments have produced a plethora of memory forms, some based on novel ways to fabricate flip-flops, others based on novel ways to retain one of two binary states using magnetic and other phenomena. Amongst these memory forms are bubble memories and holographic techniques. However, whatever physical property is used, from the system viewpoint, they can be classified as sequential, semi-random or random-by-access. They can also be classified according to reading properties, e.g. destructive or nondestructive, matrix organization and addressing possible or not.

Not infrequently, some memories do not fall naturally into a convenient grouping and must be considered with some care. The bubble memory is a case in point. It is fundamentally a form of shift register as fabricated and therefore sequential. The enormous packing densities achieved make very long shift registers possible. Unfortunately, such long shift registers lead to very long access times. It is therefore not unusual for one long register to be divided into several (8 or more) shorter registers which can work in parallel. If 8 such registers are used, the organization is very suitable for storage in bytes. However, 8 interfaces to the input/output ports are necessary. Alternatively, the 8-register outputs can be multiplexed to a single port with a

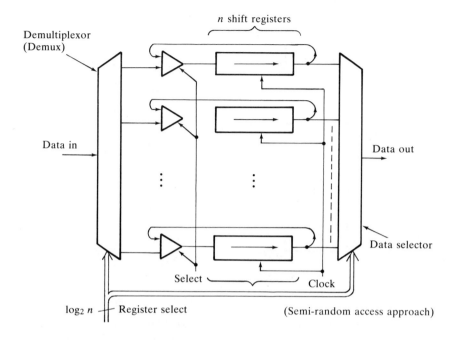

Fig. 4.29 Bubble-memory organizations.

consequent saving in interface electronics and supply power (Fig. 4.29). Such a memory is again bit serial in organization, but semi-random in its access characteristics. It is interesting to compare the multiplexed bubble memory with the disk memory organized on a head-per-track basis, in which each shift register is likened to a track.

4.6 MEMORY TECHNIQUES (Axford and Fiske, 1971; Corsini, 1975; Lewin, 1980, Section 9.4)

Throughout the existence of computers, there has been pressure on memory designers to develop faster, more capacious but cheaper systems (Fig. 4.30). This shows that, as might be expected, fast memory is also expensive memory so it must be used in limited quantities if system costs are not to be excessive. The trick, therefore, is to use a variety of memories in which a sufficiency of fast memory is used to maintain performance and the bulk of memory is provided by cheaper forms. A typical combination might be 6–10

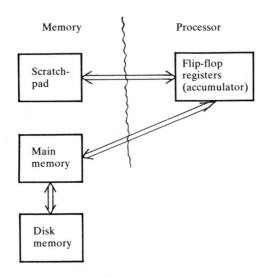

Fig. 4.30 Elementary memory hierarchy.

fast flip-flop registers in the processor, 50–100 bytes of scratch-pad, several K bytes of main MOSRAM memory and 10 Mbytes of disk memory for a minicomputer. The actual numbers vary enormously according to application and organization, but the greater use of slower (backing) memory still persists.

A problem in the use of several "layers" of memory is that of forming an effective interface between them. The ultimate goal is to give the user the illusion that he has memory performance approaching that of flip-flop registers but with a capacity at his disposal equal to that of the disk. In order to approach this ideal, it is necessary for the maximum of data in use at any time to be available in fast memory—at the time of requesting it. To do this requires an element of "precognition" for clearly if data were sought at random from disk, this could not be achieved.

However, several practical factors come to the rescue:

1.   Program instructions are put in contiguous memory locations so that if a given instruction is being executed, we know from where the next instruction will come. Exceptions to this are jump (branch) and subroutine call instructions. However, for a wide variety of programs and algorithms, these occur on only about 20% of occasions and are frequently to nearby destinations, i.e. loops are frequently quite short.

2.   Data are frequently organized in arrays and tables so that blocks of data in contiguous locations are processed at around the same time.

Taking each memory interface in turn, we see that it is not difficult to capitalize on the orderliness of data requests. The interface between scratch-pad and the processor is the simplest one and usually takes the form of making the scratch-pad the origin of one or both operands in arithmetic instructions. Much arithmetic is of the subtotalling variety in which, for long periods, a limited set of operands and subtotals is processed time and again.

Example   Use of Newton's method to derive a square root. The algorithm is given by

$$x_{n+1} = \tfrac{1}{2}\left[x_n + \frac{A}{x_n}\right],$$

where x_n is the estimate of $\sqrt{A}$ on step n. The flowchart, after a suitable x_0 has been chosen, is shown in Fig. 4.31 (ε is a suitable small positive number which serves as a measure of closeness).

A, x_n and B would use three scratch-pad locations and would each be called from scratch-pad to the processor's arithmetic unit on many occasions

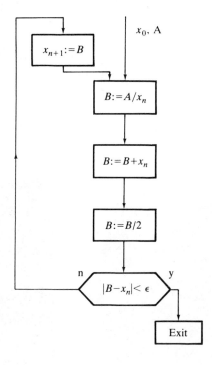

Fig. 4.31 Square-root Flowchart showing scratch-pad utilization.

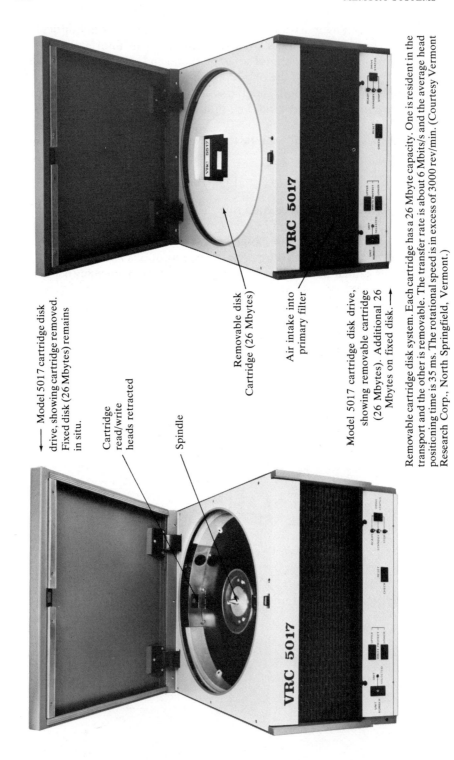

⟶ Model 5017 cartridge disk drive, showing cartridge removed. Fixed disk (26 Mbytes) remains in situ.

Cartridge read/write heads retracted

Spindle

Removable disk Cartridge (26 Mbytes)

Air intake into primary filter

Model 5017 cartridge disk drive, showing removable cartridge (26 Mbytes). Additional 26 Mbytes on fixed disk. ⟶

Removable cartridge disk system. Each cartridge has a 26 Mbyte capacity. One is resident in the transport and the other is removable. The transfer rate is about 6 Mbits/s and the average head positioning time is 35 ms. The rotational speed is in excess of 3000 rev/min. (Courtesy Vermont Research Corp., North Springfield, Vermont.)

in the execution of this routine. The use of the scratch-pad has released the main memory from all accesses bar those for instructions.

If the main memory is fairly slow, then a scratch-pad like interface or "buffer" memory could be placed between it and the processor to hold small sections of program which are in current use (Ackland and Pucknell, 1975). (Such a memory is also sometimes known as Caché.) Main memory would be called only once, to bring information down to the buffer. Considerable time savings would be realized on subsequent requests for the same data. The organization of such a scheme needs care. Clearly the buffer must be much smaller than the main memory, otherwise it would be too expensive. To be effective, it must be built in a fast technology compared with the main memory. (If it were of comparable size to the main memory, there would be no point in having a main memory in the first place!) Thus, if the buffer is small, each location must, over a period, contain information from many *different* main-memory locations. Each buffer-memory location must have a label indicating, at any time, the main-memory location with which it is associated. One arrangement is shown in Fig. 4.32.

The memory is shown as a matrix, not because it is different from the memories so far described, but because it is convenient to think of it in this

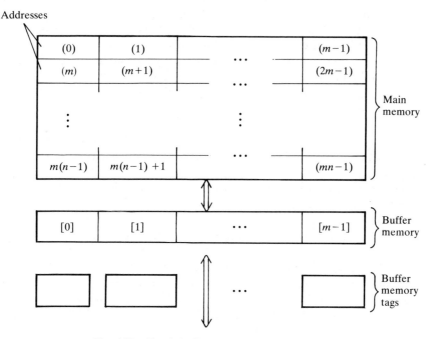

Fig. 4.32 Simple buffer-memory organization.

manner to understand the buffer's operation. A suitable system for Fig. 4.32 would have $m=64$, $n=512$ (giving a total main-memory capacity of 32K bytes). The buffer would then have m ($=64$) registers each of the same number of bits as each memory location.

Accompanying each buffer register is a "tag" register which indicates with which main memory *row* the buffer register is associated. In this example, each tag register would have 9 bits ($=\log_2 n$).

To access a main-memory location, a 15-bit address ($=\log_2 32\,768$) is needed. In effect, the least significant 6 ($=\log_2 m$) bits indicate the main-memory column and the remaining 9 bits indicate the row. If the byte required has been previously deposited in buffer, then it must be in a particular buffer register. The column organization of the whole system is modulo 32.

Example   Main-memory location 129 will always pass its data to the processor via buffer register 1 ($129/64=2$: remainder 1). (There is no point in looking elsewhere for a buffer copy of that particular main-memory location's contents.) It is only necessary to check buffer 1's 9-bit tag contents against the 9 most significant (ms) address bits sent from the requester to ascertain whether a main or buffer access is required (Fig. 4.33). If the two 9-bit address portions are equivalent, the required data are in the buffer: otherwise, they are only available in the main memory.

An important factor in the design of such a buffer is to what extent the decision logic of Fig. 4.33 degrades the performance of the buffer memory. Before anything else can happen, this logic must make the decision of whether a main or buffer access is required. If the system is working correctly, the majority of decisions should be in favor of the buffer. So this decision must be made very quickly if the full potentialities of a buffer are going to be realized.

Example   If the main memory is a 32K bytes MOSRAM with an access time of 1 μs and the buffer is 64 bytes of bipolar RAM with an access time of 100 ns, it would be hoped that the tag address processing would take only about 30 ns to make a decision. Such an overhead degrades the buffer memory by around 30% if the decision is a buffer access, but by only 3% if the byte to be acquired is only available in main memory. Some overhead cannot be avoided but it must be minimized (by fast hardware).

If the buffer is being used to interface a moderate size (say 32K bytes) main memory of around 0.5 μs access time with a mass memory of 3–4 μs access time, the decision logic can be allowed more time to operate and the tag registers could be more compactly held in a bipolar RAM rather than,

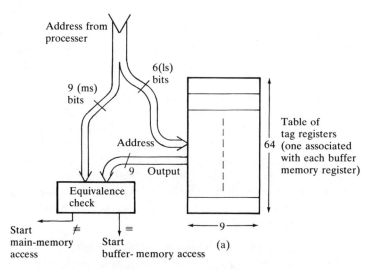

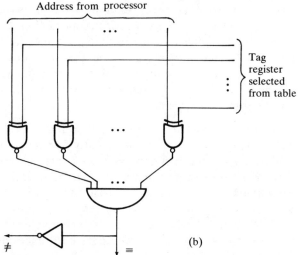

Fig. 4.33 Addressing system for a simple buffer memory: (a) organization; (b) address-equivalence logic.

say, a register file or flip-flop array. The decision time, including tag access, could be allowed to stretch to 0.1 or even 0.15 μs under such circumstances.

A final design point is the algorithm for use of either buffer or main memory when writing is to take place. Two options exist:

1. Write to buffer only,
2. Write to both buffer and main memory.

The first option is faster as only a buffer cycle is involved, but it does mean that the main memory is "out of date". As long as the out-of-date memory location is not accessed from elsewhere or the corresponding up-to-date buffer register not required to hold data from another row in the same main memory column, all is well. However, when either of these circumstances arises, the buffer must be copied to main memory before it is reused. Although complex, such an option has the advantage of eliminating unnecessary transfers from buffer to main memory [which would character-ize option (2)]. As most memory accesses, such as for instructions and program constants, do not cause updating of memory, a useful amount of time can be saved by having a flag (flip-flop) associated with each buffer register to indicate whether or not that particular buffer register has been written to. A flowchart for a buffer/main memory access, which would be realized in hardware, is shown in Fig. 4.34.

A disadvantage of the buffer system so far described is that, under certain circumstances, the tag registers will have similar contents i.e. refer to the same main-memory row (Fig. 4.32). A simple example is furnished by the circumstance in which a small loop of instructions (iterative loop) is being executed and the complete loop has been deposited in the buffer. The loop of instructions is from contiguous main-memory locations and hence, probably, from the same main-memory row. Better utilization of tag regis-ters can be effected if a "block" of contiguous main-memory locations is associated with the same tag register.

To make best use of such an arrangement, it is preferable if all the buffer registers for a certain tag can be loaded concurrently. This can be done if the main memory is *actually* rather than notionally segmented into columns, as in Fig. 4.32. The same row, for all columns, can be fed with the same row address. (A column is frequently referred to as a submemory and forms an electronically independent unit.) A typical system might consist of 8 sub-memories each of 8K bytes (8192 bytes) to make a complete main memory of 64K bytes (65 536 bytes). The system would have a number of rows (2^p) for the buffer, each row having its own tag register and flag to indicate if *any* buffer in that row had been written to (Fig. 4.35). As each submemory column is of 8K bytes i.e. 2^{13} bytes, each tag thus needs 13 bits to give row identification. As before, the buffer registers are of the same length as the main-memory locations. To access this system, a 16-bit address is needed ($2^{16} = 65\,536$). The least significant (ls) 3 bits determine the column and the remaining 13 bits are compared with the 2^p tag registers. All the comparisons are carried out concurrently (Fig. 4.36). The tag register and comparison logic forms what is known as a content addressable memory (CAM). If any equivalence is obtained, the required byte must be in buffer and can be accessed immediately. If no equivalence is found, main memory must be

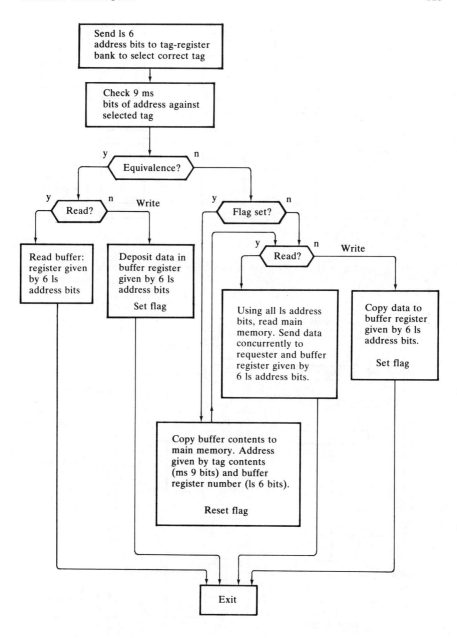

Fig. 4.34 Buffer-memory flowchart.

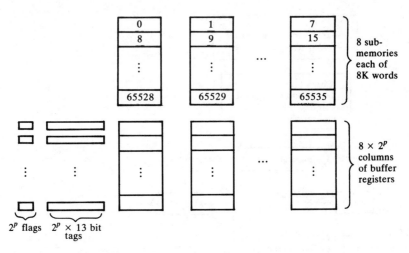

Fig. 4.35 8×8K-word main memory/buffers memory.

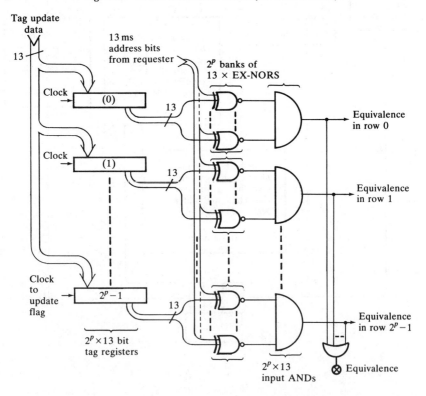

Fig. 4.36 Content-addressable memory.

accessed. The procedure is therefore exactly the same as that for Fig. 4.32, except that there are 2^p possible buffer places where the required word may be lodged. Use of the flags and the flowchart are the same as for Fig. 4.32. There are, however, some important differences.

1. If the option which defers writing to main memory is used (when a buffer register is updated), then the flag is set the first time writing to a buffer row occurs and is left set until that row is copied to memory. Use of this option is, in practice, very beneficial to this system as several buffer registers may be written to over a period. The whole row will then be copied to main memory, updating several memory locations concurrently.

2. The question arises as to *which* buffer-memory row data should be written to from main memory. In other words, some form of algorithm is needed which will remove the data *least* likely to be needed in buffer, and put it in main memory. This will create room for a new row of data. Of course, if the row to be removed has not been updated since it was first drawn from main memory (flag reset), then the copying operation, as such, is not necessary. The fresh data from main memory can just overwrite the redundant buffer row.

Several algorithms are employed, but the following one is very popular:

It is assumed that the *least* likely row to be used in the near future is the one that has least recently been requested. (A request would be either a read or write command to any word in that row.) In this context, a request to *any* byte in a row constitutes a request to that row as a whole.

To keep a history of requests, it is necessary to have a system of registers whose contents are related to such a history. The operation of these registers can be likened to that of a card-index system in which 2^p cards are arranged in a stack. Each time a card is referenced, it is placed at the top of the stack. By so doing, all cards which *were* above it move down one place. Clearly, the cards arrange themselves according to the order of referencing with the most recent at the top. If a new card has to be introduced to the stack from outside, the bottom card is the least recently referenced and must therefore be evicted. The new card is placed at the top of the stack.

To implement this system in hardware, it is much easier to keep the buffer rows (represented by the cards) static and to keep a record of where they are in a notional form. For a 2^p row buffer, $2^p \times p$ bit registers are needed, one for each row. These are called *priority registers* and their contents can represent priorities from zero to (2^p-1) for the most and least recently referenced buffer rows. In reality, p bit counters are used in this application as they are required to be zeroed when a particular row is referenced or incremented if the row is above one being referenced. The handling algorithm for any one priority register is shown in Fig. 4.37.

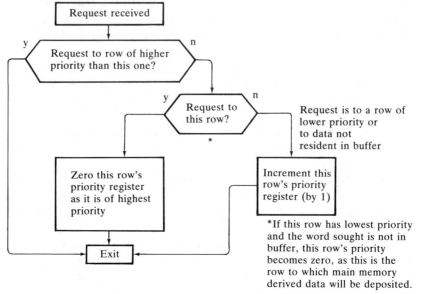

Fig. 4.37   Priority-register manipulation.

Interface for a backing memory (Kluge, 1973; Lavington *et al.*, 1971; Lewin, 1980, Section 9.5)

The buffer memory of the previous section must be implemented solely in hardware as even the slowest accesses are from a relatively fast memory. In instances where a buffer is placed between, say, a main memory (access time between 0.5 μs and 10 μs) and a magnetic disk, a slightly different approach can be applied because some hardware functions can be replaced by software ones. Clearly, a total software replacement is not possible as the decision and allocation mechanism must not seriously degrade the main-memory performance.

We will take the example of interfacing a 1 μs main memory to a fixed head (head per track) disk with a latency time and data rate of 10 ms and 100K words per second, respectively. As explained in the section on rotating memories, the latency time must be amortized over a transfer of several hundreds of words, arranged contiguously on the disk surface. For this example, the transfer of 1K (1024) words would take an average of 10 ms for latency plus 1024 $\times$ 10 μs for the actual transfer, giving a total of approximately 20 ms. If the data required are not in main memory, the organization of a disk to memory transfer and allocation of memory space can be done by software. There is plenty of time to spare without degrading the disk performance.

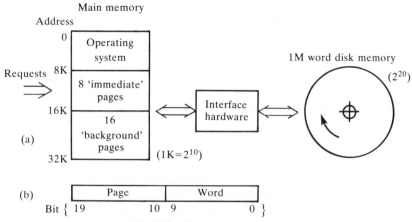

Fig. 4.38 Simple paging system.

As each disk transfer is of 1K words, then fixed (1K) areas (pages) will be allocated in main memory to receive such data. To illustrate the principle, we will assume the existence of a 32K word (2^{15}) main memory and 1M word (2^{20}) disk. It will be further assumed that 8K of main memory is required for the operating system and software to organize the interface. The remaining 24K of memory will be partitioned into 24 pages of which 8K will be "immediate" access pages and 16K will be background memory (Fig. 4.38a).

The principle of operation is as follows: from the user's viewpoint there is a 1M word memory organized like a book i.e. 1024 pages each of 1K words. The user therefore expects to send a 20-bit address to such a memory of which the most significant (ms) 10 bits refer to a page and the least significant (ls) 10 bits to a word within the chosen page (Fig. 4.38b). For the moment, the background pages should be ignored. The user sends a 20-bit address to the interface. The interface must decide whether the page, implied by the address, is available in one of the 8 pages resident in main memory or whether a disk to memory transfer is necessary. The decision logic, a content-addressable memory (CAM), can be seen to be the same as that for the buffer memory of the previous section. As it is to be hoped that the majority of decisions will indicate that the required data are in main memory, the decision must be fast compared with a main-memory access. The CAM must therefore be implemented in hardware. The CAM has only to work at the page level, i.e. compare the ms 10 bits of the user's address with the 10-bit page numbers (tags in the buffer system) in the CAM. (All 1K words of a given page are always kept together.)

In the event of an equivalence being found, the user's actual address must now be translated to a main-memory address. Again, the modification only needs to be at the page level. To distinguish between the two, they are known respectively as the logical (or virtual) address and the physical address. The term virtual arises from the fact that it is not known (nor need be known) by the user. The main-memory location occupied by a page may vary according to circumstances, i.e. the occupancy of main memory and events that have taken place prior to the page being called.

The use of priority registers to determine which page must be evicted at any time is the same as for the buffer memory system. However, in view of the size of the pages, the likelihood of any word or words in a page having been written to whilst in main memory is very high. Therefore, write flags are generally not used—a page is always returned to disk before another page is brought down to replace it in memory.

An important difference between this system and the buffer memory, and which involves software, is the use of background pages. In order to minimize the cost of CAM, a CAM with 8 immediate pages may be used (as in this example). This means that the user's 10-bit page number only has to be concurrently compared with 8 page numbers. However, if the 8 stored addresses can be arranged to refer to anywhere in main memory, then the 8 chosen ones need not be the 8 shown in Fig. 4.38(a). They could be any 8 from the 24. The 8 "immediate" pages—those registered in CAM—will just be a selection of 8 from anywhere in 24 pages of main memory.

The algorithm is subtly different for accessing a word. The user's page address is checked against the 8 page numbers in CAM as before. On most occasions, a match will be found and a page number declared. The page number (5 bits) and the word number (10 bits) from a main-memory address will be used to access the desired word (Fig. 4.39). The vast majority of requests should follow this pattern. If the request fails to obtain a match, a software routine is entered. In this, a search is made sequentially through a table of pages to see if the word requested is in a page not known to CAM but nonetheless in main memory. (These are the 16 "background" pages in main memory). If a match is obtained, the least prior page in CAM is switched to point to that page requested, thereby making the former a "background" page. No movement of data is involved and the time to do the job is not long—certainly much shorter than would be needed to bring a page down from disk.

Typical times for such a system might be as follows:

1. successful request (page entered in CAM)—1.2 μs;
2. partial success (page in memory but not registered in CAM)—10–50 μs (subsequent requests to this page would then be at the 1.2 μs rate);
3. unsuccessful request (data only in disk)—20 ms.

This sort of system is very suitable for use in a multi-access system in which a number of users are trying to operate a single computer from terminals.

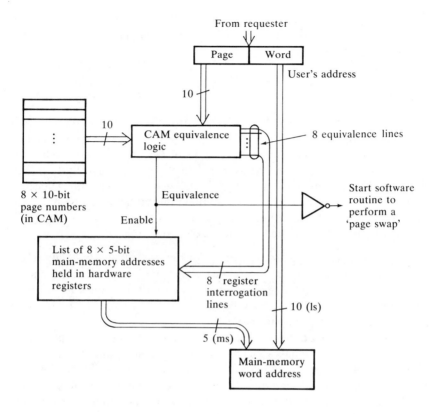

Fig. 4.39 "Successful" main-memory access in a paging system.

Each user can be allocated one or more (whole) pages which will normally be lodged on disk and brought down to main memory, as required. In this sort of environment, the choice of page size is very important—if it is too small, the latency time will reduce the disk's transfer rate; if it is too high, many small programs will waste memory through incomplete use of pages. This will necessitate the use of an excessively large main memory to cater for a certain number of (poorly utilized) pages. Pages are usually between 256 and 2048 words.

4.7 NON-ADDRESSED READ/WRITE MEMORIES

In preceding sections, memories have been discussed in which either an explicit address is used to access some data or a content-addressable memory (CAM) has been used to access data with certain attributes. In both cases, there is no particular relationship between the order in which the data are written to and accessed from the memory. Several applications exist in which the order of access (relative to writing) gives certain useful properties. If the write/access order is fixed, then explicit user addressing is unnecessary—the memory will have a hardware or software algorithm built in to achieve the correct order.

1. *The shift register* is the simplest form of non-addressed memory. It is often fabricated from concatenated flip-flops having a common clock line. Each flip-flop can be a master–slave, D-type or *J–K*, as required. Each time a clock pulse (or edge) is applied, all the data move along one flip-flop (cell) position. The last bit is lost and the first cell acquires a new bit. Such shift registers can be operated in parallel, so that multibit fields can be shifted bit parallel. A single clock, common to all cells, is then used.

There are many applications for such a shift register.

(a) *As a first-in–first-out memory* for temporarily holding data. It can only be used for this purpose in circumstances where the source for it and the recipient of data from it are working in synchronism. Failure to meet this requirement would cause loss of data because of the fixed 1:1 relationship between data acquisition and issue.

(b) *As a digital signal delay line* In many digital signal processing applications, analog signals are converted to digital form and then require to be delayed. By so doing, a time relationship can be programmed between these data and some other data. The bit-parallel shift register can synthesize a delay line because the data emerging from it are delayed by a certain time

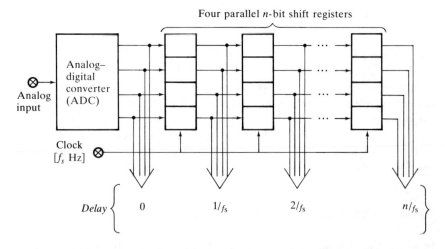

Fig. 4.40 Signal delay using a bit-parallel shift register.

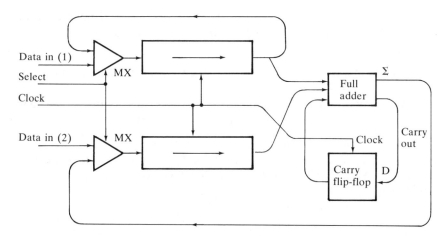

Fig. 4.41 Serial adder using shift registers.

relative to the data going in. If the shift-register clock frequency is f_s Hz and is n bits long, then versions of the original signal, delayed by $1/f_s$, $2/f_s$, ..., n/f_s seconds, can be obtained (Fig. 4.40). This sort of arrangement is useful for digital auto- and cross-correlation systems, discrete and fast Fourier transformers and digital filters.

(c) *Serial-data memory* If serial processing, i.e. serial arithmetic, is employed in a low-cost, low-power processor, then a single shift register can be used as a temporary data memory. When it is clocked, its contents can then be presented, a bit at a time, to a time-shared logic unit. A typical example is the use of a pair of shift registers plus a full adder to form a serial bit adder (Fig. 4.41).

A single clock ensures that the registers work in synchronism. Only a single full-adder is necessary. It is presented with bits of similar weight from each shift register, plus a carry-in from the previous addition. This carry has been held temporarily in a flip-flop. This flip-flop is cleared (reset) before the process starts. The multiplexers (data selectors) (MX) provide a means for entering initial data under the control of "select". After a complete "circulation" has taken place, corresponding to n clock pulses, the operand in the upper register will be back in the upper register. However, the sum of the two registers' contents will have replaced the original contents of the lower register.

2. *The read/write memory* Memory can be used to "synthesize" a delay line—in particular, one organized as n addresses by m bits wide. Read/write memory has some advantages over shift registers. Many shift registers, particularly MOS and bubble ones, do not provide many, if any,

"tapping points" along their length. Therefore, only fixed delays can be obtained for a fixed clock frequency. The reasons for such a restriction are twofold:

1.   the number of lead-outs on the chip increases as the number of tapping points rises but,
2.   more importantly, the complexity of the chip rises because of the need to provide output drivers at each tapping point.

A read/write memory has a single, time-shared, output port, so all "tapping points" are available. Furthermore, by the use of address-modification techniques, it is possible to easily obtain all delayed versions of the incoming signal (Fig. 4.42).

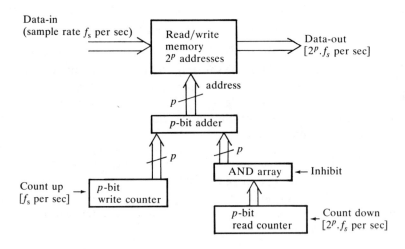

Fig. 4.42   RAM implementation of tapped shift register.

The incoming data are mapped to the read/write memory in contiguous locations (modulo 2^p). The addressing therefore "wraps-around" once per $2^p/f_s$ seconds. This simulates a shift register of 2^p cells. During writing, the read counter is inhibited from entering the adder so that the address is supplied solely by the write counter. During each period of $1/f_s$ seconds between write operations, all memory locations may be read. In order to obtain delayed versions of the input corresponding to 0, $1/f_s$, $2/f_s$ seconds, etc., the contents of a down counter are added to the write address (modulo 2^p). This is the read counter. The down counter starts at zero to obtain the data just written to memory (delay=0). It is then decremented by one to obtain the data written immediately previously, etc. In order that the system can recover if the two counters get out of synchronism, it is advisable to use a single clock source of $2^p \cdot f_s$ Hz and to use the output of the read counter to trigger the write counter. This guarantees that, even after an addressing error, the memory output will still be in the order 0, $1/f_s$, $2/f_s$ seconds delay relative to the input signal.

3. *First-in–first-out memory* *(FIFO)* This is another non-addressed memory but one not suffering the disadvantages of the shift register in demanding input and output rates to be exactly the same at all times. Clearly, any memory must match input and output rates in the long term to avoid either emptying or overflowing. However, the FIFO allows for short-term discrepancies and therefore appears to be like a shift register of variable length. For this reason, it is sometimes called an "elastic memory" or silo—reminiscent of grain silos. FIFOs are usually organized on a bit-parallel basis, typically 64 cells, each of 8 or 9 bits to a chip. It is often easier to think of them as 64 parallel register arrays, each of 9 bits.

The operation of a FIFO is not unlike that of a dentist's waiting room in which patients queue in chairs. As each patient enters the waiting room he can swiftly move along the chairs towards the surgery until he is next to an occupied chair. As each patient enters the surgery, a chair is emptied and the patients can move along. The algorithm for any given patient is therefore simply one of moving to the next chair as soon as it becomes empty. For a FIFO, a flip-flop is associated with each cell (chair) and is used to show whether the cell is empty (0) or occupied (1). This information is passed to the next cell back and can be used to effect the cell-to-cell transfer (Fig. 4.43).

FIFOs have many applications, of which the queuing of data prior to a merger (multiplexure) point is the most common. As an example, the main memory of a computer may have a cycle time of 1 μs and support a number of peripheral devices (magnetic disks, etc.) with a 10 μs/byte transfer capability. The memory is therefore clearly able to deal with up to 10 such devices as judged by average data throughput rates. However, if several devices concurrently call for access to main memory, data will be lost if they cannot be queued before the data selector at the memory's input port. If FIFOs are used, a backlog of data can be formed so that the peripheral device need not be stopped. (Most electromechanical magnetic devices are not permitted to stop once a transfer has started until an inter-record gap is reached).

How long the backlog will grow is determined by the number of devices and the data rates of the memory and devices. However, it is likely to be uneconomic to provide sufficient FIFO to *guarantee* that the backlog will not *sometimes* overflow the FIFO. Therefore, an acceptable failure rate has to be agreed as part of the system specification and software incorporated

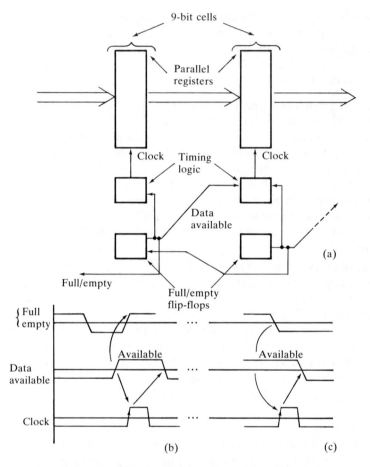

Fig. 4.43 FIFO: (a) schematic; waveforms for a cell if (b) data not immediately available; (c) data queuing.

which will allow a transfer between device and memory to be retried in the event of a FIFO overflowing. This tends to keep FIFOs down to between 16 and 128 cells (bytes) in length.

In calculating the statistics of failure, the figures obtained are usually pessimistic because devices tend to synchronize with each other. For example, devices can only be started in sequence according to the order in which I/O instructions are encountered in the software. This, straight away, spaces out their demands on main memory. Having so started, devices of similar performance tend to continue interleaving their interaction with main memory. Furthermore, as the CPU is often given the lowest priority for memory transfers, it will cease to even encounter I/O instructions (or any others for that matter) if main memory is "hogged" by outstanding I/O transfers.

FIFOs can be fabricated from parallel registers as suggested by Fig. 4.43 or using read/write memory (RAM), as for the shift register. However, as there is a danger of the RAM becoming either overfull or empty, some protection has to be provided. The logic of Fig. 4.42 can be used except that the read counter is incremented when a byte is written to the RAM (as well as the write counter). It is only decremented after a byte has been drawn from the RAM. The RAM is deemed totally empty and not able to supply data when the read counter reaches zero. It is deemed full and unable to accept more data when the read counter reaches $111 \ldots 1$.

An important parameter of a FIFO is the time it takes to pass a byte from input to output when empty. This time is proportional to the number of cells and inversely proportional to the cell-to-cell transfer rate. Typical figures are 64 cells and a cell-to-cell rate of 10 MHz. This makes the input-to-output time 6.4 μs. Notice that a bipolar RAM synthesis of a FIFO, such as that in Fig. 4.42, does not suffer this delay. It will merely be called to read from the same location as that to which the data were written. This can be as little as 100–200 ns.

4. *The last-in−first-out memory (LIFO)* This memory is the antithesis of the FIFO. Implemented (generally) in software, it is very useful, when used in conjunction with the reverse Lukasiewicz (also known as reverse Polish) notation, for software compilation. Statements containing nested parentheses can be converted to machine-executable form by being introduced to a LIFO as part of the compilation process. Implemented in hardware, it can be used for a related purpose—fast, orderly processing of chained arithmetic statements. This is frequently done in calculators and, not infrequently, utilizing the reverse Lukasiewicz technique.

Implementation can either be by a bidirectional parallel-bit shift register or by a RAM synthesis. In the former, the two shift directions correspond to the loading and retrieval of data. For the latter, a modified form of Fig. 4.42 can be used. In this, the addressing is no longer modulo 2^p, nor are two address counters needed. A single counter, which starts from zero and is incremented each time a byte is to be entered, is used. It is decremented each time a byte is withdrawn (read). If the counter reaches 2^p-1, the RAM is, of course, full. If the counter tries to decrement below zero, it is empty.

4.8 READ-ONLY MEMORIES (ROM)

A ROM is a memory in which data, once written or implanted, are permanently retained and remained unchanged (with one exception—see later paragraphs in this section). Such memories are made in a variety of forms and have wide application.

Microcomputers are frequently used in dedicated applications with a fixed program, i.e. certain process-control applications, intelligent instruments, control systems, TV games, etc. As most read/write memories (RAMs) are volatile, programs stored in RAM are lost if a blackout occurs. ROMs are not volatile so that, provided the program does not need to be changed, they are ideal program memories. In mini and mainframe computers, some routines and data remain unchanged for long periods, e.g. microcode, data constants, I/O routines, hardware macros and the like. These can also be held in ROM.

ROMs can be used and interfaced to the rest of digital systems in much the same way as RAMs except, of course, that they have no data-in ports or write control lines. Like RAMs, ROMs usually have chip-enable inputs and partial decoding mechanisms and can be connected into bus systems as described in the appendix to Chapter 3. Of greatest interest, apart from applications, is the form in which ROMs are available and the technological limitations of the various types.

1. *Mask-programmed read-only memory* (ROM). This was the original form and is still very popular. The pattern of bits issued from each memory location is determined by the final mask pattern applied to the chip. This pattern of bits is specified to the chip manufacturer who develops an appropriate mask. A schematic of a simple ROM is shown in Fig. 4.44, together with the places where the mask pattern determines the ROM contents.

The ROM uses a matrix of emitter followers to interface the address decoder to the output (column) wires. The emitter followers associated with each column from an OR gate, the connections marked * being inserted or omitted according to the final chip mask pattern. A non-connected emitter will give a logic 0 when selected by the decoder—a connected one will give a logic 1.

This form of ROM can be manufactured very cheaply and have very high bit densities (greater than 16K bits per chip). However, the per-chip cost is affected by the number of chips over which the capital cost of producing the final mask pattern has to be amortized. Normally, at least 250 chips would have to be manufactured to the same mask to make the investment worthwhile. If the pattern is incorrectly specified by the customer, considerable development time and money is wasted. Both for this reason and to make low volume production worthwhile, alternative ROMs have been devised.

2. *Field-programmable read-only memories* (*FPROM or PROM*) This type of ROM allows the user to program the ROM himself in a restricted sense. In one very popular scheme, the PROM is supplied with all logic 1s programmed in by virtue of rows and columns being interconnected by short nichrome fuses. It is as if the points marked * in Fig. 4.44 were all intact,

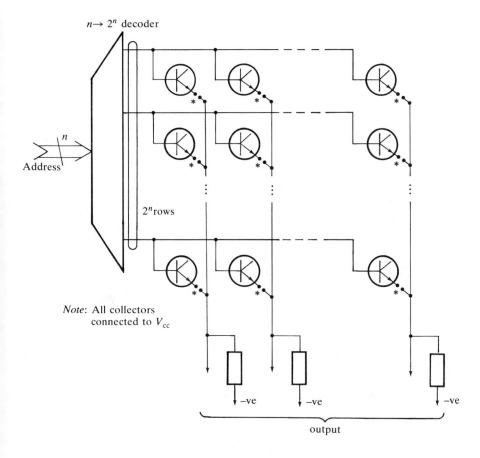

Fig. 4.44   ROM fabricated from emitter followers.

being joined by fusable elements. The fuses blow (rupture) at around 10 mA—a current which can be derived through the current gain of the emitter followers from a very moderate base current. The fuses can be selected one at a time by supplying a suitable row address and operating on an appropriate column wire. A practical bipolar version of such a PROM would have an access time of around 60 ns. The PROM is, of course, nonvolatile.

A slight inconvenience of such PROMs is the fairly high programming currents required—a function of the matrix size. A more serious problem with PROMs is that ruptured fuses cannot be repaired, so that a logic 0 programmed in cannot be changed back to a logic 1. The chip must be discarded and a fresh one programmed as required.

3. *Erasable read-only memories (EPROM* (Ogdin, 1978) *and UVROM)*
Various ROMs are available which use various modifications of MOS structures to provide a nonvolatile read-only property. One is based on the
floating avalanche-MOS (FAMOS) technology, the other on the use of a
nitride layer in the MOS make up (metal-nitride-oxide semiconductor—MNOS). In both cases, the threshold voltage of a MOS transistor, that
is, the turn-on gate-source voltage, can be altered by implanting a charge.

Two types of erasable ROM emerge. In both cases, they can have any
matrix point activated (programmed to logic 1) by setting up a high electric
field in the vicinity of the gate electrode. Erasure can be effected by

(a)   passing UV light through a window in the chip encapsulation (to erase
       the whole chip in one operation)—this is the so-called UVROM—or
(b)   by a reverse field which can be applied selectively to any given word.
       Some of these allow either a single word or total chip erasure to be
       accomplished.

Both memories are nonvolatile, have a very long data retention time measured in tens of years and therefore need no periodic refresh. However,
EPROMs can generally be read only a limited number of times without
losing a substantial proportion of implanted charge below the gate electrode.
Typically, refreshing is required once per 10^{11} accesses. EPROMs can also
only be written to a limited (10^5) number of times, and suffer damage from
excessive program pulses.

Both UVROMs and EPROMs border on being the ideal memory
element—capable of being written to and read from and nonvolatile—i.e.,
they could almost be classified as nonvolatile RAMs. Several factors make
both fall short of this ideal.

1.   Use of UV light for the UVROM is a nuisance and very time consum-
      ing. It takes about 10–20 min to erase a UVROM. At best it could be
      classified as a read-mostly memory (RMM).
2.   For both memories, the writing (programming) voltages and currents
      are relatively high and need to be applied for some time (milliseconds).
      Programming has often to be done several times to ensure sufficient
      charge has been implanted. It is doubtful whether such a procedure
      could be called writing as normally applied to RAMs!
          A version of the EPROM has been developed recently (Intersil,
      Insight, 1979); this uses a doubly formed insulated-gate technique
      which makes programming much easier. This device qualifies much
      better for the title "nonvolatile RAM" but still has some shortcomings
      in terms of ease of use relative to volatile RAM.
3.   All these ROMs are based on various breeds of MOS technology.
      Generally speaking, access times are fairly long—around several hun-
      dreds of nanoseconds.

EXERCISES

4.1 List the "ideal" attributes of an "ideal" memory form. What is a memory "hierarchy" and what does it seek to achieve (bookwork)?

4.2 Draw an S–R flip-flop using NAND gates only and determine the quiescent and active logic states needed to operate it. Take care to identify the set and reset inputs and Q and $\bar{Q}$ outputs.

4.3 Figure 4.45 shows the circuit of a pulser which can be used in Fig. 4.2(a). Determine its performance when used with a TTL gate for square-wave inputs of long, unity and short mark/space ratios.

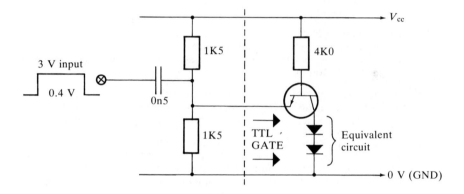

Fig. 4.45

4.4 Repeat the exercise above for the pulser shown in Fig. 4.46 and comment on its performance relative to the above one.

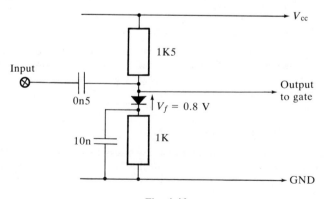

Fig. 4.46

4.5 Develop the NOR version of Fig. 4.4 and determine the polarities of the clock and data signals needed. Identify the Q and $\bar{Q}$ outputs.

4.6 Draw waveforms for *all* the gate outputs of Fig. 4.13, the D-type flip-flop, and thereby corroborate the waveforms of Fig. 4.13(c).

4.7 If reset (clear) and set (preset) inputs are required for the flip-flop of Fig. 4.13(b), to which gate inputs should they be taken in order to ensure correct operation regardless of the states of the clock and data inputs?

4.8 Check that the operation of the scratch-pad logic of Fig. 4.16 corresponds with that described in the accompanying text.

4.9 For a dynamic MOSRAM organized as a $16K \times 1$-bit memory on a square matrix, determine:

    (a)   the matrix dimensions;
    (b)   the number of address inputs (if they enter the chip bit parallel);
    (c)   the percentage of time the chip is engaged in refresh if the refresh time per row is 300 ns.

4.10 Develop the logic for a two-level row (or column) address decoder for Exercise 4.9. Do not draw the logic in its entirety but just sufficient to ascertain the number of gates used, and the load value imposed on each.

4.11 A computer processor has a power supply capable of supplying 5 V±5% at 100 A. The logic in the processor requires a 5 V supply with a tolerance of ±10%. A supply failure monitor is attached to the logic supply rail and triggers at 5 V less 8%. What is the minimum nominal capacitor needed to "prop up" the supplies if the dumping of data takes 0.5 ms after failure is signalled? The capacitors available have a manufacturer's tolerance of ±30%. Make (and state) suitable assumptions.

4.12 What is the maximum capacity of a reel of two-track cassette tape (in bytes) given the following parameters:

    Length of tape: 84 m (275 ft);
    Recording method: biphase;
    Flux change density: 43 per mm (1100 per in);
    Each byte: 8 bits plus 1 parity bit.

4.13 One "phase-encoded" method of cassette tape recording is a bit-serial method which makes a flux change at the start of every bit plus an additional one in the center of a bit if the bit is a logic 1. Sketch the waveforms for such a system for any chosen data string, develop outline logic for recording a bit-serial stream in this manner and for recreating the data from the recording. What limitations can you determine for the system and which of these is a function of the attributes of the tape transport?

4.14 A cartridge disk uses both sides of a single disk for recording. Each side has 256 tracks organized as 40 sectors, each of 256 bytes capacity. What is the disk's byte capacity and how many bits are needed to address any particular sector?

4.15 A floppy disk transport can change tracks at the rate of 1 per 40 ms. If the disk is organized into 77 tracks, what is the average time needed to change from any one track to another? Assume that the start and destination tracks are chosen at random so that you are seeking an expected track-to-track time. (*Hint*: the mean head movement is *not* 38 track positions!)

4.16 A certain processor has a main memory organized as 8 submemories and an 8×8 buffer memory (see Fig. 4.35). If a program segment, initially held in main memory, consists of 64 nonbranching instructions, followed by a loop of 16 instructions to be executed 20 times, followed by 64 nonbranching instructions, what is the total instruction access time (fetch time) for the segment during run time?

Main-memory accesses (including copying to buffer) take 1.2 μs; buffer (only) accesses take 200 ns.

What is the corresponding time if the main memory (only) is used and has an access time of 1.0 μs?

(*Note*: No writing to main memory is necessary as the data in buffer are never written to from the processor and therefore need never be copied to main memory.)

4.17 Using D-type flip-flops for the full/empty indicators of a FIFO cell, develop suitable logic for setting and resetting such flip-flops according to the full/empty status of the adjacent (upstream) full/empty flip-flops. Develop additional logic for generating the strobe pulses for passing the *data* from one cell position to another.

REFERENCES

Ackland, B. D. and Pucknell, D. A. (1975) "Studies of caché store behaviour in a real-time minicomputer environment," *Electron Letts*, **11** (24), 588–90.

Axford, J. G. and Fiske, A. R. (1971) "Method of using redundancy in very large computer stores," *Proc IEE* **118** (10) 1383–92.

Booth, T. L. (1971) *Digital Networks and Computer Systems*, Wiley International, New York, Chapter 8, Section III.

Corsini, P. (1975), "*n*-user asynchronous arbiter," *Electron Letts* **11** (1) 1–2.

Hanatek, E. (1976), "Chipping away at core: another round," *Digital Design*, July 1976, 31–42.

Hartley, M. G. and Healey, M. (1978) *A First Course in Computer Technology*, McGraw-Hill, London, Section 7.4.

Hill, F. J. and Peterson, G. R. (1978), *Digital Systems: Hardware Organization and Design*, Wiley International, New York, Chapter 18.

Intersil, *Insight* (1979): Issues 1–4, N. European H.Q., Intersil Inc., 8 Tessa Road, Reading, Berks, UK.

Kluge, W. (1973), "Content addressable memories based on magnetic domain logic," *Proc IEE* **120** (11), 1308–14.

Lavington, S. H., Kinniment D. J. and Knowles, A. E. (1971) "An experimental paging unit", *Computer J.*, **14** (1), 55–60.

Lewin, D. W. (1980), *Theory and Design of Digital Computers*, Nelson, London.

Marcus, P. (1972), *Switching Circuits for Engineers*, 3rd edn, Prentice-Hall, Englewood Cliffs, N.J., Chapters 18 and 19.

Millman, J. and Halkias C. C. (1972), *Integrated Electronics= Analog and Digital Circuits and Systems*, McGraw-Hill, Tokyo, Section 17.9.

Nashelsky, L. (1972), *Introduction to Digital Computer Technology*, Wiley International, New York, Chapter 11.

Ogdin, C. A. (1978) "Using EAROMs with your μC requires some special tricks", *EDN*, November 20, 237–47.

5 IMPLEMENTATION OF COMPUTER ARITHMETIC

5.1 BASIC PROCESSES

Whenever an arithmetic operation such as add, subtract, multiply or divide is carried out on a digital computer or instrument, a large number of (frequently) similar processes is involved (Garner, 1976). A simple example is addition in which pairs of bits from corresponding positions in words A and B are added and a sum bit and carry produced. Also, there may be a carry to be considered from a less significant operation. The operation is the same whatever the position in the words from which the bits are taken. If two 16-bit words are to be added, 16 similar operations are involved. This leads to two basic choices for the implementation (Fig. 5.1):

1. *serial*, in which a single adder is used for all bit pairs from the two incoming operands, these pairs being operated on in sequence;
2. *parallel*, in which as many (identical) adders are used as there are bit pairs.

Pencil-and-paper addition is clearly of the serial variety unless 16 people can each be talked into taking on the addition of 1 pair of bits from a pair of 16-bit words!

Serial addition is potentially cheaper than parallel because only 1 adder is used, but it is more time consuming as the 1 adder is used 16 times. This is a very simple comparison and other comparisons will be touched on later. The choice, in effect, is one between occupancy of the space and time domains for a set of n operations.

Subtraction commands the same considerations as addition above, but multiplication has far more operations. If the multiplication of two 16-bit numbers is considered, then $16 \times 16 = 256$ multiplications of pairs of bits

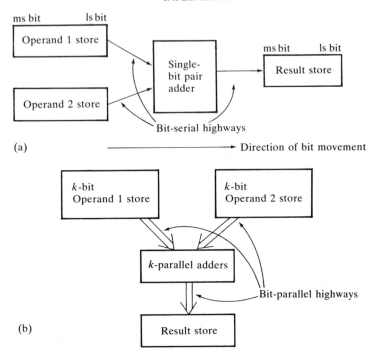

Fig. 5.1   Basic schematics for (a) serial and (b) parallel arithmetic.

from A and B are needed, plus the grouping and accumulation of these 256 subproducts to form a final 32-bit product. The situation with division is very similar. It is therefore not surprising that most machines carry out at least some of the multiplication and division processes in the space domain, i.e. using parallel arithmetic to cut down on execution time.

As a comparison, addition and subtraction of 16-bit operands using serial arithmetic and a single adder (which requires 50 ns to generate the sum and carry bits) needs 16×50 ns $= 0.8$ μs to complete its task. Using a single adder for the 256 operations in multiplication would take 256×50 ns $= 12.8$ μs.

This chapter is mainly concerned with parallel arithmetic methods on the following grounds:

1. The reducing cost of medium- and large-scale integrated circuits makes the extra cost of parallel-arithmetic techniques quite acceptable even from the cost/performance viewpoint.
2. Although serial arithmetic is less costly and power consuming, the need for timing and counting circuits to control the time multiplexure of the single adder can greatly offset these advantages.

3. As further support for (2), many parallel-arithmetic circuits need no special timing or clocking at all—merely a suitable time allocation for the worst-case settling time of the circuitry.

4. The use of a single time slot instead of a multiplicity (as for serial arithmetic) can make worst-case circuit tolerancing much easier, particularly when the operating temperature range of the equipment is considered. As a simple example, in serial arithmetic, the speed variations of the adder, the shift registers and the time-slot generators must all be taken into account over the temperature range. For parallel addition, only the adder speed variations are of great consequence.

5.2 PARALLEL ADDITION (Agrawal, 1974; Bin Nun, 1974)

If we consider two binary words A and B that are to be added, there are three bits associated with each significance position n (Fig. 5.2). A_n and B_n are the bits

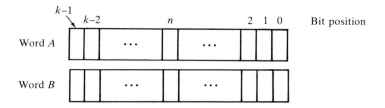

Fig. 5.2   Bit positions for k-bit unsigned operands.

from words A and B of weight 2^n and C_n is the carry from the adder in bit position $(n-1)$. The carry C_n also has weight 2^n. The adder needs to generate two outputs, one (the sum Σ) of weight 2^n and a carry of weight 2^{n+1} (Fig. 5.3).

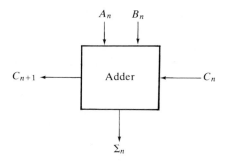

Fig. 5.3   Full-adder connections for stage n.

As n may have any value from 0 to $k-1$ (Fig. 5.2), then the circuit may be used for all adder positions. The truth table and typical NAND logic implementation for the adder are shown in Fig. 5.4.

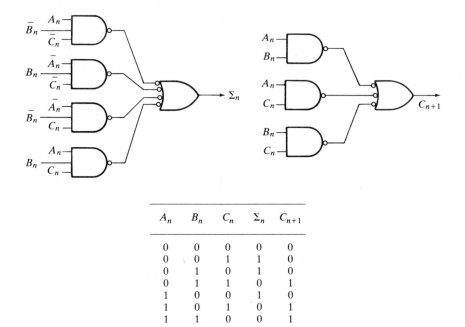

A_n	B_n	C_n	Σ_n	C_{n+1}
0	0	0	0	0
0	0	1	1	0
0	1	0	1	0
0	1	1	0	1
1	0	0	1	0
1	0	1	0	1
1	1	0	0	1
1	1	1	1	1

Fig. 5.4 Full-adder fabricated in NAND logic.

In the case of $n=0$, there is, naturally, no carry-in bit C_0. Thus the adder circuit of Fig. 5.4 has a spare C_n input. Two choices are possible. Either a degenerate version of the (full) adder above, called a *half-adder*, may be designed which has only inputs A_n and B_n, or C_n can be tied to logic 0 to indicate the lack of a carry-in. For the first case, the corresponding truth table and logic are shown in Fig. 5.5. However, for practical integrated circuits (IC), full adders are often packaged four at a time in one circuit, with the carries already internally linked. Therefore, it is usually found preferable to use a full adder with a zero carry-in rather than a separate IC to provide a single half adder. Figure 5.6 shows a typical full adder array for k bit pairs.

Unfortunately, it is clear that the array is not really parallel at all, for if the decision time (propagation delay) through each stage is, say, τ_d, then $k \cdot \tau_d$ will be

A_0	B_0	Σ_0	C_1
0	0	0	0
0	1	1	0
1	0	1	0
1	1	0	1

$\Sigma_0 = A_0 \bar{B}_0 + \bar{A}_0 B_0 = A_0 \oplus B_0$

$C_1 = A_0 B_0$

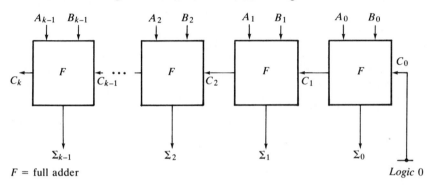

Fig. 5.5   Half-adder truth table and logic.

Fig. 5.6   A k-bit parallel adder.

required for the carries to *ripple through* from the least significant (ls) to the most significant (ms) stage. This is the *carry-propagation* time, and for the circuit of Fig. 5.6 it obviously dominates the settling time of the adder. The adder system shown, although parallel, that is it *accepts* the incoming operands together and processes them with combinational logic, nonetheless uses an *iterative* scheme for determining high-significance sum digits, i.e. less-significant result (carry) bits are necessary to the determination of higher-significance bits. The possibility of reducing this carry propagation time will be discussed under the headings of Carry-save and Carry-look-ahead (Sections 5.6 and 5.7).

5.3   PARALLEL SUBTRACTION

Although it is quite practical to repeat the exercise as for parallel addition and generate half and full subtractors, this is not done in practice both because of the expense of two separate units (plus that of the extra data paths) and because subtraction can be carried out using adders plus a little extra logic. Two methods are outlined:

Method 1   If B is to be subtracted from A, then $A–B$ may be recast as $A+(-B)$. For this purpose, B may be negated using the 2s complement method, wherein every bit of B is inverted (1s complement) and an extra 1 introduced to the $A+\bar{B}$ adder at the bottom significance (Fig. 5.7).

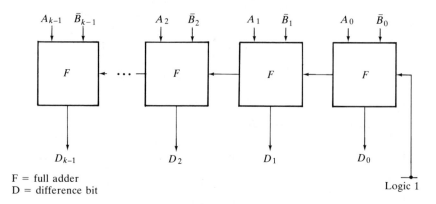

F = full adder
D = difference bit
Logic 1

Fig. 5.7   A k-bit parallel subtractor using full adders.

So far, only unsigned numbers have been considered, so that this method must be re-evaluated for situations where $A-B<0$. See the section on signed arithmetic.

Method 2   Some mini and microcomputers do not offer a subtraction facility at all. However, 1s complementation *is* frequently offered. An example is the Fairchild F–8 microprocessor. Although a programmed version of method 1 could be implemented using the complement, increment and add instructions, an interesting alternative, which does not need increment, is as follows:

(a)   complement the minuend (i.e. A);
(b)   add the minuend and subtrahend;
(c)   complement the result.

This method also works for 2s complement notation signed operands. It is quite straightforward to prove correct for 2s complement:

Step (a) forms $\bar{A}$ i.e. $-A-1$
Step (b) forms $\bar{A}+B$ i.e. $-A-1+B$
Step (c) forms $(\overline{\bar{A}+B})$ i.e. $-(-A-1+B)-1 = A-B$.

Example   5 subtract 3.
That is, 0101 subtract 0011.

Step (a) forms 1010
Step (b) forms 1010+0011=1101
Step (c) forms 0010=2.

Signed addition and subtraction

If k-bit 2s complement notation numbers are considered to have bits of weight -2^{k-1}, $2^{k-2}, \ldots, 2^2, 2^1, 2^0$, the addition of signed numbers can be implemented as for unsigned ones except at the ms bit position.

A_{k-1}	B_{k-1}	C_{k-1}	Σ_{k-1}	C_k	Σ_{k-1}^*	C_k^*
0	0	0	0	0	0	0
0	0	1	1	0	1	-1
0	1	0	1	-1	1	0
0	1	1	0	0	0	0
1	0	0	1	-1	1	0
1	0	1	0	0	0	0
1	1	0	0	-1	0	1
1	1	1	1	-1	1	0

Table 5.1   Addition of ms bits in 2s complement notation.

However, consider the addition of the ms bits of A and B (each having weights of -2^{k-1} and a carry-in of weight $+2^{k-1}$ (Table 5.1). It will be seen that, although the carry-out C_k is completely altered, the sum digit Σ_{k-1} remains exactly the same as for the normally used full adder. (This assumes that Σ_{k-1} and the carry have weights of 2^{k-1} and 2^k respectively.) However, as we usually wish to generate a sum digit of the same weight as the incoming operands [in this case -2^{k-1}] Σ_{k-1}^* and C_k^* are also given where their weights are -2^{k-1} and -2^k respectively. Again, the sum digit is the same as when a full adder is used normally. Thus, we are able to use a full adder for the ms sum-digit pair. (The carry-out is ignored.) Therefore, to add two 2s complement notation operands A and B, the circuit of Fig. 5.6 is still valid. (Use is made of this convenient fact in computers which offer both signed and unsigned arithmetic, such as the Motorola M6800 series of microprocessors.)

As parallel subtraction for unsigned operands may be implemented using parallel adders as shown in Fig. 5.7, the question arises as to whether the same circuit is valid for operands using 2s complement notation. As the process being carried out in the full-adder array of Fig. 5.7 is still *addition*, then it clearly is.

Example $k = 4$

$\qquad A = 5 \qquad A = 0101$

$\qquad B = 3 \qquad B = 0011$

$\therefore \; \bar{B} = 1100$ and $A + \bar{B} + 1$ is $\begin{array}{r} 0101 \\ 1100 \\ 1 \\ \hline 0010 = 2. \end{array}$

Example $k = 4$

$$A = -3 \quad A = 1101$$
$$B = -4 \quad B = 1100$$

$\therefore \bar{B} = 0011$ and $A - B$ is 1101
$$0011$$
$$\underline{\hspace{0.8em} 1 \hspace{0.8em}}$$
$$\overline{0001} = +1.$$

Again, the carry from stage $k-1$ is of no utility.

5.4   PROGRAMMABLE ADDER/SUBTRACTOR

In previous sections, it has already been shown that the parallel-adder array may be used as a basis for the addition and subtraction of signed and unsigned operands. Subtraction is achieved by 1s complementation of the subtrahend and the insertion of an additional "1" at stage 0 of the adder array.

To combine addition and subtraction, therefore, we need a system whereby the operand B may be inverted or not according to a control bit T, together with programmable insertion of a carry bit. A circuit which can perform this is shown in Fig. 5.8.

The EX–OR gates act as programmable inverters, for if one input T is a logic 0, the output Z of the gate $= W$ (the remaining input). Otherwise, if $T = 1$, then $Z = \bar{W}$, i.e. $Z = T\bar{W} + \bar{T}W$.

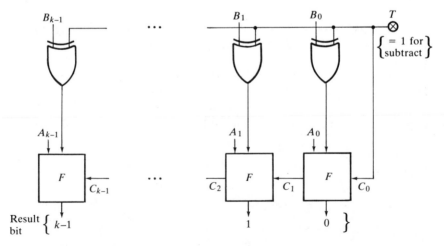

Fig. 5.8   Programmable adder/subtractor.

5.5 OVERFLOW DETECTION

If two numbers (regardless of radix) are added or subtracted, there is always the possibility of overflow if the result word length (field) is constrained to be the same as that of the incoming operands.

Example (a) To add two unsigned k-digit integers A and B of radix r gives the incoming operands the range

$$0 \leqslant A, B \leqslant r^k - 1,$$

and so the sum is of the range

$$0 \leqslant A + B \leqslant 2r^k - 2 \leqslant r^{k+1} - 2$$

and, in general, needs $k+1$ bits to accommodate it.

(b) To add two k-bit 2s complement notation integers means that the incoming operands are of the range

$$-2^{k-1} \leqslant A, \ B \leqslant 2^{k-1} - 1$$

and the sum of the range

$$-2^k \leqslant (A + B) \leqslant 2^k - 2.$$

Again, $k+1$ bits are needed. The requirement for 1 extra bit can be proved for subtraction, fractions and mixed numbers.

For most digital systems, it would be very inconvenient to have to provide larger and larger registers to accommodate ever growing operands, so overflow (out-of-range) detection circuits are normally incorporated into a structure with a fixed register length. To detect overflow in unsigned binary addition, it is necessary only to detect the presence of a bit of significance 2^k when adding two k-bit integers. This follows from the fact that the requirement for $k+1$ sum bits indicates a sum $\geqslant 2^k$ and hence the existence of a 2^k bit. In a k-bit adder, the carry-out of the ms adder provides this bit. *If $C_k = 1$, then overflow.*

For operands in 2s complement notation, C_k does not have the same meaning (see Table 5.1). Two simple methods exist to detect overflows in this instance:

1.   Use the fact that overflow can only occur if A and B are of like sign (for addition) for it is only then that the sum magnitude can exceed both $|A|$ and $|B|$. If A and B are legitimate operands to start with, then, for overflow to occur, clearly the sum magnitude must be greater than both $|A|$ and $|B|$. Twos complement notation for k-bit numbers may be thought of as a special case of a modulo-2^k system in which negative numbers exist along with positive ones. A pictorial representation of this cyclic form is shown in Fig. 5.9 for $k = 4$. Addition of numbers of like sign (Fig. 5.10) may cause the sum to enter

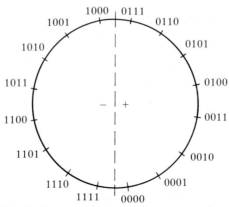

Fig. 5.9 Cyclic representation of 2s complement notation.

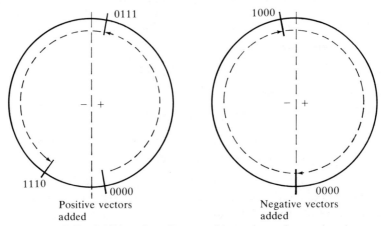

Positive vectors added

Negative vectors added

Fig. 5.10 Addition of maximum positive and negative numbers in 2s complement.

the half of the diagram of opposite sign. When this happens, we say that overflow has taken place. However, note that even with the maximum possible magnitudes of numbers (Fig. 5.10), it is impossible for the sum of the vectors to be long enough to re-enter the original half of the circle (having once overflowed). Therefore, a sufficient test for overflow for the addition of two operands of *like* sign is that the result sign is different.

The test is: overflow has occurred if:

(a) incoming operands of like sign, *and*
(b) result sign different from them.

If the sign bits of A and B and the result are $S(A)$, $S(B)$ and $S(R)$ respectively, then

$$\text{overflow} = S(A)S(B)\overline{S(R)} + \overline{S(A)}\,\overline{S(B)}S(R).$$

It is convenient to re-express this as:

$$\text{overflow} = [S(R) \neq S(A)][S(R) \neq S(B)],$$

the logic for which is shown in Fig. 5.11.

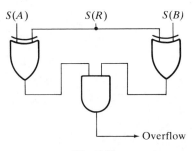

Fig. 5.11

2.   An alternative form of overflow detection, which is often easier to incorporate into an adder array's logic, makes use of the property of 2s complement notation numbers that a number expressed to $k+1$ bits can be compacted to k bits provided that bits of significance k and $k-1$ are equal.

Examples   11001 (-7) can be expressed as
                    $\underline{1}$001 and
             00111 $(+7)$ can be expressed as
                    $\underline{0}$111.

Neither can be further compacted as the two *new* ms bits (underlined) are not equivalent.

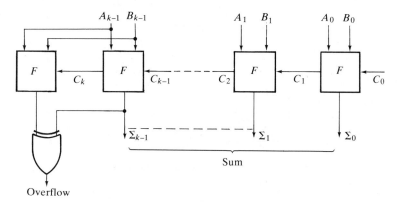

Fig. 5.12   Overflow detection: method 2.

Using this simple criterion, overflow detection can take the simple form of performing the addition of 2 k-bit numbers using a $(k+1)$-bit adder (to prevent overflows) and then checking the two ms bits for equivalence, i.e. ability to be compacted to k bits (Fig. 5.12). However, inspection of the left-hand side of Fig. 5.12 shows a certain amount of redundancy if we think of a full adder in gate form. There are only three independent signals involved: A_{k-1}, B_{k-1} and C_{k-1}. If $A_{k-1} \equiv B_{k-1}$ (input operands of like sign) then $\Sigma_k \not\equiv \Sigma_{k-1}$ (overflow) occurs only if $C_k \not\equiv C_{k-1}$ (Table 5.2).

A_{k-1}	B_{k-1}	C_{k-1}	C_k	Σ_k	Σ_{k-1}	Overflow?
0	0	0	0	0	0	
0	0	1	0	0	1	✓
0	1	0	0	1	1	
0	1	1	1	0	0	
1	0	0	0	1	1	
1	0	1	1	0	0	
1	1	0	1	1	0	✓
1	1	1	1	1	1	

Table 5.2   Truth table for Fig. 5.12.

The left-hand half of Fig. 5.12 can be reduced to the configuration shown in Fig. 5.13.

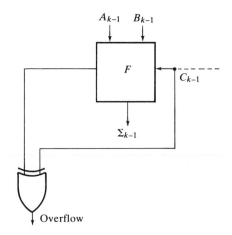

Fig. 5.13   Overflow detection: method 2 reduced.

5.6   CARRY LOOK-AHEAD

The time needed for carries to ripple through the basic parallel-adder array of Fig. 5.6 greatly degrades its performance. In practice, it can mean that a 16-bit parallel adder is probably no more than 4 times as fast as a serial adder (as compared with a hoped-for 16-fold improvement). For both the parallel and serial adders, the process time is proportional to the number of bits in each operand. The per-bit delay through a parallel adder is the time to generate the carry-out from a carry-in and this usually amounts to two gate delays. For a serial-adder system, the per-bit delay is the time for generating the sum or carry bit in the (time-shared) full adder, plus the time to write the carry-out to the carry flip-flop. Typically, this totals about 8 gate delays (around four times as much as the parallel adder). It is the iterative approach to the generation of high-order sum and carry bits that slows down the parallel adder, i.e. the high-order result bits are a function of low-order result bits rather than the incoming operands direct.

One method for ameliorating this situation (Gosling, 1971a) is to replace some of the purely iterative carry logic by two level AND–OR circuits which generate functions of the input operands direct. To do this for all high-order sum bits (carry generation would then be unnecessary) would be very expensive for all but very short word lengths (k). However, a compromise can be achieved whereby carry determination over a limited number of stages (m) can be implemented. This is called *block carry* or *carry look-ahead*.

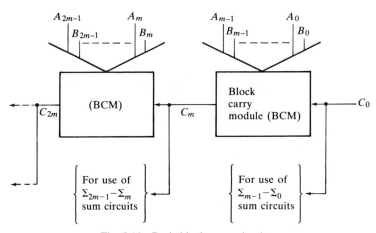

Fig. 5.14   Basic block-carry circuit.

In its simplest form, the block-carry logic would consist of a number of identical AND–OR-based modules generating the module carry-out as a function of the carry-in and the A and B bits entering the module (Fig. 5.14). A carry at C_{pm} can exist for one of two reasons:

1. It has been *generated* because the values of

$$A_{pm-1}, A_{pm-2}, \ldots, A_{m(p-1)} \quad \text{and} \quad B_{pm-1}, B_{pm-2}, \ldots, B_{m(p-1)}$$

    dictate it, regardless of the state of $C_{m(p-1)}$ (where $p=0,1,2,\ldots$) or
2. a carry at $C_{m(p-1)}$ can be *propagated* by virtue of the values of

$$A_{pm-1}, A_{pm-2}, \ldots, A_{m(p-1)} \quad \text{and} \quad B_{pm-1}, B_{pm-2}, \ldots, B_{m(p-1)}.$$

Clearly, not only is C_{pm} a function of $A_{m(p-1)}$, etc., but so too are the sum bits $\Sigma_{m(p-1)}$ etc. Therefore, the sum generation and BCM circuits are usually integrated together. However, for explanatory purposes, we shall first of all consider a BCM only.

Consider the BCM generating C_m in Fig. 5.14. C_m will be generated if $A_{m-1}B_{m-1}=11$ regardless of $A_{m-2}, \ldots, A_0, B_{m-2} \ldots, B_0$ and C_0. This is generation from the $m-1$ stage. If $A_{m-2}B_{m-2}=11$ and $A_{m-1}B_{m-1}=01$ or 10,*

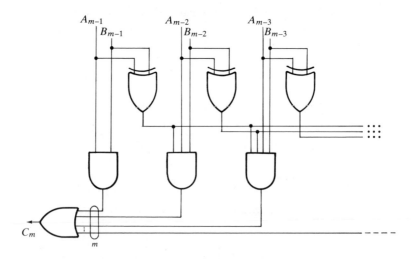

Fig. 5.15 Basic block-carry module (BCM) carry generation.

---

*That is $A_{m-1} \oplus B_{m-1}$. An EX–OR gate is needed to generate this function. It might appear that an OR gate would do just as well, but $A_{m-1} \oplus B_{m-1}$ is usually generated as part of the sum-bit circuitry and is therefore already available.

then a carry is generated at stage $m-2$ and is propagated by stage $m-1$ to appear at C_m. Similarly, $C_m=1$ if

$$[A_{m-1}\not\equiv B_{m-1}][A_{m-2}\not\equiv B_{m-2}]A_{m-3}B_{m-3}$$

(see Fig. 5.15). It can be seen that an m-bit BCM is going to need m EX–OR gates, m ANDs and an OR gate for carry generation. In addition, if $C_0=1$, then a carry may be *propagated* through this BCM. The logic expression for this is merely an extension of the carry-propagate portion of the carry-generation circuitry:

$$C_m \text{ (propagate)}=[A_{m-1}\not\equiv B_{m-1}][A_{m-2}\not\equiv B_{m-2}]\cdots[A_0\not\equiv B_0]C_0.$$

A four-stage BCM circuit is shown in Fig. 5.16.

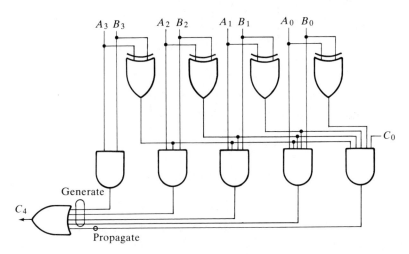

Fig. 5.16 Four-stage BCM.

There are several noteworthy points regarding this BCM:

(a)   A limit is imposed on the number of stages, either by the cost of such modules, the fan-in and fan-out limitations of the gates available or the type of technology available, i.e. whether medium-scale integration (MSI) devices are available which are suitable.

(b)   This circuit has two or three logic levels between any input port and C_{pm}. In particular, there are two logic levels between C_{pm} and $C_{m(p-1)}$. In some logic families, AND and NAND gates may have their outputs connected together. This gives a compound function of the form AND–OR (for AND gates) or AND–OR–NOT (using NAND gates). In both cases only *one* level of gating is used as far as logic delays are concerned. Emitter-coupled logic (ECL) and transistor–transistor logic (TTL) both provide this facility. However, the inversion of the output means that the next BCM must handle an inverted BCM carry input. This is not difficult if the BCM is designed with the *non*-generation and propagation of C_m in mind. A suitable design for such a BCM is shown in Fig. 5.17.

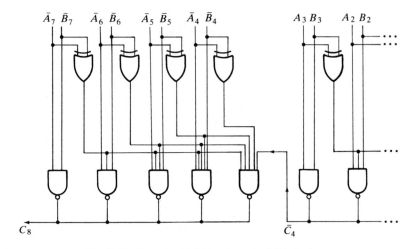

Fig. 5.17   Inverting BCMs using wired-OR logic.

(c)   As block-carry circuits are frequently associated with ECL technology, there is a tendency for only a relatively low level of circuit integration to be employed. (The dissipation per gate precludes many complex MSI circuit forms being implemented in ECL.) This unfortunate situation does, at least, lend itself to the possibility of optimizing each stage of an adder based on block carry rather than just using a chain of identical, generalized, modules. As an example of this process, an obvious way of constructing a 16-bit adder would be to use four identical building blocks each generating a look-ahead carry C_{4n} using the circuit of Fig. 5.16. Each BCM could employ, in addition, simpler versions of Fig. 5.16 to generate the carries C_{4n-1}, C_{4n-2}, C_{4n-3}, which would be used to generate the sum bits Σ_{4n-1}, Σ_{4n-2} and Σ_{4n-3} (Fig. 5.18). However, if we go away from the use of identical blocks, considerable savings can be made as the time needed for the carries C_{4n} to *ripple through* the block-carry circuits is going to be two gate

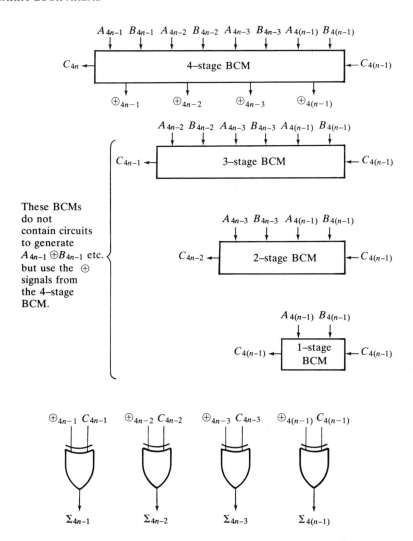

Fig. 5.18 Sum-bit generation using BCMs.

delays *per circuit*. (The least significant one is slightly longer because of the delay through the EX–OR gates to generate the first "propagate" signals.) Because of these inevitable delays, there is no point in accelerating the determination of the less significant sum bits with 1-, 2- and 3-stage look-ahead circuits. It is quite sufficient to let them generate their sums and carries by the normal iterative means until the settling time for a sum bit

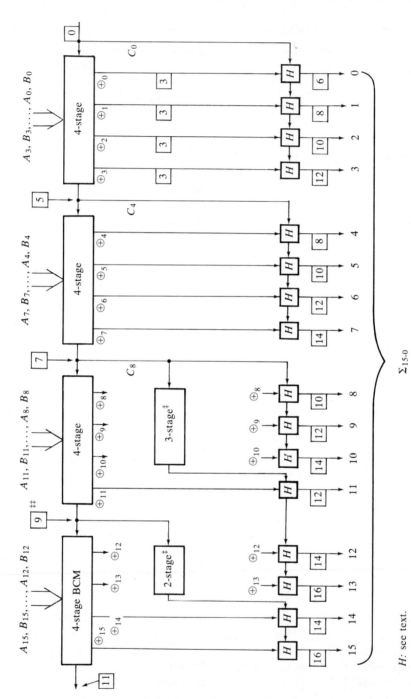

Fig. 5.19 Optimized block-carry arrangement.

H: see text.

equals that for the worst-case ms sum bit. At that point, a "look-ahead-carry" of suitable significance can be used to provide an earlier indication for the next sum bit along (Fig. 5.19).

It is assumed that the maximum allowable delay from the input operands to *any* sum bit is 16 gate delays. Each EX–OR gate is assumed to incur three gate delays. The adders (H) are modified half-adders which use the $(A \neq B)$ signals generated by the look-ahead circuits to create a ripple carry and sum bit (Fig. 5.20).

In order to get the carry to the ms end of the adder, maximum stage size look-ahead circuits are concatenated. The first one (generating C_4) takes five gate delays and subsequent ones take two. Modified half adders are wired in a ripple-through arrangement as far as gate delays will allow and then a suitable size look-ahead circuit is inserted (‡ in Fig. 5.19) to yield an earlier carry than is possible with ripple through. The rippling through is then continued up to a maximum delay of 16. The early carry is then re-established (‡‡) and so on.

(d)   The block-carry technique, in effect, creates *m*-stage carry generators rather than single-stage ones. However, carry ripple-through is still operated but on a shorter chain of units. An enhancement can therefore be made to basic block carry by gathering the generate and propagate signals

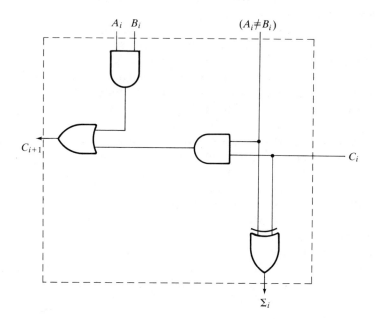

Fig. 5.20   Modified half-adder (H) for Fig. 5.19.

from several contiguous blocks (BCMs) and applying them to a second-level block-carry circuit. Thus a block-carry design may be used to look-ahead over 4 bits at the first level and the same design used to look-ahead over 16 bits by using the output from four contiguous BCMs as its input. Such a technique makes its greatest impact on very much longer adder arrays—say for $k=32$ and above.

5.7   CARRY-SAVE ADDITION

Carry-save is a technique in which use is made of the fact that the summation of a large number of items (operands) does not necessitate the generation of a normal binary weighted subtotal at each stage of the calculation. Provided that no information (particularly carries in transit up the adder array) is lost at each stage, it is perfectly in order to synchronize the propagation of carries with the generation of subtotals. This technique is sometimes known as *synchronous parallel addition*.

A typical and widespread use of this method is in multiplication (see later) which may be thought of as repeated addition and the creation of subtotals (partial products).

If we take just two levels of summation, i.e. the addition of three operands, and hold each carry generated in a flip-flop at each stage, then the subtotal registers will now have twice as many bits (sum and carry bits). After subtotalling has taken place, what is left will not be a normally binary weighted result as there will be two bits at each significance (Fig. 5.21). The clock signal is applied at a rate limited by the sum of the worst-case adder plus flip-flop delay times. Operands A, B and C etc. do not have to come from physically co-existing sources—they may just be different (or even similar) versions of the same operand from the same source. (Multiplication is an example of this situation.)

Carry-save is a form of (iterative) pipelining. It always generates subtotals with 2 bits of each weight (except the least significant bit), whatever the number of stages or operands involved. Therefore, to convert a final total back into normal binary, it is merely necessary to use a normal parallel full-adder array, assigning each pair of bits of weight 2^m to position m in A and B as in Fig. 5.6. Even better, a final adder based on block carry could be used to improve the speed of the final addition.

Carry-save can be extended for use with operands using 2s complement notation by utilizing the full adder's properties illustrated in Table 5.1.

A problem associated with the use of carry-save is the difficulty of detecting overflows. Frequently, the lengths of the adders are just increased

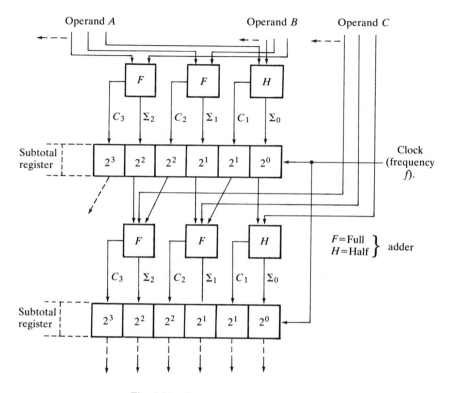

Fig. 5.21 Carry-save method.

at each stage to make overflow impossible. In the case of multiplication (see p.164) the number of operations (subtotals) is rigidly defined by the number of multiplier bits, and so it is known in advance how many bits are required in each register. Other subtotalling operations are usually less rigorously defined.

If the carry-save technique is not being used iteratively, e.g. in a hardware loop situation where only one subtotal register is used, then operands may be introduced at the top of the system at a rate of f per second (Fig. 5.21). This is a form of pipelining which enjoys a high throughput. However, the generation of any *one* subtotal may be quite slow because of the time allowance necessary for the data to pass through each subtotal register. (Removal of the registers would accelerate the generation of any *one* total, but only allow one to be generated at a time. This latter technique is therefore *not* a form of pipelining.)

5.8 MULTIPLICATION

Multiplication, being a particular form of repeated addition, is much slower than simple addition. However, even a cursory glance at computer instruction mixes will confirm that multiplication is very important and heavily used. It is not only used explicitly by the programmer but also called in the generation of trigonometric functions, roots and many other iterative procedures. It can also be used in a form of division. (See division by reciprocals.)

Multiplication requires every bit of the multiplier (r bits) to be multiplied by every bit of the multiplicand (s bits). The rs products so generated must then be added together at their correct weights to form an $(r+s)$-bit product.

Serial multiplication is very slow as the rs products are formed in one time-shared multiplication unit (an AND gate) and the products are summed in a single time-shared adder. The whole process therefore takes rs time slots to complete and is consequently very slow.

Parallel multiplication (Gosling, 1971c; Anderson et al., 1967; Gardiner and Hont, 1972; Meggitt, 1962; Houselander, 1974) can take several forms such as:

1. Use of parallel arithmetic to add preformed s-bit subproducts of each multiplier bit by the s multiplicand bits. This needs r time slots for the r multiplier bits.
2. As (1) but processing two or more multiplier bits at a time. Typical process times are 50–70% less than for (1).
3. Use of parallel-arithmetic and parallel-multiplier processing in a fully combinational device (rather like carry-save without the intermediate registers).
4. Use of look-up tables to form subproducts of slices of the multiplier and multiplicand, which are then added together. The look-up tables can be fabricated from read-only memories (ROM) (see p.171).
5. Other algorithmic variations such as the use of logarithms, i.e.

$$\log ab = \log a + \log b.$$

Multiplier 1. Parallel arithmetic: one multiplier bit processed at a time

This is the simplest parallel method and can be built very economically in MSI even if 2s complement notation is used. The strategy is shown in Fig. 5.22.

The multiplicand is assumed to be available in bit-parallel form throughout the process. If this cannot be guaranteed, a temporary buffer must be provided to store it at ∗ (Fig. 5.22). The multiplier, which is

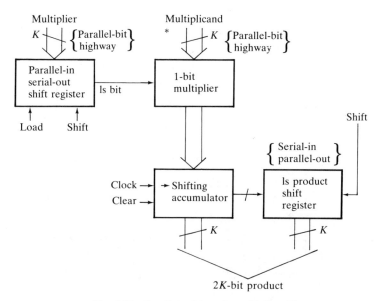

Fig. 5.22 Parallel arithmetic multiplier (1).

processed 1 bit at a time, starting at the ls bit, is held in a right-shifting register. Therefore, right-shifting of this register at each stage makes each multiplier bit available (from the ls end). To multiply every bit of the multiplicand by the current multiplier bit requires just n parallel AND gates (Fig. 5.23a).

If the current multiplier bit is 0, the AND gates produce zero output; if the multiplier bit is 1, the multiplicand contents appear at the AND gate outputs. This is equivalent to multiplication by a single bit. The shifting accumulator must add the s-bit subproduct from Fig. 5.22 into the running total in the accumulator at the right significance. This is easily done if, after every addition into the accumulator, the accumulator contents are right-shifted one place. This has the effect of doubling the weight of the next subproduct entry *relative* to the running total. The shifting-accumulator logic is shown in Fig. 5.23(b).

It will be noticed that s adders ($s-1$ full plus 1 half) are used so that intermediate overflows are prevented. The right-shifting of the new partial result at *each stage* causes a bit to be "lost" from the accumulator's ls end. Such bits form the lower half of an rs-bit product and are assembled in a shift register that allows its contents to be read out in parallel. This is often known as a *serial-in parallel-out register* (SIPO).

In order to process operands in 2s complement notation, it is necessary to be able to treat the ms bit of the multiplier as having a weight of -1. This can be done by subtracting the last s-bit subproduct from the running total.

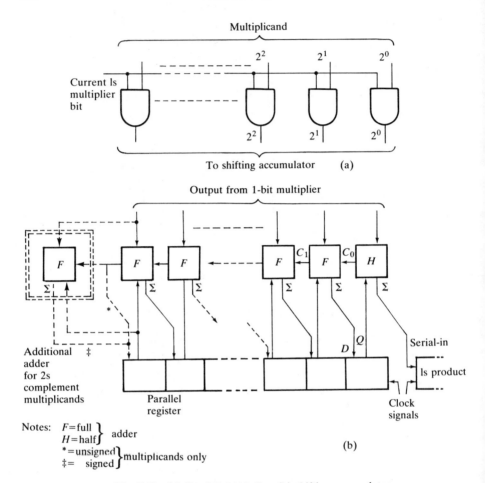

Fig. 5.23 (a) One-bit multiplier; (b) shifting accumulator.

The adder array must therefore be enhanced to a programmable adder/sub-tractor as in Fig. 5.8, using the appearance of the ms bit of the multiplier at the end of the multiplier shift register as a trigger to program subtraction. Of course, the adder/subtractor array must be capable of handling signed terms. Figure 5.23(b) shows the minor modifications necessary.

There are 3 clock and 1 clear signals to be generated for this multiplier. All 3 clock signals (multiplier right-shift, strobe-shifting accumulator and ls-product shift-register clock) may all be derived from the same source. The propagation delay through these registers will ensure fault-free operation. The (pre)clear signal, which prevents garbage from a previous multiplication being added into the current product, need only be applied to the parallel register. Any garbage in the ls-product shift register will be gradually

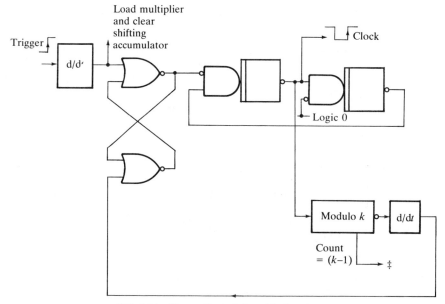

Fig. 5.24 Generation of clean/clock pulses.

removed by shifting as the product is formed. A simple circuit for generating the necessary timing signals for this multiplier, which would allow it to work autonomously from a trigger signal, is shown in Fig. 5.24.

Of course, the necessary waveforms could be generated from a ROM-based microprogram unit (see p.221).

Multiplier 2. Carry-save (see p.162) method

This system saves carries from all full adders and only fully assimilates them in a separate full-adder array. In other respects, it is similar to the previous multiplication example, except, of course, that the clock rate can be much higher (Fig. 5.25). It should be noted that two bits are generated by every adder except the one at the ls end. Only a sum bit is generated at significance 2^0 and this can be stored directly in the ls product-shift register. For 2s complement operation, an extra adder and one extra parallel register cell will be necessary to correctly handle the sign bit. Furthermore, the adder(*) in Fig. 5.25 will have to be a full adder. Although there is no room to fit in a carry of "1" at significance 2^0 during subtraction in the carry-save array, the carry-assimilate logic will have a spare input at the correct significance. Not shown in Fig. 5.25 is the s-bit parallel-adder logic needed to assimilate the saved carries in the accumulator. For extra speed this may incorporate carry-look-ahead (block-carry) logic.

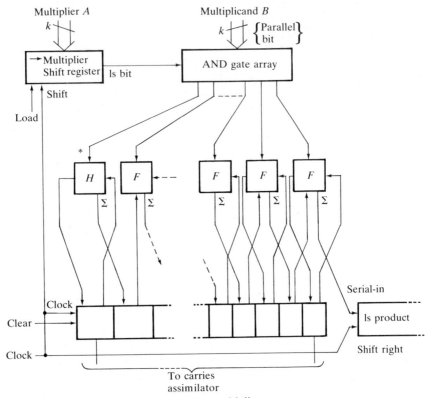

Fig. 5.25 Carry-save multiplier.

Example of operation Unsigned multiplication of 13 (multiplier) and 5 (multiplicand) with $r-s=4$ using the multiplier of Fig. 5.25.

Parallel-register (accumulator) bit weights:

$^{16}/_8$	$^8/_4$	$^8/_4$	$^4/_2$	$^4/_2$	$^2/_1$	$^2/_1$

where, for instance, 4/2 means that a bit enters a cell at weight 4 and leaves at weight 2 due to the shifting action of the accumulator (Table 5.3).

Stage	Subproduct	Parallel register	ls product register
Initial condition	—	0000000	————
1	0101	0001000	1———
2	0000	0000010	01——
3	0101	0001001	001—
4	0101	0001011	0001

— denotes garbage

Table 5.3

The final parallel register contents may be resolved into two operands A and B which must be added.

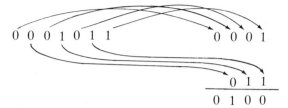

The final result is

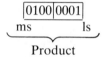

ms   ls

Product

Multiplier 3. Two or more multiplier bits processed at a time (Patel and Bennett, 1976)

The performance of the basic parallel multiplier of Fig. 5.22 can be improved if more than one multiplier bit can be handled at a time. In principle, the limit to which such a scheme can be taken depends on the difficulty of producing suitable subproducts of the multiplicand and the current multiplier bits together with provision of a suitable accumulator-shifting mechanism.

Multiplier bit pair	Value	Subproduct formation
00	0	$(0) \times$ multiplicand
01	$+1$	$(+1) \times$ multiplicand
10	$+2$	$(+2) \times$ multiplicand
11	$+3$	$(-1) \times$ multiplicand*

*1 added to next bit pair

Table 5.4

If two bits are to be processed at a time, then the current multiplier bit pair can take four possible values as shown in Table 5.4. The first two entries in the table are the same as for the basic multiplier. The third entry requires a parallel-bit left-shift of the multiplicand to be possible. The fourth entry poses a problem as $(3\times)$ cannot be created without use of another adder. However, if $(-1\times)$ is substituted, this leaves a deficit of $(4\times)$ in the total computation. This deficit can be "paid back" by adding 1 to the next bit pair (which is of 4 times the weight of the current pair). In all cases, the accumulator would perform a two-place right-shift after each bit pair has been processed. If the last "effective" bit pair is 11, a further addition of

($+1\times$) at the next bit-pair significance must be executed to complete the multiplication.

A slight variation on the above scheme, and one more suited to 2s complement multiplication, treats the "effective" 10-bit pair as ($-2\times$), adding 1 to the next bit pair. By so doing, all 2s complement multipliers are correctly handled except when the ms bit pair is 01 and 1 is added from the penultimate pair. Under these circumstances, a ($+2\times$) operation has to be performed.

Handling of three or more bits at a time presents more serious problems because of the difficult multiples of the multiplicand required. One solution is to allow more than 1 iteration to process a given group of multiplier bits, when necessary. Such a procedure makes variable shifting of the parallel-register/1s-product register necessary and causes a shortfall in the hoped-for performance. The total number of iterations (which determines the multiplication time) is not fixed, being dependent on the pattern of bits in the multiplier. One of several ways of handling multiplier triplets is shown in Table 5.5.

Multiplier triplet	Value	Multiple of multiplicand	Shift places
000	0	($0\times$)	3
001	1	($1\times$)	3
010	2	($2\times$)	3
011	3	$-(1\times)$	0*
100	4	($4\times$)	3
101	5	($1\times$)	0*
110	6	$-(2\times)$	3†
111	7	$-(1\times)$	3†

*Set current multiplier group value to 4 and repeat this step
†Add 1 to next multiplier group

Table 5.5

Other ways of handling triplets are more suitable for 2s complement working. Still others are faster but may require more shift options. Although three bits are handled at a time, 2 of the 8 combinations require a double iteration. The resulting improvement over handling 1 bit at a time is not 3 but only about 2.4.

Multiplier 4. Booth's method (Booth, 1951)

This method is a variation of the standard shift and add scheme of multiplier 1 and comes in several forms. The basic idea is that if shifting can be done much faster than adding/subtracting, then a more careful inspection of multiplier bits can alter the places at which addition/subtraction (a/s) and shifting take place. This can reduce the proportion of a/s operations.

Example   A multiplier 00111001110011 would require 8 a/s operations to be performed if applied to multiplier 1. It would require only 6 if the multiplier were recast as:

$$\begin{cases} +01000010000100 \\ -00001000010001 \end{cases}$$

In effect, groups of 0s are ignored. Groups of 1s are replaced by a single subtraction of the multiplicand at the significance of the ls 1 in the group and an addition at 1 place to the left of the last 1:

$$------011111------$$
$$\qquad\quad \uparrow \qquad \uparrow$$
$$\qquad \text{addition} \quad \text{subtraction}$$

A suitable algorithm is one which inspects pairs of multiplier bits but which progresses along the multiplier at just 1 bit per iteration. The first inspection is of the ls multiplier bit and a hypothetical zero to the right of this ls bit. (See Table 5.6.)

Bit pair	Action
00	Do nothing
01	Add multiplicand
10	Subtract multiplicand
11	Do nothing

Table 5.6

This method is of greatest use with 2s complement numbers as there are no end effects at the ms end of the multiplier. It also benefits from use in fixed-point calculations which tend to have multiplier distributions which peak close to zero. Such numbers have long chains of 1s and 0s at the ms end.

Multiplier 5. Fully combinational

All arithmetic processes are, by their nature, time-invariant. In logic terms, this means that they can, theoretically, be fabricated solely by combinational logic. However, the heavy cost of parallel logic in the quantity required, plus its repeated nature, makes iterative structures very attractive. If the fastest possible speeds are required, then combinational-logic methods must be used.

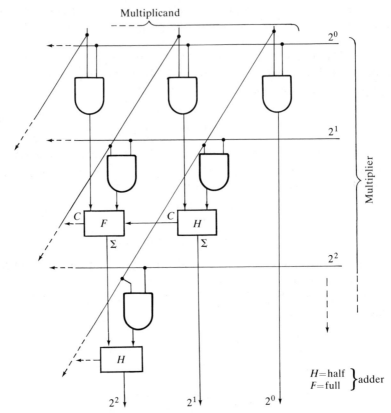

Fig. 5.26 Combinational logic multiplier.

One method of such processing lays out the basic scheme for multiplication (as Fig. 5.22) in a long tree-like structure (Fig. 5.26). The number of AND gates and adders is very high and the volume of interconnections daunting. A 16×16 multiplier would require about 270 adders and a similar number of AND gates. The number of rows can be reduced by using a "2 bits at a time" system. (The logic for (a) selectively adding 1 to each multiplier bit pair and (b) parallel-bit shifting of the multiplicand at each row must be added to the cost.)

An alternative, purely combinational, approach is to use read-only memories (ROM) in a look-up table scheme. Here, subproducts of groups of bits, taken from the multiplicand and multiplier, are formed. These are added together at the right significance to form a final product. ROMs are available (1980) which can perform the multiplication of two 16-bit operands (and the accumulation of the product with a previous result) in 115 ns (typical). The logic layout for such a device is shown in Fig. 5.27. Multipliers can also use fusable-link PROMs and be programmed by the

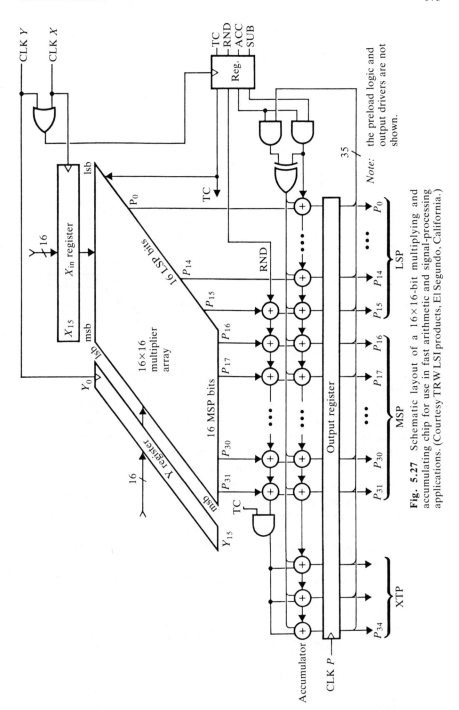

Fig. 5.27 Schematic layout of a 16×16-bit multiplying and accumulating chip for use in fast arithmetic and signal-processing applications. (Courtesy TRW LSI products, El Segundo, California.)

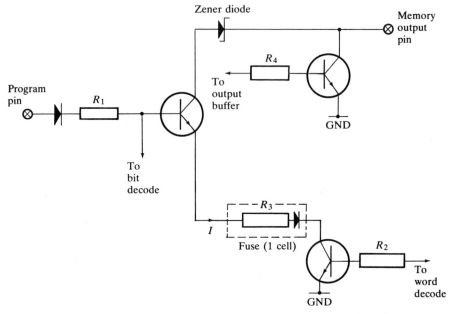

Fig. 5.28   Output (fusable-link) circuitry for a fast bipolar PROM.
(Reproduced by courtesy of MMI Inc.)

user. A typical PROM is the 6300 device by MMI Inc. The fuse-link circuit is shown in Fig. 5.28.

Practical multipliers often demand a ROM size which is prohibitively large (Chung, 1975). To obtain the product of two n-bit operands requires a 2^{2n} location by $2n$-bit ROM, i.e. a 16×16 multiplier would need a 1.4×10^{11} bit ROM. However, if the operands are partitioned into, say, 4-bit slices, subproducts of pairs of 4-bit operands may be derived from sixteen 256×8 (similar) ROMs. The subproducts must then be added at their correct significances in a tree of adders to form the final product. The technique is illustrated for multiplying two 8-bit operands using 256×8 ROMs, where what would have been a $65\ 536\times16$ bit ROM has been replaced by four 256×8 ROMs, plus a few full adders. Such a system would be slower than a pure ROM approach (because of the extra logic levels). However, the difference may be very small because larger ROMs are frequently fabricated in a slow, low-power, technology.

An interesting variation on the system of Fig. 5.29 which saves up to 50% on hardware costs has been developed by the author for signal-processing applications (Bywater, 1975; 1977). Here, it is assumed that the operands entering the multiplier are not precise, discrete quantities devoid of uncertainty, but measured values, most likely derived from transducers and converted to digital form using analog–digital converters (ADC) or synchro–digital converters. These quantities must carry an uncertainty (in

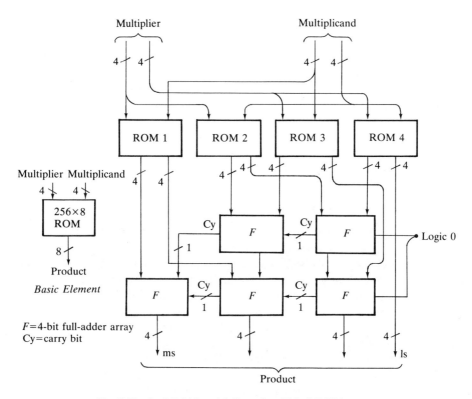

Fig. 5.29 8×8 ROM multiplier using 256×8 ROMs.

digital form) of at least $\pm\frac{1}{2}$ quantum of the ls bit, that is $\pm 0.2\%$ of full signal value for an 8-bit conversion. If two such 8-bit operands are multiplied, the product uncertainty (regardless of multiplier errors) is about $\pm 0.4\%$, which not only does not justify a 16-bit product representation, but makes 8 bits very dubious. Looking more closely at the uncertainties, let us multiply A by B, where A and B are discretized (quantized) fractions in the range $0 \leqslant A$, $B < 1$ with uncertainties of $\pm\delta_1$ and $\pm\delta_2$ respectively. The product is $A * B$—or with the uncertainties appended it is

$$(A \pm \delta_1) * (B \pm \delta_2) = A * B + B * \delta_1 + A * \delta_2 + \delta_1 * \delta_2$$
$$\text{or } A * B - B * \delta_1 - A * \delta_2 + \delta_1 * \delta_2$$
$$\text{or } A * B + B * \delta_1 - A * \delta_2 - \delta_1 * \delta_2$$
$$\text{or } A * B - B * \delta_1 + A * \delta_2 - \delta_1 * \delta_2.$$

As δ_1 and δ_2 may *usually* be considered small with respect to A and B, the term $\delta_1 * \delta_2$ can be safely neglected. However, if A and B are large (~ 1), then the uncertainty is

$$\pm (B * \delta_1 + A * \delta_2) \cong \pm (\delta_1 + \delta_2).$$

A multiplier working with such uncertainties does not justify a double-length product such as the one in Fig. 5.29. Therefore, ROMs associated with the generation of the least significant half of the product may be omitted. However, in order to avoid bias errors (due to consistently rounding down the subproducts) the system is greatly improved by assuming that the most significant half of an operand has $\frac{1}{2}$ quantum added to its value when entered to a ROM. In addition, subproducts involving the least significant bits of the retained product should be rounded to the nearest quantum of the least significant retained bit. By this means the bias produced is small compared with the product uncertainty.

Overflow in multipliers

The question of overflow in multipliers arises only if other than a full double-length product is to be generated from a pair of integers, or mixed numbers. It applies to both signed and unsigned operands but not to pure fractions. Frequently, only a single-length product is required. If the ms half of a double-length product is retained, overflow will not be encountered—just a loss of precision. (Most frequently, this technique is applied to the multiplication of fractions for which the overflow problem doesn't arise, anyway.) If the ls half is retained (i.e. as in the ICL 1900 series of computers) overflow can occur. Not infrequently, detection is accomplished by generating a full double-length product and then checking whether such a product can be compacted into a single-length form. The test method will depend on whether the operands are signed or unsigned. Checking may be carried out during the multiplication by detection of *significant* bits entering what would be the most significant area of the product. However, this procedure is difficult if signed operands are used because 1s are not significant in the ms portion of a *negative* product, or 0s in a positive product.

5.9 DIVISION

Division is frequently carried out as a reverse process of multiplication (Robertson, 1958; Tocker, 1958; Ahmad, 1972). Pencil-and-paper methods are called either "long" or "short" but short is only a reference to the digit length of the divisor and is of no general importance—and certainly of no importance to computer methodology. Pencil-and-paper methods are basically of the "restoring" type, that is, if a trial subtraction is unsuccessful, the partial remainder is restored, the divisor shifted right and another trial made. Mechanized division usually avoids the restoring method either (a) because extra storage is necessary to hold an "unsullied" version of the partial remainder before the trial subtraction, or (b) because time is wasted in restoring the partial remainder, or both. If the divisor D is subtracted from the dividend or partial remainder P, then the result is $P-D$. If $P-D$ is negative, the operation is said to be unsuccessful and a quotient digit of 0 recorded. In the restoring method, either P would have to be restored by discarding $P-D$ or D would have to be added to $P-D$ to regain P. Either way, housekeeping irrelevant to the division proper is involved. If we think in terms of binary, then the *next* trial subtraction will be with $D/2$ (D shifted) to form $P-D/2$. It is clearly quicker to form $P-D/2$ by adding $D/2$ to the *result* of the previous trial subtraction ($P-D$) rather than by restoring P, etc. This is the *non-restoring* method.

The algorithm is:

1. First iteration: subtract divisor (at its greatest significance) from the dividend. If the result is negative, quotient is 0; else 1.
2. Other iterations: if the previous result is negative/positive, add/subtract the divisor (right-shifted 1 place) to/from the partial remainder. If the new result is positive, set the quotient bit to 1; else 0.

Example $\frac{3}{8} \div \frac{7}{8}$ (see Fig. 5.30).

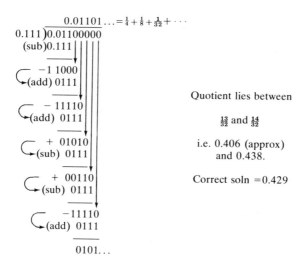

Quotient lies between

$\frac{13}{32}$ and $\frac{14}{32}$

i.e. 0.406 (approx)
and 0.438.

Correct soln $= 0.429$

Fig. 5.30

Division can produce a number of problems which must be faced:

1. The non-restoring method, when used for fractions, is quite straightforward. The process is continued until a sufficiency of quotient bits is obtained. For integer division, it can produce anomalous results as the last

trial addition/subtraction may leave a positive or negative result (remainder). The reason is easy to see. Any of the results below is correct but only the fourth one is normally acceptable:

$$19 \div 5 = 0 \text{ remainder } 19$$
$$19 \div 5 = 1 \text{ remainder } 14$$
$$19 \div 5 = 2 \text{ remainder } 9$$
$$19 \div 5 = 3 \text{ remainder } 4$$
$$19 \div 5 = 4 \text{ remainder } -1$$
$$19 \div 5 = 5 \text{ remainder } -6, \text{ etc.}$$

However, even the fifth has some "respectability" as, at least, it produces a remainder whose magnitude is less that that of the divisor. Non-restoring division, in effect, makes either the fourth or the fifth possible, depending on whether the last trial addition/subtraction is successful. In essence, we normally demand that it *is* successful so that an additional operation may be necessary, as shown in Fig. 5.31.

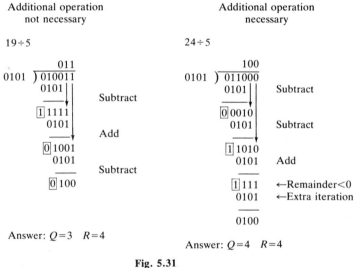

Fig. 5.31

2. The non-restoring method, when applied to signed (2s complement notation) operands, produces the same difficulties as in (1) together with the possibility of a quotient *algebraically* 1 less than expected. The additional operation mentioned in (1) can be used to adjust both the remainder and quotient. Before illustrating 2s complement non-restoring division by examples, it is necessary to establish what results are to be expected. For instance, there doesn't seem to be much to choose between:

$$-11 \div -3 = +3 \text{ remainder } -2$$

and

$$-11 \div -3 = +4 \text{ remainder } +1.$$

However, mechanization of the division process must produce *consistent* results and a relationship is usually defined between the sign of the remainder and either that of the dividend or the divisor.

A suitable algorithm for 2s complement division is:

(a) If the signs of the divisor and dividend are equivalent, then subtract; else add.
(b) For all subsequent iterations, if the signs of the divisor and partial remainder are equivalent, then subtract; else add.
(c) For any iteration, if the new partial remainder sign is equivalent to that of the divisor, then the quotient bit is 1; else 0.
(d) If, on the last iteration, the remainder and dividend are of unlike sign, and the remainder is nonzero, then perform one more addition/subtraction according to the rules of (b) above. This will guarantee that the dividend and final remainder will have equivalent signs. If the dividend is positive and the divisor negative or if the dividend is negative and *either* the divisor positive and the remainder nonzero *or* the divisor is negative and the remainder zero, then add one to the quotient.

Examples of the algorithm in action are shown in the appendix to this chapter.

3. Because division is the inverse of multiplication, it is often formatted accordingly, i.e. the dividend is a double-length (word) operand, the divisor, quotient and remainder are single-length.

Example IBM 360 series. Here, it is possible for overflow to occur if the dividend is large and the divisor small. To overcome this difficulty, the first trial subtraction/addition must, in effect, be unsuccessful. In essence, this means that the divisor, set to its first position relative to the dividend, must appear to have a greater magnitude than the dividend. For 2s complement operation, this requires that the first trial must produce a partial remainder of unlike sign from that of the dividend. (The first quotient bit may be a 1 or 0, quite legitimately.)

4. An extreme case of (3) occurs if the divisor is zero. However, it is usual for zero divisors to be trapped by a zero detector before division, *per se*, is attempted.

5. Although division with 2s complement notation undergoes some machinations in order to obtain consistent quotients and remainders, sign and modulus division does not. Such a format may be treated exactly as for

unsigned division—the result sign being determined by the normal laws of algebra, i.e. operands of like sign will produce a positive quotient and those of unlike sign a negative one. The magnitude of the quotient is, of course, not affected by the signs of the incoming operands.

There are several techniques for increasing the speed of division of which a few are outlined below.

Division by reciprocals

If the reciprocal of a number can be found (obviously without using division), then a quotient can be formed by taking the reciprocal of the divisor and multiplying the result by the dividend.

$$\text{quotient} = \frac{\text{dividend}}{\text{divisor}} = (\text{divisor})^{-1} * (\text{dividend}).$$

Newton's method is popular for finding a reciprocal and uses the iterative formula:

$$x_n = x_{n-1}(2 - d * x_{n-1}),$$

where d is the incoming operand and x_{n-1} and x_n are the previous and current approximations to d^{-1}.

Notice that only multiplication is involved, plus simple arithmetic.

The formula may be shown graphically (Fig. 5.32) to be one in which tangents are drawn from the current value of the ordinate to the abscissa in repeated attempts to seek the root of $y = x^{-1} - d$.

Once the procedure is close to the target, the convergence is very fast. The error falls on a square-law basis, causing the number of useful decimal places in the estimation to approximately double at each iteration. This can be readily shown by considering the situation at steps n and $n | 1$:

On steps n and $n+1$ the errors are respectively, say,

$$\epsilon_n = \left[\frac{1}{d} - x_n\right] \quad \text{and} \quad \epsilon_{n+1} = \left[\frac{1}{d} - x_{n+1}\right],$$

that is

$$\frac{\epsilon_n}{\epsilon_{n+1}} = \frac{(1/d) - x_n}{(1/d) - x_{n+1}},$$

but

$$x_{n+1} = x_n[2 - dx_n];$$

therefore

$$\frac{\epsilon_n}{\epsilon_{n+1}} = \frac{1}{1 - dx_n}$$

$$\therefore \epsilon_{n+1} = d\epsilon_n^2.$$

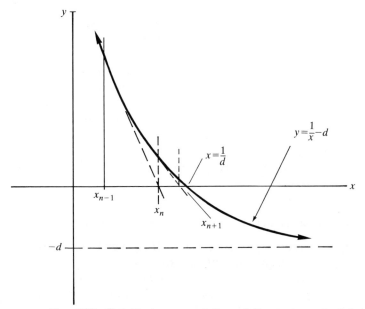

Fig. 5.32 Graphical representation of Newton's method for extracting a reciprocal.

Clearly, if x_0 (the initial guess) is badly chosen, then either convergence will be initially very slow or, if $\epsilon_0 \geqslant 2/d$, the algorithm will be unstable. Gill (1955) suggested a simple formula for an initial guess $x_0 [4(\sqrt{3}-1)-2d]$ which can be held in ROM look-up tables or, quite simply, calculated each time the algorithm is used.

Direct quadratic convergence division

A system of division which is particularly useful for use on *normalized floating-point operands*, and first used on the IBM 360/91 machine (Anderson *et al.*, 1967), operates on the dividend and divisor with *equal multipliers* so as to make the divisor converge on unity and the dividend on the quotient:

$$\frac{\text{dividend}}{\text{divisor}} \times \frac{k_1}{k_1} \times \frac{k_2}{k_2} \times \ldots \rightarrow \frac{\text{quotient}}{1}$$

The multipliers k_1, k_2 etc., are determined by inspection of the divisor. If the normalized divisor is represented by $1-x$, where the divisor $\geqslant \frac{1}{2}$, then $x \leqslant \frac{1}{2}$. (Signing may be ignored.) $1+x$ may be easily obtained by complementation of the divisor, i.e. if the divisor $= \frac{3}{4}:(01100\ldots0) = 1-x$, then $1+x = 1\frac{1}{4} = 11100\ldots0$, i.e. is the 2s complement. Multiplying the divisor $1-x$ by $1+x$ gives $1-x^2$. But x is less than $\frac{1}{2}$, therefore $1-x^2 \geqslant \frac{3}{4}$.

Similarly, $(1+x^2)$ is derived from $1-x^2$ to give $1-x^4$, which is even closer to 1; then $1-x^8$, $1-x^{16}$, etc. As the power of x rises, so the divisor converges quadratically on unity. If the dividend is multiplied by the same factors $1+x$, $1+x^2$, $1+x^4$, etc., then it will converge on the quotient, because, at all stages, the modified dividend and divisor maintain the same ratio.

Again, being a quadratically converging algorithm, it starts slowly, particularly if the divisor is close to $\frac{1}{2}$. However, a "guesstimate" for k_1 (based solely on the divisor value) may be obtained by the use of ROM look-up tables. This can give 7 or 8 binary places of accuracy before the iterative procedure is even started.

Note that, without a very fast multiplier, this method would not be worthwhile.

Cellular divider (Gardiner and Hont, 1972; Yildirim and Toker, 1972)

In order to make division fast, by whatever method, high levels of arithmetic parallelism are always required. Both iterative schemes and repeated subtraction methods lend themselves to the development of systems (matrices) of arithmetic cells for the hardware-based iterative evaluation of quotients. Not only are the steps identical (through repetition) but the process, at each bit position of the partial remainder or quotient, is the same. Thus, a single arithmetic-cell design, having linkages to similar axially and diagonally adjacent cells, can be repeatedly used to mechanize division (and many other arithmetic operations) in an array. The arrangement is usually purely combinational, making the generation of timing pulses unnecessary, and the cells are usually designed to be very amenable to implementation in IC form either as medium-scale integrated circuits (MSI) or as elements in a hybrid polycellular LSI structure.

5.10 BINARY-CODED DECIMAL (BCD) ARITHMETIC
(Gosling, 1971a; Agrawal, 1974)

The relative simplicity of binary arithmetic stems from the simple weight ratio between each adjacent pair of bits in a binary number—2:1. In 8421 BCD, this ratio only applies between adjacent bits *within* a decade. Between decades, the ratios between adjacent bits are 5:4. However, the ratio between digits of a decade is, of course, always 10:1. Implementation of arithmetic structures for BCD therefore naturally centers on the decade, not the bit, as the basic element. We must therefore think in terms of decimal full adders and subtractors involving all 4 bits of a decade, rather than individual bits. A decimal adder can accept 2 digits plus a carry-in and produce a sum digit Σ (4 bits) plus a carry-out, to give a total output range x in the range $0 \leqslant x \leqslant 19$. The weight of the carry-out is 10. As there are 6 combinations of 4-bit numbers which are not used in 8421 BCD, many BCD arithmetic logic designs consist of two parts:

1. a first part which treats the two incoming operands as if they were binary, producing an essentially binary result;
2. a post-correction to convert the "binary" result to BCD.

For a decimal full adder, part (1) can be implemented by a simple 4-bit full-adder array and part (2) by a circuit which detects results greater than 9 and adds 6 to those which do, in order to avoid the 6 unused BCD combinations (Fig. 5.33).

Detection of sums greater than 9 is quite easy if the weight of each bit D–H is recognized. Logically $Z = D + E(F + G)$, where $Z = 1$ if the sum $\geqslant 10$. The value of Z may be used, *per se*, as the tens carry bit. It is also used to

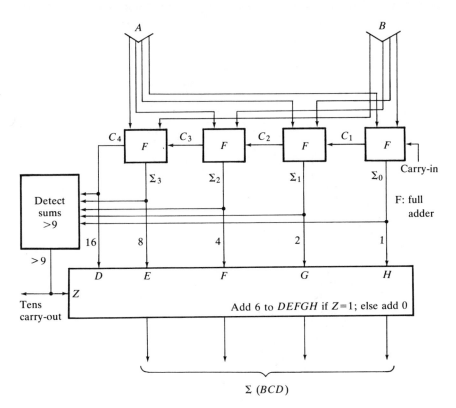

Fig. 5.33 Typical decimal full-adder logic.

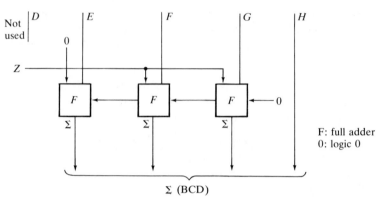

Fig. 5.34 Binary-to-BCD corrector for Fig. 5.33.

control a programmable binary adder which can be made to add 6 to the
binary sum ($DEFGH$) if it is greater than 9; else add nothing (Fig. 5.34).

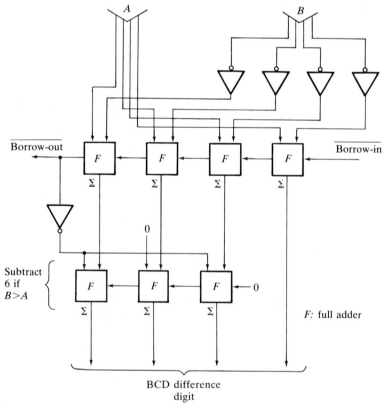

Fig. 5.35 BCD full subtractor.

A decimal subtractor may be designed on similar lines, but here negative results have to be trapped and illegal BCD combinations avoided.

Algorithm: subtract B from A as a binary operation. If the result is negative, subtract 6 and generate a borrow. (It is convenient to generate the borrow in negative logic form—Fig. 5.35.)

Figures 5.33 and 5.35 may be combined to form a programmable decimal adder/subtractor equivalent to the binary type of Fig. 5.8 (see Fig. 5.36).

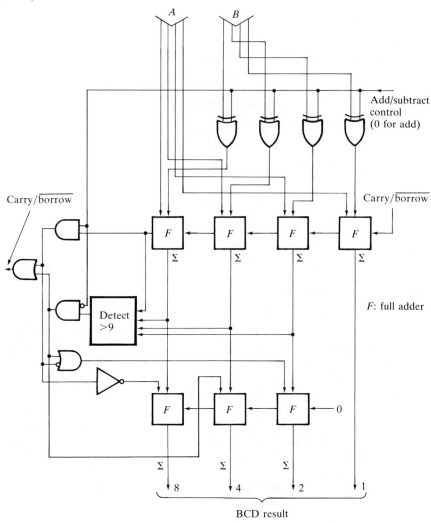

Fig. 5.36 Programmable decimal adder/subtractor.

Just as with any other purely arithmetic device, the BCD adder/sub-tractor is only combinational and can, in principle, be replaced by a ROM array. For Fig. 5.36, a ROM with 10 address lines and 5 output lines would suffice. Because of the restriction on combinations allowed for A and B, the ROM would not be fully utilized. However, the convenience of using a ROM, plus possible speed gains, makes such an implementation very attractive. Furthermore, the ROM size required is readily available in a single chip (IC) form, albeit having 8 rather than 5 output bits (Fig. 5.37).

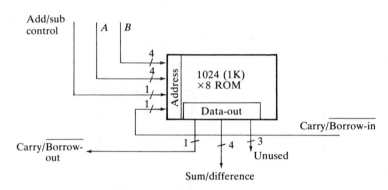

Fig. 5.37   ROM implementation of Fig. 5.36.

Excess-3 coded arithmetic

Adders, subtractors and programmable adder/subtractor units may be designed for the unweighted excess-3 system in much the same way as for the weighted 8421 code. Furthermore, a ROM version, similar to Fig. 5.37, may be created but, of course, would contain a different mask pattern.

Excess-3 algorithms are:

1. *Addition*: add $(A+3)$ and $(B+3)$ as if binary. If the "true" sum is greater than 9 (i.e. $A+B+6 \geqslant 16$), then add 3 and generate a carry. The 3s are involved because the result required is $A+B+3$ but the addition operation yields $A+B+6$. The addition/subtraction of 3 is a combined operation of removing a 3 and skipping over the 6 unused BCD combinations if the true result is greater than 9.

2. *Subtraction*: subtract $(B+3)$ from $(A+3)$. If the "true" result is negative, i.e. the carry from the ms adder is 0, then subtract 3; else add 3.

The excess-3 notation has the advantage that only two post-correction operations are required (even for a combined adder/subtractor) as against

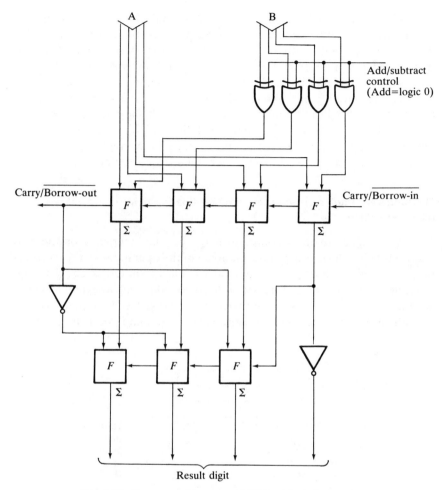

Fig. 5.38 Programmable excess-3 BCD adder/subtractor.

three for the 8421 system. Furthermore, if desired, subtraction may be carried out as a 10s complement operation by complementation of B. A typical programmable adder/subtractor is shown in Fig. 5.38.

5.11 BINARY FLOATING POINT

The basic processes for floating-point arithmetic have already been discussed in Chapter 2. However, there are several aspects of its implementation which are noteworthy.

All the methods for addition, subtraction, multiplication and division are applicable for the mantissae of floating-point numbers. The characteristics of floating-point numbers only ever have to be compared, added, subtracted, incremented or decremented. They do not normally have to be multiplied or divided. This has led to the quite common use of unipolar codes for the representation of characteristics. This is because clearing (zeroing) of a characteristic register is equivalent to setting the highest negative power of 2 by which the mantissa can be multiplied. So, for example, "zero" can be represented by a cleared mantissa and characteristic indicating $0 \times 2^{-(2^n - 1)}$, where n is the number of bits in the characteristic register.

The hardware implementation of common floating-point micro-actions
(Gosling, 1971b)

Scaling Scaling involves comparison of the characteristics of the two operands and right-shifting of the mantissa of the operand with the *algebraically lower* characteristic. The number of places shifted is equal to the difference in the characteristics. In order to avoid having a scaling mechanism for each operand, it is common to employ a register "swapping" system which is used after the characteristics have been compared (Fig. 5.39).

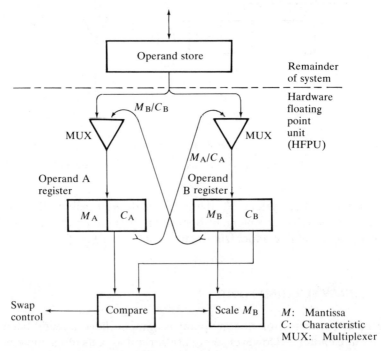

Fig. 5.39 Floating-point scaling (schematic).

It is assumed that the operand to be scaled is lodged in M_2/C_2 so that if the characteristics comparator indicates otherwise when the operands first enter the HFPU, they are swapped. The scaling mechanism can be either a right-shifting register which operates a number of times determined by C_1-C_2 or a parallel-shift mechanism which returns a single-place right-shifted version of M_2 to the M_2 register. Each time M_2 (shifted) is returned, C_2 can be incremented and a fresh check made of C_1-C_2.

Whatever the method of shifting used, the sign bit of M_2 must be correctly handled. If M_2 is expressed in sign and modulus form, the sign bit takes no part in the shifting operation and zeros enter the ms bit position of the modulus as shifting proceeds. If 2s complement notation is used, the sign bit of the mantissa must be replicated in the vacated bit positions (Fig. 5.40).

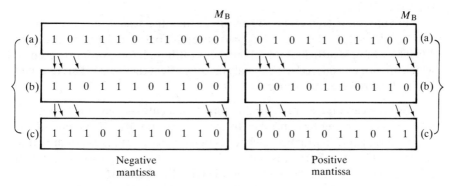

Fig. 5.40 Scaling of mantissae in 2s complement notation.

Scaling of an operand necessarily causes bits to be lost from the ls bit position of the mantissa. This raises a question as to whether the internal hardware of an HFPU should retain some, or all, of these bits for use in the final mantissa of an add or subtract instruction. Clearly, these bits will be of no use if no post-normalization of the result mantissa is necessary, as they would not gain sufficient significance to re-enter the mantissa.

Consider the addition/subtraction of two operands A and B, where it is assumed that the characteristic of B (C_B) is not greater than that of A (C_A); that is, $C_A \geqslant C_B$.

Situation 1. $C_A = C_B$. Here, there is no scaling necessary, no lost bits from M_B and therefore no bits available to re-enter the result mantissa (M_R) if post-normalization is necessary.

Situation 2. $C_A = C_B + 1$. Here, 1 bit is lost from M_B due to scaling and may be usefully retained in the HFPU hardware for re-entry to M_R. If the two operands A and B were originally normalized (as would normally be the case), then $\frac{1}{2} \leqslant |M_A|, |M_B| < 1$.

Scaling of M_B by 1 place would reduce M_B to the range $\frac{1}{4} \leqslant |M_B| < \frac{1}{2}$. The range for M_R (before normalization) taking account of all possible signing situations for M_A and M_B and whether the operation is add or subtract, gives:

$$0 < |M_R| < 1\tfrac{1}{4}.$$

This result indicates that left-shifting post-normalization of the result may be necessary, and hence retention of the lost bit of M_B through scaling is justified.

Situation 3. $C_A = C_B + 2$. Here, 2 bits are lost from M_B during scaling. However, the range for $|M_B|$ after scaling is only $\frac{1}{8} \leqslant |M_B| < \frac{1}{4}$. Thus, M_R must lie in the range $\frac{1}{4} < |M_B| < 1\frac{1}{8}$, indicating that only a *1-place* left-shifting post-normalization will ever be necessary. Retention of *1 bit* of M_B is therefore sufficient.

In general, if $C_A = C_B + n$, where $n > 1$, then the scaled range for $|M_B|$ is $2^{-(n+1)} \leqslant |M_B| < 2^{-n}$. Therefore, $|M_R|$ can never fall below $\frac{1}{4}$. Thus, retention of 1 lost bit of M_B is sufficient for all purposes (although round-off procedures, which are not considered in this analysis, may affect the issue). This retained bit is often referred to as a *guard bit*.

Scaling can take a very variable time to execute—from almost nothing when $C_A = C_B$ to the time it takes to completely run M_B off the end of the mantissa register. In practice, a check is made before scaling is attempted to see if $C_A \geqslant C_B + m$, where m is the number of bits in the mantissa register. If this inequality is true, the instruction is trivialized and $M_R = M_A$.

Frequently, the scaling unit works autonomously on a handshake/interrupt basis. A micro-action called "scale" would be sent to the scaling unit, which would reply with a "busy" signal. The "busy" signal would freeze the microprogram on the scale step. When scaling had been completed, the "busy" signal would be removed and the next micro-instruction started.

Normalization   Normalization may take place before the arithmetic, proper, of an instruction is executed (operand pre-*normalization*), or after the arithmetic (*result post-normalization*). In most cases, it involves left-shifting of the mantissa and decrementation of the characteristic. When fractions overflow (see p.42) occurs, it will also involve right-shifting of the mantissa and incrementation of the characteristic. Whatever the form the normalization takes and at whatever point in an instruction, the same hardware may be used for the purpose.

The following actions must be taken as part of normalization:

1.   Before normalizing, the mantissa must be zero checked. If it is zero, normalization is impossible and the operation must be aborted.

2. During normalization, the characteristic must be incremented/ decremented by 1 for each place the mantissa is right/left-shifted. Characteristic overflow/underflow must consequently be checked at each stage (Fig. 5.41). The mantissa register must have an extra bit a to hold mantissae which have overflowed in the adder/subtractor. If 2s complement notation is assumed, then the left/right-shift control may be determined by inspection of bits a and b of Fig. 5.41.

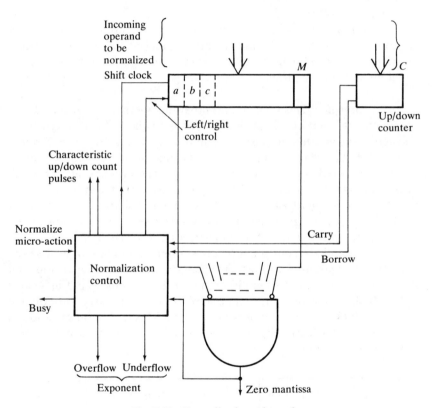

Fig. 5.41 Normalization schematic.

If bit $a \neq$ bit b, then right-shift; else left.

If left-shifting is taking place, then bit $b \neq$ bit c may be used as the test for completion. For right shifting, only a 1-place shift is ever necessary.

If the characteristic is held in an up/down counter, then the carry/borrow signals may be used to indicate characteristic overflow/underflow.

5.12   MISCELLANEOUS DATA-HANDLING OPERATIONS

Arithmetic and logical shifting

As part of the provision of bit handling, editing and significance modification facilities for data, most computer systems offer a variety of shift operations. In some cases, only the basic nature of the shift can be specified, i.e. direction and handling of end effects, whereas others allow the number of places to be specified as well. In the case of the former, a 1-place shift is implied. Most microcomputers offer the first variety, most mini and mainframe systems offer the latter. Many computer systems give a choice (through the operation code) of three basic types of shift—arithmetic, logical and rotational. However, in most cases, implementation is by the use of either shift registers or parallel-bit shift mechanisms.

1.   *Arithmetic*   This type assumes that the operand to be shifted is in 2s complement notation. Thus, if the shift is to the right, the sign bit is replicated in the vacated bit position, and if to the left, zeros are entered at the 1s end of the register (Fig. 5.42). The operations are equivalent to multiplying a signed quantity by 2 (left) or ½ (right) for each position shifted. However, in the case of right-shifting, errors are introduced if 1s are lost from the 1s end of the register, and in the case of left-shifting, overflows can occur by raising the magnitude of the operand excessively. Overflow detection is very straightforward—it is simply necessary to check that the ms two bits of the operand are equivalent *before* shifting takes place otherwise the operand will "apparently" change sign when shifted. In some micro and mini systems, the lost bit (be it from either end of the register) is put in a carry flip-flop. If shifting is by more than one place, then the carry flip-flop will hold the *last* bit lost at the end of the operation. This is a useful variation as the contents of the carry flip-flop may be invoked as the test for some conditional instructions.

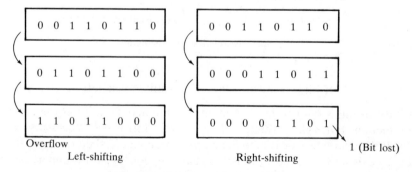

Fig. 5.42   "Arithmetic" data shifting.

2. *Logical*   This is the same as arithmetic shifting except that over-flows are not detected (overflow is not meaningful) and zeros fill vacated bit positions at both ends of the register shifted. The carry flip-flop may be invoked in the shifting operation.

3. *Rotational*   This is a variation of the logical shift, except that bits that would otherwise be lost are fed back into the other end of the register in a circulatory motion. Such a facility finds use in, amongst other applications, serial arithmetic and cyclic (polynomial) code generation and checking.

4. *Multiple register shifting*   The limited length of computer words (particularly micros) frequently leads to the need for multiple register opera-tions to synthesize long registers. A single 8-bit word in a microprocessor can only represent quantities to a precision of a few parts per thousand. Greater precision can be obtained by using, say, pairs of words and operating on them as if they were a single 16-bit word. This concept of *variable length* working can be extended to 3, 4 or more words. However, carries and borrows must be sent from the top of a "less significant" word to the bottom of a "more significant" one to give the effect of having 16, 24 or more bits of precision.

Many mainframe computers are internally organized to handle multiple-length words directly in their hardware—this is particularly true for floating-point operations which call 2 or 4 computer words. In mini and micro systems, multiple-length operation is generally handled through software with a necessary minimum of "inter-register" linkage facilities made available in hardware. The carry flip-flop is often the basis of the linkage in mini and micro systems, so that a double (word) length left arithmetic shift might be implemented by the following software operations:

(a)   shift left logical the least significant word (the ms bit enters the carry flip-flop);

(b)   shift left arithmetic the ms word (the contents of the carry flip-flop enter the vacated ls bit position of the ms word).

The first shift is logical as the ls word has no sign bit and, in any case, should not set the overflow flag under any circumstances. For 3, 4 or longer word operation, a series of carry flip-flop linked logical shift instructions would be executed, followed by a final arithmetic shift instruction.

Dyadic logical operations   Shift facilities provide only part of a bit-manipulation facility in a computer. In addition, it is usual to provide instructions which allow Boolean operations to be performed on fields of bits. A monadic operation—complementation (see p.148)—has already been encountered. In this, each bit of the field is inverted as if each were passed through a NOT (inverter) gate. Dyadic operations usually provided are AND, OR, EX–OR and sometimes EX–NOR, NAND and NOR. They involve two operands and the operations are carried out on pairs of cells (bits) in the same corresponding positions in the two fields. The result bits form a third field which usually replaces the original contents of one of the source fields.

1.   *AND*   This is often used for extracting part of a field from the remainder, i.e. 1 digit (4 bits) from a 2-digit (8-bit) register, as shown in Fig. 5.43. The result may replace the "mask" leaving the original data field intact. The result, in this case, would be $0000\delta\delta\delta\delta$, where $\delta\delta\delta\delta$ is digit (2).

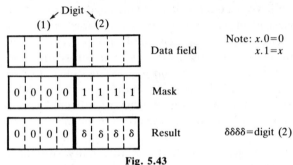

Fig. 5.43

This operation is also sometimes called *masking* or *collation*. A result bit is always 0 adjacent to a mask bit of 0, and equal to the data bit adjacent to a mask bit of 1.

2.   *OR*   This is often used for merging fields (Fig. 5.44).

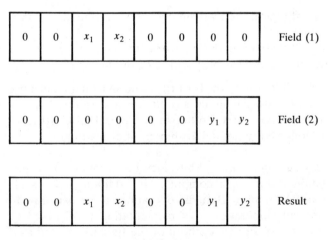

Fig. 5.44

The operation is *inclusive–OR*, which means that if either or both of adjacent bits in the two fields are 1, the corresponding result bit is also a 1.

3.   *EX–OR*   This may be used for field swapping or for checking the equivalence of two patterns of bits, without using subtraction and selected bit complementation.

Field swapping   If the two fields (registers) need to have their contents exchanged by software, this may be done without invoking any other addressable memory locations by use of the EX–OR instruction, as shown in Fig. 5.45.

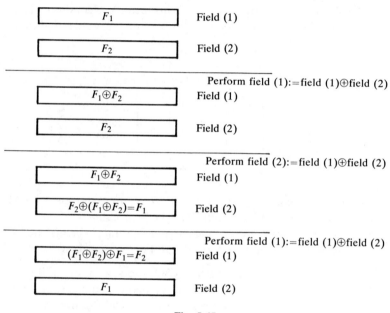

Fig. 5.45

Equivalence checking   Unlike subtraction, EX–OR yields information about *where* two fields are non-equivalent. If two fields are equivalent, the EX–OR instruction will yield an all-zeros result. If two fields are non-equivalent, the EX–OR instruction will yield 1s where non-equivalence exists. Simple shift and test instructions will reveal the bit positions at which non-equivalence exists.

Selected bit complementation   Occasionally, some of the bits in a field may need to be inverted (complemented) and some not. If an EX–OR instruction is performed on such a field, this can be done in a single operation by arranging that the mask field has 1s in the bit positions that require inversion and 0s in the rest.

5.13   ARITHMETIC AND LOGICAL RESULTS SUMMARIES
AND DECISION MAKING

Decision making in computers and hardware digital systems is frequently based, not on the detailed results of calculations and operations, but on a "summary". As an example, it is not usually necessary to know by *how much* an addition operation has overflowed—merely that it has. A flip-flop can be set if overflow occurs but it will give no quantitative information. A machine instruction may then be arranged to be executed or not, depending on the state of the flip-flop. Such an instruction is termed *conditional*. Typical *conditional* instructions are: branch (jump, go to) branch to subroutine, interrupt, subroutine-return. Which flag is inspected in a conditional instruction is either implied in the instruction code or by a flag field (condition code field).

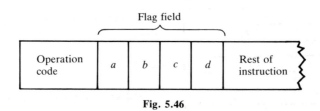

Fig. 5.46

Example of flag field   In Fig. 5.46, *a*, *b*, *c*, *d* might be "RESULT $<0, =0, >0$, OVERFLOW" respectively. The instruction is executed if a 1 is in the flag position consonant with the current flag state. The instruction can be made unconditional by covering *all* flag field positions with 1s.

In most micro, mini and mainframe computers, a variety of flip-flops is provided, each signifying by its state, an element of the results summary from the most recently executed instruction. Typical flip-flops (flags) provided are: overflow, result negative, result zero, carry and interrupt enable.

Some flags are relevant to some instructions and others not. As a consequence, there is a total of four possible situations for a flag at the end of an instruction:

1.   It is to be set or reset according to the result of the instruction (such as the overflow flag at the end of addition).
2.   It is always to be set by an instruction (such as the result zero flag after a register clear instruction).
3.   It is always to be reset by an instruction (such as the overflow flag after a register clear instruction).
4.   It is to be unchanged by an instruction (such as the overflow flag after a logical shift—as it is irrelevant).

Which flags fall into categories 1–4 for each instruction must be carefully considered according to the instruction's most likely application. This comes about because an instruction which uses the state of a flag to determine what it does may not come *immediately* after the instruction which operated the flag.

Example Addition of two multiword operands in a single accumulator microcomputer.

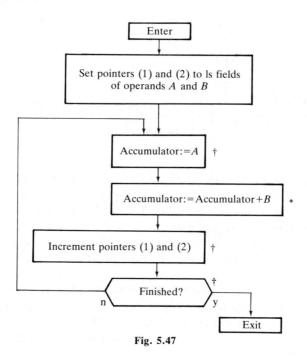

Fig. 5.47

In Fig. 5.47, the operation ∗ will use the carry flip-flop to link the registers in the multiple register field. Thus, operations † must not interfere with the state of the carry flip-flop—otherwise the link will be broken. Therefore, MOVE, ADDRESS POINTER and BRANCH instructions do not generally alter the state of the carry (and frequently any other) flag.

Multiple use of flags

Very effective use can be made of flags in decision making if they are inspected in combinations. Just by use of the result zero, arithmetic overflow and result negative flags, it is possible to infer a number of other arithmetic summaries. This is done extensively in the Motorola M6800 microprocessor which provides a number of branch and subroutine-call instructions, which are dependent on the states of combinations of these flags for allowing execution. Some examples appear in Table 5.7.

Result summary	States of flags		
	Zero	Negative	Overflow
Positive (i.e. $\geqslant 0$)	$\begin{cases} x \\ x \end{cases}$	0 1	0 1
Greater than zero (>0)	$\begin{cases} 0 \\ 0 \end{cases}$	0 1	0 1
Less than zero (<0)	$\begin{cases} x \\ x \end{cases}$	0 1	1 0

Table 5.7

At first glance, it might appear that a test for "positive" would be completely covered by inspection of the "negative" flag. If the "negative" flag is reset, then "positive". However, Table 5.7 is drawn up for the *results of calculations*, not the state of a single operand. This means that "positive" is true if the result is non-negative *regardless of whether the result overflowed the result register*. We have already seen that overflow causes an apparently anomalous result sign in 2s complement notation, so the complete test is: "positive" result if no overflow OR "negative" result if overflow signalled. Although the zero flag is not used in the test, zero is covered by those tests. Zero is a non-negative value in 2s complement. "Less than zero" is the exact opposite of "positive" and covers all results that *should be* negative, regardless of overflow. "Greater than zero" can be achieved by a "positive" result in the absence of overflow, or an "apparently negative" result if overflow occurs. Under all circumstances, "zero" being true invalidates the test.

5.14 APPENDIX: COMBINATIONS OF POSSIBILITIES FOR SIGNED-INTEGER DIVISION

The following examples deal with the variations occurring in the signs of operands and in the existence or otherwise of a remainder. (*Note*: In the context of these examples, adding 1 to the quotient means adding 1 algebraically. Thus $+2$ becomes $+3$ and -3 becomes -2.

A: Positive/Positive

1. +8/+3

```
           010
011)001000
        0011    Subtract
       11110
        0011    Add
       00010
        0011    Subtract
        1111
Q=2     0011    Extra add
R=2     0010
```

2. +9/+3

```
           011
011)001001
        0011    Subtract
       11110
        0011    Add
       00011
Q=3     0011    Subtract
R=0     0000
```

3. +10/+3

```
           011
011)001010
        0011    Subtract
       11111
        0011    Add
       00100
Q=3     0011    Subtract
R=1     0001
```

B: Negative/Positive

1. −8/+3

```
             101←+1
011)111000
        0011    Add
       00010
        0011    Subtract
       11110
        0011    Add
        0001
Q=−2    0011    Extra subtract
R=−2    1110
```

2. −9/+3

```
           101
011)110111
        0011    Add
       00001
        0011    Subtract
       11101
Q=−3    0011    Add
R=0     0000
```

3. −10/+3

```
             100←+1
011)110110
        0011    Add
       00001
        0011    Subtract
       11100
Q=−3    0011    Add
R=−1    1111
```

C: Positive/Negative

1. +8/+3

$$
\begin{array}{r}
101 \leftarrow +1 \\
1101\overline{)001000}
\end{array}
$$

            1101   Add
        11110

            1101   Subtract
          00010

              1101 Add
            1111

$Q=-2$ 1101 Extra subtract
$R=+2$ 0010

2. +9/−3

$$
\begin{array}{r}
100 \leftarrow +1 \\
1101\overline{)001001}
\end{array}
$$

            1101   Add
        11110

            1101   Subtract
          00011

$Q=3$ 1101 Add
$R=0$ 0000

3. +10/−3

$$
\begin{array}{r}
100 \leftarrow +1 \\
1101\overline{)001010}
\end{array}
$$

            1101   Add
        11111

            1101   Subtract
          00100

$Q=-3$ 1101 Add
$R=+1$ 0001

D: Negative/Negative

1. −8/−3

$$
\begin{array}{r}
010 \\
1101\overline{)111000}
\end{array}
$$

            1101   Subtract
        00010

            1101   Add
         11110

            1101 Subtract
          0001

$Q=+2$ 0011 Extra add
$R=-2$ 1110

2. −9/−3

$$
\begin{array}{r}
010 \leftarrow +1 \\
1101\overline{)110111}
\end{array}
$$

            1101   Subtract
        00001

            1101   Add
         11101

$Q=+3$ 1101 Subtract
$R=0$ 0000

3. −10/−3

$$
\begin{array}{r}
011 \\
1101\overline{)110110}
\end{array}
$$

            1101   Subtract
        00001

            1101   Add
         11100

$Q=+3$ 1101 Subtract
$R=-1$ 1111

EXERCISES

5.1 (a) Using any microprocessor's instruction set, write a subroutine for adding two 8-bit (1 byte) signed operands assumed to be expressed in (i) sign-and-modulus (ii) unipolar notation.
(b) Extend your subroutine so that 2-byte operands may be handled.

5.2 Devise algorithms which can operate on 1-byte microprocessor fields as if they were in 8421 BCD and incorporate them in microprocessor subroutines for BCD addition and subtraction. (Use may be made of the carry or link flip-flop for introducing and temporarily storing carries when generated by subroutines.) Do not use decimal adjust instructions.

5.3 Design a block-carry module (BCM) which maximizes the number of stages over which it can operate using gates with a fan-in and fan-out limitation of 8. What is the maximum size of adder that could operate with such BCMs if the propagation delay is not allowed to exceed 12 gate delays? AND, OR and NOT gates only to be used.

5.4 Develop the multiplier of Fig. 5.25 so that it may handle 2s complement operands. Test the design with $k=4$, $A=-5$ and $B=-7$.

5.5 Develop the combinational multiplier of Fig. 5.26 such that it may handle 2 *bits* at a time, i.e. at each row position. Details of the logic for determining if 1 needs to be added to the next row multiplier bit pair should be included. The design should be able to operate with 2s complement operands.

5.6 How could the ROM multiplier design of Fig. 5.29 be arranged to give results rounded to the nearest (ms) 8 bits?

5.7 Determine the ROM contents for the initial estimate of the reciprocal of d for the method of Fig. 5.32. Assume that the ROM available is of 16 locations by 4 bits and that d is an unsigned normalized mantissa ($\frac{1}{2} \leqslant d < 1$). (*Hint*: The ms bit of d should not be entered to the ROM (it must always be equal to 1). However, the *next* 4 bits *should* be used.)

5.8 Using a tree of 4 input multiplexers, develop a combinational logic normalization unit for incoming operands with 24-bit unsigned mantissae and 8-bit unipolar coded characteristics. (*Hint*: the multiplexers should be used for parallel-bit shifting—not necessarily 1 place at a time! Exponent underflow should be trapped. All mantissae should be assumed fractional.)

REFERENCES

Agrawal, D. P. (1974a), "Fast binary coded decimal/binary adder/subtractor," *Electron Letts*, **10**(8), 121–2.

Agrawal, D. P. (1974b), "Fast BCD multiplier," *Electron Letts*, **10**(12), 237.

Ahmad, M. (1972), "Iterative schemes for high speed division," *Comp. J.*, **15**(4), 333–6.

Ali, Z. M. (1978), "A high-speed FFT processor," *IEEE Trans. Comm.*, **Com-26**(5), 690–6.

Anderson, S. F., Earle, J. G., Goldsmidt, R. E. and Powers, D. M. (1967), "The IBM System/360 model 91 floating point execution unit," *IBM J. Res. Devt*, **11**, 34–53.

Barnes, C. W. and Fam, A. T. (1977), "Minimum norm recursive digital filters that are free of overflow limit cycles," *IEEE Transactions on Circuits and Systems*, **CAS-24**(10), 569–74.

Bin Nun, M. A. and Woodward, M. E. (1974), "Halfadders modulo-2^n using read-only-memories," *Electron Letts*, **10**(11), 213–14.

Booth A. D. (1951), "A signed binary multiplication technique," *Q. J. Mech. Appl. Math.*, **4**(2), 236–40.

Bywater, R. E. H. (1975), "A binary multiplier for signal processing applications," *Digital Processes*, **1**(1), 261–5.

Bywater, R. E. H. (1977), "Error reduction in ROM multipliers," *Electron Eng.*, **49**(593), 17.

Chung, T. J. and Bedrosian, S. D. (1975), "Iterative digital multiplier based on cellular array of ROM's" *Electron Letts*, **11**(18), 426–8.

Gardiner, A. B. and Hont, J. (1972), "Cellular array arithmetic unit with multiply and divide," *Proc. IEE*, **119**(6), 659–60.

Garner, H. L. (1976), "A survey of some recent contributions to computer arithmetic," *Trans. IEEE, Comp.*, **C-25**(12), 1277–82.

Gill, S. (1955), "Standard routines for Mercury," Internal Communication.

Gosling, J. B. (1971a), "Review of high speed addition techniques," *Proc. IEE*, **118**(1), 29–35.

Gosling, J. B. (1971b), "Design of large, high speed floating point arithmetic units," *Proc. IEE*, **118**(1), 493–8.

Gosling, J. B. (1971c), "Design of large high speed binary multiplier units," *Proc. IEE*, **118**(1), 499–505.

Houselander, L. S. (1974), "Cellular array negabinary multiplier," *Electron Letts*, **10**(10), 168–9.

Liu, B. (ed.) (1975), *Digital Filters and the Fast Fourier Transform*, Benchmark Papers in Electrical Engineering and Computer Science/12, Dowden, Hutchinson & Ross, Stroudsburg, Pa.

Meggitt, J. E. (1962), "Pseudo-division and pseudo-multiplication processes," *IBM J. Res. Devt*, **6**, 210–26.

Moore, F. R. (1978), "An introduction to the mathematics of digital signal processing," *Computer Music Journal*, **2**(2).

Narasimha, M. J. and Peterson, A. M. (1978), "Design and applications of uniform digital bandpass filter banks," Conference record of International Conference on Acoustics, Speech and Signal Processing, pp. 499–503.

Oppenheim, A. V. (ed.) (1978), *Applications of Digital Signal Processing*, Prentice-Hall, Englewood Cliffs, N.J.

Patel, M. R. and Bennett, K. H. (1976), "Analysis of speed of a binary multiplier using a variable number of shifts per cycle," *Comp. J.*, **19**(3), 254–7.

Robertson, J. E. (1958), "A new class of digital division methods," *Trans. IRE Elec. Comp.*, **EC-7**, 218–22.

Schirm, L. (IV), (1979), "Getting to know the FFT," *Electronic Design*→ April 26, 78–85.

Tocker, T. D. (1958), "Techniques of multiplication and division for automatic binary computers," *Q. J. Mech. Appl. Math.*, **11**, 364–84.

Yildirim, N. and Toker, C. (1972), "Cellular logic array for redundant binary division," *Proc. IEE*, **119**(10), 1452–6.

6 DIGITAL SYSTEM CONTROL AND TIMING METHODS

6.1 INTRODUCTION

In preceding chapters, we have considered the digital computer as being a simple two-level hierarchy consisting of hardware, that is, the logic, adders, registers, memories and peripheral devices on the one hand, and software—the various programs, on the other. The two levels of the hierarchy are concerned with the same aims—that is, the execution of the various tasks and algorithms defined by the user.

The break point between hardware and software is a somewhat arbitrary one and is largely set by the economics of providing hardware to enhance system performance. If cost is of paramount importance, there is a tendency to minimize the amount of hardware provided, so that fewer instructions, of longer execution times, are offered. A greater burden is then thrown upon the software, both in terms of the amount that must be written (in order to make up for the lack of instructions) and the system facilities that are offered. An additional element which impinges on this breakpoint is the point at which the user wants to be able to modify facilities as against having them fixed, for all time, at manufacture. Software is readily alterable—hardware is not.

In modern, practical, digital systems, the simplistic picture of alterable software and unalterable hardware is somewhat inaccurate. This will become clear when we consider the interface between the instructions, as defined by the (software) user, and the sequences which take place within the processor (Fig. 6.1). So far, consideration of processor activity has been limited to 'broad-brush' concepts of registers, arithmetic/logic units, data buses and memory systems. The intricacies of organizing the exchange of

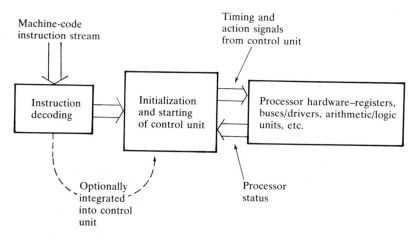

Fig. 6.1 The control unit provides a hardware and software interface between the machine-code software and the processor hardware.

information between these registers, etc., has been left largely unmentioned. It has just been assumed that, by some suitable logic design, the various activities which will culminate in the correct realization of, say, an ADD instruction, *can* happen.

When looked at from the point of view of a sequence of events, e.g. the movement of data from register to register, the implementation of the instructions in a processor does not appear much different, in principle, from programming a machine, using a set of instructions, say, in assembly language. Clearly, the individual events are much more elementary in the processor, but they have the essential programming elements of data movement, decision making, conditional actions and the like (Tables 6.1 and 6.2). Starting with a processor consisting of a set of registers, data paths, etc., the sequences which will realize any given instruction are obviously going to be implemented by applying suitable waveforms to the clock and conditioning inputs to these registers and ALUs. These waveforms and logic levels are known collectively as *control signals*. Some examples are "strobe

Mnemonic	Operand	Remarks/comments
⋮	⋮	⋮
DIV	B	Divide accumulator by B: result to acc.
ADD	B	Add B to accumulator : result to acc.
RRA	1	Rotate acc right 1 place (Arithmetic)
JMP	L23	Jump unconditionally to instruction labelled L23

Table 6.1 Assembly-language statements.

Step	Mnemonic	Next step address	Comments
$\vdots$	$\vdots$	$\vdots$	$\vdots$
k	IR←MM	$k+1$	Main memory (instruction) to instruction register
$k+1$	MMAR←IRA (ADD,SUB); PC←IRA (JUMP); NOP (ROT)	Q (SUB) R (JUMP) S (ROT)	If add or subtract then address portion of instruction register to memory address port. If jump then IRA to program counter. If rotate, do nothing. Next step addresses show 4-way branch
$k+2$			
$\vdots$	$\vdots$	$\vdots$	$\vdots$

Table 6.2   Control-unit sequence

register A", "set the ALU to subtract", and such like. If we set out the sequence to realize each one of the instructions in a processor's menu, a set of (micro) programs will evolve. Because of the similarity between a number of instructions, it may also be possible to 'merge' many of these sequences to cut down on the total number of microprogramming steps and microactions. (A *microaction* is a single action within the processor, such as transfer the contents of register A to register B.)

As an example, we can take the processor of Fig. 3.6 and determine the microsequences and control waveforms needed to implement the instructions:

1. ADD the contents of a memory location to the accumulator
2. SUBTRACT the contents of a memory location from the accumulator.
3. JUMP (Branch) to a location given by the address portion of the instruction.

A merged flowchart for these three instructions is shown in Fig. 6.2. It will be noticed that, whichever instruction is being executed, the same first few (fetch) microactions are carried out. Once fetching has taken place and the operation code is available to the opcode decoder, the instruction can be identified and branching to the appropriate sequence undertaken. Figure 6.2 shows a very representative situation in which only a limited amount of such branching is necessary because of the great similarity between certain instructions (in this instance ADD and SUBTRACT). Only a two-way

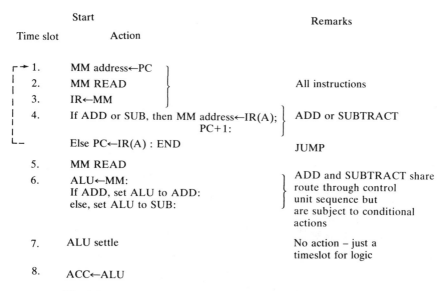

Fig. 6.2 A merged set of sequences for add, subtract and jump as executed in the processor of Fig. 3.6.

branch is therefore necessary at Step 4. For ADD and SUBTRACT the sequence continues to Step 5; for JUMP it terminates at Step 4 to return to Step 1, in readiness for the next instruction.

Because we are, essentially, dealing with the control of hardware at the microprogramming level, it is possible to define these microsequences in some ways which are unfamiliar to the programmer. Clearly, the use of flowcharts, familiar to programmers, is still a valid way of approaching the job, but the use of waveform charts, showing clock, clear and set-up logic levels, plotted against time, is another popular approach. Figure 6.3 (a) shows a flowchart representation of the merged sequence of Fig. 6.2, where the numbers in the top left-hand corners of the 'boxes' correspond to step numbers of Fig. 6.2. Fig. 6.3 (b) shows the same steps by waveform and is clearly a much more difficult representation than either of the methods of Fig. 6.2 or 6.3 (a). It can be used for simple systems having few instructions or short sequences. It cannot be used for large systems except to show short parts of sequences. One area in which it *is* extensively used is in indicating how the fetch, interrupt, input/output handling and other specific procedures are handled in microprocessors.

In this chapter, we will explore the various ways in which timing and control of a computer's hardware can take place; in particular, in the processor. It will be seen that techniques are drawn both from the software and logic-design arenas, for this side of digital system design lies midway between the two.

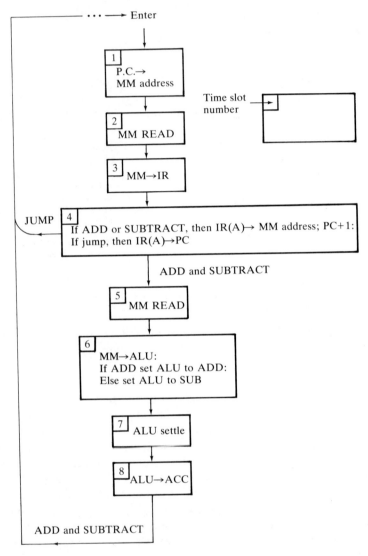

Fig. 6.3 (a)

6.2   SPECIFICATION FOR A CONTROL UNIT

Looking at timing and control of a processor from the hardware viewpoint, it is apparent that this is an area lacking in the symmetry and logic uniformity of the parallel data structures that make up the registers and other data-handling units. It is an area which is often less amenable to automated design

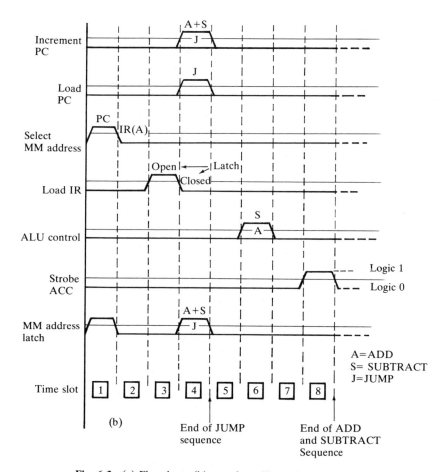

Fig. 6.3 (a) Flowchart; (b) waveform illustrations of Fig. 6.2.

processes and is often "shrouded in mystery" because of the high level of individual human skills needed to realize it. Timing and control is a difficult area for the following reasons:

1. Its design is a mixture of logic, programming, and the tolerancing of electronic circuits (to make sure they will operate over the specified temperature range and supply voltages).

2. In many realizations, it is difficult to modify the control unit if design errors are found. This is partly because it is implemented in hardware and partly because it is common to merge many of its activities (to cut costs). Once merging takes place, an alteration in one area can affect others, so that a simple alteration can have far-reaching consequences in other parts of the hardware, or in the execution of other instructions.

3. As hardware is used as the basis of the realization of instructions, it
    follows that the logic needed to provide the timing signals to control
    this hardware is likely to have to operate at great speed. The design of
    such fast logic is difficult and so is its most effective use. In very
    high-speed processors, not only does the delay imposed by each gate
    have to be taken into account, but also the transport delay of logic
    signals along printed circuit traces and discrete wires (Fig. 6.4).

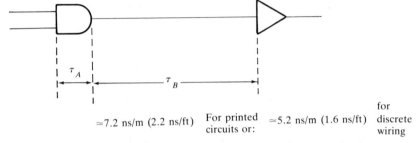

≈ 7.2 ns/m (2.2 ns/ft)   For printed ≈ 5.2 ns/m (1.6 ns/ft)   for discrete wiring
circuits or:

Fig. 6.4 "In-circuit" delay for a gate $= \tau_A + \tau_B$, where τ_A and τ_B are
the gate and interconnection delays respectively.

Although the concept of an algorithmic approach and the element of
sequency make control/timing realization appear similar to ordinary programming, there *are* a number of essential differences:

1. In some respects the pressure to maximize performance is greater in
    timing and control systems. A poorly structured or devised program
    can be modified, if not satisfactory. Once a processor is in production,
    the timing and control circuits are committed.
        To maximize performance, use is made of concurrent steps, that
    is, several non-interacting microactions may be timed to occur on the
    same microstep. In most computers, instructions are carried out in a
    sequence (Fig. 6.5).
2. Not infrequently, the many branching microinstructions are combined
    with the "action" part of a microinstruction to form a compound step.
    This saves execution time. (The practice of merging microinstruction
    sequences tends to make the incidence of branches very high so that a
    very worthwhile saving can be made by compounding actions and
    branches.) (Fig. 6.6).
3. Merging of microsequences also tends to make multidestination
    branches necessary. In a simple computer, software branches are
    usually only two-way. The branch is to a single possible destination (if
    taken) or to the next instruction (if not taken). Merging of microins-
    tructions can often make up to 20 or more destinations desirable, from

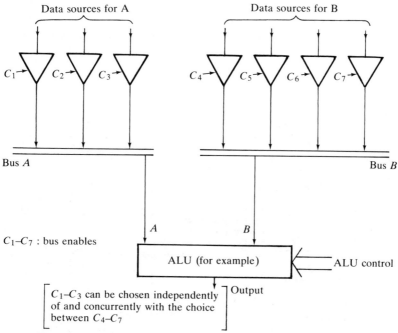

C_1–C_7 : bus enables

$\begin{bmatrix} C_1\text{–}C_3 \text{ can be chosen independently} \\ \text{of and concurrently with the choice} \\ \text{between } C_4\text{–}C_7 \end{bmatrix}$ Output

Fig. 6.5 Example of microaction concurrency (parallelism) in a bus-orientated processor.

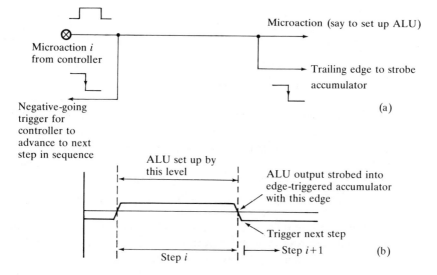

Fig. 6.6 A single microaction can be used to set up the control of programmable logic, provide a time interval for the logic to settle and an edge to record the results in a register (accumulator).

a single microstep. To implement this by 19 conditional branch microinstructions would clearly waste a great deal of time. It would also be very wasteful in ordinary software, but the incidence of such a need is negligibly small (Fig. 6.7).

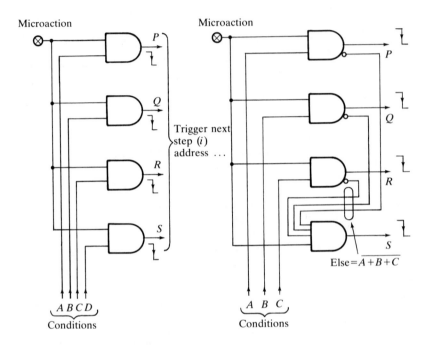

Fig. 6.7 Multiple-destination branching. Examples of logic.

4. Considerable savings in instruction execution time can be made if microactions are made conditional. In normal software this is usually done by prefixing an instruction with a conditional branch so that if it is not to be executed, it can be skipped round. In microsequences, such branching would take too much time so that the condition and action are usually combined into a compound decision-action microaction (Fig. 6.8).

5. Other time-saving schemes are often employed at the control/timing level which, although feasible in software, are frequently ignored. A simple example might be the inspection of the bit patterns in arithmetic operands to see if processing can be curtailed. An example might be the inspection of multipliers for leading (non-significant) zeros so that the number of iterations can be reduced. This can yield useful savings,

Microaction (step *i*)

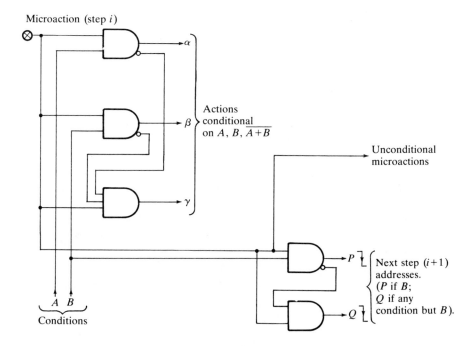

Fig. 6.8 Any combinations of conditions can be used to control the issue of microactions on any step. (The same conditions may also be used to determine the next-step address.)

as many variables encountered in computer programs make poor use of the dynamic range offered by the computer word length. A mainframe computer may have a 32-bit word length, offering integer operands in the range $\pm 2^{31}$, i.e., approximately ± 2 billions. Such operands, used as multipliers, will often have no more than 16 significant bits used, i.e. the multipliers used will often not go outside the range $\pm 65\ 000$.

6. Simple computer processors often arrange that all instructions are tied to some master clock, possibly running at 1 MHz or more. Each instruction is constrained to take an integral number of clock cycles to execute. This can waste valuable time if the last clock cycle is not fully utilized. As the number of clock cycles is usually kept small to simplify the control circuitry, the wastage can be a significant percentage of the allotted execution time.

   In high-speed timing/control systems, where time is at a premium, such wastage is usually avoided by tailoring the time slots for each microaction according to its needs and not to some fixed time source.

6.3 CONTROL AND TIMING WAVEFORMS

The waveforms that have to be generated by the processor controller fall neatly into two major categories:

1. *Logic levels* which will be needed, either to set up some process or to continuously condition an action, until complete. A simple example is a level needed to control whether a programmable adder/subtractor shall add or subtract. This signal will need to remain at the desired logic level for the duration of the settling time of the adder array. If it were to change part way through the microstep, a transition would propagate through the adder carry path and give an erroneous adder output.

2. *Pulses and edges* (logic transitions) needed to time the beginning and ends of microactions or to write the results of microactions to registers and memories.

    A typical microaction has a leading edge when it is initialized, a logic 'plateau' for the duration of the step and a trailing edge at the completion of the step. The plateau can satisfy the requirement for conditioning logic levels and the leading and trailing edges can be used to operate edge-triggered flip-flops and registers. The leading and trailing edges can also be processed into pulses, either to operate latches or to give a time delay for the initialization of some special action, which must start part way through a microstep. The latter situation often occurs on microsteps having compound microactions to realize (Fig. 6.9).

The necessity to avoid time wastage in control/timing systems has already been mentioned. It is not always either desirable or practical to arrange that every microstep has its own customized time slot. A compromise which is often used involves the further compounding of microinstructions above that already described. It can take two related forms:

1. Each microstep can be made relatively long and the microprogramming made such that almost all microsteps are compounded to involve several sequences of microactions. This has the advantage of making possible a slower microprogram clock but makes efficient microprogramming difficult, because of the pressure on the designer to efficaciously use *every* microstep.

2. Microsteps can be made very short but long microactions may take several microsteps to complete. This certainly makes programming easier, but the number of microsteps for a complete microprogram can rise alarmingly.

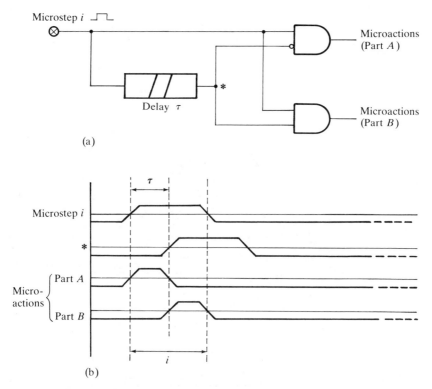

Fig. 6.9 Compound microsteps can initiate a sequence of microactions (parts *A* and *B*).

Both of these approaches amount to fitting a number of small integers into a large integer—the classic "filling the suitcase" problem. In the case of (1) we are trying to fit a number of microactions into a long step; in (2) we are fitting fixed-length steps into a complex microaction.

6.4 CONTROL-UNIT REALIZATION

Control units are all implemented in hardware because of the speed requirement: but some designs follow more closely the tenets of software practice and others are clearly just part of the processor hardware. The two types are called "microprogrammable" and "hard-wired" respectively. Each has its advantages and disadvantages—speed and flexibility being the main issues in contention.

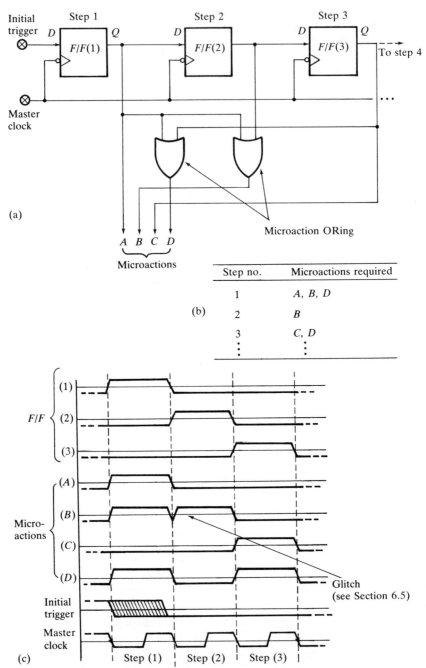

Step no.	Microactions required
1	A, B, D
2	B
3	C, D
⋮	⋮

Fig. 6.10 "One flip-flop per step" processor control/timing unit: (a) part of logic; (b) allocation of microactions to steps; (c) waveforms for (a).

Hard-wired control units

As microprograms clearly implement series or sequences of events, then hard-wired control units are naturally based on the flip flop for defining each microstep. The simplest approach is to have one flip-flop to define each microstep and for only one flip to be set at any one time. Each time the master clock, connected to all flip-flops, cycles, control is passed from one flip-flop to the next one. By interconnecting the Q outputs of flip-flops to the D inputs of others, any sequence of flip-flops can be arranged to be set (Fig. 6.10). Various programming aids can be incorporated into this simple system:

1. *Branching* is simply effected by having as many AND gates connected to the output of a given flip-flop as there are branching destinations. Each AND gate is "primed" with a condition from anywhere in the processor such that the AND gates are primed mutually exclusively. That is, only one AND gate can be primed, whatever the combination of conditions supplied to the group. Whenever the driving flip-flop is set, there must be one and only one AND gate giving a logic 1 output (Fig. 6.11).

If there is, say, a three-way branch to be implemented, it is quite possible that only two conditions will be needed, as AND gates 1 and 2 can be primed with conditions A and B respectively, and AND gate three can be primed with $\overline{(\text{condition } A + \text{condition } B)}$. In effect, the condition for AND gate 3 is "else".

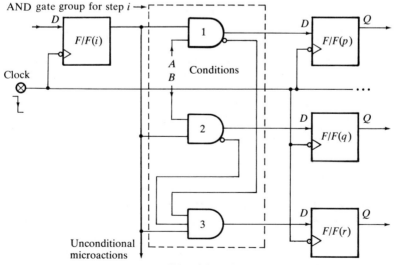

Fig 6.11 Three-way conditional branch implemented as part of a "one flip-flop per step" control unit.

2. *Several microsequence paths can converge* on a single flip-flop, merely by ORing. The inputs to the OR gate must be mutually exclusive as only one microsequence path should be operational at any one time—in fact, only one flip-flop should be set at any one time.

3. *Conditional actions* can be implemented in the same way as conditional branches, although the "mutually exclusive" rule can be waived. On a given microstep, some actions may be unconditional, some dependent on one condition and some on another. Any combinational logic and any combination of conditions can be invoked to determine whether any one of the microactions, associated with any step, are to be activated.

A grave disadvantage of the "1 flip-flop per step" method is the large number of flip-flops needed. If a computer offers, say, 100 instructions in its menu, even with merging, the number of flip-flops needed can easily exceed 200.

A couple of alternatives are available which can greatly reduce the number of flip-flops needed:

Alternative 1   This method takes what is essentially a string of flip-flops as represented by the "1 flip-flop at a time" method and translates it into two or more dimensions. In the most straightforward approach, a two-dimensional matrix of AND gates is formed, with flip-flops driving each axis (Fig. 6.12). On each step, one flip-flop, from each axis, is set. This ensures that only one AND gate, the one on the node connecting the two set flip-flops, is activated. The output of this AND gate can be used to drive actions, conditional and otherwise, and to provide the same logic 1 as the outputs of the single flip-flop method to set another *pair* of flip-flops.

In this system, a controller needing 256 steps no longer needs 256 flip-flops, as in the previous system, but only 32 (16 on each axis). However, there are 256 AND gates needed to form the matrix nodes, but some of these can be absorbed into conditional microaction circuits. A more important disadvantage is that each of the 32 flip-flops will need a large fan in OR gate, regardless of whether a "branch merge" is taking place. This is because a given flip-flop will be addressed at least 16 times (by AND gates), simply because each flip-flop is now associated with 16 steps.

Alternative 2   The most efficient use of flip-flops occurs when they represent the microstep in encoded form. If we wanted to realize a 256-step controller, then theoretically only 8 flip-flops would be necessary. Each combination of set and reset flip-flop states would then represent a certain microstep. The obvious disadvantage of this system is only an extension of the objection to alternative 1. On every microstep, *all* flip-flops must be supplied with either a logic 0 or a logic 1 to define the next microstep. However, the saving in flip-flops is often considered worthwhile and the technique, with many modifications, is often used.

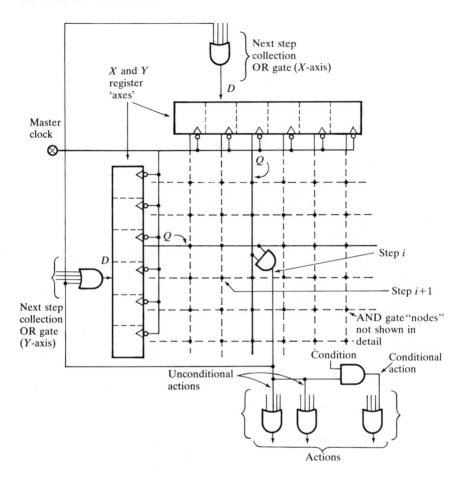

Fig. 6.12 Two-axis flip-flop matrix control unit.

At this point, it must be apparent that a major drawback of all the methods described so far is the irregularity of the combinational logic that is inevitably going to occur. By this is meant that little, if any, of the logic is in the form of repeated patterns or units, as occurs with data paths, registers and adders. For the latter, whatever logic is used for processing one bit is repeated for all other bits. This gives rise to "regular" patterns (both in the logic design and even, sometimes, on the printed-circuit layouts). Control logic isn't particularly amenable to implementation in other than small-scale (SSI) and medium-scale integrated (MSI) circuits. The controller will be difficult to package, expensive to implement, relatively unreliable because of the high package count, difficult to maintain because of the lack of structure to the logic, and very difficult to enhance.

There are two types of integrated circuit now available which can ease many of the above difficulties:

Programmable logic array (PLA)

This is, in essence, a form of read-only memory (ROM) in which the complete "n-wire encoded-address input $- 2^n$-wire decoded output logic" is replaced with an implementation of the Quine–McCluskey construct. Such logic only provides a partial decode. If the PLA is incorporated into the logic of alternative 2, it will be seen to implement all the irregular "next state" logic and, possibly, some of the "conditional actions" logic, in one or a small number of packages. This would appear to solve the objections to hard-wired logic. However, there are several penalties and outstanding problems left unsolved by the PLA:

1.   In any but a trivial controller, a number of PLAs will be necessary. Generally, PLAs are limited to about 20 inputs and 10 outputs so that the amount of combinational processing possible in one package is quite small. PLAs are generally only available in mask-programmed form (i.e. the intraconnections are defined by the manufacturer's mask patterns), which means that each design carries a masking charge and a turn-around time of many weeks for (re)processing by the semiconductor manufacturer. If more than one PLA is required for a controller, there is no chance that a single design will suffice for all PLAs. There will almost certainly be a separate mask charge associated with each.

2.   All the hard-wired designs described so far have been for use with a fixed-frequency master clock, for moving from one microstep to the next. Some steps may be required to be of less duration than others. Unless the clock frequency can be altered for each step, an inevitable waste of time will occur. Each of the above designs can be modified to operate with a small selection of different clock periods, if the clock period can be specified as part of the "action" information for each microstep. This is certainly an improvement over a fixed-period clock. Nonetheless, it is usually difficult to provide more than two or four choices of step length, so that *exact* tailoring of step length to microactions is still not possible.

Uncommitted logic array

Such an array gives the original equipment manufacturer (OEM) choice as to the gate and flip-flop content of a chip, within the limitations of the cells offered by the semiconductor manufacturer, and for our purposes, within the limitations of package leadouts. A suitable controller schematic for use with a ULA is shown in Fig. 6.13. As with the PLA, the limited number of

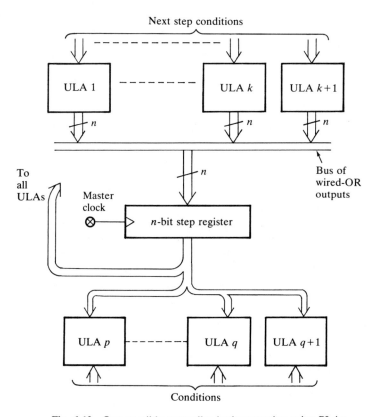

Fig. 6.13 One possible controller inplementation using PLAs.

package leadouts makes the ULA most effective when used with encoded flip-flop arrays, as the number of inputs and outputs required of the ULA is minimized.

As a postscript on methods based on flip-flops, it is sometimes possible to further reduce the leadout requirements. This can be done if some of the ULA cell positions are used for flip-flops as well as combinational conditioning logic. Then both the flip-flop outputs and inputs can be kept within the package—only the condition signals, which prime the combinational logic and the microaction outputs, then have to be brought out of the ULA.

Controller based on read-only memory

As early as 1951, M.V. Wilkes of Cambridge (Wilkes, 1951; Wilkes and Stringer, 1953) proposed a method for controlling the execution of instructions by the use of memory. The argument was, as it still is, that control of the sequence of (hardware) events inside a processor is only a variety of programming in the normally accepted sense. The use of memory to hold the "conditioning" and "next microstep" generating information makes possible a much more understandable and readily modified logic structure. Indeed, if the content of the memory, or the memory itself, can be replaced at will, then modification of the "appearance" of a processor by altering its instruction menu becomes a possibility. Of the many uses for such a facility, the *emulation* of one processor by another is one of the most important. If a manufacturer produces a new range of computers, with a different structure and instruction menu from an existing series, it may well be desirable to offer an alternative microprogram with the new system which can, effectively, make it appear like the existing series (Fig. 6.14). By so doing, purchasers of the original equipment may well be prepared to change to the new system, as it can be made software compatible with the old one. From the user's point of view, this means that the expense of recoding all existing software is avoided. This will also save time when the new system is installed. Of course, emulation need not be confined to one's own brand of machines. The technique can be used to emulate other manufacturers' equipment.

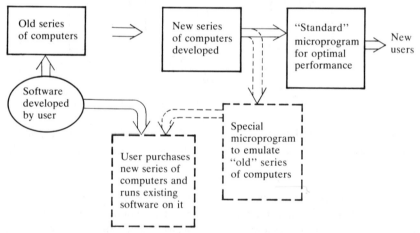

Fig. 6.14 An alterable controller (microprogram) can make software for one machine executable on another.

The basic scheme for using a read-only memory (ROM) is shown in Fig. 6.15. The ROM contains the information pertaining to a given microstep, in a certain location. That location must have sufficient bits to encode all possible actions, next step addresses etc., that may be needed. In practice, this can mean that up to 60 bits may be associated with each ROM location. The information can be split into two major parts:

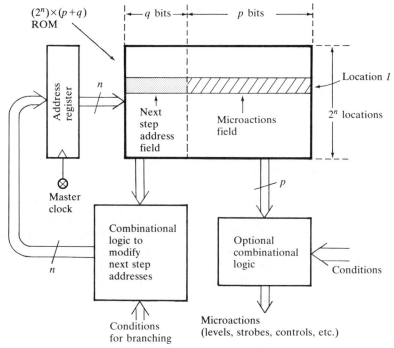

Fig. 6.15 Elementary ROM-based controller (microprogram).

1. *A next step address*, that is, the address in ROM of the next microstep to be executed after this one. It should be noted that, although there is complete freedom as to what this address can be (so long as it has not already been used), it does not constitute a branch. Branching implies a *choice* of two courses. On what has been described so far, only one has been offered.

2. *The microactions to be executed on this step*. For simplicity, at this stage, we will assume that each action bit is associated with a unique action, i.e. set the programmable adder/subtractor to add or transfer the contents of register *A* to register *B*, etc. The pattern of 0s and 1s in the microactions field will therefore determine which actions will and will not take place on this step. With such a system, there would be no restriction as to what combination of actions was possible. In fact, some ridiculous combinations would be possible, such as "pass the contents of the program counter to the main-memory address register" and "pass the contents of the address portion of the instruction register to the main-memory address register". If permitted, this combination would cause chaos.

In a practical implementation of the Wilkes scheme, a number of enhancements and additions are made to Fig. 6.15:

1.   Because many microactions are not desirable in combination, they are made mutually exclusive by grouping into a "mutually exclusive set". Thus, if a certain group of 8 microactions were such that only one was ever to be allowed to operate at a time, they could be coded into 3 bits, instead of 8, in the ROM. For each combination of the 3 bits, 000,001, etc., one of the microactions would be invoked. This guarantees that only one can occur at a time and it also greatly reduces the number of ROM bits per location. Quite a large number of groups can be formed in a practical microprogram unit, making useful savings possible in the size of the ROM (Fig. 6.16).

2.   Frequently, an extra field is introduced to the ROM, which determines which one of a number of external conditions shall be tested as part of a conditional action or next microstep address. As several microactions on one step may be conditional, there may be several such conditions selecting fields (Fig. 6.17). Care must be taken in the design of such conditioning systems, as the number of ROM bits needed can rise dramatically, both for conditions selection and, say, alternative branch addresses. To keep the facility of multiple branches, without needing too much extra ROM, it is common for the next step address to be incompletely specified where n-way

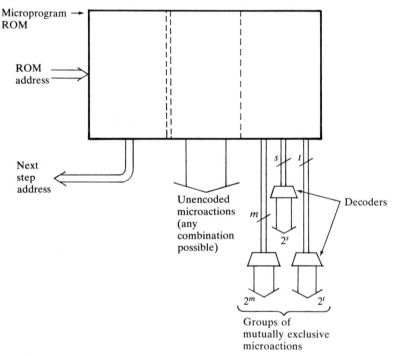

Fig. 6.16   Use of decoders to group mutually exclusive microactions to save ROM by disallowing untenable combinations of microactions.

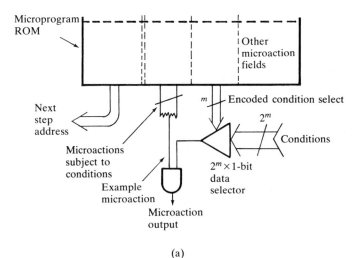

(a)

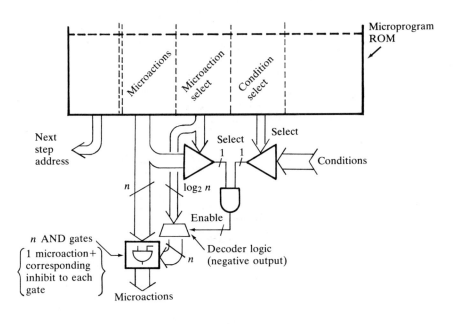

(b)

Fig. 6.17 Two (of many) approaches to providing conditional microactions: (a) flexible conditioning (one data selector and AND gate per conditional microaction); (b) one conditional microaction per microstep.

branching takes place. External conditions are used to define the remaining address bits. As an example, if branching is required to a maximum of 8 different destinations in a given controller, then only the first $n-3$ bits of a next microstep address would be supplied, straight from the ROM field. The other 3 bits would be obtained via combinational logic using the current step address plus external conditions to determine the values of these bits. The combinational logic could be provided by hard-wired logic, PLA, ULA, or even another (smaller) ROM (Fig. 6.18).

3.   In order to make a number of different microstep durations possible, a short field could be associated with each microstep. Two such bits could give a choice of 4 durations—probably sufficient for most purposes. The logical implementation of such a scheme is shown in Fig. 6.19.

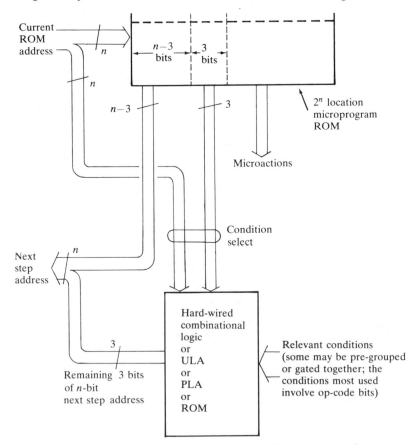

Fig. 6.18 Schematic of an eight-way branch facility for a ROM-based controller.

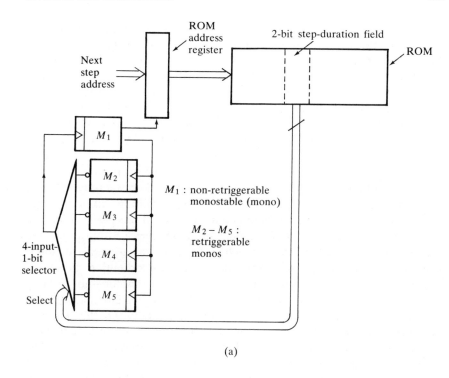

(a)

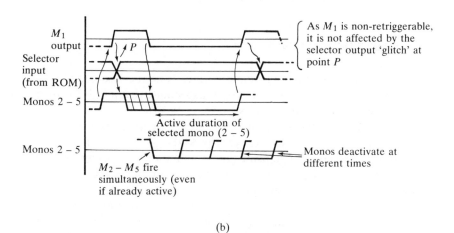

(b)

Fig. 6.19 (a) Schematic diagram and (b) waveforms for a ROM-based microprogram able to select four microstep durations.

4. Practical design of microprograms involves decisions as to how microinstructions (actions) should be grouped. On the one hand, maximum speed is obtained from a microprogram only if each step is full utilized. This usually means that all non-interacting actions should be carried out on the same step, where possible. In order that the designer can call any combination of such actions for each step, each may, in extreme circumstances, need its own ROM bit. Clearly, the ROM is very wide if this is done. However, it does not *necessarily* mean that the total number of ROM bits is substantially higher, as the number of microsteps needed is obviously less. (Each microstep carries out a greater proportion of each instruction.)

On the other hand, if the opposite extreme is taken whereby only one microaction is allowed on each step, then, by definition, all actions are mutually exclusive and the minimum number of ROM bits per location will be needed. In effect, the ROM supplies no more than a form of encoded operation code to the hardware—much in the same way as an instruction is formatted. Mutually exclusive instructions cause the execution time to be maximized, although the programming task is much simpler—not to mention the fact that the grouping and assigning problem is eliminated.

Practical microprograms usually compromise between the so-called *horizontal* approach, which allows complete freedom of action concurrency, and the *vertical* approach, which is hardly microprogramming at all. The result is a microprogram with a selection of ROM bits assigned to groups of mutually exclusive tasks and other ROM bits assigned to actions which do or may be carried out on the same microstep.

6.5 A SIMPLE DESIGN EXAMPLE

It is difficult to devise a design example which is neither too complex, such that it obscures the points to be raised, nor so simple that it fails to illustrate important features of control units.

Let us consider the single address processor of Section 6.1 and, in particular, the control needed to execute ADD, SUBTRACT and JUMP (BRANCH) instructions. Choosing this combination gives a chance to show how microcode can be merged, how branches take place and how concurrency of processing on a single microstep can be used to advantage. It will also show the difference between the control methods outlined so far.

It is assumed that the design of the processor, from a data-flow viewpoint, has already been fixed (Fig. 3.6). Table 6.3 shows the time slots needed for each relevant microaction. Because this is a simple example, it is also possible to show the waveforms to execute these instructions. However, this would be quite impossible for a practical system offering, say, 50 or 100 instructions.

Microaction	Timeslot needed (ns)
MM address←PC	150
MM read	400
IR←MM	100
MM address←IR (A)	150
PC←PC+1	100
PC←IR (A)	50
ALU←MM	100
ALU settle	200
ACC←ALU	50

Table 6.3 Typical microaction timings for the processor of Fig. 3.6 with the sequences shown in Fig. 6.2.

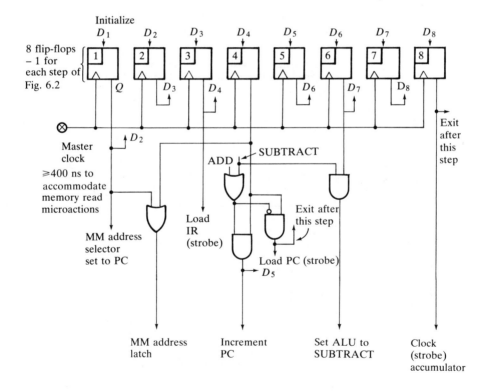

Fig. 6.20 "One flip-flop per step" controller for add, subtract and jump instructions.

Flowcharts for the three instuctions would have been derived quite independently. Figures 6.2 and 6.3(a) show how they can be merged. In this example, it is quite obvious how this has been accomplished, but in a large system a great deal of trial and error, coupled with previous experience, may be employed to achieve a reasonable merger. There is no doubt that merging

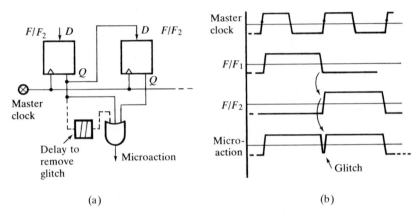

(a)   (b)

Fig. 6.21   (a) Logic and (b) waveforms showing glitch occurrences and its removal when more than one clock period is used for a long microaction.

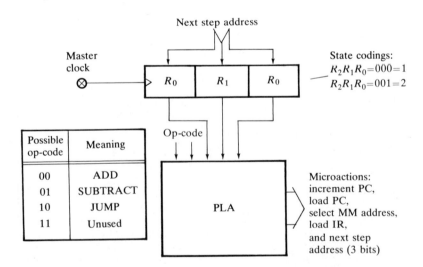

Fig. 6.22   PLA implementation of the controller for the sequence of Fig. 6.3(a).

is wholly worthwhile, as it drastically reduces the ROM size needed, the additional logic requirements and sometimes even the processor's instruction times (by reducing the levels of ANDing and ORing required at the microaction level). Figure 6.20 shows how this (part) microprogram might be implemented with the "1 flip-flop per microstep approach" and a fixed clock. Note that many steps are considerably longer than necessary, in order that the slowest microactions can be completed in one microstep. An improvement to this scheme might allocate multiple microsteps to the longer tasks. If this is done, care must be taken to avoid "glitches" (transient, short term, disturbances to an otherwise steady waveform) in the microaction waveforms, as they may cause unreliable operation (Fig. 6.21).

A register and PLA implementation is shown in Fig. 6.22. This looks deceptively simple, because only three instructions are being executed. It would be much bigger for a full microprogram.

A ROM-based approach is shown in Fig 6.23. It is only one of a large number of possible implementations but represents a reasonable compromise between the vertical and horizontal schemes.

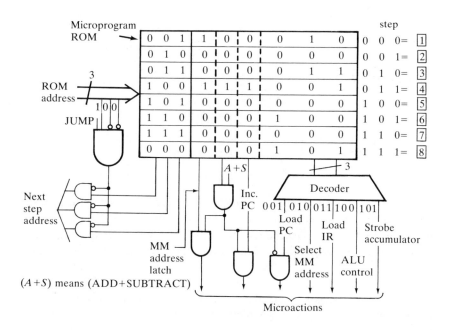

Fig. 6.23 ROM-based equivalent of Fig. 6.22.

6.6 PERFORMANCE OF CONTROL UNITS

Because they are controlling hardware activities, the *performance* of control units is of great importance. Regardless of the control strategy used, be it flip-flop or ROM-based, certain performance characteristics are shared.

In all cases, control is handed, from microstep to microstep, from one source of microactions to another. For the flip-flop system, control is handed from one flip-flop to another. For the ROM-based system, control is handed from one location to another in ROM. Before any microactions can be asserted on any microstep, the hand-over must take place, the new flip-flop set or ROM location be accessed, conditional logic processed and the microactions distributed (Fig. 6.24). Therefore, the time allocated for a microstep is

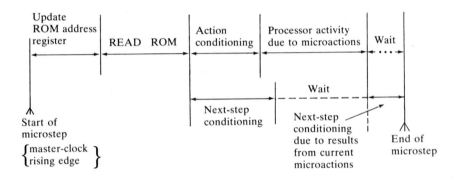

Fig. 6.24 Interaction of addressing and microactions logic in a ROM-based microprogram (shown as a time chart).

the sum of the control-unit process time and that due to activity in the processor hardware. In many computers, the control unit can take as long as the main hardware to operate, particularly for the simpler microsteps. A number of techniques are employed to avoid this control-unit overhead. Some of them are listed below.

1. Use of specially selected logic (and ROMs) for the control unit. As the control unit should represent a relatively small proportion of the processor hardware outlay, it might be possible to consider the use of more expensive but faster logic in this area. In the case of ROM-based systems, the ROM can be the dominant component in determining speed, and the use of fast bipolar devices is quite common.

2. *Microinstruction pre-fetch* As in normal machine-code programming, it is quite feasible to fetch microinstructions before they are needed. If a string of short microsteps is encountered in a microprogram, it may be all the control unit can do to keep up with the demand for microinstructions. However, there is no reason why a fresh microinstruction should not be fetched from ROM before the completion of a long, maybe compound, microinstruction. A hazard with such a technique, shared with normal programming, is that conditional branches make it impossible to be certain which of two or more paths are going to followed (Fig. 6.24). (It has already been stated that branches are very common in microprograms as a consequence of merging.) The situation is not as gloomy as might at first be thought. There is only indeterminacy associated with the path taken through a maze of branches if the condition determining the path is not resolved until the microstep before the branch is taken. The vast majority of branches through a microprogram come as a consequence of merging and are thus only conditioned by the instruction being executed. This is known from the beginning of the microprogram sequence for that instruction and does not change until the end of the instruction. Such branches do not cause difficulties and the path to be taken can be predicted with confidence. Clearly, resolved and unresolved branch conditions must be differentiated in the control-unit hardware so that a hold is placed on pre-fetch for those which are as yet unresolved.

3. *Multi-phase ROM operation* This technique is usually only applied to ROM-based systems but it has also been applied successfully to the flip-flop matrix method (see later). Section 4.6 described how the overall throughput of a memory system could be increased by having several memories operating in parallel. As the access time of the ROM tends to be dominant, then use of parallel ROMs would seem to provide a solution. This technique is sometimes used in microprogram systems. Usually, the ROMs don't actually work in parallel but in a multiphase arrangement. The next step issued by one ROM is always routed to the address input of another ROM, so that during the remainder of the control unit and processor hardware operations (associated with the microactions sent by the first ROM), the second ROM is being addressed. Normally no more than two-phase operation is attempted. This system has the same disadvantage as pre-fetching insofar that there is a commitment to a ROM address before processing is completed for the previous step. However, the same comments as to incidence and approach apply equally to multiphasing as to pre-fetch.

4. *Complex and long duration microinstructions* Some microactions can take a long or variable time to complete. For example, memory access (for instructions and operands) takes a long time in comparison with

1. a simple register-to-register transfer and

2. shift (rotate) operations which take a time dependent on the number of
    places over which shifting is to take place.

In both of these cases, it is probably better to arrange a "clock halt/restart"
system. In this, a single ROM bit indicates that the master microprogram
clock should be halted until a *completion signal* is received from the (shifting) hardware being actioned. A typical logic arrangement is shown in Fig.
6.25.

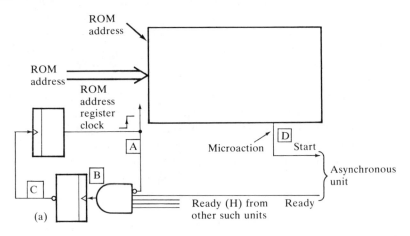

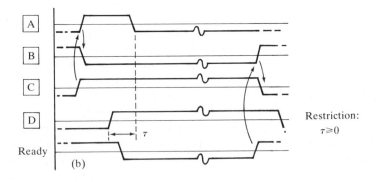

Fig. 6.25 (a) Logic and (b) timing of microactions that drive
hardware of unpredictable process times.

Notes. 1.   It is not necessary to specify which unit should be inspected for a completion signal as the one actioned should be the only one to become "unready" as a consequence of the microaction being sent. In fact, it is quite in order to initiate two or more such units, each of which may take a different time to complete its task. In this case, the conjunction (logical AND) of "ready" signals will be used to indicate when the microprogram clock can be restarted and the next microinstruction accessed.

2.   Both multiphase operation and clock holding can be applied to encoded flip-flop, matrix flip-flop, ULA and PLA control units as well as the ROM-based ones. There is also little difference in the logic needed to accomplish these refinements.

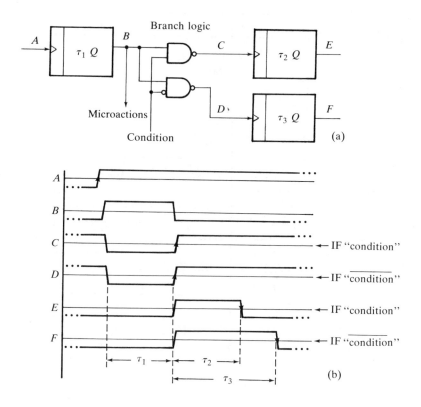

Fig. 6.26   Controller implementation using monostables: (a) logic; (b) waveforms.

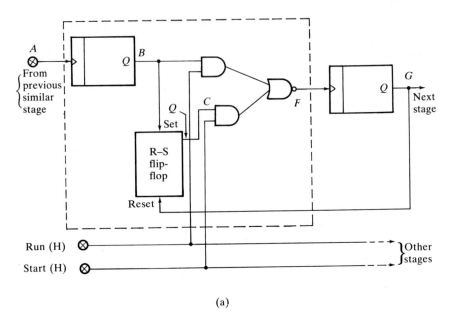

(a)

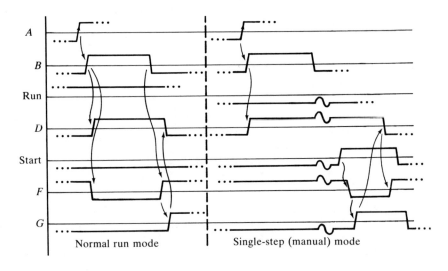

(b)

Fig. 6.27 A monostable-based controller with single-step facilities:
(a) logic; (b) waveforms.

5.   *Controllers with time-tailored microstep lengths*   The controllers so far described have, at best, only provided a microstep duration which *approximates* to the actual time of execution of the various microactions for that step. In each case, the next longer duration to the actual time required would have been chosen, from a limited menu of durations. Where performance is so important that even small wastages of time must be avoided, then *unlimited* choice of step durations may have to be provided. One approach is to use monostables or multi-tap delay lines to provide the variety of durations required. Such delay lines are often fabricated as single-layer (solenoid) windings on a cylindrical core (in effect a lumped "artificial" line requiring a termination network). In such a system, *each* step has its own monostable or delay line for this purpose.

A simple example of this system is shown in Fig. 6.26. Each monostable triggers on the trailing edge of the one feeding it. Like other controllers, the "monos" provide the necessary edges and logic levels for controlling the processor hardware at their Q outputs. Generation of branching and merging, and of conditional and unconditional actions, is implemented in much the same way as for the "1 flip-flop per step" method.

There are a number of points to note:

1.   With all previously described methods, it has been possible, by holding the clock, to trace microsequences one step at a time. This is very

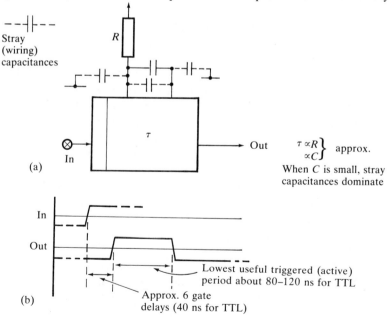

Fig. 6.28   (a) Simplified equivalent circuit and (b) short-period performance of a typical monostable.

useful when commissioning a system or carrying out fault-finding. Mono-stables and delays cannot be halted unless a flip-flop is associated with each step (Fig. 6.27). The flip-flop provides a record of the last mono to be triggered, so that "restart" or "single stepping" is possible.

2. Monostables do not operate satisfactorily at very high speeds. In particular, their performance can be erratic and difficult to reproduce or predict. There are two reasons:

(a)   Monostables do not respond to input trigger signals immediately. A typical mono may take the equivalent of 5 or 6 ordinary gate delays before its Q output goes to logic 1. At high speeds this may be a sizable proportion of the delay time being generated (Fig. 6.28).

(b)   Very small capacitances are required to give short delays. These often have wide tolerances and, moreover, may only represent a small prop-ortion of the actual circuit capacitance when circuit strays are also taken into account. Designing for short delays is therefore very dif-ficult and prone to error.

6.7   MICROPROGRAMMING LANGUAGES AND EMULATION

The design of microprograms is complex and laborious if carried out manu-ally. In order to alleviate the time taken, both in the initial design and enhancements, some language and development aids have been produced.

Languages tend to be confined to variations of assembly languages, simply because of the machine dependence of any tasks written. However, such languages must reflect the parallel-processing element that can be present and the hardware limitations that are particular to the processor being developed. These assemblers must also be able to trap a wider variety of invalid operations—in particular, groups of microactions made mutually exclusive by the processor hardware. For example, clashes may occur when enabling talkers on bus-orientated systems as only one should be active at a time. In the case of the latter, the use of mutually exclusive groups does not *necessarily* prevent certain combinations of talkers and listeners arising on a given microstep. Traps must also be laid for invalid time slots, handshakes and unreasonable conditions. Extra assembler traps may also have to be present if multiphase operation or pre-fetch is used.

As most branches are dependent solely on the instruction being executed, a microprogram assembler (microassembler) should also be able to take the burden of specifying such branches away from the programmer. Only conditions of a local and ephemeral nature should have to be explicitly specified. When merging takes place, each instruction sequence should be separable so that when simulation of a microsequence is carried out, each instruction will automatically follow the correct sequence of microprogram addresses (through ROM).

As each microassembler is particular to the hardware being developed (machine dependent), writing suitable microassemblers represents a sizable outlay in skill and time. It is not undertaken lightly and many quite large computers have been fully developed at the microprogram level, with little more than a crude simulator. This çan handle one instruction at a time with little or no reference to the existence of other microsequences, at the time of simulation.

EXERCISES

6.1 Discuss the relative advantages and disadvantages of the various methods of providing digital-system control: "1 flip-flop per step", "encoded register", monostables, ROM-based microprogram.

6.2 Using the processor layout of Fig 3.6, write control sequences for a variety of simple instructions, including conditional jumps, store and load accumulator. Merge these sequences as much as possible and observe how many fewer microsteps are required for the controller.

6.3 Using normal TTL logic, determine the amount of time required for each microstep of Exercise 6.2. Design the controller logic using each of the methods described in this chapter and determine how much controller processing time is required by each design. The controller should also be fabricated with TTL or TTL-related components.

6.4 Using Fig. 3.6 as a base design, determine what modifications it would require in order to be able to handle multiword instructions. Show how the microsequences, developed in Exercise 2, would have to be modified.

6.5 Using the programmable adder/subtractor as an approach to parallel arithmetic, design a single cell of a programmable arithmetic/logic unit which could perform the following functions: add, subtract, rotate right, rotate left. (Rotation should be 1 place only, on each pass through the unit.)

6.6 Enhance your design of Exercise 6.5 to include the logical operations AND, OR, NOT and EXCLUSIVE-OR.

6.7 Write microsequences for the processor of Fig. 3.6 and arithmetic/logic unit of Exercise 6.6 to take advantage of the functions now provided. Implement the controller using the "1 flip-flop per step" method.

6.8 If the utilization of multiplier values in an arithmetic unit follows a negative exponential law, by how much does the time-saving scheme of Fig. 6.29 reduce the mean time to multiply, expressed as a percentage?

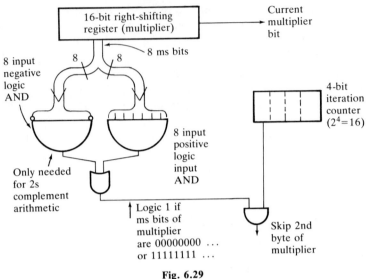

Fig. 6.29

6.9 Assuming the use of normal TTL logic with a gate delay of 10 ns, what would be a suitable value for the anti-glitch delay of Fig. 6.9 if delays can be manufactured to a tolerance of ±30%?

6.10 Redesign the branching logic of Fig. 6.11 so that normal, single-output, NAND gates (only) are used in the combinational logic.

6.11 Take any (moderately long) microsequence, preferable containing a number of conditional branches and microactions, and determine by how much, if any, the controller is reduced if the matrix flip-flop implementation of Fig. 6.12 is used instead of either the "encoded flip-flop" or "1 flip-flop per step" methods.

6.12 Repeat the exercise for Exercise 6.11 but consider implementation as shown in Fig. 6.15.

6.13 Explain why the non-retriggerable and retriggerable monostables were so specified for the variable step duration controller of Fig. 6.19.

6.14 Compare the process time results you obtained for question 3 with those quoted in Table 6.3.

REFERENCES

Agrawala, A. K. and Rausher, T. G. (1974), "Microprogramming perspective and status," *IEEE Trans. Comp.* **C-23,** 817–37.

Chu. Y. (1972), *Computer Organization and Microprogramming*, Prentice-Hall, Englewood Cliffs, N.J.

Clare, C. R. (1973), *Designing Logic Systems Using State Machines*, McGraw-Hill, New York.

Mick, J. R. and Brick, J. (1977), *Microprogramming Handbook*, Advanced Micro Devices, Sunnyvale, Calif.

Wilkes, M. V. (1951), "The best way to design an automatic calculating machine," Report of Manchester University Computer Inaugural Conference, July, 1951, pp. 16–18.

Wilkes, M. V. and Stringer, J. B. (1953), "Microprogramming and the design of the control circuits in electronic digital computers," *Proc. Camb. Phil. Soc.*, **49**(2), 230–8.

7 INPUT/OUTPUT SYSTEMS

7.1 INTRODUCTION

So far, the computer system has been largely referred to in terms of a self-contained processor/memory combination. In order to enter programs and data to it, retrieve results from it, and, possibly, interact with it during a computer run, methods must be found to communicate with the system. They must be effective, economical and flexible. Amongst the more important considerations are:

1. Will the input/output (I/O) methodology allow connection of many different types and speeds of devices—possibly at the same time?
2. Will control of input/output routines be easily programmed with a minimum of special instructions?
3. Can expansion of I/O facilities be undertaken easily from a small beginning?
4. When I/O transfers take place, to what extent will traffic (data) flow affect other computer activities such as processing and memory accesses?
5. Will the introduction of additional hardware, say, input/output processors, be worthwhile to improve the rate of data flow or to minimize interference with other computer activities?
6. How will the processor be kept aware of the progress of I/O transfers so that it does not, for instance, attempt to use data which have yet to be acquired from outside the computer?

The I/O data-flow problem is shown schematically in Fig. 7.1. The first question that arises from consideration of Fig. 7.1 is where exactly are the I/O connections to the processor/memory sub-system? Ostensibly, connection can either be made to the processor or the memory. Both of these will be discussed in this chapter and the implications of each choice outlined.

242

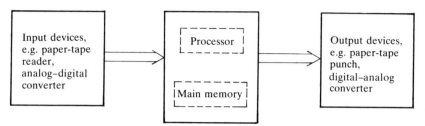

Fig. 7.1 Schematic connection of input/output devices to a computer.

7.2 PROGRAMMED TRANSFERS OF DATA

In principle, the simplest I/O connection must be to the processor (rather than the memory) if only because it contains physically co-existing (separate) registers. No address needs to be supplied as for a memory connection—just access to the chosen register (Fig. 7.2).

Frequently, the chosen register is the accumulator. This may be because it is the only register in the processor accessible to the user (via his software) or because it forms a "focus" of activity in the processor and is the obvious choice. If the processor contains a scratch-pad or register file, the accumulator will still be chosen by addressing that scratch-pad location designated "accumulator". This would be accomplished by having

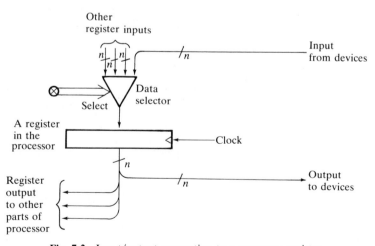

Fig. 7.2 Input/output connection to a processor register.

input/output instructions as part of the processor's repertoire and which, by using suitable addressing, always involve the accumulator in an I/O transfer.

Two instructions would normally be made available:

1. transfer the contents of the accumulator to the machine's output port "output";
2. transfer the information at the machine's input port to the accumulator "input".

Such a scheme is very easy to implement, particularly if the system has only one input and one output port. Even if more than one port of each type is involved, little additional complication arises as the address field of the input and output instructions can be used to designate the device or port (Fig. 7.3).

Logic for a data selector has already been described in Chapter 3. A demultiplexer performs the opposite function. It routes a single channel of information to one of 2^m routes according to the "route-select-bit pattern" of

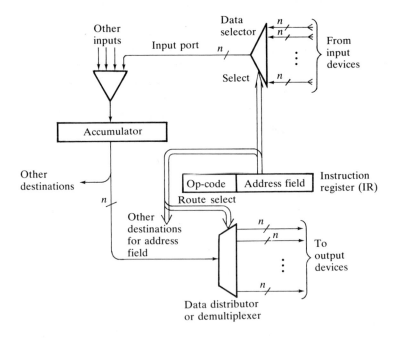

Fig. 7.3 Programmed transfer for several input/output devices.

m bits. The logic for a 2-bit, 4-way demultiplexer is shown in Fig. 7.4. As with the data selector (multiplexer), it is basically a decoder with a data path attached to each AND gate. In some designs, the decoding is done separately with *each* decoder output being applied to another AND gate along with a data bit. Such an arrangement uses more gates—but each gate has fewer inputs. Figure 7.3 indicates that a large number of input and output routes can be supported as the instruction address field can frequently be of 8 or more bits. This would allow up to at least 256 input and 256 output devices to be connected.

Many micro, mini and mainframe computers operate on a bus system to which subsystems are connected. The subsystems consist of processors, main memory, input and output ports, bulk memory, interrupt systems and the

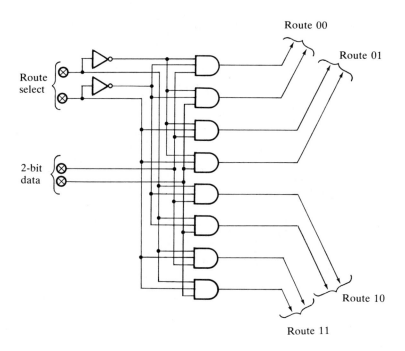

Fig. 7.4 Two-bit, four-way demultiplexer.

like. Programmed transfers can operate in such a system. The processor
normally controls the protocol between the subsystems participating in the
transfer; normally these subsystems consist of the processor itself and a port.
Typical examples of such systems can be found in many microcomputers.
Figure 7.5 shows a typical arrangement in which the minimum set of data,
address and control lines are used to control the selection of the desired port
and the subsequent flow of data to or from it. In a typical microcomputer, the
accumulator and I/O enable gates are integrated into the microprocessor
and I/O port chips, respectively.

Each subsystem can normally deposit data on the bus or read data from
it. In order that the bus is protected from those subsystems not permitted to
deposit data at any given time, three-state gates are used (see Appendix to
Chapter 3). Each subsystem decodes the address bus to determine if it is the
one involved in a transfer of data. Additional timing and control lines from

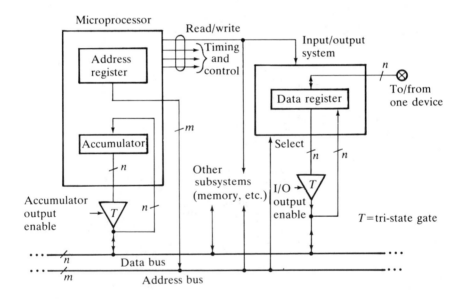

Fig. 7.5 Schematic of typical microprocessor bus-connected
programmed-transfer input/output system.

the microprocessor, broadcast to all subsystems, indicate the direction and time of data flow. In most cases, the system is not general, i.e. it is not possible for any subsystem to "talk" to any other subsystem. Generally, the microprocessor is always one of the participants together with *one* other subsystem. Transfers in a microcomputer can therefore be of the form:

microprocessor to memory;
memory to microprocessor;
microprocessor to input/output system;
input/output system to microprocessor.

This restricted set of allowable data movements allows the use of a single control wire from the microprocessor to indicate whether a READ (transfer to the microprocessor) or WRITE operation is required. In practice, a second timing signal is also often sent by the microprocessor to synchronize the other subsystems activities with the microprocessor's clock and control unit. These two signals provide the subsystems "output enable" when they deposit data on the bus. They also provide a "register strobe" or RAM write signal when data are to be taken from the bus and entered to another subsystem.

An important facet of the bus method just described, which is largely followed in the Motorola M6800 series of microprocessors, is that every subsystem has a set of addresses associated with it, regardless of its function. (This does not apply to the microprocessor, per se.) Therefore, if a 16-bit address bus is used, there are $2^{16}=65\ 536$ addresses available which are subdivided amongst the various memory, I/O and timer units and other bus-connected subsystems. The advantages of such a method lie in control simplicity and the fact that the same type of microprocessor instructions can be used for transferring data anywhere on the bus. Any device which can be addressed as if it were just another memory location is called 'memory-mapped', e.g. memory-mapped I/O.

Example The ubiquitous MOVE instruction in a microprocessor is normally associated with the transfer of data from one microprocessor register to another or between a register and a memory location. However, suitable choice of "memory" address can cause such an instruction to move data between the processor and the I/O subsystem. I/O is, in effect, treated as part of memory. In this way, separate input/output instructions are rendered unnecessary.

There are two possible disadvantages if this system is adopted, neither of which is, in practice, difficult to overcome.

1. The available address space, typically 65 536 locations, is shared between memory, I/O and other subsystems, thereby making less available than in a system in which the subsystems are "identified" by the microprocessor (e.g. the Intel 8080/8085 microcomputers). Most microcomputer systems do not need to use all the address space provided, so that the problem rarely arises. In a system large enough for this to matter, some I/O subsystems can be connected to mass-memory devices to make up memory space, e.g. floppy disk, cassette disk or magnetic tape. There is, however, a performance penalty when electromechanical memories are introduced.

2. In most circumstances, the number of I/O subsystems is very much smaller than memory locations so that, although it is reasonable to expect to have to decode wide address fields for RAM and ROM devices, it would seem an unnecessary burden to be carried by I/O subsystems. (A typical microcomputer may only have 1–8 I/O subsystems connected to its bus.)

Most microcomputers and minicomputers can make use of a method called *partial decoding* to overcome the cost of full decoding.

Example A particular microprocessor has a 16-bit address bus, contains 4K bytes of memory fabricated from 1K byte ICs and has 8 I/O channels serviced by 4 I/O subsystems. Memory and I/O share the same address space. A suitable addressing arrangement is shown in Fig. 7.6.

Each memory module, being of 1K locations, has 10 address bits ($2^{10} = 1024 = 1K$). In addition, it has a 5-input AND gate which can enable or disable the chip. Such an AND gate has a selection of logic 1 and logic 0 inputs so that different combinations of the states of the remaining address bits from the bus can be used to control whether the chip is operational or not. (The allocation of logic 0 and 1 inputs is often mask-defined by the manufacturer of the chip so that the same chip type may have several versions—some with more logic 1 than 0 inputs and vice versa.) Enabling can be carried out in several ways according to the chip electronics. The way shown in Fig. 7.6 is arranged so that the ENABLE signal forms an extra input to the decoder AND gates. In the event of ENABLE being at logic 0 , all decoder outputs are set to logic 0 and no memory location is selected or presented at the chip's output. An additional input to the chip would determine whether the chip was to be in the READ or WRITE mode. The read/write and enable inputs to the chip are often gated together to provide overall control of the chip's activities. (Alternative schemes operate on the chip's data lines to the memory matrix rather than on the address lines. However, the aims and results are the same.)

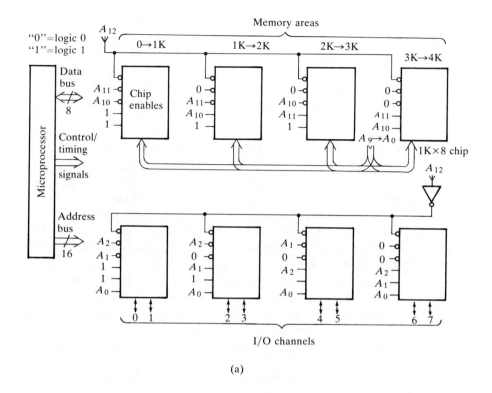

(a)

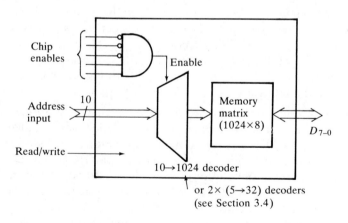

(b)

Fig. 7.6 Partial decoding of bus addresses: (a) schematic; (b) partial decoder logic.

For the I/O chips, it is assumed that each contains two registers, one for the data of each I/O channel serviced. A 5-input AND gate is again used which can enable or disable the chip. It therefore controls the data flow into and out of the chip. For an I/O chip, the 10 address lines are replaced by a single "channel select" line. In effect, an I/O chip is a two-location memory as seen by the microprocessor. Using the addressing system of Fig. 7.6, the first 4K memory locations (0 to 4095) are accessed by "address values" H(0000) – H(0FFF) (H denotes hexadecimal (hex.)) and I/O channels 0–7 using "address values" H(1000)–H(1007). However, because the decoding is only partial, a given memory or I/O location is not unique, that is, it is possible to use more than one "address value" to access the same location. For example, in Fig. 7.6, address values H(0000), H(2000), H(4000),..., H(E000) will give access to memory location zero. Thus, partial decoding wastes the addressability of the system. Only full decoding can achieve a full 2^{16} addressability. To achieve this for Fig. 7.6 would require a 13-input AND gate for address lines A_{15}–A_3 on each I/O chip!

Parenthetically, the AND gates for these chips would need to have a variety of true and inverse (complementary) inputs according to the address space to be occupied by the chip. Such an arrangement is neither practical nor desirable in most circumstances. A more reasonable arrangement would merely *increase* the scope of partial decoding by the use of off-chip decoders.

Example   A partial decoding scheme for a 4K memory having only two ENABLE inputs on each 1K byte chip would be as shown in Fig. 7.7. In effect, the decoding takes place at two levels–in the decoder chip and in the memory chip enable AND gate. The two levels perform a partial decoding task on A_{12}, A_{11} and A_{10} to give effective memory chip enables corresponding to $A_{12}A_{11}A_{10}=000$, 001, 010 and 011. These correspond, in turn, to memory locations 0, 1K, 2K and 3K. Combinations involving $A_{12}=1$ are available for the I/O chip.

Partial decoding trees of more than two levels can be formed at will according to the number of uniquely addressable locations needed. However, "trees" of decoders can impose high propagation delays which must be taken into account when designing the microcomputer. The time allowance made by a microprocessor between its issue of an address and its expectation of having valid data returned is fixed for a given system. Partial decoding time must be added to the raw memory access times when deciding if data are to be returned to the microprocessor in time for its next cycle. If the required speed cannot be obtained, it will be necessary to resort to one of the following:

1.   Reduce the system clock speed—this will reduce the microcomputer's performance at all levels, not just for memory accesses.

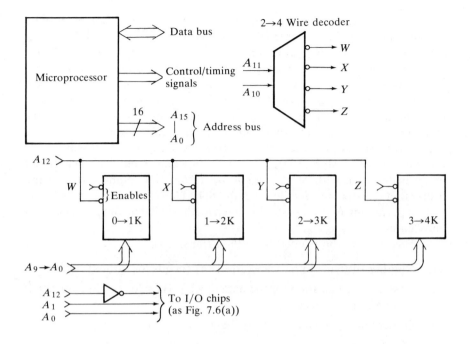

Fig. 7.7 Development of Fig. 7.6 using a decoder and fewer chip enables.

2. Use the *hold* facility made available on many microcomputers so that memory accesses can be of any duration and data are returned by handshaking. This wastes time in whole numbers of machine cycles but is frequently used.

3. Change the memory/address decoding technology used, that is, use faster memory chips if they are available or maybe faster decoders, such as Schottky clamped TTL, so that the total access time is within specification.

7.3 DIRECT MEMORY ACCESS (DMA)

Programmed I/O transfers are relatively simple and generally provided as standard on most micro, mini and mainframe computer systems. However, such transfers are slow, and create a heavy processing overhead for the central processor.

Generally, an I/O transfer requirement is for a "block" of n bytes to be moved between main memory and a particular I/O device. The block of data will be moved either to or from *contiguous* main-memory locations. Therefore n bytes might be moved, starting with memory location m with subsequent bytes drawn from locations $m+1$, $m+2$, ..., $m+n-1$.

If we consider a bus-orientated system with memory and I/O subsystems, there is no reason why data should not move directly between memory and I/O. The processor can therefore be freed to carry on other processing (within constraints listed later in this section). Clearly, the processor will be involved before the start of a transfer as the data movement must be initiated by an instruction, with some suitable operation code being found in the instruction register (see Sections 3.3 and 8.4). However, after certain information pertaining to the transfer has been made available, the processor can be released.

The information needed for a data transfer is:

1. Number of bytes to be transferred (n) (needs $\log_2 n$ bits).

2. First memory location for the data block (m) ($= \log_2 p$ bits, where p is the main-memory capacity).

3. Direction of transfer, i.e. to or from memory ($=1$ bit).

4. First location in the I/O device (up to 16 bits, typically).

The only item of information whose function is not self-evident is (4). If the I/O device is "simple", such as a teletype (TTY), paper-tape reader (PTR), paper-tape punch (PTP), etc., data have pre-assigned device locations, i.e. a character output to the PTP would automatically go in the next character position on the paper tape. However, a transfer to floppy disk would have to specify a track and possibly a sector for the first byte. Subsequent bytes would then follow on through the sector (until full) and then to the next sector. If the end of a track were reached, the next track would be started, and so on.

Example   A cartridge disk contains 40 sectors of 256 bytes per track. Each of the two disk recording surfaces can have 256 tracks. Item (4) above would then need 1 bit to define a surface, 8 bits to define a track and 6 bits for a sector. Total$=15$ bits to define any sector. If we assume 100 I/O devices are connected to the computer, each requiring sufficient information bits for items (1)–(4), then a considerable volume of memory will be needed (maybe 500 to 600 bytes).

For a microcomputer DMA controller, memory requirements can be kept low by various means:

1. keep the number D of I/O devices small—typically 8;
2. fix n to some value so that its value is implicit;
3. fix m to make it implicit.

Various microcomputer DMA controllers use some or all of the simplifications (1)–(3). Most DMA controllers maintain generality and keep items (1)–(3) explicit.

A bus-orientated system is shown in Fig. 7.8.

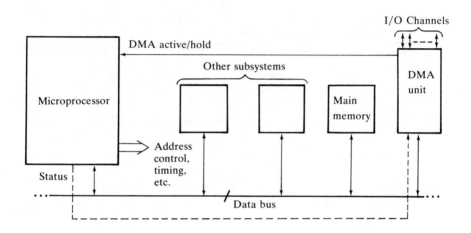

Fig. 7.8 Bus-orientated DMA system.

The information needed for the transfer of data will eventually be needed in the DMA controller but is generally generated by a program sequence *prior* to use in an I/O instruction and *parked* in an area of main memory. Each I/O device is numbered and allocated an area of memory for this information. A typical arrangement appears in Fig. 7.9, where it will be seen that the device number defines its reserved memory area. In this example, it is assumed that 8 bytes are sufficient to hold all the transfer information for each device. Such a system allows any or all of the devices to have their transfer information set up in main memory at any time, as required and when convenient. The area of memory from t to $(t+8D-1)$, although not available to the user for general software, is nonetheless readily accessible by him to deposit "transfer set-up" information.

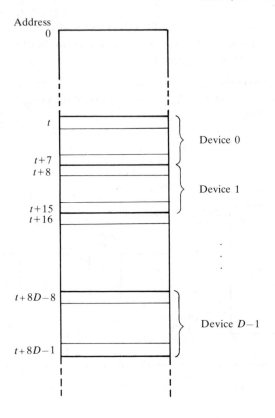

Fig. 7.9 Memory allocation for multidevice driving DMA system.

A typical sequence of events leading to a transfer is as follows:

1. Enter a software sequence which generates the transfer information pertaining to device A and deposit it in memory area $(t+8A)$ through $(t+8A+7)$. (The format for these 8 bytes is fixed for a given computer and is therefore generally the same for all A.)

2. Encounter an I/O instruction. The address portion of the instruction would probably be used as a device number (A in this case).

3. A would be sent to the DMA system via the bus.

4. Whilst the processor proceeds with the next and subsequent instructions, the DMA unit would use A to address the main memory, obtain the eight bytes and use them to effect the main memory/device transfer.

5. When the DMA transfer is completed, a finished signal is sent to the processor to let it know that the data movement is complete and that the device in question can receive further commands.

A number of points should be noted for DMA operation:

The processor is only directly involved for a very short time and can operate concurrently with the DMA transfer to make better use of the total equipment.

The organization of the transfer is largely under the control of the DMA system—which includes counting the bytes transferred and halting the transfer when completed. It also generates the main-memory addresses for each byte transferred. If the required byte count is deposited in a down counter before the transfer, the counter can be decremented as each byte passes through. A zero detector, attached to the down counter, can be used to halt the transfer. If the first main-memory address m is deposited in an up counter, the memory address for each byte can be generated by incrementing this counter as each byte passes through the DMA controller.

If the processor attempts to operate whilst a DMA transfer is in progress, a clash for main-memory access will occur from time to time. The processor needs to access main memory for instructions and operands and the DMA unit needs memory access for I/O data transfers. Several options are available to the designer to resolve such clashes of interest:

1. Eliminate the problem by shutting down the processor during the I/O transfer. This can be done if the wastage of processor activity can be tolerated. In microcomputer systems this is frequently the case and the processor is shut down by a signal, issued by the DMA controller. This halts the processor timing unit and puts the (tri-state) data and address bus drivers, in the processor, into the "high-impedance" state (see Appendix, Chapter 3). Such action prevents the microprocessor from interfering with the DMA unit via the bus. Many microprocessors have an input line to allow this to take place—this is variously known as HOLD, HALT and SUSPEND.

2. Make use of otherwise inactive periods in the normal operation of the memory available. This is generally only possible with a small number of microcomputer systems. If a microcomputer operates with a 2-phase clock, it may only attempt to access memory during one of these phases (Motorola M6800). The DMA unit can therefore make use of the other phase to access memory.

3. Cycle stealing. This is a technique whereby the processor is prevented from access to memory only when the DMA unit requires it. A floppy disk may only be able to transfer data at, say, 20K bytes per second, i.e. 1 byte per 50 μs. The processor can therefore proceed with a great deal of work between each DMA access. When a DMA access is required, bus control is wrested from the processor and a DMA-based byte transfer made. The processor's hold line can be used for this purpose. After the transfer, the processor can regain bus control.

It is very reasonable to arrange the system such that, in effect, the DMA unit has a higher "priority" than the processor, i.e. can gain bus control at any time it likes. The processor, being just a collection of registers and logic, can be made to wait indefinitely for memory access without loss of information. However, many I/O devices are dynamic, that is, they are only able to operate as information *passes* their read/write heads. Examples are magnetic disks, drums and magnetic tape. Therefore, when operating, they demand that data are acquired (read) or disposed of (written) within a certain time. In this way, the need for data to "queue" is avoided (see Section 4.7). Such a priority system is therefore to the advantage of the devices with the processor "soaking up" spare main-memory time as it becomes available.

There are certain important variations in DMA design which can affect logic economies. In large computers, more than 1 DMA technique is often used. A fast design is needed for connecting fast devices; an economical design for handling the (majority) of relatively slow devices. A typical DMA "channel" can handle 1 device. It would normally contain several blocks of logic to do this. Up and down counters would be needed for memory-address generation and outstanding byte counting, as already mentioned. Frequently, several other registers, counters, data transfer and protocol-handling systems are also needed. The cost per device of such logic is high and is therefore reserved for fast device handling only. The utilization of such logic falls when used with slower devices to the extent that such logic can be shared between several devices. This sharing can be done at two levels:

1.   Have a local (semiconductor) memory in the DMA unit to hold the current byte counts and main-memory addresses for several devices, and to call these into the logic as each device is ready for service (Fig. 7.10). Any device requiring service sends a flag (signal) to the DMA unit where it is processed by an arbiter (Fig. 7.11). If another request is being serviced, the request is held. When the request is eventually serviced, it is first identified against its source and the status for the device drawn from memory. The status (outstanding byte count, etc.), is deposited in the shared logic unit. Normal DMA to memory protocol then takes place for the transfer of *one* byte. When finished, the updated status is written to the local memory and a search made for another device request. If none is outstanding, the DMA unit defaults to an "idle" mode.

2.   Use main memory to hold status information as well as "transfer set-up" information for each device. By this means, the need for local memory in the DMA unit is eliminated and one unit can very economically

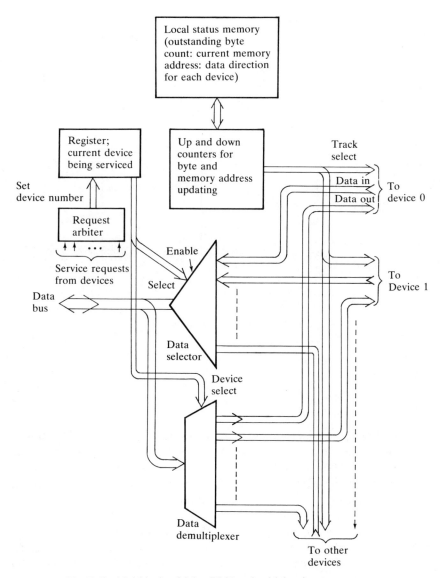

Fig. 7.10 Multidevice driving DMA unit with local status memory.

service a large number of (slow) devices. Each time a device seeks service during a transfer or the processor initiates a fresh transfer, (having encountered an input/output instruction) the status information for a device is

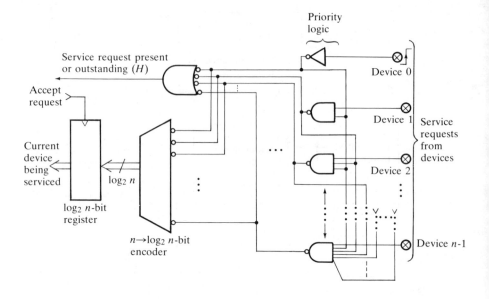

Fig. 7.11 Schematic of request arbiter.

brought down from memory and temporarily deposited in the DMA unit. A single byte will be transferred between device and memory, the status information will be updated by the DMA and the new status redeposited in memory. Given a sufficiency of data selectors and demultiplexers, a single such DMA unit can service a hundred or more devices.

The penalties for using such a system are considerable and must be balanced by the gains in hardware. The most important are very inferior performance and a heavy memory burden. Performance is poor because, for each byte transferred, the several status bytes must be drawn from memory and then redeposited. Typically, this could involve two memory-read and two memory-write cycles. In addition, a memory cycle will be required for the data byte, itself. Hence, five memory cycles are required per byte transferred—an "efficiency" of 20% or less! If 200 devices are to be serviced by this means using a 1 μs memory, the slow-device DMA unit could completely command memory time if the devices connected had an average transfer rate of 1K byte/second.

7.4 SERVICE-REQUESTS ARBITRATION

The request arbiter deserves a somewhat closer study, as pitfalls associated with its use are often overlooked (Fig. 7.11). The basic problem is one of differentiating between the arrival times of service requests from asynchronous sources. (The sources are considered to be asynchronous simply because it is not possible to synchronize the operation of electromechanical devices of widely differing performances.) If one request arrives in the absence of any other, its corresponding NAND gate goes to logic 0 and promptly prevents any other request from actuating *its* corresponding gate. The request passes through an (optional) encoder so that its source is recorded for the duration of a byte transfer through the DMA unit. The "service request present" signal ORs the requests so that the DMA unit knows when one has arrived (regardless of its source).

A problem arises if more than one service request arrives at the arbiter within a very short time span, i.e. within less than 1 NAND gate delay. Clearly, the steady-state condition of the NAND logic permits only one output to go to logic 0 at a time. Two or more "concurrent" requests induce a state of indeterminacy in this logic, which may take a long time to resolve.

In its simplest form, the situation is akin to that of an S–R flip-flop in which both set and reset lines have been previously actuated and then released at essentially the same instant. The flip-flop is left in a "balanced" condition, which can take an indefinite time to settle (Corsini, 1975). Several models for analyzing this situation have been proposed. However, it is clear that the resolution time can far exceed the normal propagation time of the basic flip-flop if the two requests occur almost concurrently.

If the requests are assumed to arrive asynchronously, a resolution-time–probability curve can be drawn (Fig. 7.12c). Of particular interest is the fact that it would appear that, however long one delays the interrogation of the arbiter (in the hope that it will resolve the time difference between two incoming requests for service), there is always a nonzero chance of the arbiter having not settled. This is particularly annoying as it is really immaterial which request source is chosen first if they send requests so close together. Nonetheless, one must be serviced first and a failure to decide—even if the outcome is irrelevant—can be disastrous. It will probably result in the two requests being handled concurrently through both logic signals giving a sufficient voltage to gate through their own demands. This is a "statistical" error. It does not arise as a consequence of an equipment malfunction or component failure—it just happens with a certain frequency. In fact, whenever work is committed to a computer, there is a chance that component failure will cause erroneous results to be produced. Statistical error occurrences are just another failure mode to be added to the list. Their rate of occurrence must be made acceptable, and this is often done by

(a)

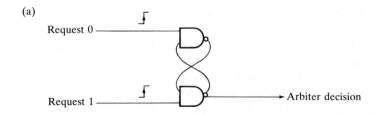

Request 0

Request 1 ——————————————→ Arbiter decision

(b)

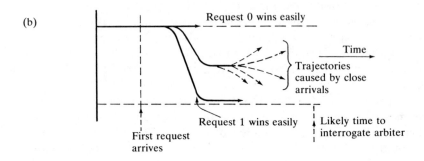

Request 0 wins easily

Time

Trajectories
caused by close
arrivals

Request 1 wins easily   Likely time to
                         interrogate arbiter

First request
arrives

(c)

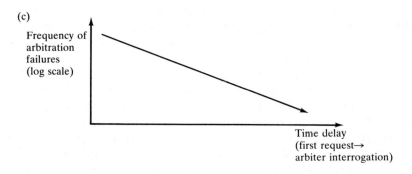

Frequency of
arbitration
failures
(log scale)

Time delay
(first request→
arbiter interrogation)

(d)

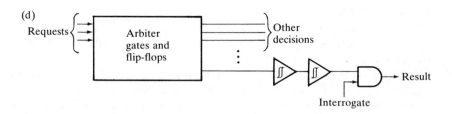

Requests

Arbiter
gates and
flip-flops

Other
decisions

Result

Interrogate

Fig. 7.12 Failure of logic to arbitrate asynchronous service
requests: (a) failure model; (b) waveforms; (c) failure rate; (d) cure.

following the arbiter flip-flops with Schmitt trigger gates to accelerate the trajectories of Fig. 7.12(b). But this is not a 100% cure and occasional failures can still occur. Because such failures do not involve component replacement (it's just a terrible coincidence that two asynchronous signals "intercepted" each other), this is known as a *soft error*. Another form of soft error is to be found in high-density MOSRAMs where a charged atomic particle may just penetrate a memory capacitor, release electron–hole pairs and discharge the capacitor. As the arrival and trajectories of particles are the subject of chance, the failure is again soft; the MOSRAM has not been damaged.

7.5 INTERRUPTS, FLAGS AND POLLING

Whether programmed transfer or direct-memory-access (DMA) type I/O is being executed, some kind of communication is needed between the peripheral devices and the processor. Such communication may be needed before a transfer to indicate the readiness of a device to participate or after a transfer to indicate completion of a task.

If many devices are involved, such communication will also involve identification of the communicator. The form of the signals depends to some extent on the type of device and the nature of the processing. For instance, if data are to be transferred to a line printer, the initiative generally comes from the processor. The line printer is idle if the processor does not require to send data to it. However, if data have been transferred, the processor will want to know when the printer has finished and is able to accept further commands and data. On the other hand, if a computer is being used in a real-time activity, that is, it does processing as and when information is presented to it, the initiative may come from outside the system.

As an example, a process-control computer may have an analog–digital converter (ADC) connected (Fig. 7.13). The ADC will be sampling the value of some variable in a process, which is available in analog form. As each sample is entered to the processor, it must carry out some procedure or algorithm on it and possibly output some results. Normally, the processor will be able to complete its work long before the ADC has converted another sample. Therefore, the processor may have nothing to do after it has completed the current task and can thus enter an idle loop. Here, nothing material happens apart from a frequent check on the ADC status.

Alternatively, the processor may handle several such ADCs. In this case, they may have data ready to be processed in an irregular and varying order. It is then incumbent on the processor to monitor all of them and service them as they become ready. When more than one ADC becomes ready at a time, a decision must be made as to which should be serviced first.

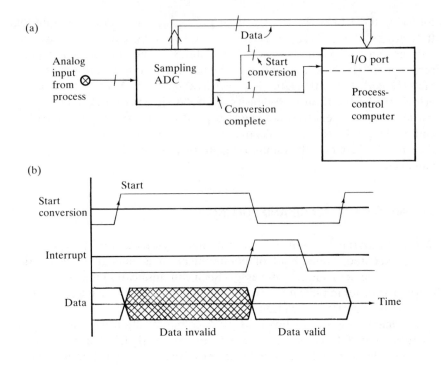

Fig. 7.13 Simple "real-time" system: (a) schematic; (b) timing.

A first-come–first-served system may be instituted or a priorities schedule devised. A decision may also have to be made, as part of the system design, on whether one device's demand for service may interrupt the processing associated with another device, or whether the processing of a given device must always be taken to completion.

Frequently, systems incorporate some or all of these combinations of process style according to the relative importance of the various devices and processes.

Central to this communications problem is device identification, and the burden this may impose on the processor. Let us assume we have a processor which is connected to a number of devices, any of which may demand service—or just wish to flag status to the processor. There are at least three ways to program the processor to acknowledge the existence of and react to an external signal.

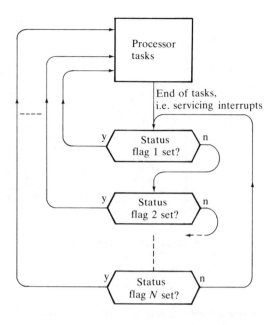

Fig. 7.14 Simple cyclic scanning of interrupt flags.

1. If the loading on the processor is light, it may be possible to simply put the processor into a "halt" state or idle mode in which the signal lines are scanned (Fig. 7.14). This is a common practice for microcomputers which, maybe, only have a simple keyboard or other low-speed data-entry form. The signals are grouped together to form a status word which can be frequently checked by software using input ports. They may also be ORed together to form a composite flag to simplify drawing to the processor's attention that at least one of the flags is active. If the latter, source identification will have to be carried out once the existence of some signal is established (Fig. 7.15). Although this system may be satisfactory in low speed microcomputers, it wastes far too much valuable processor time for most applications.

2. An alternative scheme is to scan the external signals, not on a virtually continuous basis, but less frequently. The frequency can be simply determined by considering how long any device can wait between becoming ready and the processor reacting to it. Between such scans, the processor can continue with "background" processing.

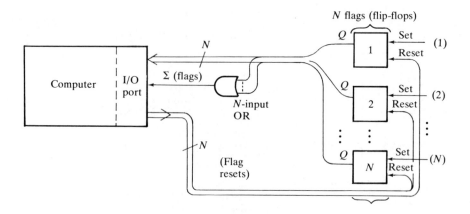

Fig. 7.15 Multiflag hardware (schematic).

However, the method is still wasteful of the processor both because of fruitless scanning of (frequently non-existent) signals and because it falls upon the processor to measure time intervals between scans. Nonetheless, this method is often used, but again it tends to be confined to lower-performance micro and minicomputers.

3. The ideal system is one in which the processor can continue with useful background processing at all times when no external signals exist. It should have to be diverted only when an external signal arrives. Ideally, the processor should react as quickly as possible to such a signal but should in no way be burdened with looking for it. Such a method is known as an *interrupt system* and can take many forms. In all cases, it involves some additional hardware which allows a signal, external to the processor, to assert itself and break into the background processing. The processor will then jump to a different program (the interrupt-service routine). Figure 7.16 illustrates the situation in some detail and provides an outline, both of the hardware involved and the corresponding software necessary. In essence, an interrupt is the same as a subroutine call except that the stimulus is an incoming logic signal rather than a special instruction embedded in software. A record of where the background program was abandoned must be kept and, like the subroutine call, this record is often kept on a stack (see Section 4.7). When the *interrupt routine* has been completed, the background program can be resumed by retrieving the old program-counter value from the stack.

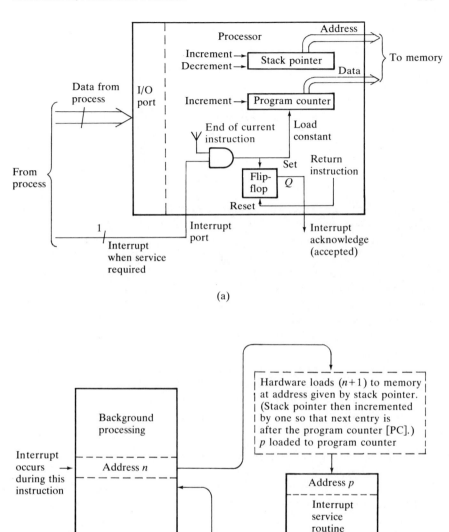

Fig. 7.16 (a) Hardware and (b) routine for handling an interrupt.

The interrupt hardware consists of logic to:

(a) record the existence of the external signal (in case it is a pulse rather than a level);
(b) operate the stack and program counter to enter and leave the interrupt routine and
(c) identify the external signal if there is more than one possibility. For a number of processors, the interrupt system frequently embraces some processor routines which might not be expected from what has been described so far. For instance, many microprocessors treat system-reset and event-timer expiry as forms of interrupt.

Examples (a) The Intel 8080 microprocessor has 8 interrupt levels each of which causes the program counter to be forced to a unique value. The original program-counter value is automatically recorded on the stack and the stack pointer advanced accordingly. One of the "interrupts" is "system reset" which forces the program counter to zero. Other interrupts force the program counter to other values. The 8080 follows the same procedure as many other microcomputers and mainframe machines by arranging that the first instructions of the interrupt service routines are clustered close together. It is impossible for a manufacturer to predict what memory space will be needed for each routine, so no attempt is made to allocate any. Sufficient room is simply given between each one to carry out one or two very elementary instructions, followed by a branch (jump). The address space allowed on 8080 is just 8 bytes between interrupt start-points. The branch will take the interrupt service routine wherever the programmer wishes, allowing the programmer to allocate memory space as he thinks fit.

(b) In contrast to the Intel 8080, the Motorola 6800 takes the above idea to its logical conclusion by having each interrupt "point" to a unique memory location wherein the programmer will have previously deposited the first address of his interrupt service routine. These are known as interrupt vectors (Fig. 7.17). Because they only act as pointers, these vectors can be in contiguous memory locations rather than spaced out.

In a practical computer, the interrupt system described so far for I/O forms only a part of a complete interrupt system for a whole machine. Other sources of interrupts can come from anywhere in the computer. Some examples are mains failure, parity error in any data transfer, algorithm and arithmetic overflows and interval timer expiry. Parity is often generated and checked in several parts of a computer such as in memory-to-processor transfers and memory-to-I/O transfers. If, during a transfer, a parity error is signalled, an interrupt is generated. As there may be more than one instance of parity checking, more than one interrupt flag may be used. These flags

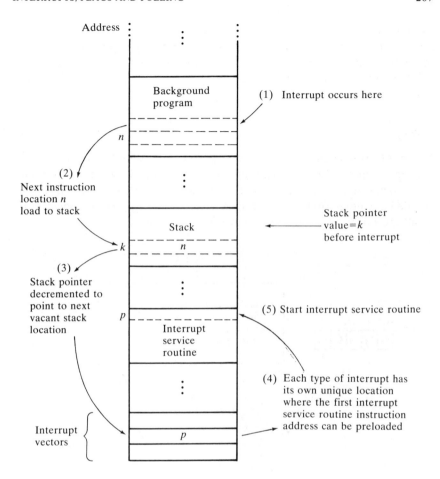

Fig. 7.17 Activity chart for Motorola 6800 interrupt vectoring.

may be assigned priority, e.g. a processor-to-memory failure will be considered to have priority over a memory-to-peripheral failure. The former would therefore be processed by an interrupt-service routine first, leaving clearing up of the memory-to-peripheral failure until later.

Apart from microcomputers and small minicomputers, many computers have distributed arithmetic. Fixed-point (integer) arithmetic may be carried out (executed) separately from floating-point or decimal arithmetic. (Frequently, separate, optional hardware units can be purchased for a computer to carry out more complex arithmetic.) Most arithmetic and algorithmic processes can give rise to overflows and other anomalous results if unsuitable data are used. Interrupt flags may be designated for each one so as to aid identification of the anomaly. In some cases, such interrupts are assigned priority. As an example, decimal overflow generally gives a quite unusable result which must be trapped immediately. However, floating-point significance error (see Section 5.11) may simply be logged, but otherwise ignored.

Polling

When interrupts can come from several sources, assigning priority gives a convenient method for overcoming the problem of which interrupt should be serviced first. Hardware in the processor can sort out which interrupt should be handled first and will also generate a single signal (the logical OR of all the interrupts) indicating that service is required.

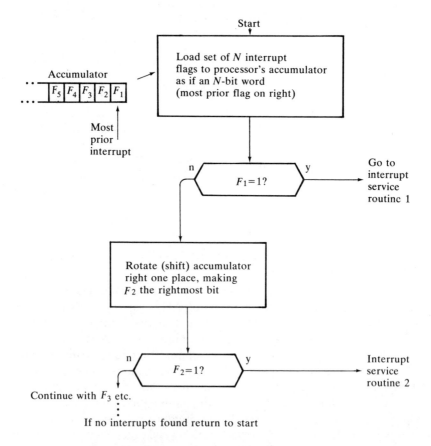

Fig. 7.18 Interrupt scanning with priorities assigned.

An alternative scheme is to use software to scan all the interrupt flags on a regular basis in a never-ending cycle—or, at least, when it is known that an interrupt has occurred somewhere. Such scanning is known as "serial polling". If it is combined with a system which indicates the existence (but not source) of an interrupt, a prioritizing system can be incorporated by suitable allocation of interrupt entry points. In Fig. 7.18, the rightmost bit entering the I/O port will be checked first and will therefore assume highest priority. All flags, having been assembled in the processor—say, in the accumulator—can be shifted using shift (rotate) instructions, in order to find the highest priority flag that is active. When the first interrupt found has been serviced, the shifting and checking can continue. This, of course, is

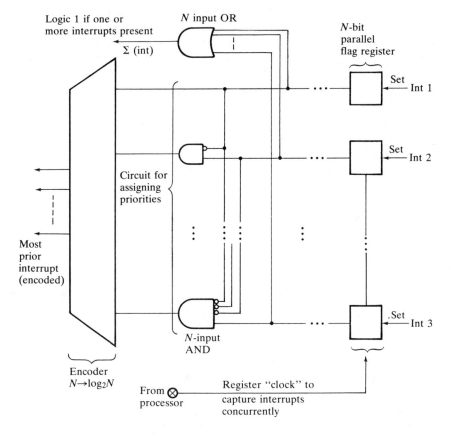

Fig. 7.19 Parallel polling of interrupts. (A similar circuit could be used to poll status.)

done only after it has been ascertained that there is still an outstanding interrupt to be serviced. Inspection of the logical OR of interrupts gives this information. If scanning is continued in this way, outstanding low-priority interrupts have a chance of being serviced. Otherwise, if the whole field of interrupts is sampled again, newly created, but higher-priority, interrupts will be serviced first.

The latter system *is* frequently adopted because some interrupts, such as "mains fail", must hold sway over all others and be serviced immediately.

The connection between sorting and handling interrupts in the sense of a polling system is easy to grasp. That the sorting may be carried out on a scanning basis makes it also easy to see why we use the term "serial polling". However, the term "polling" is applied to other, related, activities and may be carried out on a parallel basis. Unless there is more than one processor in a system, then clearly the handling and sorting of many interrupts must be done one at a time (serially). Nonetheless, the fact that one might, at least, *acquire* the status of many external devices, causes the term "parallel polling" to be used. A blur therefore exists between the terms parallel and serial polling and the distinction is only really resolved as far as the *transfer* of status is concerned rather than its *processing*. The fact that the system of Fig. 7.18 reacts to sampled status (interrupt) bits from their various sources (apparently concurrently) would qualify as parallel polling. However, there is no doubt that the processor's software carries out a sequential sort. Interrupt systems using priority logic can be considered as examples of parallel-polling systems if such logic has a parallel register to "capture" all the interrupt bits at the same time (Fig. 7.19).

7.6 BUS I/O SYSTEMS

We have already seen the several advantages of using bus systems within processors. The same principles can be applied at a higher level and involve complete subsystems, i.e. a computer, peripheral devices, control console/engineer's panel, instruments, data loggers, transducers and actuators. If a unified system of busing is adopted, all of these subsystems can be built with the same interface standard so as to be electrically compatible with each other and share an agreed communications protocol.

One example of such a system, which has enjoyed widespread adoption, is the Hewlett–Packard Interface Bus (HPIB) variously known as the general-purpose interface bus (GPIB) and Institution of Electronic and Electrical Engineers (IEEE) 488 standard bus (Fig. 7.20; see p.272 for explanation of abbreviations). Such a system, unlike the more rigidly operated system we saw involving the microprocessor in Section 7.2, permits any capable participant to be a system controller, talker or listener.

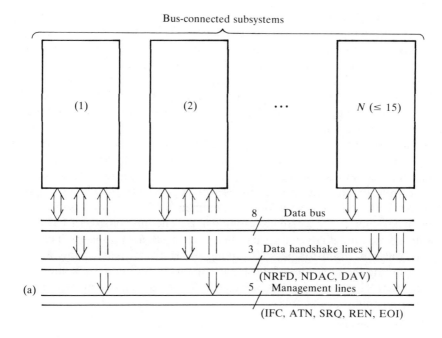

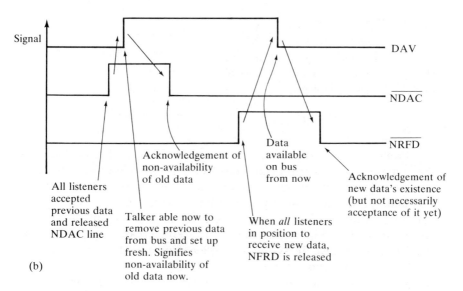

Fig. 7.20 IEEE-488 bus system: (a) schematic; (b) handshaking of data.

By software, it is even possible to change the roles of subsystems and make a participant, formerly only a listener, into a talker as well. Of course, at any one time, only one subsystem can assume command and be the controller as, indeed, only one can talk to the bus at a time. However, several may listen to the same talker, if required. The system is intended for laboratory rather than long-range communication use as it is only specified for a *total* bus length of 20 m. This limit is partly imposed by the fact that it uses a standard voltage-driven unbalanced line driving system to be TTL compatible. Furthermore, normal line termination is not observed. If greater line lengths were used, the system would be both more susceptible to interference and would have to operate at lower data rates to allow line reflections to die away between bytes sent. A good introductory description of the IEEE 488 bus can be found in Peatman (1978); however, some of the main parameters are worth mentioning here. The bus consists of 16 lines of which 8 are for data to give bit-parallel, byte-serial, data transfers. The same 8 can also be used for parallel polling the status of participants and for distributing the identities of those participants permitted to talk and listen. The other 8 lines are used to send handshake and management information. Their meanings are as follows:

Mnemonic	Full name	Comments
IFC	Interface clear	Used to initialize the bus (after power on).
ATN	Attention	Used to define whether data lines contain data or talker/listener assignments
NRFD	Not ready for data	Double handshake lines.
NDAC	Not data accepted	See Fig. 7.20 for waveforms.
DAV	Data available	
SRQ	Service request	Used to gain controller's attention
REN	Remote enable	Used to define local or remote control of a bus participant
EOI	End or identify	Used as part of parallel poll system (amongst other uses).

From the user's viewpoint, an interesting facet of this bus lies in the fact that, although a participant can use software to provide most of the data-transfer protocol and management responses, certain specific ones such as IFC and ATN require a very fast response which must be provided by hardware. Attention (ATN) requires to break in, in less than 200 ns—even interrupting a talker in mid-transfer! The essential reason for this response requirement is to give the system controller command of the bus in order to quickly retrieve status information or reconfigure the system because of some important event. The interface clear (IFC) command is less particular and requires only a 100 μs response. For many computers, this can be most conveniently met by feeding IFC to any interrupt port.

7.7 INPUT/OUTPUT DEVICES

Although it is outside the scope of this text to detail the internal operation of the many peripheral devices that may be connected to a digital computer, it may be instructive to look at their external characteristics, performance and data requirements for correct operation. Of particular importance is the enormous difference in operating speed between even the fastest peripheral devices and the central processor/memory. This leads to the possibility of connecting up to several hundred devices to the same computer.

1. *Teletype* (*TTY*) This most ubiquitous device must also be amongst the slowest normally coupled to a computer. In its simplest form, it is just an electric typewriter with the ability to send data via the keyboard or receive it to hardcopy (provide printed paper output). Data rates for both input and output are normally around 10–30 characters per second, although special versions do exist to push this rate beyond 100 characters per second. Frequently, a paper-tape reader and/or punch will be included which works synchronously with the keyboard and print mechanism.

The Teletype is an example of a device which is normally interfaced using asynchronous serial data transmission. When data are to be transferred, the I/O line, previously idling at logic 1, creates a start signal followed by a burst of 8 data bits. This is usually followed by a parity check bit and a stop signal. The 11 signals are of equal duration and are generated using some internal timing mechanism. Timing for a teletype is provided by a rotating drum running at, hopefully, constant speed: timing for the computer is provided by the computer's internal clock (suitably divided down to match the bit rate). Naturally, the two "clocks" must run at about the same speed to make error-free transfers possible. However, in order to prevent cumulative timing errors from creating problems, resynchronization of the clocks takes place at the beginning of every character sent (Fig. 7.21). In this method of

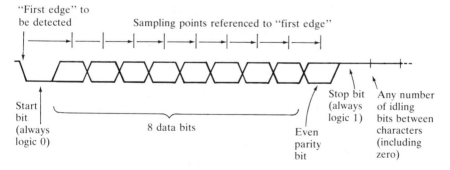

Fig. 7.21 Asynchronous character transmission timing (at 110 bauds=one 8-bit character in 100 ms).

transmission, the I/O line may operate on a voltage or current-loop basis (see the EIA RS232 standard).

Synchronization is normally achieved as follows:

(a)   A first logic 1 to 0 transition is detected and interpreted as the front edge of the start bit.

(b)   If the transmission is from TTY to computer, the computer will then start a clock and counter in which the clock may run at several times the baud rate of the TTY, thereby subdividing time within each bit. If, for instance, each bit time is subdivided into 16 intervals by using a clock running at say 16×110 Hz in a 110-baud system, then the center of the start bit would be reached at a count of 8. The centers of the 8-bit times (which would be safest place for the computer to sample the bits issued by the TTY) would be at counts of 24, 40, 56, 72, etc. By attempting to sample the bits at their centers, the maximum allowance is made for relative drifts in clock frequencies at the sender (TTY) and computer. In fact, based on 11 bits per character, a drift of $\frac{1}{2}$-bit time in $10\frac{1}{2}$ is permissible.

As every character is terminated with a logic 1 stop bit, resynchronization is possible on the front edge of the start character of each new character sent. However, in order to check that all is well, the computer would check that the last bit sent *is* a logic 1 and if it is, assume that it is the stop bit. If it is not, a framing error is signified and the transfer declared void. Of course, such a check does not trap a framing error with 100% confidence because data and parity can be logic ones as well. However, it is unlikely that many framing errors could occur over more than a few characters without detection taking place.

The great advantage of this method of data transfer is that only one I/O line or pair is used, making it very economical. However, there are several disadvantages:

1.   Transmission is serial and therefore slow: 1 character needs typically 11 bits including start and stop bits.
2.   Most computers handle 8 or more bits as bit-parallel entities. To send or receive serial asynchronous data requires special data format and (frequently) voltage translators. Format changing can be provided by special chips now available called universal asynchronous receiver/transmitters (UART) which, as the name implies, perform both the sending and receiving functions. They also generally contain facilities for checking the parity of the character sent and checking for framing errors.

The low speed of the teletype, plus its ability to be stopped after any character means that, in theory, only a single character buffer is required to separate it from the computer proper. (All devices need, at least, a single character buffer in order that data may be queued pending it being accepted by the computer). It is possible even for a 1 μs memory to be busy just when a 10 character per second teletype wants to enter data to it! The buffer is usually combined with the serial-to-parallel converter (shift register) which converts data from teletype serial to computer parallel (Fig. 7.22).

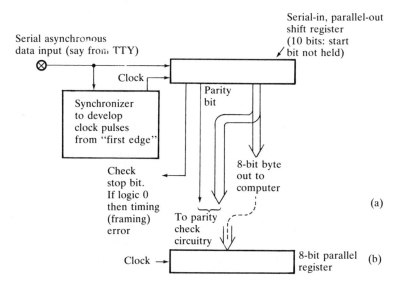

Fig. 7.22   Schematic of serial-to-parallel converter for asynchronous data: (a) single-buffered; (b) double-buffered.

Sometimes, a system called *double buffering* is used in which the assembled character is parked in a second buffer (parallel register) to await collection by the computer. By so doing, the serial-to-parallel converter is freed to accept more data. The second buffer can hold this character for almost the whole of the next character time without being pressed to accept another character from the serial-to-parallel converter (Fig. 7.22b).

2.   *Paper-tape-handling devices*   Paper-tape readers and punches can be obtained with character rates varying from 10 to 2000 per second for readers and from 10 to 200 per second for punches. They normally operate bit-parallel, character-serial and are therefore more easily connected to a computer than a teletype. As both readers and punches are normally designed to operate on a per-character basis, i.e. they can stop after handling

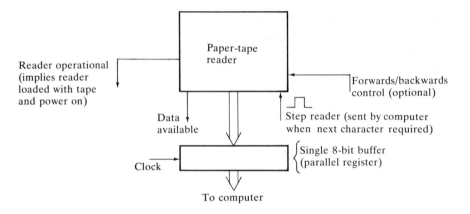

Fig. 7.23 Step-control paper-tape reader with single buffer.

any one character, a single character buffer is sufficient to queue data. A paper-tape reader is shown connected to a microcomputer in Fig. 7.23. Paper tape normally has smaller sprocket than data holes so that when the sprocket photocell fires, the data holes are centrally placed over the data-detecting photocells, thereby ensuring reliable reading. (If there were a possibility of data being read near the edge of holes, both skewing of holes and "hairiness" around the holes could give rise to unreliable reading.)

Not all readers are designed to operate on a per-character basis. Some readers are caused to operate continuously using a continuous drive command rather than individual steps. In this event, a full/empty flip-flop is associated with the buffer, which is set when the buffer contains valid data, but reset if not. If a character arrives from the reader when the buffer is still full—having not had its contents removed by the computer—the drive is removed and the reader halted. In order to give a reasonable stopping distance for the reader, this system usually incorporates double buffering in order that one more character may be read, without loss of information.

3. *Punched cards* Punched cards are normally of 80 columns by 12 rows. Each column contains a coded character. Cards can be read at rates of up to 2000 per minute using photocells to process one column at a time. Transmission of the data to the computer can either be on a per-character basis or in a burst of 80 characters after the whole card has been read. Even at 2000 cards per minute, the data rate is hardly high by computing standards, being

$$\frac{2000 \times 80}{60} \cong 2700 \text{ bytes per second.}$$

Card punches are very slow, handling around 100 cards per minute. Single and sometimes double buffering is used to queue data.

4. *Line and matrix printers* These printers very much outperform the Teletype and are worth some separate consideration. Matrix and "daisy-wheel" printers work on a per-character basis, like the Teletype, but advanced design gives them a performance up to 10 times that of the Teletype. Furthermore, some designs print on alternate lines in opposite directions (bustrophedon) to save on carriage return time.

The line printer, as its name implies, prints a line at a time. It has a separate print head (with a complete set of characters) for each character position on the paper. A line may consist of up to 160 characters, each with its own character disk. Print rates of 1500 lines per minute, or more, can be achieved. Other line printers, based loosely on the photocopying principle, are capable of 10 000 lines per minute. Even at 10 000 lines of 160 characters per minute, i.e. 27K bytes per second, the data rate is still low by main-memory standards.

5. *Rotating magnetic and other memories* So far, the devices discussed can all be operated such that a character can be transferred to the device without any destination information. This is simply because it is assumed that the next character goes to the next character position on the printer paper or paper tape, as appropriate.

Rotating magnetic memories have been considered in some detail in Section 4.4, where it was seen that destination information must be given to indicate track, sector, recording surface, etc. Such devices are mentioned in this section only because they are frequently connected to the computer as if they were peripheral devices, even though they may have no relationship with the outside world, as do printers and transducers. They are frequently connected to the computer via the I/O subsystems and use DMA methods.

The transfer rates and associated parameters of the various memories available are given in Table 7.1. Several of these memory forms can operate at data rates which begin to match the computer's main-memory rate. DMA methods then become essential to cut down on "bureaucratic overheads".

Bubble memories and holographic systems can be treated in much the same way as rotating magnetic ones, i.e. connected to the computer via the I/O system. For bubble memories, the organization is, because of the nature of their operation, serial. However, typical commercial memories are arranged to have a number of bubble "shift registers" of, say, 100K bits to over a megabit, working in parallel. This yields a system whose external characteristics are very similar to a head/track disk. In fact, many of these units are sold specifically as static memory replacements for disks. Typical

Memory type	Seek/latency time	Typical capacity	Data transfer rate	Comments
Cassette magnetic tape	Up to 30s (typical)	Up to 1M bytes/cassette	20–25K bytes/s	Several different versions including "mini" forms
Cartridge tape		Up to 3M bytes/cartridge	40–50K bytes/s	
Magnetic tape		2 to 3M bytes/reel	$\frac{1}{2}$M bytes/s	Tape speed up to 500 cm/s (200 in/s)
Floppy disk	0.6 s	$\frac{1}{4}$M bytes/disk	30K bytes/s	Based on 20 cm (8 in) disks. However 8 cm (5½ in) disks also available
Cartridge disk	50–100 ms*	5M bytes/cartridge	200K bytes/s	1 disk per pack
Removable disk	50–100 ms*	10–20M bytes/pack	200K bytes/s	6 disks per pack
Head/track disk	5–20 ms	1–40M bytes/unit	Up to 1M bytes/s	Disks not removable
Moving head multidisk unit	50–100 ms*	40–1000M bytes/unit	$\frac{1}{2}$M bytes/s	Disks not removable

Table 7.1   Magnetic memories. Capacity and performance

* Includes time for head movement.

units have a latency time of ½ or more seconds and capacities comparable with the smaller disk units. Therefore, at present, they are somewhat slower and less capacious than conventional disks, but they are expected to catch up and be even better than disks around 1985.

6. *Visual display units* (*VDU*) These units comprise a cathode ray tube (CRT) screen and a keyboard with an enhanced character set for screen management. The simplest form can just set up alphanumeric characters on the screen which can be edited either from the keyboard or the computer. When the keyboard is used, the data set up also goes to the computer.

A typical screen format consists of 40 characters per line and 24 lines. To provide flicker-free operation, the screen is scanned 25 or 30 times per second. This gives rise to a continuous (refresh) rate of $40 \times 24 \times 30 = 28.8$K bytes/second. In view of the low transfer rate of *new* information, i.e. from the keyboard, it is normal for the VDU to have its own 40×24 character memory, which is cycled to continuously refresh the screen. This can simply be a 960-character shift register. By so doing, the VDU-to-computer connection can be by the same low-speed serial asynchronous method used for connecting teletypes. Many VDUs are "plug-compatible" with teletypes so that they can form direct replacements. (*Note*: Generally, no hardcopy or paper-handling equipment is attached as standard to VDUs, so that there is a difference of emphasis in its use from the teletype.)

When data are transferred from the computer to the VDU, the shift register is simply updated at the appropriate cell and hence screen-character position. Again, no addressing information is needed, as a cursor is normally part of the screen display and indicates the current character position on the screen due for update. It is at this position that either a computer or keyboard-derived character will next be placed. Once this has been placed, the cursor is advanced. Most VDU keyboards incorporate cursor movement facilities in addition to the normal character set. This gives more flexibility for the placement of characters on the screen. Movements made available are up, down, left, right, move to top left of screen and carriage return.

More advanced (and more expensive) VDUs, called graphics terminals, also give drawing facilities. Vectors can be defined for placement on the screen using a minimum of parameters from the computer. For instance, to draw a straight line, one only needs the end points defined or one end plus length and slope. Curves can also be defined parametrically. The drawing information is stored in a shift register in parametric form. It is decoded into graphical vectors at each refresh. This greatly reduces memory capacity needed.

There are a number of low-cost graphics terminals available which do not draw true vectors, but instead have an extended alphanumeric character set which includes a number of shapes which can be placed in each character position. Use of combinations of these shapes can create rudimentary pictures.

A not unreasonable quality of picture can also be obtained on a commercial TV by resolving the screen into a 256×256 matrix. Each coordinate can be black or white (1 bit). A single 64K bit RAM (256×256=65 536) can therefore hold one complete screen's worth of picture information. Use of more that 1 RAM can make color pictures possible. This system (plus variants) is used by organizations such as the UK Open University. The University can issue commercial quality audio magnetic tape cassettes of pictures and text which are loaded to the students' home-based microcomputer. The microcomputer has an ultra-high-frequency modulator so that direct connection to a commercial TV is possible.

In some systems there is also a light-pen attachment. This consists of a photocell buried in a pen-like barrel which can be placed against the screen. When the raster scan passes the pen, it is activated, thereby telling the microcomputer where the pen was being pointed. It is a simple matter to update the RAM at the correct location to make a dot appear at that same place on the screen. Drawing then consists of slowly moving the pen about the screen to update a large number of RAM locations and give the illusion of "drawing on the screen".

EXERCISES

7.1 List and explain the main considerations involved in designing the input/output system for a computer. How does real-time computer operation affect design?

7.2 What instruction formats would be suitable for programmed transfer I/O instructions:
(a)   if a single accumulator processor were used;
(b)   if a scratch-pad (RAM) is available and transfers are to be allowed involving any scratch-pad location?

7.3 Develop an interface between a paper-tape reader and a microcomputer in which a 100 μs pulse is sent to step the reader. The reader replies with a logic 1 when data are available. Write software which will allow the reader to interrupt the processor when data are available and which creates a doubly buffered system. (The first buffer can be a register in the I/O chip and the second buffer can be a fixed memory location in the microcomputer.)

7.4 Assuming that a special chip (i.e. a UART) is not available to interface an asynchronous serial data source to a computer, write a flowchart for any computer which will input such data and check it. Checking should include parity, framing and double-buffer overrun errors. Electronic problems regarding the interface should be ignored.

7.5 The following components are available for use with a particular microprocessor and can all be memory mapped:
    UVROM: 1K byte chips
    RAM: 256-byte chips
    I/O chips: each servicing 1 port.
In addition, a 3-bit-to-8-line decoder is available. All components have a single chip-enable input.
    Design the address bus logic for a microcomputer having the following specifications:
(a)   2K bytes UVROM, 1K bytes RAM and 4 I/O ports;
(b)   8K bytes UVROM, 2K bytes RAM and 4 I/O ports;
(c)   16K bytes UVROM, 1K bytes RAM, 8 I/O ports.

In all cases, one UVROM should be located at the top of memory. (Addresses 0–1K.)

7.6 Repeat Exercise 7.5 assuming three chip-enable inputs are available for all chips and which can be logic 1 or logic 0 active in any combination.

7.7 Outline the design for a DMA system for 64 devices which can be connected to a 16-bit computer with direct access to 64K words of memory. Determine how many words per device have to be allowed, bearing in mind that some devices are rotating memories having 256 tracks split into 32 addressable sectors.

7.8 Design the logic of a synchronizer for use with an asynchronous serial data receiver. Assume the incoming data will be of 110 bauds/10 characters per second. What local oscillator error (positive and negative) can be tolerated without framing errors being incurred?

7.9 Design the logic for a discrete logic decoder which can accept standard 12-column punched-card code and output in 7-bit ASCII.
    Notes:
    1.   Card-hole positions are designated Y,X,0,1,2,3,....,9.
    2.   Card codes are 2 holes for letters: Y and (1–9) for A–I, X and (1–9) for J–R and 0 and (2–9) for S–Z. Numbers are represented by a single hole 0–9.
    3.   ASCII code can be thought of as 2 hex digits H(   ). Numbers 0–9 are coded H(30)–H(39): letters (A–Z) are coded H(41)–H(5A), with no gaps.

REFERENCES

Corsini, P. (1975), "*n*-user asynchronous arbiter," *Electron Letts*, **11**, (1), 1–2.

Dietmeyer, D. L. (1978), *Logic Design of Digital Systems*, Allyn and Bacon., Boston, Chapter 8.

Flores, I. (1970), *Computer Organization*, Prentice Hall, Englewood Cliffs, N.J.

Intel Corporation (1975), *Intel 8080 Microcomputer Systems Manual*.

Kuck, D. J. (1978), *The Structure of Computers and Computation*, Wiley, New York.

Motorola Semiconductor Products (1975), *Motorola Microprocessor Applications Manual* (6800).

Nashelsky, L. (1972), *Introduction to Digital Computer Technology*, Wiley International, pp. 519–65.

Peatman, J. B. (1978), *Microcomputer Based Design*, McGraw-Hill, New York, Section 5.10, pp. 299–311.

Slotnick, D. L. and Slotnick, J. K. (1979), *Computers: Their Structure, Use and Influence*, Prentice-Hall, Englewood Cliffs, N.J.

8 MICROCOMPUTER SYSTEMS

8.1 INTRODUCTION

It will be assumed that the reader, through first-level texts, will have some knowledge of microcomputer-based systems and their applications (Peatman, 1978; Hill and Peterson, 1978; Hartley and Healey, 1978). Apart from some recapitulation, which highlights the important similarities between microcomputer and conventional computer architectures (plus their essential differences), the chapter will be largely concerned with the technological and other considerations associated with the design of microprocessors and microcomputers. The important trade-offs available in system design, the main changes that occur as a result of going from 4- to 8- to 16-bit designs and the various features of the commonly encountered microcomputers will be discussed. Finally, trends in microcomputer design, component advances and transducer developments will be outlined.

Recapitulation

At the most fundamental levels, the microcomputer does not differ conceptually from any other general-purpose digital computer. The microprocessor—the "computational" part of the system—has a certain menu of instructions in its repertoire which would be familiar to anyone more used to mini and mainframe designs. The program material (instructions), constants and ephemeral data are retained in a memory form and executed in an orderly manner as in other computers (the stored-program concept). Finally, in common with conventional computers, various facilities are usually included which provide input/output transfers of data, processor interrupts and event timing.

There are, nonetheless, many and important differences between microcomputers and others. However, they are essentially a consequence of the technological limitations that are necessarily associated with having a processor—the microprocessor—formed on a single silicon die (Millman and Halkias, 1972). The combination of these limitations, together with the natural advantages of cost and flexibility of the microcomputer, has set a pattern of applications. Before considering these applications in detail, it is worthwhile to look at the technological limitations, to see how they have been ameliorated by system design and to study the various "styles" of microcomputer that have resulted.

Of the limitations, probably the number of leadouts that can be associated with each chip has been a consistent source of problems. This is particularly the case for microprocessors. The use of bus structures reduces the leadouts required by admitting bidirectional data flow (Fig. 8.1a). For an 8-bit microprocessor, 8 data leadouts are immediately saved. Another technique is to time-share the functions of leadouts. For example the Intel 8085 (Intel Corporation, 1978) has 8 leadouts which provide 8 of the memory address bits as well as an 8-bit bidirectional data port (Fig. 8.1b). Other time-sharing techniques are also possible, such as data bus/status output. However, for a given technology, there is a certain "bit rate" that can be supported by each signal leadout. It therefore follows that, unless non-time-shared operation of a leadout is going to result in the leadout being under-utilized, then time-sharing will not improve the chip's overall throughput in bits/second. Furthermore, time-sharing can also cause additional leadouts to be necessary to define the use of a leadout at any time. It can also lead to more chips being necessary to support the basic device. For instance, if time-shared data and address leadouts are used, latches, external to the microprocessor, will be needed to hold the address whilst data use the bus. A "latch-strobe" signal will have to be generated by the microprocessor to synchronize the latches with the microprocessor's microprogram (Fig. 8.2). Despite these shortcomings, bus structures are frequently used in microcomputer systems and, not infrequently, leadout time-sharing.

A characteristic of microcomputers which greatly distinguishes them from conventional systems is the use of semiconductor ROM for program retention (storage). This does not imply that the much cherished computer concept of having program and data material cohabiting in a single memory space has been abandoned. The normal microcomputer system has only a single memory *address space*—typically 64K bytes—but both ROM and RAM devices share this address space. ROM is used to hold the program and system constants—RAM holds the ephemeral data which are to be processed.

One of the great advantages of microcomputers is a hardware cost saving. This could be completely negated by the use of rotating electro-

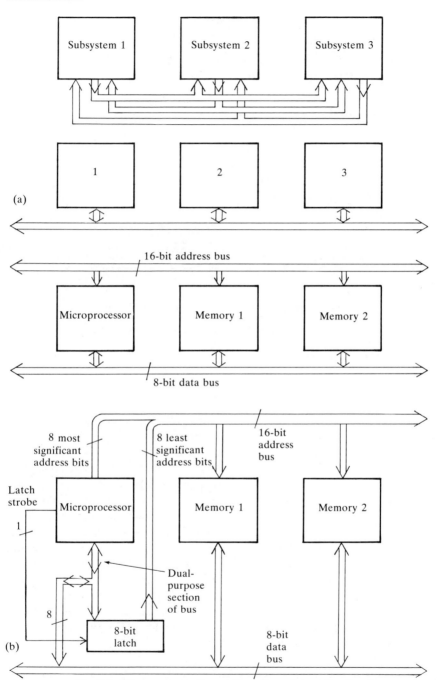

Fig. 8.1 Microcomputer bus configurations: (a) unidirectional vs. bidirectional bus systems; (b) part address/data bus time-sharing.

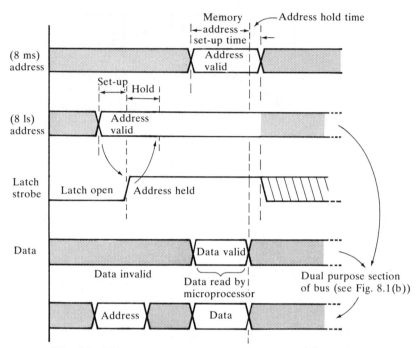

Fig. 8.2 Microprocessor READ cycle where time-sharing.

mechanical or similar memories to hold programs in a nonvolatile form (that is, data are not lost when power supply is removed). As, at the time of writing this text, a nonvolatile RAM has yet to appear in commercial quantities, it is not surprising that low-cost microcomputer systems have tended to contain fixed programs, held in ROM. For a large number of applications, restriction to fixed programs has not proved a disadvantage, if calculators, TV games, simple process controllers, "intelligent" instruments, domestic appliances and other consumer goods are considered. Where a restriction has been felt, it has usually been possible to enter small amounts of program information parametrically, just before run time. In a sense, the use of double key actuations in a calculator is an example of this. In a simple calculator, the fixed, firmware, program implanted in it causes a fixed reaction to any key pressed. That is, depression of a given key causes a fixed routine to be entered to, say, evaluate the tangent of an angle. However, some keys can be arranged to change the use of other keys so that, for instance, an "arc" key pressed before "tangent" can cause "arctangent" to be evaluated. Use of "arc" causes a different routine to be entered when "tangent" is depressed

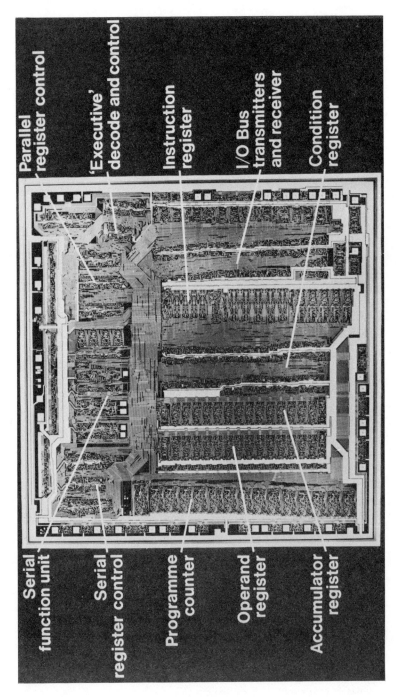

Parallel register control

'Executive' decode and control

Instruction register

I/O Bus transmitters and receiver

Condition register

Serial function unit

Serial register control

Programme counter

Operand register

Accumulator register

Layout of a 16-bit bipolar microprocessor – the Ferranti F100L. Many of the features on this chip are only a few microns wide, for which very closely controlled photographic and manufacturing processes are vital. (Courtesy Ferranti (UK) Ltd., Bracknell, Berks. UK.)

from that when only "tangent" is used. In effect, separate (read-only) programs have been implanted in the firmware for each *combination* of key actuations. Therefore, although the calculator is still fixed in terms of its repertoire, its flexibility can be increased by having a number of fixed programs, the *choice* of which is open to the operator through the use of key combinations (Hewlett–Packard Co., 1979).

Most microprocessors, like most conventional computers, have a fixed menu of instructions implanted at manufacture. Therefore, taken in concert with the remarks above about fixed program operation, it can be seen that most microcomputers are used as sequencers with fixed (micro) instruction sets at two levels (Fig. 8.3). A limited number of microprocessors are offered by manufacturers as "microprogrammable", that is, the (OEM*) user is able to define his own instruction set (Moralee, 1979). Normally, this would be carried out as a one-off design process by the OEM for a certain product line—no attempt would be made to have each unit different because of the very high development and mask or programming charges involved. (In any

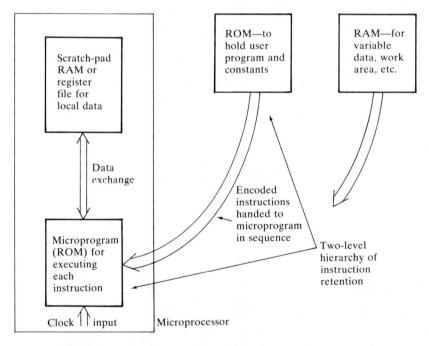

Fig. 8.3 Fixed-program microcomputer showing two levels of programming.

*Original Equipment Manufacturer—converts and assembles components and subsystems to usable products and systems.

case, very few OEMs attempt this sort of approach as the skill required to carry it through successfully is very great.) Furthermore, the chip manufacturer has as good an idea as anyone as to the most suitable instruction set for his product. The number of specialized products which need to deviate from a "standard" menu is relatively small. Microprogrammable microprocessors exist only for 4- and 8-bit systems (Fig. 8.4), and some are only part microprogrammable, such as the Texas Instruments TMS1000 series (Texas Instruments, 1976).

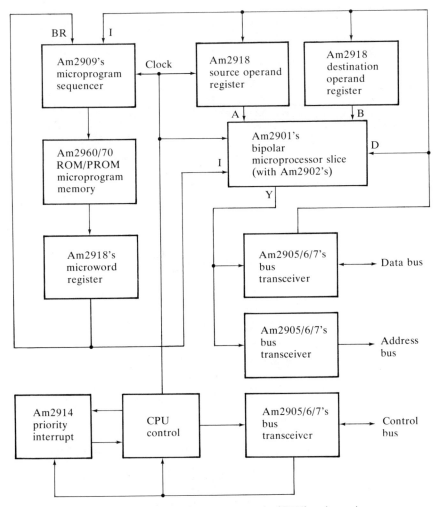

Fig. 8.4 Typical central processor unit (CPU) using microprogrammed high-speed bipolar microprocessor circuits (Advanced Micro Devices—AMD).

A range of microcomputers is available in single-chip form—the so-called "microcomputers on a chip". On a single die, typically 5–6 mm (0.2–0.25 in) square, all the components of a microcomputer are grown—microprocessor, clock source, ROM, RAM and I/O connections. For each basic design, there are usually several members to a family:

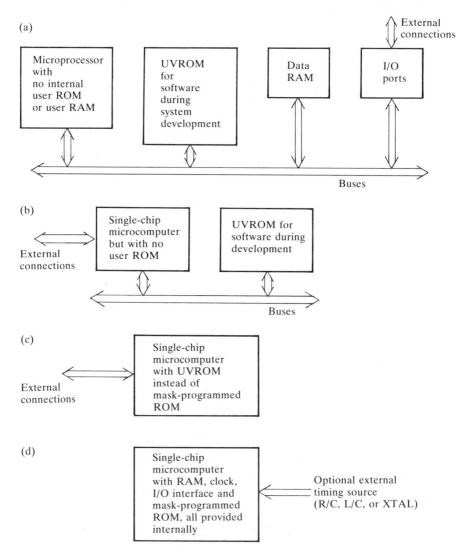

Fig. 8.5 A variety of microcomputers showing possible transitions from multichip development configurations through to single-chip volume products.

1. A multichip version which can be used for development purposes and maybe a limited production run; or a version with UVROM instead of mask-programmable ROM.
2. A single-chip version, but with no internal ROM. Again, the developer can use his own (maybe UVROM) to develop the system.
3. A single-chip mask-programmed ROM version for normal, minimal cost, production runs (Fig. 8.5).

An important facet of many single-chip microcomputers, such as the Intel 8748 (Intel, 1977) is the ability to have ROM and RAM added externally without either great difficulty or much waste of the original single-chip type facilities. This allows a single microcomputer design to cover as wide a range of applications as possible, from those which can be economically implemented in single-chip form up to those requiring considerable volumes of ROM,RAM and input/output connections.

The technology employed in the fabrication of microprocessor and support components can have a profound bearing on the performance and operational facilities offered. The range is enormous but a few examples will serve to show the possibilities:

1. Bipolar technologies, such as TTL, STTL, I²L and ECL make possible very fast microcomputers but the power required is often high in comparison with most MOS devices. For this reason, some bipolar microprocessors are available only in 1- or 2-bit "slice" form. In this form, the required word length is built up by concatenating a number of slice chips, i.e. 8×1-bit slice chips to fabricate an 8-bit unit. Slicing distributes the greater power requirements (and the greater die area per bipolar active element) over several chips. (Bipolar transistors can easily take 5 times the chip area of MOS designs because of their greater complexity, i.e. masking operations and hence mask lines.) Some manufacturers offer bipolar versions of MOS designs such as the Texas Instruments (TI) TMS 9900 as an I²L version of the MOS TMS 9900 (Texas Instruments 1975). The two designs are operationally identical and hence software compatible. Regrettably, they are not pin-for-pin compatible.

2. Standby power is an important consideration in some microcomputer designs, for protection against momentary and more permanent power failures. These are known as *brown-outs* and *black-outs* respectively (see Section 4.3).

CMOS provides a technology which dissipates power approximately proportional to operating speed. This comes about because use of complementary (totem pole) transistors gives a logic gate of about zero quiescent

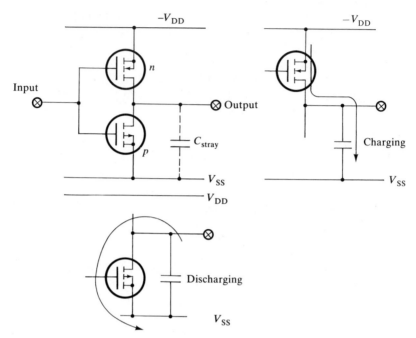

Fig. 8.6 Complementary (C-)MOS inverter showing loading effect of inter-gate wiring capacitance.

current drain in *either* logic state (Fig. 8.6). The only time when any current other than leakage is consumed is when the gate switches, and this is to charge stray circuit capacitances loading the output of the gate. As the energy required to charge a capacitor is dependent only on the change of potential difference and the capacitance, it follows that the energy required per switching operation is fixed. Therefore the power consumed by a CMOS gate is proportional to the rate of switching. If a CMOS microprocessor's clock is halted when power failure is detected, the power drawn is exceedingly small. If a whole microcomputer is fabricated in CMOS, it can be comfortably powered for weeks by a couple of mercury or nickel–cadmium (NiCd) cells. Furthermore, the standby supply-voltage tolerance is generally very wide. Microprocessor designs which use this technology include the Intersil IM87C48 and the RCA COSMAC (Peatman, 1978).

An alternative approach, used by manufacturers (maybe) already committed to other technologies, is the provision of a reduced facility under power-failure conditions. An example of this is the Motorola 6802 (Motorola, 1978), used with the 6846 ROM, I/O, timer chip. This two-chip microcomputer can support 32 of its 128 internally provided RAM locations using standby current amounting to only 8 mA, compared with the maximum operating supply current of 240 mA. So, provided data are shunted to these locations at power-failure time and processing is suspended, data can be retained using a battery standby system of only modest capacity.

3. The use of highly refined MOS technologies such as HMOS can greatly increase the performance of microprocessors without exorbitant increases in power consumption. P-channel MOS (PMOS) technologies of the early 1970s frequently incurred gate delays of up to 50 ns. In 1978–79, HMOS devices using MOS gate lengths as low as 4 μm and with gate delays of around 2 ns were possible. Such performance makes possible microprocessors having highly effective and complex instruction sets. (Complex instructions make the interface between high-level languages such as PASCAL (Wilson and Addyman, 1978) and BASIC (Cavanagh, 1978) and the machine-level languages much easier, by taking much of the software interface away from the compiler.)

8.2 MICROCOMPUTERS VERSUS CONVENTIONAL COMPUTERS

The microcomputer has found a very convenient niche in the spectrum of digitial processing as may be seen from the admittedly rather simplified groupings in Fig. 8.7. In the early 1970s, the groupings of Fig. 8.7 would have been more accurately represented by having gaps, particularly between the microprocessor and its immediate neighbors. However, the same technologies that have made the microprocessor possible (and subsequently enhanced it) have also had a bearing on other digital processors. The appearance of large and fast ROMs and RAMs and other memory forms has made possible more sophisticated discrete (hard-wired) logic systems. For

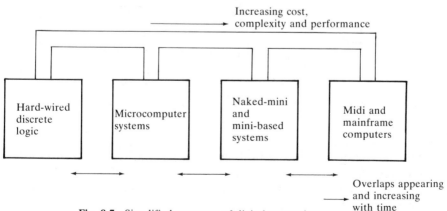

Fig. 8.7 Simplified spectrum of digital processing.

example, there are instances, particularly in simple process-control sequencers, timers and actuators, where neither the complexity nor the development cost of the microcomputer can be justified. Under such circumstances, an approach using ROM plus hard-wired logic has much to commend it. The types of structures that can be so formed are manifold but include, most importantly, ROM-based look-up tables for invariant or parameter-set sequences. The hardware structures that often evolve are based on that postulated by Wilkes and Stringer (1953) and which form the kernel of many microprogram controllers (Fig. 8.8). In a sense, such a

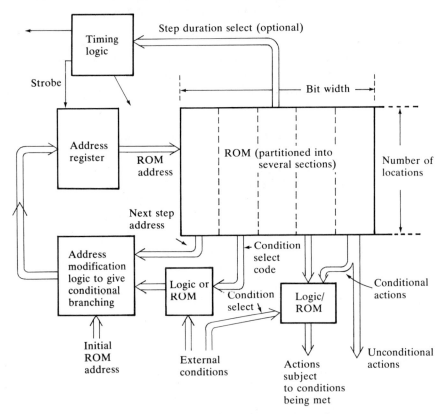

Fig. 8.8 Simplified ROM-based microprogrammer for use as a microprocessor controller.

system is merely a customized subset of a special-purpose microprocessor. However, both the customization and the use of discrete components can lead to greater performance than can be obtained by a straight microcomputer.

Technological differences

Considering the micro/minicomputer border of Fig. 8.7, it is clear that minicomputers have benefited from the advent of LSI technology.

Low-cost "naked" minis have appeared and are very attractive for small-systems design. They have made commercially possible many small computer and control systems that would have been unthinkable 10 years ago. Such "scaled-down" minis are frequently to be found as built in "super components" in slave-processor systems, word and graphics processors and the like. There is so much interchange of components and architecture now possible between micros and minis that it is often difficult to discriminate between the upper end of the micro range and lesser minis. This is illustrated by the fact that some of the larger micros such as the TI TMS 9900 (990/4) and DEC LSI-11 (PDP 11/03) devices are now incorporated into computer systems that are not only architecturally similar to minis and have a performance to match, but even form part of a range of computers based, ostensibly, on minis. At the mini/micro border, the only real distinction is whether the processor is monolithic (i.e. formed on a single chip) or based on having several chips on a PC card. Furthermore, the development time for a micro is usually somewhat shorter than that for a mini, with the consequence that marketed micro products often appear more "advanced" than mini products at any given point in time.

To illustrate the upper-end performance of micros, a shortlist of 16-bit devices is given in Table 8.1, together with some of their characteristics.

One way in which the "average" micro may be distinguished from the "average" mini is to consider the technological effects of having a monolithic (micro) or a multichip (mini) processor. If a single chip is used, then die (chip) area and dissipation can limit performance. The considerations are roughly as follows:

1. A monolithic design is limited to a low dissipation per gate for a given gate count and chip cooling method. Most gate technologies yield faster gate switching if the gate supply current (and hence dissipation) is allowed to rise. Higher currents mean faster charging of stray capacitances (associated with interconnections).

2. Nothwithstanding 1, a monolithic design keeps all interconnections very short and hence stray capacitances low. Therefore multi-chip designs, although allowing higher dissipation per gate by spreading the gates over several ICs, do not gain as much as might have been hoped. Stray capacitances, due to inter chip connections on a PC, can easily rise as high as 100 pF per connection.

Manufacturer/ device	TI TMS 9900	Intel 8086	Fairchild 9440	Motorola MC68000
Technology	NMOS	HMOS	I^3L	HMOS
Second sources	AMI	Siemens Mostek	—	Rockwell
Memory addressing	64K	1M	64K	16M
Registers	16*	8*	4+4	34
Languages supported	P,F,B†	M,F,C,P†	B,C,F,P†	P,F,C†
Mult/div	y	y	—	y
Relocation	y*	y	—	y
1979 (100 up) Price (approx.)	$30	$85	$75	$250?

Manufacturer/ device	Zilog Z8000	Ferranti (UK) F100–L	Digital Equipment Corp. (DEC) LSI 11–23	NS 16000
Technology	NMOS	CDI	NMOS	—
Second sources	AMD	—	—	—
Memory addressing	8M (Z8001)	64K	64K	16M
Registers	16*	2	8	8×2
Languages supported	F,B,C,P,Z†	CORAL	F,B	P ‖
Mult/div	y	y‡	y	y
Relocation	y	y	y	y
1979 (100 up) Price (approx.)	$100–140	$125	only avail.** assembled into complete microcomputers (1979)	Not known 1979

Table 8.1 Shortlist of 16-bit micros available 1979/80

Manufacturer/ device	Plessey MIPROC 16	Nat. Semi PACE	Data General mN602	General Instruments CP1600A
Technology	Bipolar	PMOS	NMOS	NMOS
Second sources	AME Norway	—	—	ITT, EMM
Memory addressing	64K	64K	128K	64K
Registers	256 (in memory)	4+3	4+3	8
Languages supported	PL MIPROC (Agol-like)	SM/PL (instructions NOVA-like)	F, B, NOVA instruction set	F
Mult/div	y		y	
Relocation	y			
1979 (100 up) Price (approx.)				

*But see text.
†B=BASIC, F=FORTRAN, P=PASCAL, M=PLM–86, C=COBOL, Z=PLZ.
‡Separate multi/div. chip connected via DMA.
‖Especially oriented to PASCAL.
**See also Western Digital MCP1600.

Table 8.1   Shortlist of 16-bit micros available 1979/80 (continued)

3. Although the very small gates used in current micros have little drive power, this is of no significant consequence provided all the connections are intra-chip. The result is that modern, high performance, microprocessors using refined technologies, such as HMOS and XMOS or bipolar ones such as I^3L, can achieve very high individual gate speeds achieved with emitter-coupled logic (ECL), Schottky-clamped TTL (STTL) or advanced STTL (ASTTL). (The very fastest ECL went subnanosecond in the middle 1970s).

As outlined earlier, the rather low leadout count of a monolithic processor is a major stumbling block for high performance, because of the tremendous data "funnelling" that takes place. Many microprocessor designs use multiplexed address and data leadouts to keep the leadout count down. From a simplistic viewpoint, this does not affect potential throughput—which might be defined as the product of signal leadouts and

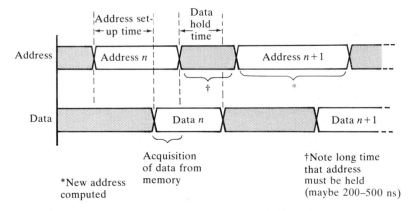

Fig. 8.9 Successive memory-read operations showing the relatively long time that the memory address must be held steady.

bandwidth in bits per second. However, the picture is not as simple as this because of the enormous difficulties associated with achieving anything approaching maximum throughput on any leadout (over a long period). An extreme case of this is the chip's reset input which may be used less than once per hour! However, an address or data leadout (Fig. 8.9) will be more consistently heavily used as it will be used at least once and possibly up to 6 times per instruction. However, even an address leadout will, from time to time, show periods of relative inactivity. Consider a memory-read cycle (Fig. 8.10). It will be seen that the address, once set up, has to be held for a long time, in comparison with the raw-chip gate performance, whilst the memory is being read. Furthermore, the delay in obtaining the data also means that

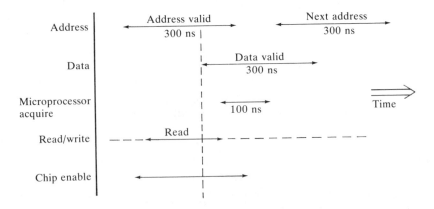

Fig. 8.10 Typical memory-read cycle for a microcomputer.

the data leadout is also poorly utilized. It is therefore not surprising that multiplexure of these lines into combined address/data lines is very attractive. The throughput *is* improved simply because leadout utilization is improved. Multiplexing leadouts does carry a couple of penalties:

1. An extra leadout or two will be needed to indicate to other chips whether data or address information is being carried by a leadout at any given time.
2. Off-processor chips, especially latches (Intel Corporation, 1978), are required to separate signals emitted by such a leadout. For our example, the address must be held in a latch for addressing memory, not only during the access time, but also for a short time afterwards, whilst the data are being read by the microprocessor. Such a latch must be supplied with a signal, from the microprocessor, to clock in this address (Fig. 8.1b).

Differences in application

The technological differences between the "average" micro and mini lead naturally to differences of application. We talk of "average" here because high-performance micros and lower-cost minis share application areas—indeed, some microprocessors have been designed specifically to fulfil the instruction sets of "parent" minis. (An example of this practice is Fairchild's 9440 "Microflame" which executes the Data General "Nova" minicomputer's instruction set.) The lack of overall throughput, lack of exotic data-handling instructions, inferior performance and lack of relocation (ability to move whole program blocks about memory without altering addresses in them) and other program-management facilities tend to relegate most microcomputers to single-user, dedicated applications. Where "performance" is required in a specific, but limited, sense, e.g. cathode-ray (TV) tube (CRT) refresh, then the possibility of using low-cost, add-on, hardware still makes the micro feasible. Examples of such applications, which illustrate comformity to such limitations, are process control and sophisticated sequencers, telephone-equipment monitoring systems and control, point-of-sale terminals, instruments (both for electrical and non-electrical measurements), data logging, teleprocessing and time-sharing-system front-end processors, data-base management front-ends, word processors and a host of single-user domestic and industrial applications. Examples are domestic-equipment control, gaming machines, manufacturing processes (control, management and statistics) and robotics. Many such systems could have been fabricated several years ago using either tailored, hard-wired logic or minicomputers (as most appropriate). However, they would have been too expensive both to develop and to produce and would have, in many cases, grossly under-utilized the processing capabilities of either logic or minis. The "average" micro has neatly filled the gap between logic and minis and opened up a wide variety of new markets and processes.

As a somewhat negative footnote to this section, the micro has, not surprisingly, also encroached on existing market places—not all electronic. A fine example is the mechanical-calculator market, which has withered into virtual non-existence in the space of 5 years.

One characteristic of many, but not all, micro applications, is the use of ROM-based "user" programs, i.e. programs which are fixed as a consequence of the product development. For the technologies extant at the end of the 1970s, this was not inconvenient, as ROM represented the only really economical nonvolatile, non-electromechanical data and program memory medium. As most microcomputers find applications in the low-cost market place, it follows that low-cost memory is essential. This indicates ROM. (Nowadays, some so-called nonvolatile RAMs (NVRAMs) (Intersil, 1979), based on multigate MOS technologies, are gradually emerging and will undoubtedly alter the situation.) ROM does not necessarily mean single-program because:

1. Several different programs can be burned into memory and chosen by key selection.
2. Data and parameters entered at run time can affect which computation is carried out.

The fixed-program concept seems to permeate through most of the very successful micro-based products such as calculators, TV games and other consumer products, small intelligent instruments, etc. These products also reflect another area of economy in micro hardware—economy of I/O systems. Transducers, code and voltage converters and the like can be very expensive and completely overshadow the cost of the micro. The most successful products have been very simple in terms of I/O, using just keypads and displays in the best examples. Calculators, TV games, for instance, involve an absolute minimum of real measuring equipment and electromechanical devices.

8.3 MICROCOMPUTER WORD LENGTH

The word length of a microcomputer may be defined as the maximum number of data bits that may be handled as a single entity in a single execution of a single instruction. Notice that the grouping is for data and not address bits and does not *necessarily* imply the width of the data bus. These points will be apparent if some specific microcomputers are considered:

1. The Motorola M6800 (Motorola, 1975) is considered an 8-bit unit because it handles 8-bit entities in arithmetic logical and I/O instructions. That it has a 16-bit address bus is irrelevant—that merely indicates memory-addressing capability.

2. Many single-chip microcomputers do not necessarily need an accessible data bus at all (external to the chip) so that the number of bits per data entity is the only measure of word length (Fig. 8.11).

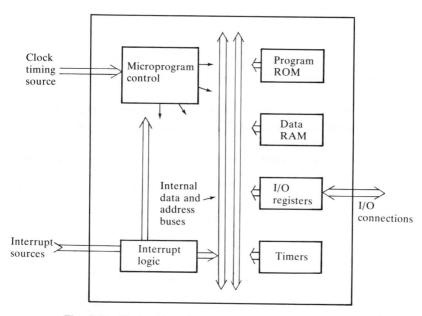

Fig. 8.11 Single-chip microcomputers often have inaccessible internal buses so that bus width can be freely chosen by the manufacturer.

3. It would be quite possible to have a micro with an 8-bit data bus but capable of handling double byte (16 bits) in a single instruction. Such a unit would lack the performance of a "true" 16-bit micro because of the need for 2 data-bus transactions per word accessed. However, it would still qualify as a 16-bit device. The term "maximum" is included in the definition of data bits as many microprocessors are capable of operating on shorter words with more economical instructions. As an example, the TI TMS 9900 (Texas Instruments, 1975) can address bytes as easily as 16-bit words.

The word length of a microcomputer has a profound effect on its design, cost and support components. Taking extreme examples:

1. The original microprocessor, the Intel 4004 (Peatman, 1978) was a 4-bit device, used a time-shared 4-bit bus for both data and addresses and, as a consequence, could be packaged in a low-cost, high-yield, 16-pin chip. However, it was a very slow device, due largely to bus multiplexure.
2. At the other extreme, the TMS 9900 is a 16-bit unit using an expensive 64-leadout frame and has separate 16-bit address and data buses. Amongst the many differences between these devices are very different word lengths and hence precision to which quantities can be held. Also the memory addressing capabilities are very different.

The difference in word length can have one of two effects from the applications viewpoint:

1. It can mean that 4-bit micros are used for "logical" operations rather than those for measurement, i.e. they will be used more in sequencers, process control etc.
2. It can mean that quantities, to be held to a certain precision, must be represented by, not one, but several words (probably stored in contiguous memory locations). 4-, 8- and 16-bit quantities are represented to precisions of 1 part in 2^4, 2^8 and 2^{16} respectively, i.e. approximately $\pm3\%$, $\pm0.2\%$ and $\pm0.0008\%$ (Fig. 8.12).

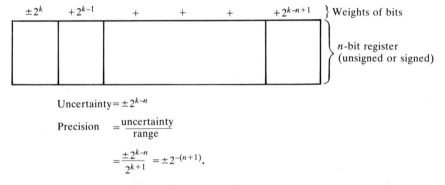

Fig. 8.12 Precision of n-bit digital numbers (signed and unsigned).

Eight-bit microprocessors are frequently used in process control, signal processing, sequence and data-processing applications—although for the latter, 2- and even 3-byte representation of quantities is necessary to obtain the required precision. Arithmetic, particularly the most complex operations involving multiplication and division, can be very slow to execute in multibyte form. This is despite the fact that most microcomputers have "carry" flags and other facilities that help to link one byte with the next more significant one during addition and subtraction. The loss of speed comes about not only because of the larger number of arithmetic operations involved (see below) but also because it is necessary for a significant number of data movements because of the lack of free registers in the CPU. If we compare the multiplication of a pair of 16- and 8-bit operands in an 8-bit microcomputer, it can be seen that each 16-bit addition and shift is now on 2 bytes and that twice as many operations are necessary to cope with the 16-bit multiplier (Fig. 8.13). A typical "software" multiplication on an 8-bit micro can take upwards of 1 ms. This can be compared with $20\,\mu s$ for a "hardware/firmware" one, which would be typical for a current 16-bit micro featuring multiplication in its instruction set.

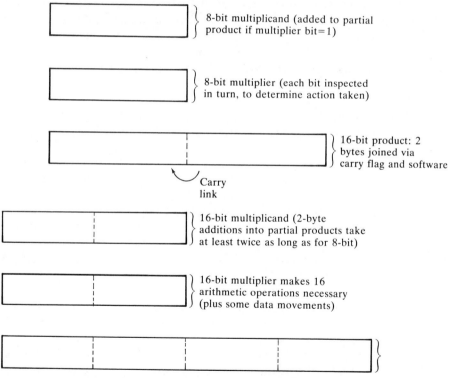

Fig. 8.13 Eight- and sixteen-bit multiplication in an eight-bit microcomputer.

With such great differences between the costs and capabilities of micro-computers of differing word lengths, it is not surprising that application areas, and therefore development techniques, are quite distinct. The 4-bit units were originally used in calculators and are now used in domestic equipment, consumer items and cheap process controllers—in fact, any-where that processor power or performance is of secondary importance to cost. The wide range of applications, each with a large market, made the 4-bit microprocessor the largest selling unit throughout the 1970s. (This was despite the fact that many more 4-bit units must be sold than, say, 8-bit ones, for the same market value.) Because a number of OEM users of 4-bit units are not themselves specialists in microcomputing (see applications above), it is not surprising that a considerable market has grown up wherein semicon-ductor manufacturers are asked by OEMs to undertake part or even all of the system-development responsibility for a product, including software development, mask design for ROMs, PLAs etc and, of course, quantity production of devices. Such a semiconductor manufacturer is TI who market the single-chip, 4-bit TMS 1000 series of microcomputers. (Simulators and emulators (see Section 8.6) are offered for in-house development work but the development is sometimes carried out, in toto, by TI.) Parenthetically, the TMS 1000 series is quite different from conventional micros insofar that it has:

1. user-definable instructions through user-definable microcode; and
2. two PLAs which must be developed along with the user ROM.

This level of flexibility makes conventional EPROM or UVROM type implementation unattractive, because PLAs, microcode ROMs and user ROMs would have to be field programmable and erasable. Therefore the TMS 1000 series is offered only in mask-programmable form. It is highly suitable for the low-speed, high-volume, applications cited above. Finally, several preprogrammed versions of the TMS 1000 series are available which do not need development. They include units suitable for the high-volume markets such as microwave-oven control, etc.

The 8-bit microcomputer has proved very popular in a wide variety of applications, stretching from the point at which the performance of the 4-bit units is inadequate. Examples are complex process and manufacturing pro-cess control through to real-time control and signal-processing applications, at the top end. For relatively low-speed process control, the Fairchild F–8 series of 8-bit micros offers more performance than is obtained by 4-bit units. There is also a single-chip version available, although it is not designed for RAM and ROM expansion in the same way that the more powerful Intel 8748 or Zilog Z8 are.

No 8-bit units compare very favorably even with the lower end of the mini spectrum, either in terms of raw processing power or data-handling capacity. It is therefore not unusual to see the performance and capabilities of 8-bit units enhanced by the addition of peripheral hardware. Examples of such hardware are add-on fast-memory units for refreshing CRTs (Intel Corporation, 1978) (whilst leaving slow updating of such memory to the micro); peripheral arithmetic units such as calculator chips, hardware multipliers (TRW LSI products, 1979) trigonometric look-up tables (burned into ROMs), shift registers (for correlators and filters), analog integrators (connected via ADCs and DACs) and a host of other specialized hardware. The resulting structures all tend to have certain characteristics in common:

1. The fast processing is taken up by this add-on hardware, thereby relieving the microprocessor. However, these add-on units are relatively inflexible and "unintelligent".
2. The organization and management of the system, as a whole, is the microcomputer's responsibility. These tasks include handling of data and parameters, acceptance and conditioning of initial conditions, collection and organization of results, display processing, operator-panel interface, management of interfaces to other equipment, and preparation of data for, and retrieval of results from, the add-on peripheral hardware. Generally, none of these latter activities requires great processing speed as they are not generally "real-time" activities. (Otherwise, they only have to match human or slow mechanical speeds.) The "intelligence" of the microcomputer is well suited to such tasks.

A final task, which is also executed by the micro and which also does not require extremes of performance, is instrument self-check, i.e. the exercising of the various sections of the system to ascertain that it is in working order before use. This is usually achieved by the running of a set of programs using fixed data stored in the instrument's memory. The results can be checked against known results which are also held in the instrument's memory. Care has to be exercised in the choice of such programs so that, on the one hand, the system is fully exercised, but on the other, does not take too long to carry out.

The 16-bit microcomputer fills the gap between the 8-bit units (with their limited basic precision and processing capabilities) and the minicomputers. They are very much more expensive than 8-bit units for the following reasons:

1. They are far more complex: compare the Motorola M6800 with about 5000 and the MC68000 with 68000 active devices.

2. The manufacturing costs are higher, the technology is more refined and the yield of good devices is lower.

3. Testing costs of complex devices is far higher as the combinations of tests to be performed soars with active device count.

4. 16-bit units are newer and manufacturers are at an earlier stage in their production-learning process.

5. Because manufacturers want their products to have a long life, i.e. be specified for OEM equipment for many years, the units are deliberately designed to "stretch" the technology to the limit, at the beginning of the product life cycle. Around 1979, most 16-bit units fell into this category and were therefore very expensive (from $50 to $200 for 100 up at 1979 prices).

6. Support chips, such as memory, I/O interfaces, interrupt processors, timers, etc, are more expensive—either to accommodate 16-bit operation or because they must be that much more flexible and powerful to justify inclusion with a powerful microprocessor. (Some 16-bit microprocessors require extra support chips, anyway, to demultiplex data and address buses at the microprocessor. Otherwise, some microcomputers require additional chips to provide system control when complex systems are built up, i.e. with large memories and numerous I/O connections.)

The 16-bit microcomputers have architectures which, in most cases, are undeniably "mini-like". This can be seen in terms of the instruction sets, the support chips and the processing style adopted.

The instruction sets tend to reflect the fact that high-level languages are likely to be used rather than assembly languages (as for 4- and 8-bit units). As a consequence, they offer instructions which make multiprogramming (several RAM resident programs, each given access to the processor as circumstances permit) and high-volume general data-handling much easier. Examples of such instructions are multiply, divide, decimal arithmetic (including ASCII format), byte and string operations (including translation), string search and compare instructions and data-stacking facilities. Special support chips, which can be directly interfaced to the microcomputer data and address buses, include:

1. direct memory access (DMA) controllers for fast I/O to memory data transfers;

2. CRT interfaces for visual display units (VDUs), including refreshing and code conversion for raster scan systems,

3. direct interfaces to standard buses such as the Hewlett–Packard interface bus (HPIB, GPIB, IEEE 488 bus) (IEEE, 1975) and

4. fast arbiters for priority resolution of request clashes between I/O devices and bulk memories.

Aspects of 16-bit processing which reflect a relationship with mini architecture are:

1. Use of memory-to-memory instruction architectures so that interrupts can be quickly processed by changing a pointer value rather than moving the contents of CPU registers out of the CPU to make room for those of the interrupting program (Fig. 8.14). The TI 9900 processors use this technique.

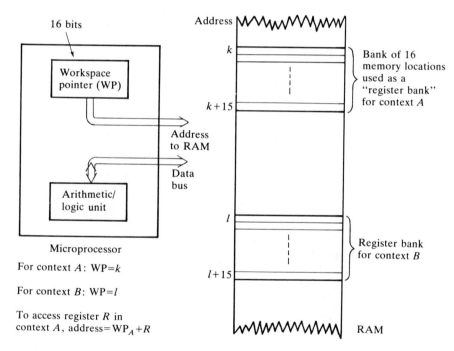

Fig. 8.14 Use of a "workspace pointer" to access memory-based "register banks" in a memory–memory architecture.

2. Use of base and index addressing for program code and data so that dynamic relocation is possible, and the use of memory as a stack area of almost unlimited depth (Fig. 8.15).

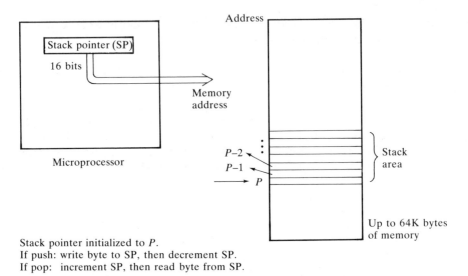

Stack pointer initialized to P.
If push: write byte to SP, then decrement SP.
If pop: increment SP, then read byte from SP.

Fig. 8.15   Use of memory to give a stack accessed by a stack pointer.

8.4 INSTRUCTION FORMATS AND INSTRUCTION-CODING METHODS

For whatever purpose it is intended, it is possible to break down (decode) a computer instruction into two portions—the operation code (op-code) plus an address field. The address field may have only one component if all addresses, bar one, are implicit. For instance, in arithmetic instructions, the use of an accumulator can reduce the number of address-field components to 1 by using it both for the source of one operand and the result destination. However, many of the larger microprocessors do use more than one address component because of the flexibility it gives to the programmer. This may be in the form of multi-accumulator or scratch-pad memory banks.

Alternatively, use may be made of a "memory-to-memory" architecture. In this, areas of memory, say 16 contiguous words, are given the status of processor registers. They can take part in arithmetic operations in the same way as the registers of a register file or scratch-pad. Because they need addressing as memory locations, a full 16-bit address is needed to access any one of them. Because the registers are in blocks, it is normal to define the address of the first one fully by way of a 16-bit "workspace pointer register" and for references to any of the sixteen registers to be defined by its position *relative* to the first one. Use of the workspace pointer as part of the address is implied and therefore is not needed as part of the instruction. A microprocessor which uses this technique is the Texas Instruments TMS 9900.

Each block of (16) registers is associated with a "context" or "interrupt level". Switching contexts merely means exchanging one workspace pointer for another. No other data movements need be involved.

The manner in which instruction formatting is tackled in microprocessors is dependent on several factors, of which word length and practices adopted in the microprocessors in a given manufacturer's range are amongst the most important. On the first point, the word length of a microcomputer refers specifically to the basic *data* field length. This is important because micros, particularly 4- and 8-bit ones, have data and address buses of differing lengths. As examples: the TI TMS 1000 handles 4-bit data (internally) but has a 10- or 12-bit address bus. Instructions in the TMS 1000 are fixed at 8 bits. A typical 8-bit design is the Motorola M6800 which uses an 8-bit data bus, a 16-bit address bus and handles instructions of 8, 16 or 24 bits (1, 2 or 3 bytes). With regard to manufacturers' practice, instruction formats for the Intel 8086 show a deliberate move to make it an upwards-compatible version of the 8-bit 8080 and 8085 devices. On the other hand, the Motorola MC68000 and Zilog 8000 16-bit micros show a break-away from the original M6800 and Z80 designs, respectively.

Comparing practices in 8- and 16-bit units, it will be seen that subtly different design pressures have been at work. The 8-bit micros have a 16-bit address (rather than the obvious 8) simply to give a reasonable ROM/RAM address range (space). Although an 8-bit bus could have been used both for data and address handling (in a time-multiplexed mode) with a consequent saving of leadouts, a performance penalty would have been incurred. Furthermore, latching of the first 8 bits would have been necessary, pending the arrival of the second 8 bits. As an example, the Intel 4004 micro used a system like this in which 12-bit addresses were built up in ROM and RAM address generators from 4-bit components sent down the bus from the microprocessor. This address assembly was actually carried out in the memory chips for the 4004. This made the ROMs and RAMs special chips, not compatible with more normal micros. (Where address assembly or address/data demultiplexure has to be carried out on more conventional micros, additional latch chips are used to keep ROM and RAM design standard.)

Generally speaking, 16-bit micros are provided with 16-bit address buses giving the same 64K bytes memory access as 8-bit micros. (It should be noted that, in respect of using the letter K to indicate address space or memory size, the value 1024, i.e. 2^{10} is implied. Therefore 64K really means 64×1024 or 65 536. This should not be confused with the term "hex K" or 1000_{16}, which equals 16^3 or 4096 in decimal.) The TI TMS 9900 and SBP 9900 micros are fabricated on a 64-leadout frame in order to accommodate separate 16-bit data and address buses. On the other hand, the Intel 8086 uses a part-shared data and address bus so as to keep the leadout count to 40.

The argument in favor of a 40-leadout micro must be balanced against the need for latches to separate the data and address buses outside the micro. As most support components for micro systems, e.g. ROM and RAM, are based on 4- and 8-bit organization, it raises the issue, for 16-bit microprocessors, as to whether memory access should be based on 8-bit (1-byte) or 16-bit (2-byte) units. (The fact that memory accesses are based on units of 1 byte does not invalidate assigning the label "16-bit" to a microprocessor if it can handle 16-bit operands in a single instruction.) The trend of manufacturers of 16-bit micros, understandably, has been toward 16-bit accesses using 8-bit ROMs and RAMs in pairs. The obvious disadvantage of such an approach is that minimum systems are more complex than strictly necessary. Greatly outweighing this is the argument that 16-bit devices are meant for the top end of the market and 16-bit accesses give twice the data per access of 8-bit ones. The minimum system is therefore of relatively little interest. Again, comparisons between manufacturers' practices are of interest because of the often contradictory pressures of upwards compatibility of products and processing performance. The Intel 8086 accesses 16-bit words from memory but retains the byte as the minimum indivisible instruction unit. Any odd unwanted bytes accessed are not discarded as the 8086 micro uses a 6-byte instruction queue for pending instructions (pre-fetch). The approach based on bytes means that software written for the 8-bit Intel 8080/8085 micros can be run on the 8086 using just those 8080/8085 instructions which have been copied into the 8086 design. Based on bytes, instructions can have any length from 1 to 6 units. This means that instructions can have been developed with relatively little regard for the number of bits needed to define them. (A poorly composed n-byte instruction need only waste 7 bits in the last byte used. 16-bit architectures could waste up to 15.) The Intel 8086 has followed the typical 8-bit micro practice of using a fixed-length 8-bit op-code as the first part of every instruction (but variable-length instructions of variable format). This op-code not only defines what sort of instruction is to be executed, i.e. add, branch etc., but also the format of the remainder of the instruction and addressing modes to be used. 8086 instructions can therefore be defined as being of fixed op-code length but variable instruction length.

The Texas Instruments TMS 9900 has adopted a rather different approach. Instruction accesses to memory (fetches) are based, like the 8086, on 16-bit units, with a few 32-bit accesses (immediate addressing mode). However, instructions have a minimum length of 16 bits. This simplifies fetching, especially for a system which can align instructions on even byte boundaries, because identical memory addresses can be sent to the two memory modules, which each supply one byte of the instruction (see Section 4.6). The TMS 9900 is not tied to any previous 8-bit system, and therefore, in effect, can look at 16 bits as the basic unit—much as many minicomputers do. In order to make the most use of 16-bit instructions, both in terms of the number of different instructions offered in the menu and address-field lengths, the TMS 9900 uses variable rather than fixed-length op-codes to make differing address field lengths possible in the (largely) fixed instruction length available (Fig. 8.16).

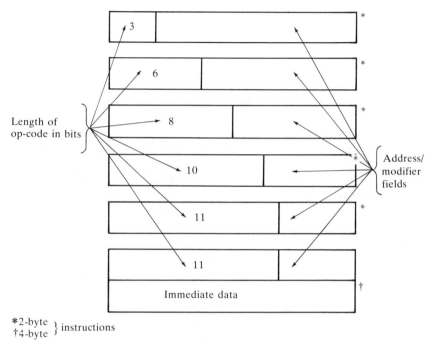

Fig. 8.16   TMS 9900 instruction formats indicating use of variable-length op-codes. (Courtesy Texas Instruments Inc.).

An instruction having a variable-length op-code must make it quite clear where the op-code ends and where the address fields begin. Furthermore this determination must be easy to implement in the processor at instruction fetch/decode time.

Variable-length op-codes

Generally speaking, there is no restriction on the pattern of 1s and 0s that may be used in address fields in an instruction. Therefore, instructions with short op-codes must differ from those with long ones in the part of the instruction which *both* types of instruction use as op-code. If this rule were not observed, a short and long op-code might be indistinguishable, given an unlucky pattern of 1s and 0s in the address field adjacent to a short op-code. Such a restriction reduces the number of combinations of distinguishable op-codes, as illustrated in Table 8.2.

Op-code	Instruction
1-bit 1 x x x x	1 address field ———————————————
2-bit 0 1 x x x	0 1 address field —————————————
3-bit 0 0 1 x x	0 0 1 address field ———————————
4-bit 0 0 0 1 x	0 0 0 1 address field —————————
5-bit 0 0 0 0 1	0 0 0 0 1 address field ———————

Table 8.2

Here, a 1-bit op-code has been set arbitrarily at 1. It therefore follows that all op-codes of length greater than 1 must be prefixed by a 0. If a 2-bit op-code is to be available, it must start with a 0. However, as it must be distinguishable from op-codes of length greater than 2, one possible 2-bit combination must not be used, so that that combination can be used as a prefix for op-codes of length greater than 2. This leaves only one combination of 2-bit op-code, say, 01. The rest of the table follows by induction. It is clear that very few different op-codes can be produced by this method, although it is equally clear that the logic needed to determine where the op-code ends and the address field begins is easy to design.

The system described fails to find many combinations because every op-code length from 1 upwards is being used. If gaps are left between each op-code length used and the next one used, the number of combinations rises rapidly. If we consider using only op-codes of length 1, 3, 5, etc., then 3 combinations of each op-code length (apart from the first) can be found (Table 8.3).

Although a large number of bits need to be committed to the longer op-codes when gaps are left in the lengths used, in the long run, many more op-code combinations become available and it is therefore always preferable to have gaps. In general, if the gap between op-code lengths is n bits, then 2^n-1 combinations of op-code are possible at each length (after the first). There are many, fairly trivial, variations on these coding schemes. Some use unique combinations of bits to make it easy to ascertain where the op-code ends. The TMS 9900 uses a system of op-codes with a simple end-of-op-code combination which can be easily detected. It also has variable-size gaps between op-code lengths to give the number of combinations at each length that is required for the instruction set (Fig. 8.17). The TMS 9900 uses

Op-code	Instruction
1-bit 1 x x x x x x	1 address field ———————————
3-bit 0 1 1 x x x x	0 1 1 address field —————————
0 1 0 x x x x	0 1 0 address field —————————
0 0 1 x x x x	0 0 1 address field —————————
5-bit 0 0 0 1 1 x x	0 0 0 1 1 address field ———————
0 0 0 1 0 x x	0 0 0 1 0 address field ———————
0 0 0 0 1 x x	0 0 0 0 1 address field ———————
7-bit 0 0 0 0 0 1 1	0 0 0 0 0 1 1 address field —————
0 0 0 0 0 1 0	0 0 0 0 0 1 0 address field —————
0 0 0 0 0 0 1	0 0 0 0 0 0 1 address field —————

Table 8.3

op-codes as short as 3 bits to leave sufficient bits for a complex address field (Cavanagh, 1978). However, some op-codes use up to 11 bits to give a larger number of op-code combinations at the expense of address-field bits. The variable op-code length system can have the disadvantage that many more combinations of instructions are needed for instructions which need a long address field and are therefore stuck with a short op-code. The shorter op-codes tend to present fewer combinations. In the case of the 9900, the shortest op-code is 3 rather than 1 to offset this limitation. In addition, some 9900 instruction bits are used as address modifiers, e.g. to discriminate between byte and word-oriented operand formats. Strictly, these form part of the address field in the terms discussed above. However, in practice they do extend the number of combinations of instructions that can be offered.

Although the 9900 uses variable-length gaps between its op-codes, decoding of instruction length is quite easy. A possible solution is shown in Fig. 8.18.

Another micro that uses fixed-length instructions with a variable-length op-code is the 4-bit TMS 1000. As a comparison, it uses an 8-bit instruction with op-code lengths of 2, 4, 6 and 8 bits. The latter, of course, leave no room for an address field at all and are therefore of the "implied-address" type. Fig. 8.19 shows the abbreviated instruction set of the TMS 1000, together with the instruction formats.

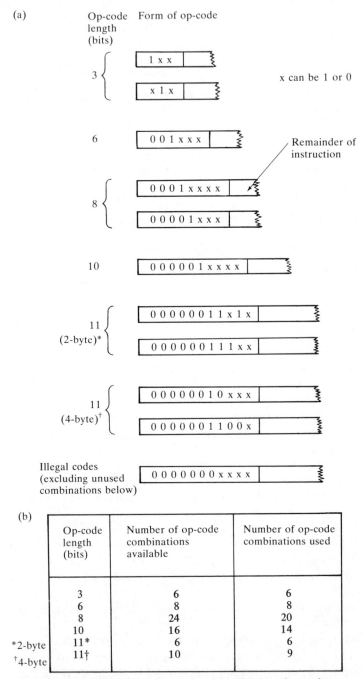

Fig. 8.17 TMS 9900: (a) op-codes; (b) utilization of op-code combinations. (Courtesy Texas Instruments Inc.).

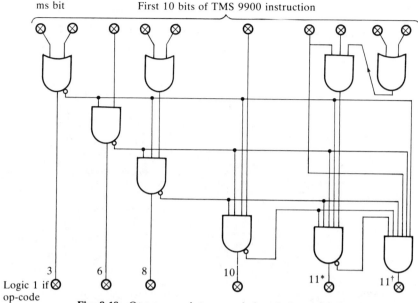

ms bit   First 10 bits of TMS 9900 instruction

Logic 1 if
op-code
= x   bits

Fig. 8.18   One approach to op-code length determination for the TMS 9900.

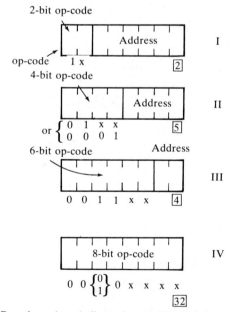

2-bit op-code

op-code   1 x   I

4-bit op-code

Address   II

or $\begin{cases} 0 & 1 & x & x \\ 0 & 0 & 0 & 1 \end{cases}$ 5

6-bit op-code   Address

0 0 1 1 x x   4   III

8-bit op-code   IV

$0\ 0 \begin{cases} 0 \\ 1 \end{cases} 0\ x\ x\ x\ x$ 32

Boxed numbers indicate the number of possible combinations.

Types of instructions

Branch and call subroutine. Address portion is destination.

Arithmetic instructions on registers. "Address" is an immediate operand (constant).

Bit operations on RAM where RAM address defined by preceding instructions. Address selects one of 4 bits in memory location to be operated on.

Operations of implied address—either accumulator or memory locations whose addresses have been defined by preceding instructions. Data are often part of the op-code, i.e. separate op-codes exist for adding 2 and 3 to the accumulator.

Fig. 8.19   TMS 1000 instruction formatting. (Courtesy Texas Instruments Inc.).

Operation codes (op-codes)

In principle, the assignment of op-codes to instructions can be quite arbitrary provided that, in the case of variable-length op-codes, the choice is within a

M.s. quartet of op-code				Condition code						Comments	
(0x)	(1x)	(2x)	(3x)	H	I	N	Z	V	C		
*	SBA: A−B→A	Uncondit- ional	TSX: SP+1→X	·	·	↕	↕	↕	↕	←TSX ←SBA Settings differ	(x0)
NOP: NO-OP	CBA: A−B	*	INS: SP+1→SP	·	·	↕	↕	↕	↕	INS/NOP CBA=compare CBA accumulators	(x1)
*	*	C+Z=0 i.e. higher	PULA: STACK→A	·	·	·	·	·	·	Remove 1 byte from stack and put in A	(x2)
*	*	C+Z=1 i.e. lower or same	PULB: STACK→B	·	·	·	·	·	·	As above but→B	(x3)
*	*	C=0	DES: SP−1→SP	·	·	·	·	·	·	Decrement S.P.	(x4)
*	*	C=1	TXS: X−1→SP	·	·	·	·	·	·		(x5)
4	TAB: A→B	Z=0	PSHA: A→STACK	·	·	↕	↕	↕	↕	←PSHA condition code ←TAB settings offer	(x6)
4	TBA: B→A	Z=1	PSHB B→STACK	·	·	↕	↕	↕	↕	←PSHB as above ←TBA	(x7)
INX: X+1→X	*	V=0	*	·	·	·	↕	·	·	Increment index register	(x8)
DEX: X−1→X	DAA: A*→A	V=1	RTS: return from subroutine	·	·	·	↕	·	·	RTS DAA is decimal DEX adjust for BCD DAA	(x9)
4	*	N=0	*	·	·	↕	↕	↕	↕		(xA)
4	ABA: A+B→A	N=1	RTI: return from interrupt	↕	·	↕	↕	↕	↕	RTI CC comes from stack with other registers	(xB)
4	*	N⊕V=0 i.e.>0	*								(xC)
4	*	N⊕V=1 i.e.<	*								(xD)
4	*	>0	WAI: wait for interrupt	·	·	·	·	·	·	Interrupt mask bit of CC set when interrupt occurs	(xE)
4	*	<0	SWI: software interrupt								(xF)

$$\left(\begin{array}{c}\text{Implied}\\\text{addressing}\end{array}\right)\left(\begin{array}{c}\text{Branch}\\\text{relative}\end{array}\right)\left(\text{Specials}\right)$$

x = index register
SP = stack pointer
CC = condition code
* = not used

Notes: 1. Branch instructions do *not* affect the condition code.
2. PULA, PULB, PSHA, PSHB adjust SP accordingly.
3. Entries in (2x) column are branch conditions.
4. Condition code operations.

Table 8.4 Motorola instruction set for the M6800 shown in matrix form: operation codes for the binary form 00xxxxxx.

certain code length set. When the op-code length is fixed, there is no restriction as to which instruction is assigned to which code. However, in practical microprocessors an element of coding orthogonality (attributes which are largely independent of each other) exists insofar that instructions

M.s. quartet of op-code

	(4x)	(5x)	(6x)	(7x)	H	I	N	Z	V	C	Comments
(x0)	NEGA: −A→A	NEGB: −B→B	NEG: −M→M		·	·	↕	↕	↕	α	Negation
(x1)		*									
(x2)		*									
(x3)	COMA: Ā→A	COMB: B̄→B	COM: M̄→M		·	·	↕	↕	R	S	1s complement
(x4)	LSRA: Shift A	LSRB: Shift B	LSR: Shift M		·	·	R	↕	↕	↕	Shift right: LSB→ carry: 0→MSB
(x5)		*									
(x6)	RORA: Rotate A	RORB: Rotate B	ROR: Rotate M		·	·	↕	↕	↕	↕	Shift right: LSB→carry carry→MSB
(x7)	ASRA: Shift A	ASRB: Shift B	ASR: Shift M		·	·	↕	↕	↕	↕	Shift right arithmetic: MSB→MSB & bit 6:LSB→carry
(x8)	ASLA: Shift A	ASLB: Shift B	ASL: Shift M		·	·	↕	↕	↕	↕	Shift left: 0→LSB: MSB→carry
(x9)	ROLA: Rotate A	ROLB: Rotate B	ROL: Rotate M		·	·	↕	↕	↕	↕	Shift left: carry→LSB: MSB→carry
(xA)	DECA: A−1→A	DECB: B−1→B	DEC: M−1→M		·	·	↕	↕	↕	·	Decrement
(xB)		*									
(xC)	INCA: A+1→A	INCB: B+1→B	INC: M+1→M		·	·	↕	↕	↕	·	Increment
(xD)	TSTA: Test A	TSTB: Test B	TST: Test M		·	·	↕	↕	R	R	Nothing changes except condition code
(xE)		*	JMP: jump		·	·	·	·	·	·	Offset is 8-bit unsigned binary
(xF)	CLRA: 0→A	CLRB: 0→B	CLR: 0→M		·	·	R	S	R	R	Clear

Condition code

Address implied   Indexed   Extended   Addressing mode
                         address   address

*=not used
α=result=0?

Table 8.5 Motorola instruction set for the M6800 shown in matrix form: operation codes of the binary form 01xxxxxx.

	(8x)	(9x)	(Ax)	(Bx)	(Cx)	(Dx)	(Ex)	(Fx)	H I N Z V C	Comments
(x0)	SUBA:	A−M→A			SUBB:	B−M→B			· · ↔ ↔ ↔ ↔	Subtract
(x1)	CMPA:	A−M:	A.M	unchanged	CMPB:	B−M:	B.M	unchanged	· · ↔ ↔ ↔ ↔	Compare
(x2)	SBCA:	A−M−C→A			SBCB:	B−M−C→B			· · ↔ ↔ ↔ ↔	Subtract with borrow
(x3)	*		*	*	*	*		*		—
(x4)	ANDA:	A∧M→A			ANDB:	B∧M→B			· · ↔ ↔ R ·	Logical AND
(x5)	BITA:	A∧M			BITB:	B∧M			· · ↔ ↔ R ·	Logical COMPARE
(x6)	LDAA:	M→A			LDAB:	M→B			· · ↔ ↔ R ·	Load accumulator
(x7)	*	STAA	A→M		*	STAB:	B→M		· · ↔ ↔ R ·	Store accumulator
(x8)	EORA:	A⊕M→A			EORB:	B⊕M→B			· · ↔ ↔ R ·	Exclusive OR
(x9)	ADCA:	A+M+C→A			ADCB:	B+M+C→B			↔ · ↔ ↔ ↔ ↔	Add with carry
(xA)	ORAA:	A∨M→A			ORAB:	B∨M→B			· · ↔ ↔ R ·	Logical OR
(xB)	ADDA:	A∨M→A			ADDB:	B∨M→B			↔ · ↔ ↔ ↔ ↔	Add
(xC)	CPX:	Compare M and index register			*		*	*	· · ↔ ↔ ↔ ·	Compare index
(xD)	BSR: branch subroutine		JSR:	jump to subroutine	*		*	*	· · · · · ·	—
(xE)	LDS:	M→stack pointer			LDX:	M→index register			· · ↔ ↔ R ·	—
(xF)		STS: stack pointer→M				STX: index register→M			· · ↔ ↔ R ·	—
	Immediate	Direct	Indexed	Extended	Immediate	Direct	Indexed	Extended		Addressing mode

← M.s. quartet of op-code →

Condition code

* = not used

Table 8.6 Motorola instruction set for the M6800 shown in matrix form: operation codes of the binary form 1xxxxxxx. (Courtesy Motorola Semiconductors Inc.).

(op-codes) have two or more components: type (add, branch etc.), addressing mode (immediate, direct, extended, relative, etc.) and possibly components such as flag-setting conditions.

In order to simplify decoding, the various bits in the op-code (or combinations of them) can be assigned particular functions. Of course, there will be a small hard core of "different" instructions which cannot fit this pattern, either because they require special addressing modes or modifier bits or because some instructions are nonsensical if associated with a particular addressing mode. As an example, the Motorola M6800 instruction

Instruction	Defined bit pattern* (x=optional)							Notes
Move	0	1	x	x	x	x	x	x	
Immediate operand	0	0	x	x	x} 1 1 0				1-byte operand
	1	1	x	x	x}				
	0	0	x	x	x	0	0	1	2-byte operand
INR/DCR INX/DCX	} 0	0	x	x	x{ 1 0 x / 0 1 1				
Add/Subtract	1·	0	0	x	x	x	x	x	
Logical	1	0	1	x	x	x	x	x	
Rotate	0	0	0	x	x	1	1	1	
Conditional jump	1	1	x	x	x	0	1	0	
Conditional call	1	1	x	x	x	1	0	0	
Conditional return	1	1	x	x	x	0	0	0	
RST	1	1	x	x	x	1	1	1	
Push/pop	1	1	x	x	0	x	0	1	
Others									

*Some exceptions exist

Table 8.7 Simplified partitioning of Intel 8085 instruction set

set is shown, in abbreviated form, in Tables 8.4–8.6. This can be compared with the Intel 8085 set in Table 8.7. The CPU structures are shown in Figs. 8.20 and 8.21 respectively.

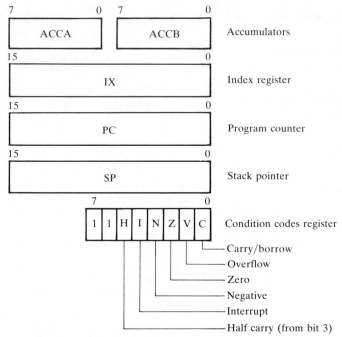

Fig. 8.20 Motorola CPU register structure. (Courtesy Motorola Semiconductors Inc.).

Miscellaneous effects of instruction methods

There are a few final points to note in instruction practice.

1.   The somewhat rigid rules of word length for data, addresses, instructions, etc. can be considerably relaxed in single-chip microcomputers because the factors are all internal to the chip and can be arranged, at will, by the semiconductor manufacturer. Only when, for instance, memory or I/O expansion is contemplated, do such considerations take on any importance. In the case of simple process controllers, which are not subject to expansion, this arbitrariness of word length can be taken to its limit. The TMS 1000 is basically a 4-bit device but uses several word lengths internally, not to mention quite unrelated I/O port widths.

2.   In order to squeeze the maximum performance from the powerful 16-bit microprocessors, it is desirable to reduce communications between the microprocessor and its support components. There are two reasons for this. The lead-out frame of a micro tends to funnel information because of a sparsity of leadouts possible on a package of a given size. Secondly, memory components are generally slow compared with the microprocessor. A typical memory-to-processor transfer, including addressing, takes 400–1000 ns. In comparison, modern microprocessors use internal gates with propagation delays of the order of 2 ns. It therefore follows that not only should data

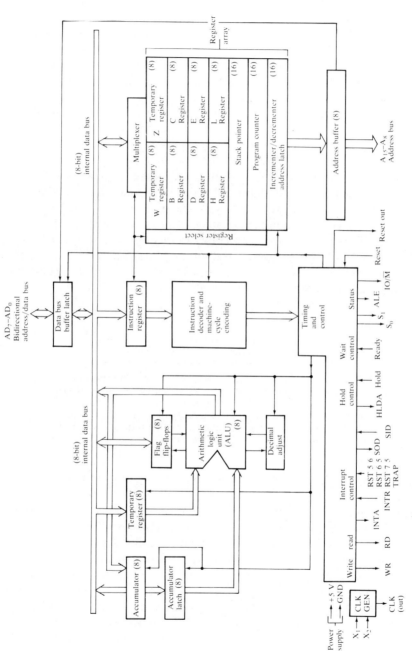

Fig. 8.21 Intel 8085 CPU structure. (Courtesy Intel Corporation).

transfers from memory to processor be minimized by the use of register banks in the processor, but that the number of fresh instructions drawn from memory should be kept down. One way of achieving this is to use "repeated" instructions. Such repeated instructions are usually associated with incremental addressing (pre- and post-indexed—the memory pointer is advanced each time an instruction is executed so that it is already pointing to the next data element in a string, table or matrix when the instruction is next executed) plus some loop-escape algorithm. Applications of such instructions include string processing whereby the same basic operation is performed on each element of a string as it is presented to the processor. The end of the string is either detected by some unique end-of-string code or by counting string elements as they pass through. Detection of an end-of-string code or element-count completion allows escape from the instruction. Not only can instruction fetches be reduced if the instruction can be held in the processor but also the number of bytes of code to carry out the whole operation. The "body" of the instruction can vary but might take the form of a code translation through access to look-up tables whose base address is held in another processor register. Some examples of these instructions are shown for the Intel 8086 processor (Table 8.8).

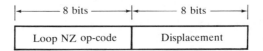

Fig. 8.22 Compound instructions applied to control transfer (jump) instructions (Intel 8086): if the zero flag (in the processor) is not set *and* the counter (C) (in the processor) has not reached zero, having been decremented at the beginning of the instruction, then transfer control to the instruction at the address given by the program-counter value plus the displacement.

3.   In addition to reducing the total number of memory accesses (fetches), it is also possible to reduce the overall number of bytes of code for executing algorithms by the employment of powerful instructions. As an example, the simple control-transfer instructions such as CALL SUB-ROUTINE, JUMP and RETURN can have conditional forms which test more than one condition as part of the decision-making process. To make multiple decisions on simple processors, more than one conditional control transfer instruction has to be used. As these tend to be amongst the longer instructions (byte length) and longer to execute, this is very wasteful. As an example for string operations, it can be very useful to be able to abort on the end of transmission (EOT) character in the source field or on expiry of byte count. Under these circumstances, the transfer address is going to be the same, i.e. the loop is continued no matter which condition dictates it. The

Instruction type	Comments
Move	1
Push/pop to/from stack	Registers/flags
In/out	Input/output transfers
Add/subtract	With/without carry/borrow, 1
Increment/decrement	1
Decimal adjust	2 for add/sub/mult/div
Multiply/divide	3
Sign extend	
Logical/not/and/test/or/ex-or	1
Rotate/shift	4
String operations	(Scan Load Store Compare)
Call subroutine	1
Jump	1, 5
Interrupt entry	5
Flag control	6

Notes:
1. Several addressing modes available including use of a base register, immediate addressing, byte or word (2-byte) operation. (Not all available in all combinations and cases.)
2. For ASCII or packed (2-digits/byte) decimal.
3. Signed/unsigned, integer.
4. Shift count in register C. Left or right shifting.
5. Several flags/conditions can be invoked.
6. Set/reset selected flags.

Table 8.8 Summary of instructions available on the Intel 16-bit microprocessor type 8086. (Reproduced by Permission of Intel Corporation, Copyright 1979.)

escape would be to continue with the next instruction rather than looping back. Therefore the control transfer instruction for multiple conditions is made only marginally more complex by invoking the extra condition—it does not have to provide extra address components (Fig. 8.22).

8.5 STYLES OF MICROPROCESSORS

The register and arithmetic/logic layouts of microprocessors vary enormously according to word length, applications, cost and technology. Variations have also occurred with time as the most effective use of active elements in a chip has become apparent. So, although the basic Von Neumann concepts of sequential instruction processing and the Wilkes methods for control and timing at the microprogram level tend to permeate most designs, there are still major variations in the implementation. We will consider some of the differences that can be readily found just by making reference to manufacturers' data.

Multi- vs single-chip microcomputers

The first microcomputers were, understandably, multichip designs, simply because this distributed the hardware over a number of chips and reduced the density of active devices on each. For many applications, simplicity is the keynote and the minimum number of chips to fabricate a viable microcomputer is an important factor. Simple designs using a scratch-pad in the microprocessor and chips that combine memory and I/O functions can reduce the chip count to two, e.g. the Fairchild F-8 (Peatman, 1978). This system can support 1K bytes of ROM, 64 bytes of scratch-pad RAM and 32 bidirectional I/O lines. Middle-of-the-road 8-bit microcomputers such as the Motorola M6800 and Intel 8080 need 5 and 6 chips respectively in the minimum configuration as RAM and I/O are on separate chips from the processor. Using the Intel 8086 as representative of 16-bit designs, a minimum system can be fabricated from 7 chips. However, as most 16-bit units are used for their performance and I/O capabilities, specification of a minimum chip count is not particularly meaningful.

In the mid 1970s, single-chip microcomputers became available, starting with "compaction" of the simpler multichip designs. Typical amongst these is the Mostek MK3870, based on the F-8, having 2K bytes of ROM, 64 bytes of scratch-pad and 32 I/O lines on one chip. It also has an internal clock generator and event timer. This chip is particularly suited to process control and logic replacement applications. Soon afterwards, more complex single-chip units became available, particularly those which were readily expandable in terms of memory and I/O. Extra chips can just be added to buses which emerge at the microcomputer's leadouts. It is quite difficult to achieve a high-performance single-chip design which is expandable, without incurring component redundancy or having many extra leadouts on the microcomputer. A good example of a device which achieves just this is the Intel 8748—one which is not a compaction of a previous design but a completely new one. The 8748 is available also in CMOS form from Intersil and is designated IM87C48 (Intersil, 1979). Up to the end of 1979, no single-chip 16-bit microcomputers were available. There is little incentive to produce one because of the emphasis on performance rather than minimum system cost for 16-bit designs. It seems doubtful, therefore, whether such a device will emerge—at least in the near future.*

Power-supply variations

Early microcomputers, particularly, were based on relatively unrefined PMOS technologies. The threshold voltages of the active components were high and necessitated high supply voltages. This also made them somewhat incompatible with conventional logic, i.e. TTL. Some designs got round the

*Two single-chip devices now available (1980): TI 9940 and INTEL 2920.

interface problem by the use of split-power supply systems. As an example, the Intel 4004 needs a 15 V supply which is split into +5 V, −10 V and ground (0 V). PMOS was favored in the early days because of its lesser susceptibility to contamination during manufacture (compared with NMOS). However, the carriers associated with PMOS are holes which have only about half the mobility of electrons. Eventually, the processing (and yields) improved to the point whereby NMOS is now offered almost exclusively in current designs. The Intel 8080 uses N-channel silicon-gate technology—but still needs more than 1 power rail +5 V, −5 V and 12 V).

Various processing refinements including nitriding, use of an alternative crystal orientation (100) has resulted in sufficiently low threshold voltages to be achieved that +5 V (only) single-rail devices are now commonplace. Examples are the Motorola M6800, Mostek 3870 and the Intel 8748. The majority of 16-bit microprocessors also require only a single 5 V supply.

The power consumed by microprocessors varies considerably, being least for 4-bit devices (90 mW for the TMS 1000), 274 mW for the MK3870 and 1400 mW for the 8086.

The use of a single +5 V supply rail raises the issue of the compatibility of microcomputers with conventional external logic, such as TTL and CMOS. The transmission of signals *from* the micro *to* external logic is of particular interest as the term "TTL compatibility" is frequently used. For those used to standard TTL this term might imply that microcomputer sources are capable of sourcing 400 μA at logic 1 (2.4 V) and sinking 16 mA at logic 0 (0.4 V). This would be the requirement for 10 loads attached to the source. This capability is usually not present. As an example, a typical interface component is the Intel 8255A programmable peripheral interface (PPI). This can connect 8080 and 8085 micros to external logic. It can sink 1.7 mA at 0.45 V and source 200 μA at 2.4 V. It is therefore just capable of driving 1 standard TTL (74 series type—Texas Instruments, 1974) load or several low-power devices.

Choice of technology

PMOS and NMOS technologies have already been mentioned above. Apart from the various bipolar technologies such as integrated injection logic (I^2L), modified I^2L (I^3L), TTL, ECL, etc., a technology of growing popularity (for microprocessors) is complementary MOS (CMOS).

For most technologies, the chip-supply current varies very little with operating (clock) speed—particularly if no attempt is made to run the clock faster than specified. However, CMOS takes a supply current roughly proportional to the clock speed. As a consequence, it is particularly suited to applications wherein loss of data due to supply blackout must be avoided at all costs. CMOS allows long-term battery back up—if processing can be halted during use of the batteries. For a system to take full advantage, all the components carrying volatile data must also be CMOS, particularly RAM. An early example of a CMOS system is the RCA COSMAC in which the typical standby processor current is only $100\,\mu$A. For each 1K bits of RAM the standby current is less than $1\,\mu$A. Intersil's CMOS version of the 8748 (IM87C48) is also available and has a full clock-speed supply-current requirement of 10 mA, which varies *pro rata* with clock speed. At standby, the current is just $100\,\mu$A. Not only is the low standby current useful, but if the system is always run off batteries and loss of operating speed can be tolerated, the run-time supply current can be reduced simply by reduction of clock speed. (In many micro applications, the performance far exceeds that actually required.)

A different approach, using non-CMOS technology, can be adopted. If a microprocessor has a few registers (or on-chip RAM locations) which can be powered from a separate source (which probably enters by a separate micro leadout), these registers can be loaded with vital data when power failure is forecast by the mains-fail monitor. The chosen registers are powered by batteries, whereas most of the processor operates from the mains. There are generally few such standby registers in a chip (so that standby power is low)—just enough for a software "linkage" to restart the processor when mains power is restored. An example is the Motorola 6802, which is a microprocessor having 128 bytes of on-board RAM, of which 32 bytes are powered in the standby mode. The chip-current requirements are 240 mA at full clock speed and a maximum of 5 mA in the standby mode.

Arithmetic/logic processing

Previous sections have already outlined the types of instructions that are normally found in microprocessor repertoires. However, the handling of operands and results has not been described. A "typical" instruction has 1 (monadic) or 2 (dyadic) operands and produces a single result. If the totality of computer memory were held in one (monolithic) medium, then a location for each operand and a result destination would have to be specified for each instruction. In practice, this can lead to an excessive number of bits being needed to define an instruction and its addresses. Most microprocessors, like most conventional computers, have one or more user-accessible registers in the processor which can be used either for temporary retention of data or as part of an arithmetic processor, i.e. an accumulator. There are many variations on this idea, as some of the examples below will show.

1. The *Intel 4004*, the original 4-bit microprocessor, has an accumulator which forms a "focus" for arithmetic, plus a bank of 16 registers in the form of a scratch-pad. Data to be used in a current calculation are

loaded to the scratch-pad locations to make it available more readily and quickly than would be the case if it had to be brought down from memory every time an operation was to be carried out.

2. The *TI TMS 1000* is a single-chip microcomputer with no ready expansion capability. Therefore, apart from an accumulator, no bank of registers is provided as all data storage is "on-chip".

3. Of the 8-bit microprocessors, the *Fairchild F-8* has 64 registers in a scratch-pad arrangement, which is quite sufficient storage for ephemeral data without additional off-chip RAM having to be provided. Note that the single-chip version of the F-8 is also based on 64 bytes of data storage, which tends to uphold the contention that 64 bytes can suffice for simple control and logic-replacement applications. (More general data processing is another story.)

4. The *Motorola M6800* goes to the other extreme by providing just two on-chip data registers, both of which are configured as accumulators. Therefore main memory (RAM) must hold all data, both foreground (current) and background (archival). However, the instruction set has powerful addressing facilities including page-zero (for 2-byte (16-bit) address systems, the ms byte can define a "page" and the ls byte a "word"; "page-zero" is therefore the first 256 bytes of memory) and indexed, which makes data access easy, especially for tables, matrices and multibyte quantities. Choice of addressing mode also tends to keep instructions short and makes them faster to execute by reducing the number of byte fetches.

5. A compromise is used in the *Intel 8080/8085* series, wherein 7 registers are provided within the microprocessor. This means that some data can be held locally in the CPU and indeed some small processes can avoid interaction with main memory (for data) for the duration of the process. However, despite this, a data exchange is always necessary between processes to dump data from the previous process in memory and to bring forward data in readiness for the next process.

6. Two examples can be taken from the range of 16-bit microprocessors:

The *Intel 8086* has eight 16-bit registers in a general file. However, several of them are normally used for specific (e.g. addressing) functions. It would probably be fairer to say that only four are available for data retention in the normally accepted sense—and, of these, one is the accumulator. Instructions in the 8086 set include base and indexed addressing modes to handle transfers efficiently into and out of this somewhat limited register set. The small number of registers is also compensated for by the fact that four of them can be accessed on a byte basis, making them appear as eight 1-byte registers. (Compare this with the *Zilog Z8000,* which has sixteen 16-bit registers, any of which can be used for data storage, accumulators or address pointers.)

The Texas Instruments *TMS 9900 (SBP 9900)* uses a memory-to-memory architecture, that is, no data storage is provided on the microprocessor chip—merely arithmetic/logic handling facilities. Instead, user-definable blocks of 16 contiguous words of memory can be set aside as a "workspace". Each block of 16 memory locations replaces 16 registers that might otherwise have resided in the microprocessor hardware. Each block of 16 locations is associated with a "context" or "interrupt level". The advantage of this system is that time-consuming data movements between register and memory and to and from the stack are eliminated when an interrupt occurs. It is necessary only to switch context, i.e. alter the pointer value which indicates the memory location of the currently used block of work registers. The disadvantage of this system is that a memory access is required for every word of data to be processed in the microprocessor—there is not even a resident accumulator to act as a source for one of the two operands entering the arithmetic unit or to act as a repository for arithmetic results. This disadvantage is somewhat offset by an instruction set which is tailored to the memory-to-memory architecture. To this end, indexed, indirect and auto-incrementing addressing modes are made available. The number of bits needed to define each instruction is necessarily long for a memory-to-memory system and for the 9900 is as great as 1 or 2 words, i.e. 2 or 4 bytes. The addressing modes are illustrated in Table 8.9. There are no one-byte instructions, as in the Intel 8086.

Code	Type	Address	Example address
00	"Register"	WP+2 * [S or D]	Hex (1014)
01	"Indirect"	(WP+2 * [S or D])	Hex (3800)
10	"Indexed"	(WP+2 * [S or D])+(PC)	Hex (6800)
10	"Symbolic"	(PC): PC←PC+2	Hex (3002)
11	"Indirect with auto-increment"	(WP+2 * [S or D]): then increment effective address	Hex (3800) then Hex (3802) after execution

WP = workspace pointer
S or D = source or destination "register"
PC = program counter
(x) = contents of x

Example (used for calculating example addresses above):

Content of WP = hex (1000)
S or D = hex (A)
Content of S or D = hex (0300)
Content of PC = hex (3000)
Content of hex (1014) = hex (3800)

Table 8.9   Addressing modes for the TI TMS 9900 microcomputer. (Courtesy Texas Instruments Inc.).

8.6 DESIGN FOR MICROCOMPUTER-BASED PRODUCTS

Microcomputers, probably more than any other type of computer, force the designer to consider both hardware and software aspects of systems, not only separately, but also in terms of their interactions. This comes about partly because it is doubtful that the microprocessor is "just another logic chip" with a catalog number and an accompanying logic diagram. On the other hand, it is not a complete computing entity which can be used with little or no reference to its performance and operating limitations. Furthermore, microcomputers are frequently used in real-time applications which require a knowledge of the form and timing of interactions between the computer and external events. The fact that hardware and software considerations must be taken together applies not only at the design level but also right through development, testing, commissioning and any subsequent enhancements or modifications.

At the development level, there is verification of peripheral hardware interfaces, transducers, displays and the hardware aspects of the microcomputer and its support components to consider. There is then verification of the software, which may well have to be committed (eventually) to ROM. Finally, the system must be tested with a suitably complete set of conditions, both external and internal. These conditions must include both valid parameters and anomalous ones (such as power failure or out-of-range data), checking that system recovery can be achieved in all circumstances and times of occurrence. When that has been achieved, correct reactions to combinations of valid and invalid circumstances must be confirmed.

There are two techniques frequently used to test systems at a fairly sophisticated level. They both involve the use of both hardware and software, additional to the system being developed.

One of these is known as a *simulator* and generally takes the form of a software check on the target system (i.e. the system being developed as a product) without considering external events (data entry, interrupts, etc.) and their interactions with the target. In effect, a simulator is a system which can accept the same software as the target and will predict the target's response to that software. The simulator contains a similar microcomputer to the target but, apart from a ROM (which acts as the simulator's operating system), will hold the target's software in RAM. By so doing, the trial software can be readily modified (Fig. 8.23). The simulator can run this software (entered from a keyboard or any other attached peripheral device) and display the results. The ROM-based operating system would be able to provide a user and program entry interface and possibly also assembly and other software preparation facilities, i.e. editing and initialization. In particular, it will allow the software to be "single-stepped" through each

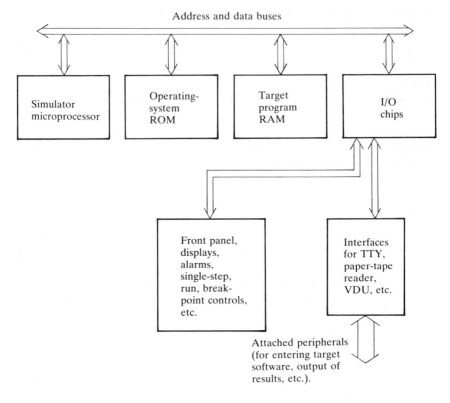

Fig. 8.23 Simplified block diagram of a microcomputer simulator.

instruction so that register and memory content can be monitored. It might even be such that "halt", "trap" or "breakpoint" instructions can be inserted in the software. This would allow the simulator to run at full speed to the breakpoint. It would then halt and display registers, etc. Using breakpoints allows checked-out parts of the software to be used and passed through quickly and yet give an opportunity for single-stepping to be carried out in a later section which contains bugs. Frequently, this sort of facility is used to allow a long, tested, loop of instructions to be executed the requisite number of times before being trapped on exit from the loop. Some simulators provide a "trace" facility, i.e. they are able to display a "post-mortem" of the simulator's response, over the n previous instructions executed, prior to halting. Display here means processor registers and possibly a selection of memory locations. Interactions with devices and

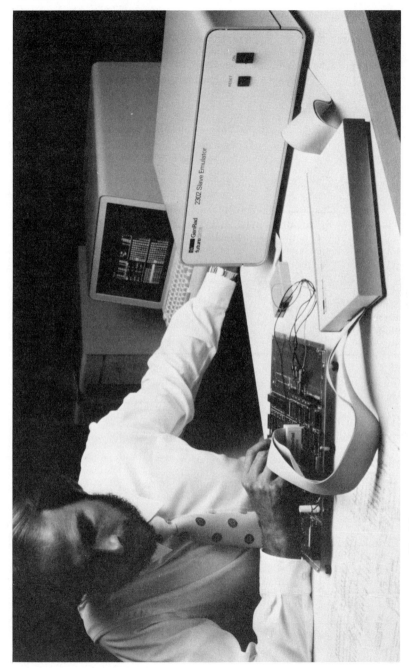

Fig. 8.24 A microcomputer development system showing the incircuit emulator connected to the user's hardware under test. (Courtesy Gen-Rad Futuredata, Los Angeles, California.)

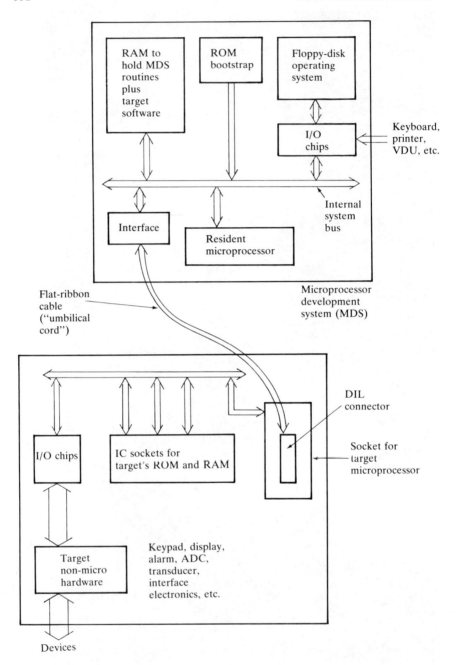

Fig. 8.25 (Micro)emulator connected to a target micro by an "umbilical cord".

systems external to the microcomputer probably have to be entered by hand to the simulator, using breakpoints to stop the simulation at the points where data are entered or interrupts encountered. The Motorola "Exorciser" is a good example of a versatile microcomputer simulation system with a wide variety of facilities.

The other development aid is the *emulator*. Again it is characterized by a hardware unit capable of accepting and running the target software. It therefore consists of a microcomputer system based on the target configuration with additional operating-system ROM and program/data storage RAM. However, the emulator, unlike the simulator, allows the designer to introduce external interactions with the emulator and, in effect, run the system realistically.

An example of such a development aid/emulator is the Futuredata microprocessor development system (AMDS), manufactured by Gen–Rad. This equipment (Fig. 8.24) is based on a floppy-disk operating system in which the system and target software is held, edited and even assembled or compiled. An "umbilical cord" is available to connect the AMDS to the target system via the target's microprocessor socket (Fig. 8.25). When emulation is first carried out, all target software is held in the AMDS RAM. The AMDS clock and microprocessor is used instead of the target's, but external interactions are with the target's I/O chips and peripheral hardware. The set-up, thus configured, can work at full speed and therefore interact with external stimuli in real time. Therefore, full testing is possible under realistic conditions. (If it were not for the cost of the development system and emulator, they could form the major part of a full working product!) The AMDS keyboard and VDU can be used to monitor and control the emulation and to do all software editing, file management, assembly and compilation control. Gradually, responsibility for providing memory (both ROM and RAM) can be relinquished by the AMDS to the target (Fig. 8.26). The target clock generator can be brought into use instead of the AMDS one. Finally, when the only component furnished by AMDS is the microprocessor (via the cord), the cord can be removed and a microprocessor plugged into the socket in the target. AMDS, in common with some other emulators and development systems, provides EPROM programming facilities so that no manual handling of programs is necessary. A socket for holding a freshly erased memory chip is provided and connected to AMDS via another umbilical cord. AMDS provides the requisite programming currents and addresses for burning in the (binary) software, and facilities for reading back the patterns programmed, in order to verify a successful exchange. (The software is simply decanted, location by location from AMDS, when it is in the emulation mode, i.e. it contains the target software, in binary form, in its RAM.)

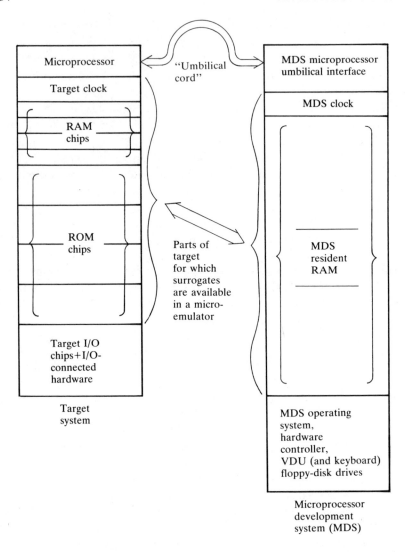

Fig. 8.26 Starting with all services, bar I/O, being emulated in the MDS, each part of the target machine can be brought into operation and checked out.

If neither a simulator nor emulator approach is possible, it is quite feasible (although time consuming) to develop a system with just an oscilloscope and the use of repeated program loops in an evaluation kit. (Evaluation kits are relatively simple microcomputers, having a small amount of RAM, a few I/O connections, possibly a TTY interface and a pre-programmed ROM, which makes possible simple protocol between the micro and the user.) Repeated program loops provide a convenient way to obtain steady traces on the 'scope. This can also be done in real-time. A major disadvantage of such an approach is the difficulty of putting all the software sections together and tracing faults (particularly those involving hardware/software interactions) or those which only become apparent when a number of simple routines are put together to form a complex, complete algorithm. Furthermore, programming must be done at machine-code level. Otherwise, assemblers/compilers must be provided to convert assembly or high-level language programs into machine-executable form. These may be cross assemblers/compilers, which are able to assemble/compile programs for a target machine on another computer. The other computer does not need to be the same type as the target, but the cross assembler/compiler must have been written specifically with the target in mind.

8.7 FUTURE DEVELOPMENTS

Microcomputers have developed very significantly since the appearance of the first units in the early 1970s. Greater memory densities, gate counts and refined manufacturing techniques have greatly increased the capacity and performance of both microprocessors and their support chips. Additionally, many single chips can perform complex interface functions which previously required a card or more of logic. These chips can frequently be interfaced directly to the microcomputer bus to give greater throughput and economy of components. Amongst these chips are:

1. complex DMA controllers capable of supporting up to eight peripheral (I/O) devices of differing throughput and protocol;
2. direct raster scan CRT interfaces for the display of alphanumeric information (including programmable user choice of code, format and scan mode);
3. analog-to-digital converters with tri-state bus-drive capability;
4. a host of communications interface chips which can provide connections from the microcomputer's bus to parallel or serial, synchronous or asynchronous data channels in user-definable formats. Parity, framing, overrun, synchronizing and timing facilities are provided on-chip.

Several of the above devices are just about as complex as the microprocessor itself, and certainly qualify as "intelligent" if the microprocessor does. In a sense, many are a form of primitive "front- or back-end" processor. In future, the number and variety of such chips is likely to rise, necessarily so if the full capabilities of the newer 16-bit microprocessors are to be realized.

There has been a tendency to standardize on the 40 leadout frame for most chips, including most 8- and 16-bit microprocessors. As the complexity of these devices grows, it might be expected that extra pressure will be exerted to increase leadout frame size. However, large leadout frames are expensive, have poor yields and are difficult to handle. (In this respect, it is interesting to note that of the 16-bit microprocessors available in 1980, only two have 64 leadouts. These are the TI TMS 9900 and the Motorola 68000, (of which the 9900 is a device dating back to 1976).) Another device, the Zilog Z8001, has a 48-leadout frame, and the rest use 40 (Intel 8086, Zilog Z8002 and Fairchild 9440). It follows that apart from the multiplexing of leadout functions (address/data sharing, etc.), there is pressure to do more inside the microprocessor for each unit of information entering or leaving it. This pressure will result in more complex instructions (taking more processing per instruction byte) and more use of repeated instructions to avoid instruction fetching. In addition, more memory, either in the form of register banks or scratch-pads, will be needed to hold working data and intermediate results of algorithms, for as long as possible, without having to make memory references.

At the economy end of the microcomputer spectrum, more standard chips may be produced for standard functions, at low cost. At present, standard chips exist for microwave-oven control and the like. In future, we would expect to see standard automotive components for fuel control, instrumentation and hazard alert. Standard chips may also be produced for most other volume uses such as point-of-sale terminals, word processors, telephone exchanges, telephone-traffic monitors, call translators and computer-network exchanges and monitors.

On the technological front, the non-volatile RAM must be high on the priorities listing. In a sense, it already exists in the form of the EPROM but, of course, the high disparity between write/erase and read times, milliseconds vs. less than a microsecond, relegates it to the read-mostly category (RMM). Developments in double-gated MOS devices, whose thresholds can be changed by rapid charge transfers, is one approach. Once such a RAM can be produced, with a competitive cell density, price and life expectation comparable to that of conventional ROMs and RAMs, it will pave the way to unified memory systems and eliminate the difficulties and inconvenience currently experienced with UVROMs and EAROMs.

Software developments for microcomputers have varied according to the word lengths of the systems used and the applications to which they are put. For simple process control and logic replacement using simple 4-bit and

8-bit units, machine-dependent languages have been widely used. Sometimes, actual machine code is used (albeit rarely). The software is usually entered to the memory in hexadecimal or, more often, from an assembly language which has been assembled on another machine (cross-assembly). The use of assembly languages, at least, gives the convenience of mnemonic operation codes, symbolic address labelling and some macro facilities. It also makes editing easier and eliminates most tendencies to introduce program "patches" when bugs are found. BASIC has been one of the more widely used high-level machine-independent languages together with (subsets of) FORTRAN (FORmula TRANslation) and ALGOL (ALGOrithmic Language). However, where performance is at a premium, many designers tend to default to assembly languages and accept their inconveniences, rather than risk being at the mercy of a possibly inefficient compiler.

The larger, more complex, microcomputers are really meant to be used with high-level languages and provide facilities, such as instructions which can be used as "high-level language hooks", for this purpose. Generally, they are virtually impossible to program by machine code, often inconvenient to program in an assembly language, but very easy to program in, say, PASCAL or PLZ, without loss of "contact" with the hardware system. Some languages, such as PASCAL, are almost self-documenting, which makes them readily transported from programmer to programmer. Apart from PASCAL, most 16-bit microcomputer manufacturers are also supporting combinations of FORTRAN, COBOL (COmmon Business Orientated Language) and BASIC.

Many microcomputers, partiularly the simple, low-cost ones, are used in process control and instrumentation. Applications include electrical measuring instruments with digital readouts and self-scaling and calibrating facilities, digital weighing and price-calculating machines, three-term furnace and suchlike controllers. In many cases, phenomena of a nondigital and non-electrical nature have to be measured to some prescribed precision. The transducers and digital converters for such machines can be very expensive, error prone and unreliable. They can certainly present far more design difficulties than the microcomputer itself. The introduction of micros has prompted a great deal of research into low-cost measuring and transduction techniques. It is anticipated that this work will be accelerated, so as to widen the *economical* applications to which micros can be put. In this respect, transduction includes not only information coming into the micro but the conversion of low-power signals from the micro into a suitable form for activating output devices—mechanical handling gear, actuators, relays (solid state and otherwise), pneumatic controllers, servo systems and others.

Many microcomputers, particularly multichip ones, present special difficulties for field maintenance personnel. Not only does the complexity of the individual components make pinpointing of faults difficult, but so does the fact that several components may be connected on a bus. If, say, a memory device fails because of a fault in a cell, a simple set of (software) tests will provide the necessary evidence. However, if the fault is at the chip interface, it may well have the effect of "locking" one of the bus lines into a certain logic state. As several chips use the same bus, it is almost impossible to isolate the culprit, unless the bus can be broken up. In the future, it is to be hoped that instruments and techniques will be developed which aid rapid diagnosis of faults peculiar to microcomputer systems, both in terms of hardware and software.

The final area of concern is that of development costs. Although, for volume production, the high cost of software development can be amortized over all the units marketed so as to be a small proportion of the cost of each unit, many low-to-medium-volume products are not economically viable to develop. In simplistic terms, we have the problem of the "5-buck chip and the $10 000 worth of software". The adoption of suitable programming languages and sophisticated hardware and software development aids will certainly help to reduce the disproportionate software burden. However, for some time—maybe a very long time—the cost of a suite of software (and the thorough exercising of it in a simulator or emulator) is going to be a major cost factor in microcomputer development.

EXERCISES

8.1 Compare the architectures of a variety of microcomputers and minicomputers. Note, particularly, the efficiency with which data can be moved about the machines and through the I/O channels. Compare instruction sets and the use of variable-length instructions. Compare, also, the ease with which multibyte (word) operands can be handled and what optional hardware (such as floating-point units) is available.

8.2 If the Intel 8085 had separate data and address leadouts and could therefore use memory-read cycles similar to the 8080, by how much could the memory-access time be increased without having to alter the clock period? State your assumptions.

8.3 A calculator has 16 *function* keys arranged in a 4×4 matrix. A 4-bit parallel-bit output port drives one axis of the matrix and another inputs the pattern output from the other axis. One of the keys is a function modifier which can be (optionally) used before pressing any one of the other keys. Write a flowchart and detailed coding for directing the software to any one of the 30 possible routines indicated by the key actuations.

8.4 (a)   By reference to the TMS 1000 microcomputer, deduce which micro-instructions are required to execute each of the 12 fixed and 31 "standard" instructions. (Use the instruction-set table and microinstruction listing only: then check your answers against the ones declared in the instruction decoder listing (Texas Instruments, 1976).)

(b) Assuming all instructions are limited to use of:

> up to 1 from CIN, MTN, CKN, ATN, ISTN, NATN
> &/or up to 1 from MTP, CKP, YTP
> &/or up to 1 from C8, NE
> &/or up to 1 from CKM, STO
> &/or up to 1 from AUTY, AUTA
> &/or STSL

(i) How many instructions are possible if use of constant and kl logic is limited to those offered in the manual?

(ii) List *some useful* instructions which are not in the standard list of 43 and state which format and op-codes they would use.

8.5 The Intel 8748/8048 single-chip microcomputer has a limited number of on-chip registers, which must be used carefully if excessive numbers of instructions are to be avoided. Draw up a flowchart and write code for deriving the 4-digit square root of an 8-digit number (expressed in BCD) using Newton's method.

Notes: 1. Although a decimal adjust instruction is available, subtraction is not.

2. Use should be made of subroutines to partition activities, but the 8748 imposes a depth limit of 8. However, if less than 8 levels are used, spare RAM becomes available.

8.6 Use the ROM-based microprogram unit of Fig. 8.8 to design a controller for the Intel 8085 (whose CPU is shown in Fig. 8.24b). The basic timing and control signals need first to be identified; mutually exclusive ones can be grouped and separately decoded and the conditional signals found.

About what word width and ROM capacity is required for your ROM? Indicate the conditional and timing logic needed in your design.

Note: Make use of Table 8.6 to decompose instructions and to establish the identities of some of the conditional signals.

8.7 Compare the speeds, chip count and power requirements of a 16-bit bipolar "slice" type processor, such as the one based on the AMD Am2900 series components, with a second-generation MOS 16-bit microprocessor.

8.8 Write software listings for at least two different 8-bit microcomputers to perform multiplication using 16-bit 2s complement notation with the "shift-and-add" algorithm. Compare performance and code length for the two units.

8.9 Write a test program for the above multiplication algorithm to give some confidence that it works, from a hardware viewpoint. (The application for this program might be as a field-maintenance aid.) The trial multiplications should cover all instruction and branch paths in the coding. It should also be arranged that all memory and register locations are caused to change state once (at least), in order that stuck-at-one and stuck-at-zero faults are detected. (The program should only be a "go–no go" test; it does not have to identify a faulty chip or location.)

8.10 Form an instruction matrix, on the lines of Tables 8.3–6, for any of the 16-bit microprocessors with fixed op-code length. Identify any areas of "orthogonality".

8.11 Assuming that op-codes of up to 10 bits are permissible in an instruction format with variable op-code length, compare the number of combinations of op-codes that can be generated, if the gaps between op-code length chosen are fixed. Present your results with gap and shortest op-code length used as parameters.

8.12 Study the facilities and costs of a number of microprocessor-design aids, including simulators, emulators and development systems. Which do you consider "best-buys" and for what reasons? Take account of such factors as other equipment and facilities that may be needed for any of the systems, i.e. peripherals, cross-software, etc.

REFERENCES

Advisory Council for Applied Research and Development (ACARD) (1978), Cabinet Office, *The Applications of Semiconductor Technology,* HMSO, London.

Cavanagh, B. M. J. (1978), *BASIC for Beginners,* Holmes and McDougall, Edinburgh.

Clough, I. D. (1979), "Reliability assessment for communication equipment," *Electronic Eng.,* **51**(620), 48–63.

Hartley M. G. and Healey, M. (1978), *A First Course in Computer Technology,* McGraw-Hill, London, Chapter 9.

Hewlett-Packard Co. (1979), *HP-45 User's Guide,* Santa Clara, Calif.

Hill, F. J. and Peterson, G. R. (1978), *Digital Systems; Hardware Organisation and Design,* (2nd edn) Wiley International, New York. Chapters 8 & 12.

IEEE (Institution of Electronic and Electrical Engineers USA) (1975), *Specification for a General Purpose Interface Bus,* Standard 488.

Intel Corporation (1977), *MCS-48 Microcomputer User's Manual,* 3065 Bowers Ave, Santa Clara, Calif. 95051.

Intel Corporation (1978a), *MCS-85 User's Manual,* 3065 Bowers Ave, Santa Clara, Calif. 95051.

Intel Corporation (1978b), *MCS-86 Microcomputer User's Manual,* 3065 Bowers Ave, Santa Clara, Calif. 95051.

Intersil (1979), *Insight,* Nos. 1–4. N. European HQ, Intersil Inc., 8 Tessa Road, Richfield Trdg Est., Reading, Berks, UK.

Intersil (1979), "IM87C48–The First CMOS Microcomputer with Built-in EPROM Memory", *Insight,* No. 3. N. European HQ, Intersil Inc., 8 Tessa Road, Richfield Trdg Est., Reading, Berks, UK.

Millman, J. and Halkias, C.C. (1972), *Integrated Electronics,* McGraw-Hill Kogakusha, Tokyo, Chapter 7.

Moralee, D. (1979), "Bit slices come in larger bytes," *IEE News* (Industrial spotlight), October, p.6.

Motorola Semiconductor Products (1975), *6800 Applications and Programming Manuals,* Box 20912, Phoenix, Ariz, 85036.

Motorola Semiconductor Products, (1978), *MC6802*, Box 20912, Phoenix, Ariz., 85036.

Peatman, J. B. (1978), *Microcomputer Based Design,* McGraw-Hill, London.

Texas Instruments (1974), *System 74 Designers Manual,* Houston, Texas, 77001.

Texas Instruments (1975), *9900 Series Microcomputers,* Houston, Texas, 77001.

Texas Instruments (1976), *TMS1000 Series Microcomputers,* Houston, Texas, 77001.

TRW LSI Products (1979), PO Box 1125, Redondo Beach, Calif, 90278 (Device TDC 1008J–1010J).

Wilkes, M. V. and Stringer, C. (1953), "Microprogramming and the design of control circuits in an electronic digital computer," *Proc. Camb. Phil. Soc.,* **49,** 230–8.

Wilson, I. R. and Addyman, A. M. (1978), *A Practical Introduction to PASCAL,* Macmillan, London.

Young, D. C. (1979), "Designing non-volatile memory arrays with CMOS RAMS," *Electronic Eng.,* **51** (620), 71–82.

9 ASPECTS OF SOFTWARE AND FIRMWARE

9.1 INTRODUCTION

9.1.1 Hardware, firmware and software: the designer's role

This chapter is concerned with total systems, but in particular with the way in which software, firmware and hardware interact. These three constituents can have their properties summarized as follows:

Software is that aspect of the system in which the programs and data, that is instructions and operands, are contained in memories of a read/write form. This makes possible ready alteration of such instructions and hence the task to be carried out. The memory form can be of any type ranging from fast semiconductor memory through to the various electromechanical forms.

Firmware is that aspect of the operation of the system which, together with the hardware, defines the structure or shape of the system as seen from the user's viewpoint. This aspect can include the microprograms which will, in part, define the machine (order) code and some of the fixed routines, which may not be made alterable by the user. Firmware is generally, but not always, held as a form of program material in read-only memories (ROM) and is therefore alterable but only by reprogramming or replacement of the relevant integrated circuits (IC).

Hardware represents the fixed equipment of the machine—the logic wiring and palpable components. Together with timing logic and/or microprograms it defines the elementary facility for use by the programmer at the lowest level of operation.

342

The designer's role is a critical one because both the cost and performance of a system will depend on the right decisions being made—in particular, that tasks are apportioned to these three areas in the best way. In typical computer systems, the software costs usually dominate those of hardware development. This is especially true with the advent of sophisticated microcomputer components and large-scale integrated circuits (LSI).

Digital systems are hierarchical and this gives the designer considerable freedom of choice regarding task allocation (Fig. 9.1). On the one hand, he must decide which routines and facilities must be provided in hardware because of frequency of use or performance demands. On the other hand, many tasks are better executed in software, particularly where operational flexibility is required.

In this chapter, the structure of software and firmware will be considered, the way in which tasks can be implemented in software and the requirements for software languages to assist both the designer and user. The chapter will be an introductory one, exploring some of the more important areas of software and firmware. Through its references, it will act as a *link* for the engineer into software systems and design but at the same time it will indicate what provisions can be made by the hardware designer to relieve the burdens on the programmers and users.

9.1.2 The user's viewpoint

Users and operators would like to define tasks in a language which is at least closely related to English, or is in some existing mathematical form. The computer hardware generally operates in binary or some closely related binary code such as binary-coded decimal (BCD). Language translation therefore forms one important aspect of 'bridging the gap' between user and hardware. In practice, this is done at several levels, because the mere entry of data to a Teletype keyboard or VDU keypad brings an immediate translation of human coding into a binary-coded form. (Each key punched closes a switch contact or suchlike mechanism so it is bound to create a binary type response.) In effect, software provides a bridge from one form of binary coding to another—it provides a user/hardware interface. The presentation of results to the operator also involves translation (at the terminal) through the actuation of a Teletype print mechanism or VDU character generator. This hardware translation is often carried several steps further in order to relieve the software burden at the peripheral devices. If combined with firmware, quite sophisticated pre-processing of operator-entered data can take place. Post-processing of raw results is also possible so that they may be correctly formatted for presentation to a VDU screen or printer.

If the user is placed at the top of the hierarchy of Fig. 9.1, then the definition of his task is at the highest level. At this level, it is either in English

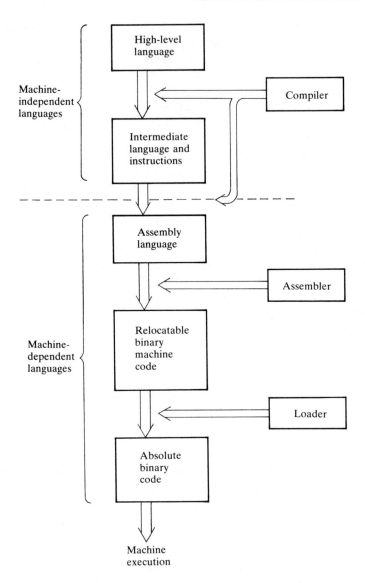

Fig. 9.1 Idealized software "edifice" showing stages of translation
from a high-level language into executable machine code.

or some conventional mathematical form. The lower-level activities of this
hierarchy, associated with "getting the job done", are less apparent to him.
This is known as the "top-down" view. It is also a way of looking at system
design—not that the view becomes less clear as levels are descended, merely
that a start is made at the highest level and the approach is downwards.

Although this is a more accepted way of designing systems today, it is the opposite from some 20–30 years ago when there was a tendency to look at the hardware first and worry about the software and systems later. It was understandable that a more "bottom-up" approach was taken as the provision of even the simplest, reliable, hardware was such a major obstacle to viable system design that most attention was drawn to it.

There is another source from which the bottom-up view comes—getting to understand a system. The tendency is to grapple with small, low-level chunks of the system, and when understanding emerges, to piece together the understood parts to make a whole concept.

9.1.3 Programming languages

Whether we consider computers from the engineering viewpoint and look at the machine as a "box of parts" or from the software side and see it as an edifice of procedures, routines etc., the focus is usually the machine-code repertoire.

For the engineer, the machine-code set can be a specification for the hardware and microcode. For the software designer, machine code is the starting point for building the software edifice in a bottom-up approach. (In terms of software, the top-down approach is one based on the realization of a specification, whereas the bottom-up one represents the order in which language implementation and achievement will arise.)

Although it would be ideal if the software engineer could dictate what machine code he wanted, and get it, a compromise is bound to be struck with what the hardware designer can economically provide. Eventually agreement will be reached and from this the software designer can decide how to create the hardware/user link. This will be a series of translators and languages, starting at the user and ending with the machine-code set.

Languages which can interface the user to the system at the task or problem level, rather than demanding a translation of his problem into a form suitable for the machine's hardware, is known as "machine-independent" or "high-level." Such languages are also often known as "problem" or "procedure-oriented" as against machine-dependent or machine-oriented.

Whether a language is high or low-level, it must have an unambiguously and rigidly defined syntax (grammar) and semantics suitable for a wide range of applications. The language must provide those required facilities using a minimum of coding for each task and follow the spirit of an "edifice" in its concept. Users' programs written in high-level languages should also tend to encourage the user to stratify his tasks so that commonly used "service" routines can be written just once and can then be called upon by the body of his program when required.

The frequency with which a particular program is to be run is crucial in deciding which programming language should be used. One which is only going to be run once or twice must take as little time to write as possible, to be worth the effort in the first place. This implies the use of a language as near natural English as possible to reduce user effort. It is then the system's task to provide the translation to machine form. Several intermediate-language levels may have to be invoked in order to make each stage of translation manageable. Each level is a compromise in terms of the effectiveness of its use of the machine's facilities. The result is that programs, initially written for high-level languages, being far removed from the hardware, do not use the hardware as effectively as those written at lower levels and which are therefore more "in-tune" with the machinery.

Preparation of programs in lower-level languages requires far more understanding of the characteristics of the computer being used. As a consequence, lower languages are generally used for frequently run programs or those requiring a maximum of machine performance. Under these circumstances, the greater effort required of the user is amply rewarded. Typical programs so written (coded) include operating systems (Section 9.6) and those connected with real-time processing. In addition, programs which translate high-level language programs may also be written in machine-oriented languages, especially as they are amongst the first programs ever written for the machine in question. Frequently run application programs for such purposes as automatic plant control, numerical tool control and other areas involving decision making and logical processes often use low-level languages as the decisions can easily be expressed in a binary form.

We are now in a position to recognize two quite distinct forms of programming language. At the machine-dependent level, the user is tied to what is provided in the machine-code set. The machine-code forms a kernel for what can be coded. On the other hand, looking from the top, tasks are generally quite independent of the machine—they just need to be processed.

There are several languages and techniques used to connect the user to the hardware. However, three levels dominate:

1.   machine level in which the 1s and 0s are entered directly to the computer;
2.   the assembly level, in which the labor of using 1s and 0s is obviated by the use of "mnemonics";
3.   quasi-English or algebraic languages.

Assembly languages are so called because the machine-code form is assembled from the binary equivalents of the mnemonic instructions and symbolic labels which make it up. The program which does this is called an assembler, and would, itself, be binary coded. There is normally a one-to-one correspondence between each assembly instruction and a machine-code counterpart. Assembly language is thus machine-dependent—it is merely a rather more tractable form of machine code.

Each line in a high-level language can define quite a complex arithmetic or logical operation, and as such may give rise to a large number of machine instructions, when translated. Each statement is therefore said to be compiled into machine code, and the program for doing this is called a compiler.

Frequently, high-level language programs are compiled into assembly code and then into machine code rather than direct to machine code. This is in keeping with the "edifice" concept and makes compiler writing that much easier. Compilers are usually written in an assembly or suchlike language. To be accurate, even the jump from a high-level to an assembly-language is sufficiently great that an intermediate language is often invoked. This will not necessarily be machine dependent, but may well be constructed to recognize some of the shortcomings of the machine-code set. Suitable choice of language can make the transition from machine independence to dependence an easy one (see Section 9.4).

9.1.4 Microcomputer systems

Here, there are several approaches to system design. For calculators, the use to which any key is put is fixed. This restricts the machine's repertoire as seen by the user. The interpretation of key punches can be written as a set of programs (in machine code) but committed to ROM. This is a form of firmware. The program never changes and the cost of firmware development can be amortized over thousands of units sold. The machine therefore has three major levels: hardware, microcode (probably part of the microprocessor) and firmware in a hierarchy. If the calculator is programmable, a fourth level, above the others, comes into existence. Its language will be the equivalent binary codes of the sequence of keys pressed in defining the user program. (The order of keys pressed in the "learning phase" determines the order of user instruction execution during run time.)

Some microcomputer systems use the same software edifice as that for conventional computers as shown in Fig. 9.1.

9.1.5 Structured versus unstructured programming

The volume of software needed for a computer, be it a single user program or a suite of compilers, operating systems, etc., usually requires a number of people to work on it in sections. Regardless of this, the understanding of a set of software requires the reader to break up the text into sections which are then linked together into a coherent whole. For either case, there is good cause that the software should consist of a number of manageable and identifiable pieces, each with an interface to the next section. To simplify the interface as much as possible is very desirable, i.e. each section should be quite self-contained and carry as few variables and conditions as possible into the next section. This is called a *structured* approach and is widely used. However, in order to make each interface so simple carries a penalty which shows itself as an inefficient handover from section to section. Each section must terminate with a "clean-up" operation and the next start by performing operations which prevent corruption of one section by another. This wastes time and means that structured programs usually need more run time than unstructured ones. However, structured approaches are very popular and again fall into the spirit of an edifice mentioned earlier.

9.2   SYSTEM ORGANIZATION

9.2.1   The hardware/software interface—machine code

If the computer is simply split into two hierarchical levels, then aportionment of tasks merely involves the simple choice: can a particular facility be better provided in hardware or software? (If firmware is involved as well, the issue is more complex as, in a sense, firmware forms a third level between the two.)

Generally speaking, the only hardware functions provided are those which are of low cost and which also either are frequently used or make use of existing resources, or at least are sufficiently closely related to such resources. More exotic functions may also be provided if their use can radically improve machine performance in a large enough number of applications. Software then has to pick up the remainder of tasks, except where firmware can provide an intermediate choice. Firmware is discussed in more detail in Section 9.5, but at this point it is worth mentioning that firmware and hardware can be used in combination to give faster execution of functions than software and at a cost which a special hardware provision may dwarf. As an example, a computer's hardware may be able to handle all integer arithmetic up to division on single-word operands but need firmware routines to handle floating-point operations or variable-length decimal instructions. Software might then be used for multi-word binary arithmetic floating-point instructions and all functions generation.

Much computer activity is not concerned with complex operations but just with mundane tasks such as data movements and conditioning. Examples of instructions which fall into this category are:

MOVE (register/memory to/from register/memory);
MASK (logical AND of fields of bits);
ROTATE (bitwise shifting of fields);

Many variations exist but most only operate on small amounts of data at each instruction execution. Program loops are usually necessary to move large volumes of data (strings). Analysis of the mix of instructions used in a computer depends both on the instruction repertoire offered and the type of computer. An analysis by Motorola (Ritter and Boney, 1979) suggests that instructions are used in a typical 8-bit microcomputer in the following proportions:

Load/store	39%
Subroutine call/returns	13%
Branches, etc.	17%
Add/subtract	3%
Tests	6%
Others	22%

It clearly indicates what a small percentage of instructions actually do arithmetic compared with those which simply move data around. The above analysis is known as static, i.e. it represents the mix of instructions as written by programmers. This contrasts with dynamic analysis which shows the number of times instructions are actually *executed* during run time. (A given instruction may be executed many times if it is embedded in a loop.) If a computer offers multiply hardware (larger micros, most minis) or if it can perform floating-point operations (as can many minis and almost all main-frames) the mix can vary markedly. Many data movements are often part of the software implementation of functions not available in hardware.

9.2.2 Hardware/software interaction

Hardware and system designers can play a vital role in providing a selection of low-cost facilities in a computer processor for reducing the number of simple, but run-time consuming, software tasks faced by the machine-language programmer. If this task is eased it will reflect in the execution speed of high-level programs which use machine-dependent facilities as their base.

From the previous section, it is clear that many tasks are associated with data movements. One way in which these can be made more effective is by the provision of a number of hardware addressing modes. Each one of these modes is given a unique operation code so that it may be selected by the programmer. Typical tasks encountered by the user are:

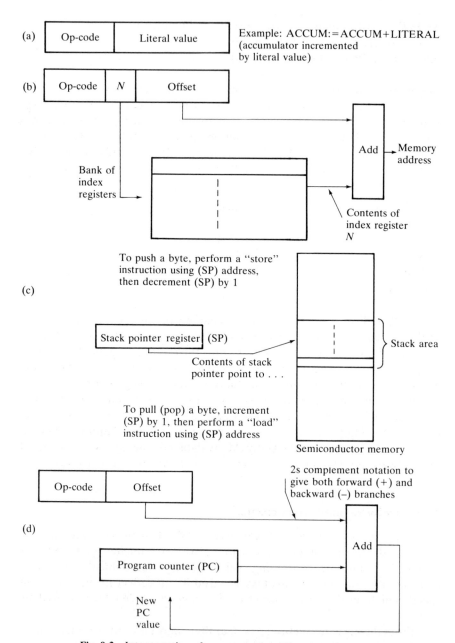

(a) Example: ACCUM:=ACCUM+LITERAL (accumulator incremented by literal value)

Fig. 9.2 Interpretation of some common addressing modes; (a) literal (immediate) addressing; (b) general scheme of indexed addressing; (c) schematic use of a stack pointer (SP) for addressing; (d) PC relative branching (jumping, controlling transfer); (e) PC relative addressing (schematic); (f) base-plus-index addressing.

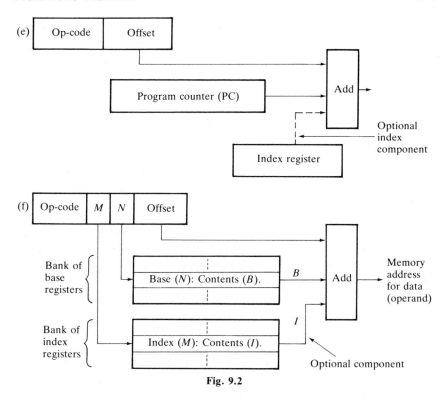

Fig. 9.2

1. Provision of constants or literals for programs. Without an immediate addressing mode in which the instruction contains the constant required, the constant would have to be stored in a table and accessed by a normal (direct) address instruction (Fig. 9.2(a)).

2. Access to tables of data through the use of index registers which can be incremented or decremented each time they are used. This allows each element of a table to be accessed in turn without the use of a separate instruction for each element. Index registers can also make multibyte operations easy by allowing each significance (byte) to be executed in turn. Index registers also avoid instruction modification (Section 1.4) to achieve the same object. In this way corruption of the original program is prevented (Fig. 9.2(b)).

3. Access to hardware or software stacks so that stack-oriented high-level languages can be efficiently implemented or even emulated (Section 9.5.3). Many languages are organized around a stack concept. PASCAL (Jensen and Wirth, 1976; Grogono, 1978) is a good example (Fig. 9.2(c)).

4. The ability to achieve position-independent code. When a computer handles several tasks in a multiprogramming scheme, i.e. several pro-

grams are resident in memory at any one time, absolute addressing presents a problem. Each programmer would undoubtedly like to think that he is the only one resident in memory and as such should be able to write code starting from location zero. All his memory references could then be with respect to zero whether they were branches (jumps) or memory-based data references. However, not everybody can be at location zero. In fact, many programs may actually be moved around memory according to space available. Position-independent code is a concept which allows the programmer to write his code as if he were actually based on zero. Either hardware or software sorts out the actual addresses he needs, taking account of his start-of-program address.

The software version of this concept arranges that all memory references he makes are modified when the program's actual memory position has been determined. This may happen as part of the assembly or compilation process (Section 9.3.4) and is known as *relocation*.

The hardware version arranges that memory references are of a relative nature, with respect to some register, at run time:

1. Branch instructions may be provided which add the user's destination to the current program counter (PC) value. This is known as *relative addressing* and clearly achieves position-independency as the user's address is only an increment of movement (Fig. 9.2(d)).
2. Data references can also be made relative to the program counter. This addressing mode is known as *PC relative*. The effective address may also contain a component from the index register, but this will not affect position-independency (Fig. 9.2(e)).
3. Use of a separate register, usually known as a *base*, to offset both destination and data addresses called by the user. This is only a slight variation of the above but is often more convenient as a separate base can be associated with each program. There is only one program counter (Fig. 9.2(e)).

The designer can help the machine-code programmer in several other ways as well. In particular, it is common for many computers to use variable-length operation codes (Section 3.5). If each byte of an instruction is accessed in turn from memory, then long instructions are likely to have long execution times. (It is assumed that the total execution time is dominated by the instruction fetch time.) If the hardware designer knows in advance that certain instructions are likely to have a high utilization, they might be arranged to be of only one or two bytes length. This applies particularly to data movement and simple arithmetic instructions.

The hardware designer is going to be concerned with the aportionment of tasks between pure hardware (logic, registers, etc.) and microcode. Microcode is concerned with the timing and sequencing of elementary data movements through the processor to implement the machine-code instructions (Section 6.4). If the microcode generator is based on the use of read-only memories (ROM), or even better, read/write memories (RAM), then the content of the microcode generator can be altered at will. Such a facility allows the movement of tasks up and down the processing hierarchy of Fig. 9.1, according to overall system requirements.

For example, if a series of computers is to be developed having different facilities and performance but the same machine-code set, then the use of programmable microcode generators allows tasks to be executed at any one of several levels from hardware up to a software level.

1. In a high-performance version of the system, decimal floating-point operations may be carried out by hardware under the control of the microcode generator. Such instructions would have unique operation codes.

2. Lower-performance versions may use more elementary hardware and therefore need a different microprogram to realize the same instructions. It may be that for this case the microcode generator would, itself, be hierarchical, using a low level for direct hardware control to realize integer–decimal arithmetic and a higher level to call such subprograms (to realize the instructions specified in the machine code).

3. Very lowly members of the computer "family" may have machine-code routines written for complex instructions. These routines would be written to reserved (privileged, shaded) areas of memory or be contained in read-only areas of main memory. The instructions available to such routines would be very elementary in nature due to the simple hardware available. Whenever such a complex instruction was encountered in a program, its operation code would be identified and the appropriate, fixed, machine-code routine entered. Essentially, the execution of such instructions would be quite transparent to the user. All machines in the family would be capable of handling such instructions but because of differences in approach to execution, would take different times to complete them. They would also make different demands on the hardware, microcode and memory facilities.

The use of stacks and stack pointers has already been mentioned in Section 8.3. They are another, important, example of the provision of low-cost hardware facilities to ease the software burden. Some of the software implications associated with the use of stacks are introduced in Section 9.7.

9.2.3 Microprogramming

The concept of a microprogram as a vehicle for implementing machine-code instructions has already been touched on in Section 6.4. However, a microprogram is more than just a hardware convenience for rationalizing the untidy timing and control-sequence logic that tends to "grow" around a hard-wired processor. It is a concept in itself which can radically alter the approach to system design. In particular, it allows for more flexibility of task allocation in a computer by allowing tasks to be performed at several different levels. In some computers, special instructions, not declared to the user, are "invented" by the computer manufacturers for special purposes. These have an unique operation code, like any other instruction, and possibly have their own area of microprogram for their execution. Of the many uses to which such "pseudo-instructions" can be applied, those for assisting in the emulation of other (target) computers are of special importance (see Section 9.5.3).

It is impossible for the designer to exclude microprogramming from the hardware/software design equation or even to deal with it in isolation. Microprogramming interacts with the hardware and software in terms of the facilities it makes possible and according to the performance achieved; it is not just another level in the processing hierarchy. In a typical computer, interfaces exist between hardware, microprogramming and software in all possible combinations and they must therefore be considered together in order to determine the interdependencies. Microprogramming is considered in more detail in Section 9.5.2.

9.2.4 Data structures

Although it would be difficult for the hardware designer to predict from what has been said so far what forms of data structures will be required in a computer system, some of the shortcomings of hardware memory organization can be illustrated by taking some real-life situations. Most memories are based on the concept of direct addressing and fixed-length entities (data). Direct addressing means that for each entity there is a certain address. Fixed length means that each address is associated with a certain invariant number of bits. In practical situations, neither of these attributes is particularly desirable or applicable.

Data are not normally just collections of freestanding pieces of information. They are generally associated with some particular name, activity or *key*. For instance, a list of all automobile model names could use manufacturers' names as keys to the models. Such a list would have the following properties:

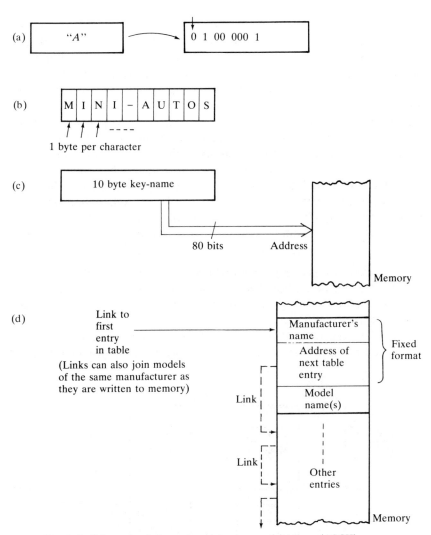

Fig. 9.3 Schematic of elementary data storage: (a) binary (ASCII) coding of a character; (b) multibyte organization of key-names; (c) linear key-to-memory address transformation; (d) linear table construction.

1. Neither manufacturers' nor model names would be of fixed length. They might typically consist of a number of ASCII characters, each of which could occupy 1 byte of memory (Fig. 9.3(a)).

2. The number of manufacturers and model names is likely to both grow and wane with time.

3. References will be made both to manufacturers' and model names during use of such a file.

A central issue is that if, say, 10 characters are allowed for any manufacturer's name, then 10 eight-bit bytes are needed for each (Fig. 9.3(b)).
Assuming the available characters to be upper and lower-case letters and
digits, this permits 62^{10} ($\approx 8 \times 10^{17}$) possible names. Normal direct hardware
addressing, that is, making a linear transformation of a name bit pattern, into
an address pattern, would imply the need for a 62^{10}-location memory (Fig.
9.3(c)). This is clearly impractical and a more compact packing method is
needed. Another extreme alternative would be to put all names in a long
linear list starting at the top of memory. This is a *linear* table (Fig.9.3(d)).
This approach is also undesirable as the list may have to be scanned from end
to end in order to find a particular entry. On average, half the list is
scanned—a time-consuming process if it is at all long. There are many
improvements possible but any usable one must take account of the need to
add or delete items from time to time. Amongst the techniques employed
are:

1. Use of *links* or *pointers* which can connect one item of data to
another (related) one. For this example, each model name could have an
associated address value pointing to the next model in the list under the same
manufacturer (Fig. 9.4).

2. The use of *relatively* small sub-lists or tables of models in which
linear address transformation is replaced with simple distribution of the

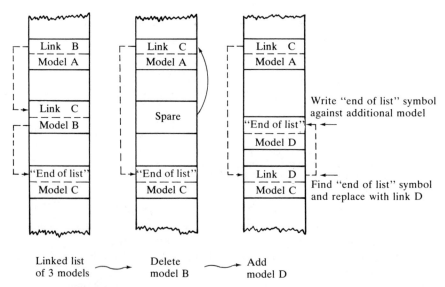

Fig. 9.4 Linking of data under the same key showing additions and
deletions to list.

items amongst the tables in an orderly but fairly even manner. If it is estimated that there are around 40 manufacturers, the 62^{10} possible manufacturers' addresses could be replaced with say 64 addresses (a number of "slots" not greatly in excess of the actual number). The trick is then to create an addressing method that causes the manufacturers to be associated with separate tables, but in such a way that searching for a certain manufacturer gives an almost certain hope of a "hit" at the first table searched (Fig. 9.5).

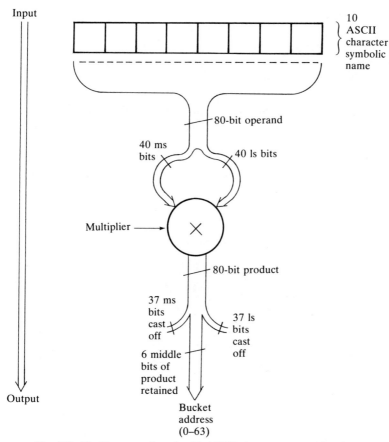

Fig. 9.5 Hashing procedure for 10 ASCII character names (keys) using multiplication. This example could handle around 40 names which would be distributed (scattered) amongst 64 buckets. About 30% of names will attempt to occupy already-occupied buckets.

This is known as "*hashing*" and the table generated known as a *hashing table*. Hashing, in effect, means mixing up the entries in such a way that each manufacturer will probably gravitate to a different location from any other.

As an example, suppose the 80-bit manufacturers' names are split into two fields each of 40 bits. These two could be treated as 40-bit integers and multiplied to create an 80-bit product. The middle 6 bits of this product could be used as an address in which to put the model names for that particular manufacturer. It is unlikely that two manufacturers' names would produce the same 6-bit product field so that each should go into a separate location in memory. If during this assignment to memory, any one entry computed an already occupied location, then it could just be entered in the next location (modulo 64). If that is occupied, the next could be tried and so on.

In order to locate a manufacturer (read), the same multiplication process is done and the same 6-bit field used. If the wrong name is found associated with the computed memory location, the one next door is tried, etc. Usually, most correct names are found first time. However, if this is not the case and the trials at adjoining addresses are ever to reveal an unoccupied location, this indicates that the name sought has never been entered to the table (Fig. 9.6).

A design difficulty associated with hashing tables is the decision as to the time at which the table should be expanded if more than the expected

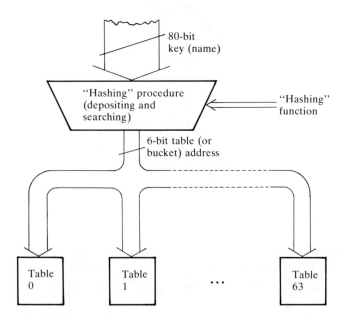

Fig. 9.6 "Hashing" system for allowing about 40 (10 ASCII character) keys to a set of 64 tables or buckets. Each table may be able to hold more than one key. When it becomes full, additional keys have to be passed on to neighboring tables to find room.

number of keys requires allocation to memory. Clearly, if too much "moving next door" is permitted as the table fills, searching becomes very protracted. On the other hand initial allocation of excessive space is obviously undesirable as well. Generally speaking, it is best not to let the table get more than about 60% full before expanding it.

Apart from hashing, there are several alternative techniques open to the designer for coping with generalized data storage:

1. *Associative memory* This has already been described in its hardware form in Section 4.6. In this, all keys can be inspected simultaneously to determine the availability and location of data. However, the technique is costly and cannot be applied to the larger systems encountered here. Nonetheless, low-performance software simulations of associative memories are quite feasible and are sometimes employed, especially where some order can be achieved in the mapping of the data to memory (Fig. 9.7).

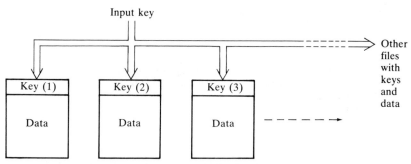

Fig. 9.7 Associative memory concept — concurrent search of all key names in memory.

2. *Binary search trees* We have already encountered the concept of cross-referencing blocks of data by the use of links, i.e. one type of data can refer to another by means of a forwarding address in the first item. Of course, in principle, there is no limit to the number of such links that can be formed between any one "parent" item of data and its "children". However, to refer from a parent to the correct child involves a computation.

A special case of this approach is the binary search tree (Fig. 9.8). The number of children is restricted to two to make the computation very easy. A simple method arranges that the key for one child (the left one) appears alphabetically before the parent and the one to the right afterwards. A search for a particular key merely involves a comparison between the desired key and a parent to decide which route to take, i.e. which child to

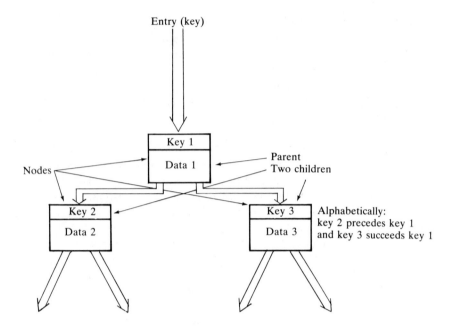

Fig. 9.8 Binary-search tree. Starting at "entry", each key is checked and the branch to the appropriate child taken. Until the key sought is found, the process is repeated from generation to generation.

choose as the next parent. If the number of generations formed in the tree is k, then about 2^k nodes (parents+children) would populate the tree if all parents had two existing children. The average search time for a particular key (node) clearly only rises as the logarithm of the number of keys. The binary search tree is therefore superior to an ordinary linked (linear) list, paricularly where the number of nodes is large (Ullman, 1976).

9.3 MACHINE-DEPENDENT LANGUAGES

9.3.1 Introduction

Any language has two important characteristics which

1. define a grammar to constrain the user's program specification to a form which can be unambiguously interpreted and translated to machine-executable form;

2. gives the necessary information to the program which carries out the translation to produce the machine code.

These are known respectively as *syntax* and *semantics*.

Of the machine-dependent languages, assembly languages are probably the most important. Symbolic rather than absolute addresses can be used for branch destinations and variables locations. These, together with easy-to-remember (mnemonic) names for operation codes are assembled by a program, known as an *assembler*, into machine-executable form. There is usually a close one-to-one correspondence between each assembly-language instruction and a machine-code instruction in the computer's repertoire.

Users can benefit by taking a multilevel approach to assembly-code programming. The main program can be split into major tasks which can, in turn, be split into minor tasks, and so on. Often these minor tasks can be made common to several major ones with a consequent saving of code. For instance, the same decimal arithmetic add routine might be pressed into service to support both root extraction and decimal division.

Examples of facilities to help a multilevel approach to user software include:

1. the ability for the user to define his own tasks, using some simple mnemonic, when needed. The task will be defined in terms of the language employed. Such an entity is called a *macro* and is available in most languages. A macro is written whenever a routine is going to be invoked on several occasions in a program. It need only be defined once and can then be "called" when required. The assembler or compiler will then fill in the code in the program, using the "macro definition" as a source of information. To be flexible, the macro will use parameters (its own variable names) which can be changed to those of the calling macro instruction. This is the "minimum link" mentioned under the heading of a structured approach (Fig. 9.9).

2. The ability to call *subroutines*. These are not dissimilar from macros and can be used interchangeably in some circumstances. Of more importance, a subroutine appears only once in the code *executed* by the computer—it does not appear as a substitute block of code against every call. The subroutine is defined and coded once and at run-time the program is diverted to it by a change in the program counter's contents, whenever it is required. When execution of the routine is completed after any call, program control reverts to the instruction immediately following the subroutine call. Clearly the switching of control takes more time than just proceeding through a set of substituted instructions in the user's program, as is the case for a macro. Furthermore, it is often necessary to move data around the computer before and after the subroutine to avoid corruption of data. This

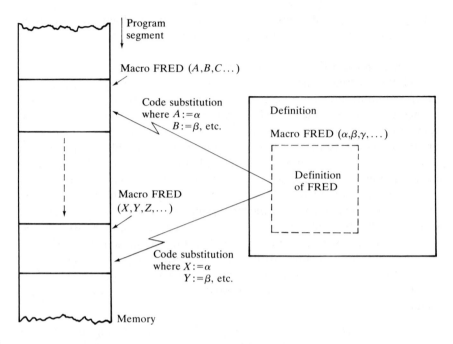

Fig. 9.9 Macro with formal parameters. After substitution of variables, the definition replaces the calling statement.

wastes more time. However, as the subroutine only appears once in the object program, memory space is saved, whereas a macro appears in object code wherever it is called.

It is usual for subroutines to be able to call themselves, making possible a multilevel nest. See Section 3.4 for an example. Some macros have the same ability. This is known as *recursion* and is permissible in some languages. See Section 9.4.2 for some applications of this facility.

(a) *Assembly language*

We can describe a language structure which applies to most assemblers simply because of the similarity between machine-hardware architectures. Generally, for each assembly instruction there is a corresponding machine-code instruction. A suitable line of assembly code is shown in Fig. 9.10.

As part of the syntax, it is important that the assembler can tell when one field of an instruction ends and another begins. This can be done either by imposing a fixed format on the layout of the line or by having agreed field separators, such as spaces. (Once the assembler knows it is dealing with a comment field, the occurrence of spaces does not matter.)

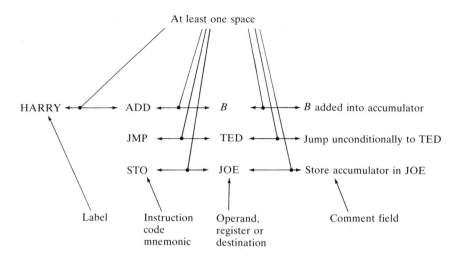

Fig. 9.10 Typical lines of assembly code showing four major fields. (*Note*: the mnemonics used vary from one manufacturer to another.)

One line of code is conveniently discriminated from another by a carriage return/line feed character or by the arrival of a new punched card. This is important, as it must be possible for the assembler to recover if it encounters an error which makes assembly or even interpretation of the line impossible. It can simply start again on the next line. By this means, most syntactic errors in a tract of assembly code should be identifiable in one pass; it will not be necessary to perform a separate pass for each error just because the assembler becomes thoroughly confused when each error is encountered.

As part of the language, assemblers allow expressions as well as symbols for defining addresses. Expressions must be simple in order neither to protract the assembly process nor to make relocation impossible (see Section 9.3.4). Typical expressions are FRED+1, BLOGGS+FRED+1. It is quite simple for the assembler to find values for FRED, etc., and to create an address from them. Such a facility allows indexed addressing for tables and array manipulation.

Assembly languages can imply addressing modes not necessarily in the hardware repertoire. A simple example is immediate addressing where the assembler would make up a table of constants for all occurrences of immediate addressing and simply substitute direct-addressing machine instructions, with an appropriate address, for the required constant. If more than one immediate-addressing mnemonic instruction called for the same constant value, the same one in the table could, of course, be used. A list of constants could be retained in a hashing table to ease the search for those already available (during assembly). Assemblers allow several representations of constants but suitable formatting must be used to discriminate between the types. Examples are: 45, H(45), *45, "true" for decimal, hexadecimal, octal and Boolean respectively. However, different assemblers recognize different formats and the correct one must be checked out before use. There is no absolute standard in this respect.

(b) *Conditional assembly*

This is an extension of the macro facility. It allows very similar macros to be defined just once and the subtle differences to be identifiable by extra parameters. The correct machine code is then assembled by reference to these parameters.

Example

MACRO FRED (A, B, CONDITION)
LOAD A
IF CONDITION   COMMENT: THE NEXT LINE IS INCLUDED
                      IF CONDITION=0

ADD B
IF CONDITION−1   COMMENT: THE NEXT LINE IS INCLUDED
                      IF (CONDITION−1)=0 i.e. CONDITION=1

MULT B
ENDM

A macro call of the form FRED W,X,0 would produce machine code equivalent to

   LOAD W
   ADD X

However a call of the form FRED U,V,1 would produce

   LOAD U
   MULT V

There are many other variations and facilities often made available.

(c) *Memory protection*

This is needed if more than one program is resident in memory at any one time, e.g. during multiprogramming. It may just prevent corruption of the operating system (Section 9.6) by erroneous user programs. It may protect one user from another by preventing cross corruption. This can be achieved by designating memory areas to users and checking on the validity of addresses generated by users. Operating systems often use systems of *bounding registers* to define the limits of applicability of individual users' addresses for this purpose. Such bounding registers would themselves be located in "shaded" (privileged) or protected areas of memory so that they could only be altered (written to) by the operating system.

(d) *Pseudo-instructions*

Because an assembly language is machine dependent, some control instructions have to be given to the assembler which are used just by the assembler and are not converted to machine code along with the rest of the user program. Examples are:

	ORG	1000	meaning the following user code is to located in memory at 1000,1001,1002 etc
	END	2000	meaning this is the end of the user program and execution will start at location 2000.
BOB	DS	4	meaning leave 4 bytes of memory space for variables called BOB
TOM	DC	45	meaning set a constant called TOM to decimal 45.

There are a number of others: see Ullman (1976).

(e) *Re-entrancy*

This property of some assemblers and compilers makes the scheduling of tasks easier because it allows programs to break off before execution is completed and go on to some other, maybe more pressing, task. When the original task can be resumed, it will continue from the point it left off.

Example 1 A data-logging system may have several inputs and each may need processing when a sample arrives. If a low-precedence task is in progress when a higher-precedence sample arrives through another channel, the first task must be abandoned in its favor. When the higher-precedence task is complete, reversion to the original one requires that a record of the status of this task can be obtained to give a clean restart. This is re-entrancy.

Example 2 Several tasks may be coded in similar languages which use common (library) subroutines. To prevent wastage of memory space, a routine could be written once to memory and shared by all users. If users can be interrupted by each other, again because of some precedence or priorities system in operation, a subroutine may only be partially used before an interrupt takes place. A record must then be kept of the progress to date through this routine so that a clean restart can take place. However, the interrupting program may well want to start this routine afresh for its own purposes. This is, again, a form of re-entrancy.

A stack system is clearly central to the realization of a re-entrancy facility to keep records of progress for each caller. However, alternatives which effectively *emulate* a stack-based system are also possible:

1. If the processor offers indexed addressing, the index register could be used to point to the beginning of a user's "workspace". Its contents would then be updated when a new user becomes active. The offset portion of indexed instructions could then be used to point to a particular byte or area of the user's workspace. This arrangement could be used in the Motorola M6800 microcomputer.
2. If a computer operates on a context basis, as does the Texas Instruments TMS 9900, then the idea of workspace operation is built into the processor's hardware. In the TMS 9900, there are no general hardware registers; main memory is used to hold work areas for each user or context. See Section 8.3 for a fuller hardware description.

9.3.2 The assembly process

An assembler is a program which would normally be resident in the main (semiconductor or core) memory of a computer when it is being used. Normal assembly implies that the assembly is being carried out in the processor (or in a processor of the same style) in which subsequent execution of the machine code will be performed. Alternatively, *cross-assembly* implies that a different processor will be used for the execution so that the user will have written his original (source) program with the second machine in mind. Either way, at this time, the assembler represents the program and the user's assembly coded program represents the data. It is quite possible that the assembler program will occupy a considerable area of memory when in use so that the whole of the user's source or object (machine) texts will not have room as well. Indeed, it is possible that the assembler may, during use, occupy a part of the memory which will *subsequently* be needed by the object code during run time. As a consequence, rather than reading the source code, *in toto*, into memory, it is normal for it to be read a line at a time and processed into object code a line at a time. The memory needed for one line is quite trivial and only one is resident in memory at a time. The only exception to this rule applies to one-pass assemblers (see Section 9.3.3).

(a) *Two-pass assemblers*

As only one line of source text is resident at any time, once it has been processed, it is not available for further processing. If that line contains a reference to a line (with a label) which has yet to be encountered by the assembler, a binary address cannot be attached to the binary operation code. This situation is known as a *forward reference* and may apply either to forward branches or to forward data memory references. To allow forward references, two passes of the source text are made through the assembler. The first one does no more than collect symbolic names and converts them to binary addresses, as they are encountered, and puts this information into a symbol table. During the second pass, the binary equivalents of the symbolic names can be substituted. During this second pass, binary operation codes will be substituted for symbolic mnemonics. However, it should be noted that, although binary operation codes are left to the second pass, the instruction length implied by the mnemonic will have been used to assess the memory address of each instruction. (Different instructions have different byte lengths in many computers.) At least two sets of tables are required for assemblers:

1. A table of symbols to be built up for labels during the first pass (which will be accessed to have binary addresses supplied as they become available). This can benefit from hashing techniques to accelerate table searching.

2. A table of operation-code mnemonics and the binary values, byte lengths and some additional information relevant to the relocation system (see Section 9.3.4).

(b) *Macros*

During assembly, the Macro definition, *per se*, causes no actual machine code to be generated. Only where it is *called* is code substituted. This can be compared with subroutines in which the one occasion that the subroutine is defined is the time that code is generated. The macro is entered to a table of operation codes during pass 1. In the above example, FRED would be the key. The associated data would be the formal parameters (in the order in which they were given). The *definition* is then deleted so that during pass 2 code will only be substituted where calls to FRED are found. In effect FRED is treated rather like a super-instruction during pass 2.

9.3.3 One-pass assemblers

It can be seen that the two-pass assembler represents an obvious implementation if forward references are to be allowed, without resorting to keeping the whole of the user's program in memory during assembly. There are some circumstances in which either adequate memory *is* available or the user's program is sufficiently short that both can be accommodated. A single pass is then sufficient just to load in the program and forward references can be handled whilst the program is in memory. Another way to a get a "free" second pass is to defer the allocation of forward references to the load phase. The load phase follows assembly and puts the user's object code into the correct area of memory for execution (see Section 9.3.4).The normal second pass can be merged with this operation as loading is in itself a form of pass. This practice is common in systems of the so-called *load-and-go* variety, whereby running of a program automatically and without hesitation follows assembly.

Reduction of passes can be important in small computers, especially if they have only slow peripheral devices for entering users' programs to the assembler. The problem is not so severe if fast disk memories are available to hold programs during these processes.

(a) *Interpreters*

There is an alternative to the conventional two-pass assembler used on a number of calculators and small computers. This is the interpreter. (It can also be used in conjunction with high-level languages.) Interpreters are related to the load-and-go approach and convert each user instruction to machine code *as it is encountered during run time*. There is no preparatory work done on the user's program prior to run time. For a calculator, the program consists of coded values corresponding to the order in which the keys are pressed during the programming operation. These are stored in contiguous memory locations. At run time, each code is retrieved from memory, converted (interpreted to machine-executable form) and causes machine actions corresponding to those which would have been obtained if the operator had pressed the keys himself.

For a computer, each source code instruction is converted to one or more machine-code instructions during run time and the instructions so produced are executed prior to conversion of the next user instruction. As this is a version of single-pass operation, certain restrictions must be applied:

1. Memory references must either be absolute or relative or of a form that requires no references to symbol tables.

2. Macros, if they are permitted, must also obey similar addressing rules.

9.3.4 Loaders and linkage editors

If a program is assembled, it must then be placed in memory ready for execution. The programmer, as suggested earlier, would like to think that he has sole occupancy of memory and can therefore start his program at location zero. A loader is a program which will place object code where there is room in memory and will adjust all address references in the user's program to take account of this. It is quite possible that the user's program will be moved to different places in memory from time to time so that address allocation may take place on several occasions.

A common practice is therefore for the loader to add suitable offsets to all memory references in the user's program according to where the program is to be loaded to memory and the addressing mode used.

Example 1 A direct address to location n in the user's program will become $n+k$ if the user's program actually starts at location k.

Example 2 A relative address $(+r)$ will stay as r because the relative movement is unaffected by the absolute placement of the program.

Example 3 An immediate address will be unaffected as the data are attached to the instruction itself.

Example 4 A reference to another program, e.g. a library subroutine, will only be affected by the *location of the subroutine*, not the placement of the user's program.

In order that the loader knows what to do with each memory reference, the assembler must pass sufficient information to it. To this end, the assembler creates, not absolute machine (object) code but *relocatable binary*, i.e. binary which has additional information for driving the *loader*. The loader will then separate the addressing directives from the user addresses in the relocatable binary program and modify the user's addresses in the absolute binary object program according to the final location of the program. The output of the loader is absolute binary object code in machine-executable form.

As programs are completed or aborted in a multiprocessing arrangement, memory space becomes available for other programs. Each program occupies a certain area of memory, for which the loader keeps records. Some programs may have to be segmented to fit into the available space. Each tract has a record kept of its memory occupancy. The record can be in several forms but the simplest ones are:

1. use of bounding registers for each tract giving start and end addresses;
2. use of base and length registers to indicate the start and byte length of a program tract.

As each area of space is made available, these registers can be interrogated to see if sufficient space exists to enter a new program. The collection of areas of memory after occupancy, ready for new programs, is called *garbage collection*.

(a) *Base registers*

Some computers have base registers to aid relocation. Again, the user writes his program from location zero as if he were the sole user. However, during run time, all his memory references are offset by the content of this processor resident hardware base register, in effect relocating at run time. The base value is set by the loader under the remit of the operating system and can be altered by it. The base is normally made unavailable to the user, in case of abuse. Modification of base values is usually done by reserved instructions in the processor's repertoire, available only to the operating system. This system makes relocation very easy and, by the use of a number of base registers, permits several programs to be handled at once. Memory references using the base take longer to execute at run time as the base value is added every time such a reference is made. However, this is often a very small penalty. Systems which include this facility are widespread, and include the IBM 370 computers.

(b) *Linkage editors*

It is necessary to be able to bring together segments of programs into a coherent whole, and for this a linkage editor is used. In particular, the linkage editor is needed to attach library subroutines to the main programs, when they are called. Part of the editor's job is to compute the memory cross-references from one segment of program to another. In some machines this process is combined with loading to produce a program called a linking loader.

9.3.5 Assembler construction

For a computer which is going to afford user flexibility, writing of the various assemblers and compilers is a step-by-step procedure. It will start with machine code and work up. Writing in machine code is very tedious and error prone, difficult to document, difficult to modify and maintain and understand for the first time.

An assembler must be written, in part, in machine code. However, only a small proportion of it will have to be so written *just* to allow mnemonic instructions to be used. This involves little more than the generation of a table of mnemonics and their associated binary values. However, even this considerably reduces tedium. Using this facility, the part of the assembler which can handle symbolic addresses can then be constructed. This facility can then be used for the generation of the next part of the assembler. In effect, from rudimentary beginnings, a complete assembler can be written, gradually increasing its sophistication by pulling itself up by its bootstraps. The binary version of it will then be put into secondary memory by a process known as a *binary dump*.

As the assembler is created, care must be taken to avoid using facilities which are not yet available, or making any errors. This is an edifice and any errors created early on will propagate into the final version of the program. Furthermore, whilst the assembler is in this intermediate state it will probably lack error-detection facilities that will protect users of the final program.

9.3.6 Uses and shortcomings of assembly languages

The closer the user operates to the hardware of a computer, the greater the effectiveness of his software and its run-time performance. Facilities provided by machine-independent languages have to serve several aims, of which breadth of applicability is one. Such facilities cannot be as effective as actually specifying down to the last register movement the details of a program, as happens in machine-dependent code.

High-level languages and compilers are used and designed with several components to optimize. These not only include run-time performance but also economy of code, ease of programming, simple syntax, speed of compilation, economy of compiler memory requirements and others. Run-time performance for many applications can have far less precedence than other factors and is usually traded with them to some extent.

In simple terms, the user's choice is between ease of programming, documentation and maintenance against run-time performance. Software with some hope of unmodified longevity such as operating systems, compilers, plant-control software, job-control languages and those demanding maximum performance are frequently assembly coded. Programs which may only be run once or a few times need to be coded quickly and give useful results with little editing if they are to be worth coding in the first instance. Here code economy and the shortest possible language-learning curve is vital. It may also mean that it should be possible for the same program to be run on more than one manufacturer's machines, i.e. it should be (*trans*)*portable*. This implies the use of machine-independent languages. In short, a high-level, machine-independent language should free the user from any consideration of the hardware characteristics of the machine on which his program is to be run. Furthermore, most of the mathematical and information-handling facilities he is likely to want should be available in an easy-to-use form. He must also be able to ignore the possible presence of other users on the machine he is using and be able to pretend he has all the machine's facilities at his disposal.

In summary, for many purposes, users require sophisticated, neo-English or mathematical languages with which to program to make possible the composition of economical but highly complex procedures.

9.4　MACHINE-INDEPENDENT LANGUAGES

9.4.1　Introduction

Machine-independent or high-level languages are designed with user requirements, rather than machine limitations, in mind. Just as for assembly languages, the specification for a high-level language comes from several sources and these have to be reconciled:

1. The language must be unambiguous.
2. It must be efficient—it must be possible to code it with a minimum of characters to define some routine or algorithm.
3. It must have a syntax (grammar) which is easy to understand.
4. The semantics (structure) must be such that the compiler can quickly translate it to machine code of an efficient form.
5. The code must be *consistent*, i.e. free from irritating conditions and exceptions in its use.

There are a number of other requirements as well which will become clearer when compilers and syntax are discussed in detail.

Just as with assembly-level languages, it is an advantage if the compiled (object) code is relocatable and can come within the ambit of a loader or link-loader. Two gains will be made:

1. The concept of a software hierarchy will be maintained and the compiler will be able to take advantage of facilities (loaders) etc. already provided for machine-dependent languages. The hierarchy in this case is compiler, assembler, machine code.

2. The possibility of mixed language operation will arise, i.e. assembly code can be inserted in the middle of high-level language procedures to make them run faster. (Many compilers produce only assembly code which is again in keeping with the hierarchical concept.)

High-level languages such as FORTRAN, ALGOL and PASCAL offer the possibility of completely breaking away from the computer's hardware limitations as far as coding is concerned. However, algorithms to compile language tracts into machine code must be found. The task is not trivial and it is quite common for an *intermediate code* to be introduced into the compilation process. This code is only used by the compiler and is unseen and unknown to most users. Such codes are discussed more in Section 9.4.2, but this is at least an indication of the complexity of compilation that more than a single language "jump" is necessary.

A typical high-level language statement shares many characteristics with its machine-dependent counterparts insofar that it defines one or more steps in a procedure or algorithm. It may well need to be labelled for branch destinations and operands and room must be provided for commentary. However, it must, to be machine independent, lack any references to specific hardware registers or memory locations. Instead, all references will be to variables, arrays and tables. Abstract names and identifiers will be used.

To reduce the user's coding problem, a number of functions, data formats and the like will be made available. In order that the letter codes (mnemonics) used for these can be differentiated from variables names, etc., certain syntax rules have to be imposed.

Example In FORTRAN (FORmula TRANslation) the following are available:

$Y=X**3$, meaning Y becomes equal to X raised to the power 3

$Y=SIN(X)$, meaning Y becomes equal to the trigonometric sine of X

$Y=X**2+Z*T*(R+W)$, meaning Y becomes equal to $X^2+ZT(R+W)$.

Several of the above do not have exact, single, machine-code counterparts even if decomposed into single arithmetic operations. Therefore routines must be substituted from libraries of functions. These libraries will define such functions in terms of formal parameters which can then have real ones substituted (when they are known to the compiler). This removes restrictions as to variables' names.

This process may be taken one stage further, if instead of X being a simple variable, it is an expression, which must be evaluated before its sine is determined.

High-level languages do not necessarily impose strict formating specifications on the user, although some, like FORTRAN, do. In the event of a "freer" format being allowed, the syntax must be such that no ambiguity exists. The reasoning is much as for assemblers, as indicated in Section 9.3.1. As there is no machine-code counterpart for each statement, the compiler must be able to identify those tasks which can be carried out by hardware (or any faster facility such as firmware) and which must be committed to software. For instance, if the hardware can handle floating-point, binary-coded decimal or Boolean expressions, then the compiler must direct such processing to the hardware. If such hardware does not exist, then software routines must be available to handle them.

9.4.2 The compilation process

In many regards, compilation is similar to assembly. It is very much more complex as there are usually a number of machine-code instructions needed to replace each statement.

In what is called *syntax-directed translation*, compilation can be segmented into seven operations (Fig. 9.11).They are not carried out in isolation or even in a strict sequence. They are activities which, like routines, are called according to the state of progress and the nature of the code currently being compiled. The parts are as follows.

(a) *Lexical analysis*

In this, the source code is scanned, i.e. read statement by statement into a buffer and generally cleaned up. Redundant spaces, delimiters, operators and other symbols are removed. Tables are created for identifiers (variables) just as in an assembler and a set of *tokens* used to substitute for functions and operators according to their class. GO TO could be treated as one type and given a token; / could be given another. Breaking symbols and groups into classes makes parsing easier. As an example+FRED−would be given the tokens "arithmetic sign", "identifier," "arithmetic sign"; +SIN (...would be given tokens "arithmetic sign", "function", expression, etc.

(b) *Syntactic analysis (parsing)*

In order to parse a statement, it is necessary to recognize its structure. A so-called context-free grammar (Ritter and Boney, 1979; Maurer, 1979; Knuth, 1968) can help in this respect.

A language can be described and its attributes and grammar defined in an unambiguous form. From such a description, the validity of statements in this language can be ascertained. A particular description is the Backus–Naur or Backus normal form (BNF description). In effect, the BNF form is analogous to the use of algebra as a substitute for arithmetic operations. Like algebra it has a semantic form, operations and rules of evaluation. Also like algebra, it provides a general description that is valid whatever the values of the variables.

Such a form allows compact recursive definitions to be used, i.e. definitions which can invoke the definition itself as part of the definition (Ullman, 1976).

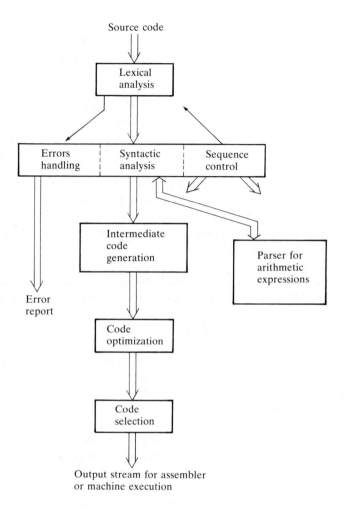

Fig. 9.11 Greatly simplified schematic of a compiler based on "syntax-directed translation".

As an example, if it is necessary to parse $A*(B+C*(D\ldots))$, then each part in parentheses can be treated as an expression in its own right. It is not necessary to define every possible valid form of expression. The parsing for this example might proceed as follows:

1. Recognize the left parenthesis and call a parsing routine for handling the assumed expression that is to follow.

2.   Trace (scan) along $B+C$ and then recognize that an expression is to follow by the second left parenthesis. However, parsing of the first expression has yet to be completed and now the parser is being asked to operate on a second one. Parsing of the first expression must be suspended (without losing track of the state of completion of the first one). The parsing routine must then carry on into a second operation (from the start). In effect, the routine is being used recursively; it is able to call itself, despite not having completed one operation. Such a recursive routine may be called or restarted several times before any given "call" is completed. The completion of all partially completed calls must be done in an orderly manner, taking due account of the delimiting (right) parentheses. The use of a stack can clearly assist in this ordering process and usually forms the kernel of such a parsing routine. Because of hardware capacity limitations, these stacks are often committed to software, using the main memory with its almost unlimited capacity.

This use of recursion is clearly non-numeric. Recursion also has uses in arithmetic work as well although there are usually better ways available. A simple example is the evaluation of factorials. To evaluate $n!$, use can be made of the expression $n!=n\ (n-1)!$ The recursive implementation would loop on itself until the factorial of *one* was required. At this point, the value 1 would be substituted and the recursion could unravel itself back to the point n. *All* recursion procedures must have a point of escape and this usually means that a particular value or circumstance, bound to occur at some point in the evaluation, is tested for.

An important function of parsing is the detection of programmer errors. Putting expressions, etc., into token form and therefore classifying them makes the detection of errors much simpler, because the structure of statements can be used as templates against which the incoming code can be checked.

Part of the ordered decomposition (parsing) of code is concerned with the creation of an intermediate code. In simple systems, the intermediate code or language may be very similar in its semantics to the final assembly language. It might ignore some hardware limitations which are imposed on normal assembly languages and might even have a few useful *imaginary* instructions in its repertoire, not shared with the hardware. PASCAL is often translated to an intermediate form called P code which is based on an ideal stack-oriented machine concept. The actual hardware may or may not reflect this concept, so P code instructions may have to be treated as macros in the final assembly language.

In complex systems, the intermediate language may not reflect the hardware system at all. A popular form is the *three-address code* which can describe operations involving two source operands plus an explicit result

$A: = B+C$

$W: = Y+Z$

Op-code	Result (output)	Source operand 1	Source operand 2

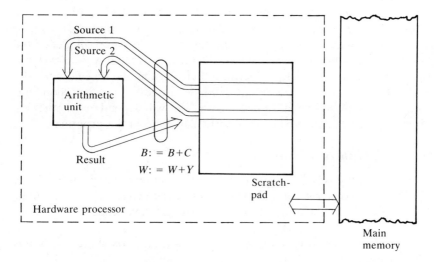

Fig. 9.12   Relationship between three-address intermediate code (as used in a number of compilers) and hardware processor based on a scratch-pad: (a) representative three-address instructions and their machine-code equivalent form; (b) ability of scratch-pad to lift the constraints of the single-accumulator processor.

variable (Fig. 9.12(a)). (Most hardware operates so as to replace one of the source operand locations with the result.) To use an intermediate language which uses three addresses makes possible some code optimization, because all options for addressing have been left open.

As an example: a processor, although restricted to one or two address instructions, may have a fast scratch-pad. If a three-address intermediate code is used, the final phase of compilation (the translation of intermediate to assembly code) can be optimized to use these registers (Fig. 9.12(b)). If the result of an intermediate instruction is placed in a scratch-pad register, the register can be accessed if its contents can now be used as the source operand for a following instruction. Tight loops of instructions occur very frequently in programming so that early reuse of variables commonly occurs. In Newton's method for finding the square root of a number A, the following formula can be used:

$$x_{n+1} = \tfrac{1}{2}(x_n + A/x_n).$$

If a scratch-pad is available, A, x_n and possibly x_{n+1} can be held locally. The use of a three-address intermediate code will highlight the possibility of the use of scratch-pad for such variables. However, if an assembly-language version of the routine were produced direct, it would be difficult, if not practically impossible, to identify such "scratch variables". Little or no use would be made of the scratch-pad and its incorporation would be a waste of money when high-level languages and their compilers were implemented. Of course, intermediate-code statements must be treated with care during the final phase of compilation, because there is generally no guarantee that each intermediate code statement will have a one-to-one correspondence with some assembly-language instruction. This will depend on whether any optimization was achieved at that particular point in the program.

(c) Intermediate code generation

This phase is almost self-explanatory after the comments made in (b) above. However, it should be noted that the intermediate code has certain important properties not shared with the original high-level code:

1. Each statement has only one operator—a property shared with most assembly instructions.
2. The order of the intermediate code statements defines the order of the resulting assembly-language instructions and hence the order of hardware execution. This is not a property shared with the original (source) code. (The operators in the source code are subject to precedence rules, parentheses and other constraining influences.)

On the other hand, like other non-machine-code languages, it uses symbolic addresses. It also, usually, generates a fixed number of machine instructions per statement.

(d) Code optimization

This has already been mentioned in the context of justifying some of the earlier steps in the compilation process. However, it is at this stage that optimization takes place. Use can be made of any hardware attributes to make the final code more efficient. Not only should the existence of processor scratch-pads be taken into account but also addressing facilities and compound conditions testing. Examples are:

1. use of short-address (direct-addressing) modes to cut down on instruction length and execution times at the machine-code level;
2. use of relative addressing schemes in the hardware to avoid the use of long explicit branch-destination addresses;
3. use of immediate (literal) addressing where it can replace direct addressing;
4. use of optional hardware facilities when they are available. For instance, the National Semiconductors NS16000 microprocessor offers only basic arithmetic instructions. However, the use of slave processors can make even floating-point operations available in hardware. From the compiler's point of view, there are several versions of the NS16000 hardware and the existence or non-existence of useful hardware options must be made known to the compiler if it is to be worthwhile incorporating them.

(e) Code selection

The form that this routine takes depends on whether direct translation to machine code (probably relocatable machine code) is to be undertaken or whether assembly code is to be generated. In the first instance, the operation codes are going to be generated in binary form together with binary addresses. In the latter, symbolic form can be maintained. In both cases, translation will be from intermediate code, with its three address properties, to individual machine-executable instructions.

(f) Errors handling

So far, it has been assumed that the source code has been error-free so that a bug-free program would have a straight run through the compilation process. In practice, this is rarely the case. The various stages (a)–(e) outlined above will identify errors of different forms. Some errors will be syntactic and others will be those of inconsistency, e.g. the invocation of labels which are not declared anywhere in the source code. Not only must the compiler find these errors, but as there is likely to be more than one in any but trivial programs, the compiler must not be "thrown" by the first error it encounters. If it were, it would be unable to continue scanning the source code with a view to correctly identifying more. Several factors can help. The use of a separate line on a VDU or card for each statement means that, even if the compiler is confused by a subtle error, it can at least start the next card afresh on the basis that it is the start of a new statement. (A small exception exists where continue codes are used to indicate that a statement goes on to the next line or card. However, even here, the compiler can start afresh when the first"non-continue" card is found.) The use of tokens greatly simplifies the handling of code through stages (b)–(e). By stage (b) no further ambiguity should exist between groups of letters representing an identifier and special functions such as SINE or LOG, etc.

Typical types of error that might be found at each stage are:

1.   Failure to find a token from a string of source characters or failure to find one which fitted with tokens generated earlier in the statement. (This would be discovered during lexical analysis.)

2.   Parsing has many attributes of the ordering processes discussed under the heading of Polish notation (Section 9.4.3). Such a process could find a right-hand parenthesis with no previous left-hand parenthesis to go with it.

3.   Intermediate code would pick up inconsistencies in the operators used with respect to the operands.

Where possible, it is desirable that the compiler corrects relatively trivial coding errors. This is most commonly done only at the lexical-analysis stage, as commitment to the code will have become too great at later stages. Generally, only error *detection* is possible at these stages. However, during lexical analysis, simple programmer blunders may be compensated provided that the compiler has kept the context of the statement and is not struggling too much on "hunches". Simple spelling errors of routines and identifiers might be attempted as might very simple inclusions and exclusions of punctuation characters. To date, the amount of such correction possible is fairly limited and of course requires that the changes made are referred to the programmer.

Correction carries no certainty of being correct. Sometimes a simple programmer blunder has the capability of completely throwing the compiler off the scent and the corrections it makes, although syntactically correct and consistent in terms of functions and symbols used, may nonetheless actually make the source code worse in terms of numbers of characters in error.

(g) *Routine organization*

The routines (a)–(f) are not carried out in sequence in a never-to-be-repeated manner. As the source code is scanned, it is clear that each element of code will be treated to lexical analysis, parsing and code generation. Thus, even a single statement may be subject to several passes through each routine. The "key" routine is probably the parser, which forms the kernel of the decomposition process. It can delegate jobs to the other routines after it has prepared each section of code.

Code optimization can be taken to any desired degree. Because of this, it is not really "optimization" at all—merely a "refiner" of code. If a program is to be run only once or a few times, it may be preferable to ignore time-consuming optimization altogether. On the other hand, a program may be run many times, in which case it is very worthwhile.

Earlier it was construed that frequently run programs may be better assembly-coded. This is true, but some programs are so complex that the labor of assembly coding them is too awesome. Furthermore a barrier is reached by many programmers in which the improvement they can make over procedure-orientated languages rapidly falls off with program complexity. It is then often better to consider a high-level language, particularly if it has a sophisticated code optimizer.

9.4.3 Arithmetic expressions

During compilation, a particular problem arises because of the complex arithmetic expressions that are permitted. Compilation is required to convert such arithmetic expressions into a form suitable for machine execution. The most important part of this process is to convert expressions having syntactical constraints of a normal algebraic form into a series of intermediate instructions, whose order will give precisely the same results.

First, let us consider how the original expression might be written. The normal form allows for precedence rules based on first, exponentiation (raising to a given power); then multiplication and division; and finally addition and subtraction. Where parentheses occur, the expression they embrace is treated as a separate entity from the rest of the expression and evaluated as such. The parentheses are then removed and normal precedence observed. Where more than one + or × operator appears in a row no ambiguity exists and the order of processing is irrelevant (examples are $A*B*C$ and $D+E+F$.) Parentheses may be used to impose an order of execution; otherwise it is normal for the order to be from left to right in accordance with the direction of scanning of the expression. Non-associative operations are also executed from left to right; for example, $A-B-C$ is interpreted as $(A-B)-C$. If a different order is required, parentheses must be used: for example, $A-(B-C)$.

A computer's machine code does not recognize parentheses. Furthermore, the placement of operators between the operands, which is used in paper-and-pencil notation (otherwise known as *infix*), is not easily translated to a series of machine or intermediate-code instructions.

Sorting out the first problem—the use of parentheses in the source code—a Polish mathematician, Lukasiewicz, devised a parenthesis-free notation. This is consistent with parenthesis notation in the execution of complex arithmetic expressions. He found that by putting the operator immediately *after* the operand or operands to which it relates, precedence is maintained. Furthermore, where more than one operator is needed, it is in order to chain operators, provided scanning is left to right and the evaluation of expressions proceeds as operators are encountered.

We can define some terms associated with arithmetic processing, which will often be met. Some operators such as $-$ may be *unary* or *binary*, that is they can be associated with one or two operands. Examples are $-(A)$ and $A-B$ for unary and binary respectively. A few operators are called *ternary*—they are associated with three operands. Some can work with a variable number, such as those for finding the maximum or minimum amongst a set of operands, e.g. MIN $(A,B,C,...,G)$. The operand with the smallest value yields the value of MIN $(A,...,G)$. Such operators are called *variadic*. Different notations allow us to put the operator in different positions relative to the operands. The unary minus (above) is an example of a *prefix* operator. The binary minus is an example of an *infix* operator, as it appears between the operands. The reverse Polish notation (Booth, 1971) puts the operator after the operands and is known as *postfix*.

As an example, the expression $(A+B)*(C+D)+E*F$ can be recast as $AB+CD+*EF*+)$ The operator rule forces the product $E*F$ to be formed before addition to $(A+B)*(C+D)$ takes place.

It is much easier to convert from Polish notation to a series of instructions than from the original infix expression. However, we now have two processes that need mechanization. It is clear that sometimes operands or even expressions must be "held" whilst others are in progress—according to the precedence rules.

Conversion from infix to Polish notation is quite easy if it is remembered that operands and subexpressions must be held if they have no corresponding expressions with which to be associated.

The algorithm, based on the use of a stack, is:

1. Identifiers pass straight through to the output stream.
2. Operators and parentheses are compared with the operators and parentheses on the top of the stack on the following precedence basis:
   exponentiation (raising to the power of)
   multiply/divide
   add/subtract
   left parenthesis (lowest precedence).

For the above example, the incoming symbols, stack contents and outgoing stream are shown in Table 9.1. If the incoming item has a lesser precedence than the top-of-stack item, the stack item is ejected from the system via the output stream. This reveals another stack item. The process is repeated until the incoming item is of greater precedence than the current top-of-stack item. When this occurs, the incoming item is added to the stack. Left

Incoming symbol	Stack		Outgoing stream	
	Top	Bottom	First	Last
(	(			
A	(		A	
+	+(		A	
B	+(		AB	
)			$AB+$	
*	*		$AB+$	
(	(*		$AB+$	
C	(*		$AB+C$	
+	+(*		$AB+C$	
D	+(*		$AB+CD$	
)	*		$AB+CD+$	
+	+		$AB+CD+*$	
E	+		$AB+CD+*E$	
*	*+		$AB+CD+*E$	
F			$AB+CD+*EF*+$	

Table 9.1 Example of infix to Polish conversion
$(A+B)*(C+D)+E*F$

parentheses are placed straight onto the stack and right parentheses are used as a signal to unload the stack onto the output stream (until a left parenthesis is found). The left and right parentheses are discarded. (The two parentheses may be discarded as they, in effect, have been matched together.)

The two unary operators must also be taken into account. These operators may precede an identifier to condition its sign. Thus $-A$ and $+A$. Unary minus is given precedence between exponentiation and multiply/divide so that it stays with the operand/identifier with which it is initially associated. Unary plus, when identified, can just be discarded. The final precedence is thus:

exponentiation
unary operator
multiply/divide
add/subtract
left parenthesis.

If functions such as EXP (exponential) are used in expressions, they must, of course, be given an even higher precedence than exponentiation. Such functions normally enclose their arguments in parentheses to bring home this point.

Having now removed parentheses, it is necessary to convert from Polish notation to a sequence of instructions. We will not concern ourselves with whether a single machine-code instruction exists for each operator encountered. It is sufficient to assume that the operator can be identified and when encountered, a routine can be substituted. It must be placed at the right point in the tract of program, to replace the operator. Therefore, all we need to do at this point is sort the notation into a set of instructions in the right order for processing.

This sorting can also be done by use of a stack. Using the example from the infix to Polish conversion $AB+CD+*EF*+$, the correct order of execution can be written straight down on paper as:

Add A to B (one calculation)
Add C to D (a separate calculation)
Multiply the above two sums
Multiply E and F (a separate calculation)
Add the results of the previous two lines.

Here, we can see the advantage of not committing ourselves to any processing which takes account of the hardware architecture of the computer. We have enough to do just ordering the instructions, without having to worry about addressing modes; one, two or three operand-address instructions; use of one or two accumulators, etc. The three-address intermediate code is just what is required for the output notation at this stage.

Use of a push-down memory (stack) allows us to defer calculations and to hold results until they can be associated with other results. Thus if we scan the Polish expression from left to right, identifiers (operands) are pushed onto the stack until the first operator is found. The requisite number of identifiers are then drawn from stack according to the requirements of the operator and an instruction generated from them. A temporary identifier is used to represent the result of this calculation and is placed on the stack instead of the identifiers and operator just associated (Table 9.2).

Input stream	Calculation/(temporary identifier)	Stack contents	
		top	bottom
A	—	A	
B	—	B,A	
$+$	Add A and B/(result 1)	result 1	
C	—	C, result 1	
D	—	D,C, result 1	
$+$	Add C and D/(result 2)	result 2, result 1	
$*$	Multiply results 1 and 2/(result 3)	result 3	
E	—	E, result 3	
F	—	F,E, result 3	
$*$	Multiply E and F/(result 4)	result 4, result 3	
$+$	Add result 3 and result 4/(final result)	result	

Table 9.2 Example from Table 9.1 undergoing Polish to three-address intermediate) code conversion.

The arithmetic expressions that result from this manipulation are shown under "calculation". This form is quite suitable for a three-address intermediate code. If it is to be translated to a form which recognizes some of the processor's hardware attributes, either this can be done in a following process or the process above can be modified. Generally, if the amount of such post-processing is high, i.e. the processor is complicated by the existence of scratch-pads, etc., or if there may be several hardware options, it is best that a separate process is used. However, if the hardware is simple, it may be possible to incorporate such refinements at this stage.

As an example, if the processor has a single accumulator, then all we need to do is arrange that scanning of the identifiers and operators recognizes when a "separate" calculation is to take place. In our example, result 1 would have to be removed from the accumulator before C and D could be added. However, the sum of C and D could be left in the accumulator for the subsequent multiplication by $(A+B)$. The refinement consists simply of detecting that two or more identifiers have been found between the last operator and the next one in a left-to-right scan. This is the case between the generation of $A+B$ and encountering the add operator for C and D. This is not the case for the $*$ operator for $(A+B)$ and $(C+D)$.

9.4.4 Commentary

Amongst the many high-level languages, certain ones stand out as being particularly important.

For engineers, FORTRAN is very popular (Blatt, 1968). Despite being short of some of the more elegant features, it provides an easy-to-understand, machine-independent language which is suitable for a wide variety of applications. Being relatively simple, compilers for it are straightforward and use little memory.

A more sophisticated language is ALGOL (Wijngaarden, 1968), which allows a structured approach to programming. Variables can have global or local status meaning that they can be effective either in some small self-contained area of a program or be available for use anywhere. Dynamic memory allocation for tables, arrays and variables is possible together with the status of program segments which allows mutually exclusive routines to share memory space. (If it can be ascertained that one routine will not call another, the same memory space can be used for both without the one corrupting the other.) On the other hand, FORTRAN tends to use memory without such regard.

SNOBOL (Maurer, 1976) is particularly suited to string and logical processing. All identifiers are allocated dynamically so that the complete set of identifiers is determined only at run-time (when, in effect, the identifiers come into existence).

PASCAL was originally devised by Jensen and Wirth (1976) as a language to teach programming. Although written in the 1960s, it has only recently gained general acceptance. A standard may well be adopted for PASCAL which will relieve it of the threat of modification by the various manufacturers wishing to offer it on their equipment. It has some features in common with ALGOL such as block structure, but is easier to implement. CONCURRENT PASCAL is a real-time version which puts constraints on subroutine nesting so as to avoid undue run-time hold-ups. Both versions are becoming popular with microprocessor manufacturers as a standard high-level language. The reader is recommended to refer to the appropriate source manuals and reports for other languages such as LISP, PL/1 and APL (Berkeley, 1964; Murrill, 1973; Iverson, 1962).

9.5 FIRMWARE

9.5.1 Introduction

Firmware is that aspect of computer organization in which information about the structure or role of the computer is generally held in a read-only-memory form. Such information may be altered by chip replacement or reprogramming but can often remain constant throughout the life of the equipment. This statement is not particularly helpful unless put in some context. A few examples will set the scene:

Example 1 The microprogram for a computer will, together with the hardware it controls, define the processor, by way of the order (machine) code. As seen by the programmer, the structure or architecture of the processor is defined through the order code. The hierarchical levels are

(a) machine code,
(b) microprograms, and
(c) registers and general logic.

In practice, of these, only the microprogram can be altered, but to do so radically alters the "appearance" of the machine.

Example 2 Many procedures and routines for a digital system can be committed to read-only memory (ROM). For instance, when a computer is first powered up, it is, in principle, totally helpless. Any hardware registers, particularly the program counter, will settle to quite random values and so will the contents of the main-memory locations. In this state, no useful computing can be carried out, nor can a program be read from paper tape or disk.

In order that the first, most elementary, routines can be read into the machine and executed, so that more complex tasks can be attempted, the system must be initialized. If a reset signal can be asserted, either as a direct consequence of power being applied or though a user-key, then the program counter (PC) can be cleared to zero and thereby made to point (vector) to the first of a sequence of instructions in a ROM. The ROM will contain just sufficient code to allow the computer to load its first proper program from, say, disk. This is known as a *bootstrap* because the machine gradually pulls itself up by its bootstraps to a point of being able to operate normally. The sequence is

(a)   initialize PC;
(b)   very elementary loader program (ROM based);
(c)   first program execution.

Example 3   Microprocessors and calculators are often configured in a *turnkey* arrangement. This means that programs, routines, tasks and overall control are fixed by the manufacturer for the user's application. If the programs for doing this are contained in ROM (by the ROM-containing binary machine-code patterns) then no expensive, nonvolatile, program memory, such as disk, is needed. Furthermore, no special program-loading procedure is required to be learned by the operator.

For a calculator, A ROM-based program contains procedures for identifying keys pressed, carrying out the calculation implied by that key and displaying results. In this example, firmware is replacing software as it does not have to be altered. The key functions are fixed, *ab initio*.

In all three examples, the ROM contents *could* be altered so as to give a completely different system. For Example 1, the order code of the computer could change; for Example 2, the power-up procedure could change; and for Example 3, the interpretation of the keys, display format, etc., could change.

9.5.2   Microprogramming

Early processors had hard-wired control. This consisted of a great deal of tailored timing and sequencing logic to control the movement of data between the registers and other logic of a processor. Sufficient logic had to be provided in order that every instruction in the processor's repertoire would be covered (and for all data combinations).

Whether a processor has hard-wired or ROM control, we can think of the basic arrangement of processor registers, adders, scratch-pads, address generators as an "amorphous" machine. This situation, i.e. hardware without control logic/firmware, is akin to a complete computer devoid of initial instructions or bootstrap. The machinery is there but there are no instructions on how it should operate.

ROMs and hard-wired logic provide this information but in different ways and with different properties.

Hard-wired logic is still used today and it can often be justified on grounds of speed. If bespoke logic is designed and used in an application it would seem to be a fact of life that it will outperform a generalized device or system such as a ROM-based control store (memory). On the other hand, the ROM-based control memory has the advantage that it can be more readily altered, is more amenable to systematic design procedures (including computer-aided design—CAD) and is more readily understood. This leads, in turn, to easier maintenance and modifications.

An important distinction should be drawn at this point between two types of control memory. So far, only ROM-based control has been mentioned—it is the most common form. However, a control memory can be based on RAM with the attendant advantages of rapid alteration. A major advantage in application is that a processor can rapidly change its identity, through its instruction repertoire, if its control memory contents can be changed. However, the greater hardware complexity of RAMs in relation to ROMs means that such memories dissipate more power but, more important, are slower. In view of the fact that such control memories are used to control hardware and that manufacturers of high-speed processors often cannot afford the access times of ROM, this makes RAMs, from the performance viewpoint, even less attractive. Such a criticism does not preclude the use of RAMs—indeed faster RAMs suitable for control-memory applications are gradually coming onto the market. However, it does put a great pressure on designers of RAM-based systems to use horizontal control-memory organizations so that concurrency of hardware activities is maximized in the processor (Section 6.4). Without doubt, if a processor has a "rich" instruction set, the use of ROM or RAM control can greatly reduce the volume of logic and ICs used, particularly if richness implies many different styles of instructions, i.e. not large numbers of trivially different ones. Furthermore, if compound instructions are required—in a sense hardware macros—memory-based control is the ideal way to implement them.

9.5.3 Emulation, translation and simulation

Emulation is the mimicking of one computer by another. The one being mimicked is the *target*, the other is the *host*. There are a number of reasons why emulation may be attempted:

1. A manufacturer, in bringing out a new range of computers not compatible with the previous range, may wish to attract old customers to his new product by emulating the old machines with the new ones. If this is done, original customers should not need to rewrite all existing applications software. (If they have to do this, there may be no great incentive to return to the same manufacturer when old equipment needs to be replaced.)

2. One manufacturer may want to provide a second source or compete with another manufacturer's products using his dissimilar equipment.

3. A user may wish to switch manufacturers but retain software already written. This is the same as (1) but taken from the user's viewpoint.

4. An emulator can be of particular assistance when an old machine, which is part of a network of computers, is only having its processor and memory replaced. This is a common situation, for in order not to disturb the network unduly, particularly the communications system between processors, the peripherals may be left in place and connected to the system. Assuming that the new machine's architecture does not immediately suit the peripherals to which it is connected, the use of an emulator to form a "processor-to-peripherals protocol bridge" is very attractive.

There are several ways in which the activity of one machine can be emulated by another and this gives rise to terms which need definition:

1. *Translation* the program written for the target machine is said to be translated when it is reproduced in the machine code of the host computer. The coding is, in general, quite different, but the algorithms and processes executed are the same. When the new machine code has been generated, execution may or may not follow.

2. *Simulation* is a process whereby the individual instructions of the target machine are *interpreted* and executed on the host, one at a time.

(a) *Comparison of translation and simulation*

Obviously simulation is a slower process than translation as the attention of the host is constantly shifting from interpretation to execution. However, at all times, the target's status is known on an instruction-by-instruction basis. This eliminates most of the run-time difficulties of translation. In translation, there is no "feel" for the outcome of actions until execution is complete. In simulation, there is a tight protocol maintained between host and target programs and status. A simulator can be thought of as a software emulator. It can be arranged to be independent of the target—an advantage in itself but bought with the penalty of being unable to take advantage of the hardware and firmware attributes of the target.

(b) *General-purpose emulators*

Because there has been a tendency for processor hardware, in particular, to become rationalized over the years, emulation has become more easy. It is now possible to construct what is known as a general-purpose emulator which consists of a hardware processor of fairly nondescript form having timing and control signals generated by a ROM (whose bit pattern can be defined by the user). The processor is known as *amorphous*. When the user defines the ROM-bit pattern he gives the emulator "shape" and character and it can therefore emulate any fairly closely related processor.

In order that redundancies of word width, etc., do not exist, it is not unusual for such hardware to be bit-sliced in the manner of some microprocessors. By coupling a number of such emulators, a word width equal to that of the target can be achieved.

(c) *Emulators and their implementation*

Emulators can be very inefficient, particularly if there are considerable differences in the hardware of host and target. As a consequence, firmware and sometimes even hardware changes are made to the host in order to improve performance. This may include the addition of instructions *alien* to the host and used only during emulation. Such instructions will be recognized as particular to the target. If the host has a ROM- or RAM-based controller, it is not difficult to insert these instructions provided sufficient controller address space and operation codes are available. An emulator, having spare control space, might be implemented as follows.

The emulator could consist of a simulator (software emulator) plus extra control memory for the target's fetch phase. This phase is very important as it tends to dominate the total execution time for most instructions in the target's repertoire. It is passed through by all the target's instructions. Most other places in which control-memory enhancements are made affect only a subset of the instructions and have less overall effect on performance.

Several emulation techniques may be applied, separately or in concert, according to the facilities available in the host and the ease with which modifications can be made to it.

1. At the highest, and in a sense, remotest level, emulation can be achieved simply by writing a set of software routines for the host to allow interpretation of the individual target instructions. Emulation is slow, as no hardware concessions are made, but at least tampering with host hardware is avoided.

2. At a closer level, the control memory can be enhanced to provide partial or complete coverage of the target's instruction set. Clearly this would be impossible if the host had a hard-wired instruction controller. For ROM-based microprogram controllers, reprogramming or replacement fo ROMs may be all that is required. The easiest approach is when a RAM-based controller is installed in the host. Then only reprogramming of the RAM is needed, once the pattern of bits has been computed.

3. Sometimes it is possible to perform some rudimentary hardware modifications to the host either to ease emulation carried out at the two levels previously described (by providing, say, more suitable interrupt handling or status reporting facilities) or to configure the host hardware so that it more nearly resembles that of the target. (Taken too far, the latter course would result in reproducing the target hardware.)

In practice, a mixture of the three procedures is followed. Considerable experience and skill is required of the emulator designer to arrive at the optimal mix of approaches.

(d) Emulation of hypothetical targets

At this point it might be assumed that an emulator is designed with particular target hardware in mind. This does not have to be the case. It would be quite in order for a hypothetical machine to be emulated. From the emulator's view point, the processes carried out by "near neighbors"—assemblers and compilers—are emulation of hypothetical targets by lower-language hosts. A compiler inputs a program in a high-level language and translates the statements into a code for running on a target which can accept assembly-language instructions. This target is usually hypothetical. The instructions are therefore translated or interpreted again into the code of the *real* target. This is the machine-code processor.

Seen this way, it is clearly possible to emulate high-level languages such as PL/1 or SNOBOL (Murrill, 1973; Maurer, 1976).

(e) Computer families

An important distinction can be drawn between simulators and translators. Some computers, such as the IBM 370 series, enjoy compatibility between members of the same "family". A single language exists for all members in which programs may be written. For some families, the compatibility may be upwards only, i.e. programs which run on the lower members can run on the larger machines but not vice versa. However, in the case of the IBM 370 series, a hypothetical 370 *concept* exists which is implemented on a number of members. The only differences lie in performance and facilities such as peripheral device handling and memory capacity. A simulator could be based on such a concept and therefore not tie itself to any one member of the family. However, a translator would be tied to a particular machine. Emulators try to exploit some of the hardware and firmware attributes of the host and may considerably enhance their performance by so doing.

9.5.4 Commentary

Emulation is an important concept which allows a target machine to appear to exist within a host. Thus programs written for the target can appear to be executable (with identical results) on the host. The process can be a mixture of hardware, firmware and software. If a host has ROM- (or better RAM-) based control memory, emulation is made particularly attractive, either to ease a customer's transition from one machine to another—with a view to retaining existing software—or for one manufacturer to mimic another's products.

In some instances, emulation can be a replacement for a software hierarchy in small computers. It is sometimes possible to take a small computer, maybe used for process control where the software is relatively simple but long lived, and to replace the combination of assembly-level language plus the machine-code instruction set by a (firmware) based higher-level machine language. By so doing, the all important attributes of many process controllers—fast, real-time operation, etc.—are not lost, but a reasonably easy-to-understand high-level user language is kept. Indeed, by the use of "layers" of firmware it is possible to arrange that some computers have really sophisticated "machine instructions" built into their repertoires such as trigonometric functions. The firmware for such functions can call on existing firmware routines for multiply, divide, roots, etc., in order to reduce the number of steps required in the microprogram.

Finally, although it is likely that ROM- or RAM-based controllers will never match hard-wired logic for raw performance when controlling hardware processes, the use of complex micro-instructions, involving several hardware actions, the use of automomous processor units such as for normalizing floating-point numbers, scaling, etc., can take much of the pressure off the controller units. This is important, because processors which have rich instruction repertoires—and they are growing in number all the time—need the flexibility, ease of maintenance, layout simplicity and ordered design afforded by a pseudo-software approach as offered by microprogram control.

9.6 CONCEPTS OF AN OPERATING SYSTEM

9.6.1 Requirements

An operating system is required for all operational computers. In very small dedicated systems, the operating system may be a very short and relatively trivial software program. For larger systems it may be very complex and perform a number of significant tasks. Some of these are listed below.

If a computer is able to handle several users at the same time, i.e. be capable of multiproprocessing or multiprogramming, the programs must each be allocated a sufficiency of memory, be allocated suitable timeslots in the processor and be arranged not to interfere with each others' operation. In particular, in order that processor time is fully utilized, more than one program or task must be in primary (semiconductor or core) memory at any one time. If this is achieved, handover from one to another is quick and not held up by primary to secondary (disk) memory transfers. Furthermore, information pertaining to one program must not have unlawful access to information in another program. Of course, the machine may make some common resources available, but that is another issue.

In allowing more than one task in the machine at any one time, it is also necessary to arrange that disasters that may befall one program do not cause the machine to *stall*. For instance, if a program incurs an arithmetic overflow or a section of memory is subject to a parity-check error, this should not *necessarily* mean that the whole system should stop.

An operating system is needed for memory allocation, protection, prevention of inter-program corruption and the allocation of input–output channels to tasks. (Without a multiplicity of input–output channels, the concept of multiprocessing would be impossible anyway.)

An operating system must, at all times, be in control of the running of the system. This means that at least the active part of the operating system must be in primary memory at all times. (Certain parts of it may be in secondary memory, provided they are not prevented from entering primary memory by the tasks being handled by the system.) For this reason, and others, the operating system often has access to certain areas of memory and use of certain instructions which are not made generally available. They are known as *shaded* or *reserved*. It is common for part of the top-of-memory to be inaccessible to the user and for the active portion of the operating system to reside there. This area may well cover some of the system-interrupt vectors. Furthermore, instructions such as those for setting base registers, which define the relocation offsets for users' machine-code programs, are made available only to the operating system. Another responsibility of many operating systems is the scheduling of virtual memory. Many user and supervisory programs are larger than the physical primary memory in which they are supposed to be run. The programs are therefore resident in disk at all times and *copies* of active pages are passed to primary memory, when required. References to Chapter 4 will reveal that typical page sizes are from 512 to 2048 bytes. Virtual memory does not have to be implemented largely in hardware as suggested in Chapter 4. It may well be a purely software system if the cost of hardware associative memories is prohibitive.

A final activity undertaken by an operating system is the scheduling and organization of communications between independent computers which are networked. Because such communication may be required by several programs and because the communication may have to be off-line, the traffic must be optimized and timed with all communicators in mind. This is particularly important when a slow communication line is involved, e.g. a serial one using telephone networks.

9.6.2   Example system

It is very difficult to describe a "typical" operating system. It is also very difficult to describe any particular one as being "typical" and even more difficult to do its intricacies justice in a short space.

Some operating systems must be capable of running themselves, especially in a multiprocessing environment where short programs may come and go very rapidly. Others can be subject to a great deal of operator intervention, especially if the system is single tasked or processes on a "batch" rather than a timeshared basis. By "batch" we mean that the processor does one job at a time and may do no more than accept the next user's job into its secondary memory whilst processing the current one.

For simplicity's sake we will consider a dedicated system for a microprocessor-development system. This, at least, will provide some insight into some of the facilities that are made available in an operator-controlled rather than automatic environment.

A microprocessor development system has to provide a number of software and hardware aids in order to develop a complete product from specification of task to realization of working hardware and peripheral equipment. As a number of these aids are provided in software form and some, as we shall see later, are quite complex, they cannot all concurrently reside in the limited primary (semiconductor) memory. A typical microprocessor system only has 64K bytes of address space in the first instance and fully populating this with RAM is quite expensive—even with modern 64K-bit read/write memory chips. Therefore a considerable volume of secondary memory is often provided, either in the form of floppy disks or Winchester disk drives.

Floppy-disk systems are usually arranged in pairs of drives—the so-called two-spindle approach—so that the operating system and service software can reside on one disk and the user software can be on the other. In this way, the operating-system disk is in little danger of being corrupted by user programs or worn out prematurely by continuous use. A typical 20 cm (8 in) floppy disk can hold from $\frac{1}{4}$ to 1 million bytes of data according to format, bit density, etc.

Winchester disk systems are becoming more and more popular for micro systems. They are an IBM development dating from around 1973 and form a useful intermediate choice between floppies and conventional hard disks. Their distinguishing facet is a totally sealed environment for the disk so that contamination is eliminated. By this means, high bit densities can be achieved and reliability is very high as well. At present, commercial versions are not available in exchangeable disk form and this may have limited their sales so far.* Even so, the total capacity of the conventional 36 cm (14 in) diameter disks and the smaller 20 cm (8 in) (mini-Winnies) is very prodigious. The latter are commercially available, having capacities in excess of 20M bytes at a cost of around $2500 (in quantity).

The operating system has to be self-starting. That is, when power is applied and possibly a load or reset button operated, a bootstrap ROM comes into play to initalize the system. A typical arrangement is one in which sufficient code exists in the bootstrap ROM to give the operator access to any of the operating-system service software. Access in this context means that the ROM would, under software control, retrieve floppy resident programs and put them into pre-arranged locations in the semiconductor memory, ready for execution.

Once any given service program is in memory, it would be arranged that the program counter is vectored to the first instruction of the program and the program would thus start. A typical *operator interface* to the program would consist of the listing of operator options in the running of the program. In a microprocessor development system a typical set of programs may be as follows:

1. A service program to allow user files of data and programs to be set up or deleted from disk, to be updated on disk and to be displayed on a VDU.
2. A service program to allow the user to enter software to the system either via a keyboard/VDU or via cards, paper tape or any other normal input medium. Such a program might also permit editing, program renaming and writing to a predesignated area of user floppy. The user program, so-written, might be in an assembly language or one of the high-level languages. (Text editor.)
3. A set of programs for compiling, assembling, interpreting or translating the program to machine-code form. The form may be relocatable as described in Section 9.3.4 or in absolute binary or hexadecimal. Where compilers are involved, the compilation may be to assembly language or directly to binary. An option may be provided. The operating

---

*Memorex have announced a part-fixed/part-exchangeable Winchester disk system of 12.5/12.5 Mbyte capacity and costing around $5500 (June 1980).

system has to ensure that the memory space made available for these compilers and assemblers is adequate and, in the event of their needing considerable space, may be required to use virtual-memory techniques, using the floppy as secondary memory. If user program errors are found, such that the compiler or assembler cannot recover, then the operating system is required to provide reporting facilities and software recovery.

4. Other software that may be provided and which must come within the general ambit of the operating system is a relocatable program loader or linkage editor. In addition, a debugger for running the now hexadecimal user program might be required.

The operating system provides entry to each of these programs and the general software environment for the control of the floppy or Winchester disk unit. Typical activities include allocation of space on the disk, directory control, error recovery (in the event of parity of other check-time failures during writing to or reading from the disk) and user information on disk loading, utilization and hardware faults.

The operating system clearly has an overview of the status and scheduling of the total hardware/software system and provides all the necessary back-up whatever the operational circumstances or languages used.

9.7 ELEMENTS OF THE HARDWARE/SOFTWARE DESIGN PROCESS

In previous sections an outline of the software and firmware facilities needed for a computer have been outlined. Many of the facilities designed in it have to be delegated to software because:

1. hardware realization is expensive;
2. the extra hardware needed, if specified, would be infrequently used;
3. execution speed is of secondary importance in some circumstances.

However, suitable hardware design can greatly relieve the software burden. From previous sections, the following possibilities exist for hardware enhancement:

(a) Provision of stack-handling facilities

This implies the need for one or more stack pointers (SP) to keep a record of the last entry on the stack. If one pointer is used, data and return-from-subroutine addresses have to be mixed in the same stack area. This can make stack management difficult. Use of separate pointers can help considerably. If the stack itself is realized in processor registers, it may be faster than using main memory but will probably be limited in depth. Both memory- and processor-based stacks are used in current designs, according to the design situation.

The stack pointer(s) must be capable of participating in elementary arithmetic operations to make them useful. A minimum set might be:

1. Load (SP) immediate or direct;
2. Store (SP);
3. Increment (SP);
4. Decrement (SP).

If the stack pointer is used in an environment which makes use of base, index or offset registers, suitably fast adders are needed to create *effective absolute addresses* for accessing main memory.

(b) Provision of several addressing modes

These may be used for easing array, multibyte and tables operations or for making position-independent-code possible (see Section 9.2.2). Such requirements may imply the use of one or more index, base or scratch-pad pointer registers and a minimum set of arithmetic facilities to make them workable.

If the hardware designer takes the first two possibilities (above) together, and analyzes the hardware overhead to implement them, it is clear that a large number of registers, inter-register highways (data paths) adders and the like are required. Furthermore, the arithmetic and data-movement operations in which these registers are involved are not dissimilar. A design-requirements analysis might well suggest that all these registers should share a common bus, internal to the processor. The bus would connect the registers into a common adder system for calculating effective-absolute-memory addresses. Part of the requirements analysis involves deciding whether this same adder system can be shared with the main arithmetic adder in the processor (which is used for instruction execution.) If no pre-fetch system is used, sharing may be possible, and this effects hardware economies. However, pre-fetch may make two or more adders necessary to avoid process queuing.

Further examples of the ways in which hardware can, at some expense, ease the software burden are:

1. Automatic data-handling routines associated with specific processor states. If the processor is interrupted or if a subroutine is entered, automatic stacking of machine status (processor registers, flags, etc.) of the exited routine could be pushed onto stack. The converse could apply where subroutine and interrupt routine *returns* were encountered. Microprogramming could be used to implement these data movements during the appropriate control sequences. By this means, both code (programs) and

execution time could be saved. Penalties include extra hardware and control-ROM expense and possibly some loss of user flexibility. (For instance, the user does not necessarily want to stack *all* registers when entering a subroutine.) The designer must make a choice against speed, cost and flexibility.

2. Availability of instructions for handling frequently occurring situations in compilers and assemblers. In these programs, the source data are likely to be in keyboard or a suchlike code rather than in normal binary. A common code is ASCII (American Standard Code for Information Interchange). This is an eight-bit code so that each character can occupy one byte in a byte-oriented machine. If instructions are available for processing such characters, e.g. moving, masking, separating and merging them and in particular, handling strings of them, string-processing can be greatly simplified. Instructions and facilities aimed at this area are commonly called *high-level language hooks*, implying they hook the hardware into the requirements of languages and translators.

Examples of these instructions are to be found in many conventional computers and a number of the more sophisticated microprocessors. Typical of these instructions are:

1. single instructions capable of moving unlimited strings of ASCII characters from one area of memory to another;
2. instructions for providing a one-to-one transformation of characters from one code to another, say ASCII to EBCDIC (Extended Binary-Coded-Decimal Interchange Code).
3. Tests on unlimited strings of characters in contiguous memory locations to find one with a particular code.

Often these instructions can be combined with other powerful ones to create powerful routines. An example might be a test (like (3) above) which would terminate either because of the character being found, or because an end-of-string character such as keyboard EOT was encountered or because of expiry of some programmed character counter. Realization of these compound tests is sometimes achieved through the use of conditional branch (jump) instructions, themselves capable of performing more than one test as part of instruction conditioning.

9.8 THE FUTURE

Although hardware developments have lately been much publicized in the form of dramatic improvements to microprocessors and their support chips (ICs), nonetheless, considerable improvements are taking place with software as well. Of course, hardware and firmware improvements serve to relieve the software burden, whether it is the hardware implementation of complex arithmetic functions or in the processing of logical strings. However, users are continually demanding better software facilities, better run-time performance and better interaction with software. The same level of pressure therefore tends to be applied to the software designers.

Some of the detailed improvements consist of making more high-level languages available to less sophisticated machines. An example is the growing adoption of PASCAL as a language for microprocessors. Other improvements include the expanding use of teleprocessing, including remote control.

Software developments include techniques for image processing, artificial intelligence, adaptive modelling and pattern recognition. Some of these developments would not be possible if suitable hardware were not available. An example lies in the processing and subsequent recognition of speech. The software tools can be greatly simplified and enhanced by real-time hardware processors such as adaptive digital filters.

The computer is being used to an ever greater extent in computer-aided-design (CAD) activites, which often require prodigious volumes of processing to be undertaken in a reasonably short time. Improvements to both the hardware and the software will make wider areas of application possible.

EXERCISES

9.1 Write a routine in assembly language which will read a single assembly-language instruction into a buffer and clean it up. Your program can be written for any language of your choosing. However, it should be assumed that the line may have any number of spaces between each field and/or may employ the TAB character. The end of the line is indicated by a carriage-return/line-feed character.

The clean-up process should consist of arranging that a single-space character appears between each field (only) and that comments are removed. The incoming instructions are expected to consist of some combination of the following fields: label, instruction mnemonic, register/address and comments.

9.2 Write a routine in assembly language that will hash a 4 ASCII character name, held in memory, such that it will be deposited in one of 16 buckets. The characters are each of 8 bits and held in contiguous memory locations, CHAR, CHAR+1, etc. The hashing process should consist of multiplying the two 16-bit character pairs together (first/second multiply third/fourth) producing a 32-bit product. The middle 4 bits of the product should determine the bucket address to be used.

Pick any 4-character names you wish (up to 10 of them) and apply them to this process. Note how many names attempt to enter the same buckets.

9.3 Extend your routine of Exercise 9.2 so that any attempt by an item to enter an occupied bucket causes it to be ejected and the next bucket (modulo 16) to be tried.

9.4 Write an assembly-language routine for simulating a push-down (stack) memory on a computer. Assume that each item to be pushed is in the accumulator. The program should set up error messages if the capacity of the stack is exceeded or an empty stack is popped.

9.5 Translate $y=(A+B**C/(D/E+F)*G)+H$ into Polish notation and then into a series of three-address-code intermediate instructions. Check that you get the same solution if the stacking algorithms for infix to Polish and Polish to intermediate code translations given in the text are used.

9.6 (a) Write an assembly-code routine for an Intel 8080 microcomputer which can multiply two floating-point numbers where the mantissae are expressed to two bytes and the characteristics to one. All quantities are to be expressed in 2s complement notation. For this exercise, ignore characteristic overflow and underflow and significance errors.

The solution should begin with a flowchart and end with the detailed code.

(b) Identify the parts of the program which could, in principle, be executed concurrently. Rewrite the flowchart showing which activities could be made concurrent and indicate what hardware would be needed to achieve maximum concurrency.

By how much would the performance of a simple vertically microcoded unit work in comparison with one which enjoyed concurrent steps in terms of steps needed?

REFERENCES

Agrawala, A. K. (1976), *Foundations of Microprogramming: Architecture, Software and Applications*, Academic Press, New York.

Aho, A. V. (1978), *Principles of Compiler Design*, Prentice-Hall, Englewood Cliffs, N.J.

Alagic, S. (1978), *Design of Well-structured and Correct Programs*, Springer-Verlag, Berlin.

Arms, W. Y. (1976), *Practical Approach to Computing*, Wiley, New York.

Backhouse, R. C. (1979), *Syntax of Programming Languages*, Prentice-Hall, London.

Barden, W. (1977), *How to Program Microcomputers*, H. W. Sams, Indianapolis.

Barrett, W. A. (1979), *Compiler Construction*, Science Research Associates, London.

Barron, D. W. (1969), *Assemblers and Loaders*, Computer Monographs, Macdonald (London)/Elsevier (New York), Chapters 2 and 4.

Barron, D. W. (1977), *Introduction to the Study of Programming Languages* (Computer Science Texts 7) Cambridge University Press, Cambridge.

Berkeley, E. C. (1964), *Programming Language LISP*, MIT Press, Cambridge, Mass.

Blatt, J. M. (1968), *Introduction to FORTRAN IV Programming*, Goodyear.

Booth, T. L. (1971), *Digital Networks and Computer Systems*, Wiley International, New York, Chapters 11–13.

Boulaye, G. G. (1975), *Microprogramming,* English language edn, Macmillan, London. First published 1971 by Dunod, Paris.

Brown, P. J. (1977), *Software Portability,* Cambridge University Press, Cambridge.

Cleaveland, J. C. and Uzgalis, R. C. (1977), *Grammars for Programming Languages,* Computer Science Library, Elsevier, Amsterdam.

Colin, A. (1979), *Programming for Microprocessors,* Newnes-Butterworths, London.

Dijkstra, E. W. (1976), *Discipline of Programming,* Prentice-Hall, Englewood Cliffs, N.J.

Freedman, A. L. (1977), *Real-time Computer Systems,* Edward Arnold, London.

Gimpel, J. F. (1976), *Algorithms in SNOBOL 4,* Wiley Interscience, New York.

Grogono, P. (1978), *Programming in PASCAL,* Addison-Wesley, Reading, Mass.

Higman, B. (1977), *Comparative Study of Programming Languages 2E,* Macdonald and Janes, London.

Horowitz, E. (1977), *Fundamentals of Data Structures,* Pitman, London.

Iverson, K. E. (1962), *A Programming Language,* Wiley, New York.

Jensen, K. and Wirth, N. (1975), *PASCAL User's Manual and Report,* Springer Verlag, Berlin.

Jensen, K. and Wirth, N. (1976), *PASCAL: User Manual and Report 2E* (Lecture notes in Computer Science No. 18) Springer Verlag, Berlin.

Knuth, D. E. (1968), "Semantics of context-free languages," *Math. Systems Theory.* **2**(2), 127–45.

Lewin, D. W. (1980), *Theory and Design of Digital Computers,* Nelson, London, Chapters 1–3.

McIntire, T. C. (1978), *Software Interpreters for Microcomputers,* Wiley, New York.

Maurer, W. D. (1976), *Programmers' Introduction to SNOBOL,* Elsevier, Amsterdam.

Maurer, W. D. (1979), An Introduction to BNF, *Byte Magazine,* **4**(1), 116–25.

Murrill, P. W. *PL-1 Programming,* International Textbook Co, New York.

E. I. Organick *et al.* (1978), *Programming Language Structures,* Academic Press, N.Y.

Richards, M. (1969), "A tool for compiler writing and system programming," *Spring Joint Computer Conf.,* **34,** 557–66, AFIPS Press, Montvale N.J.

Ritter, T. and Boney, J. (1979), "A microprocessor for the revolution: the 6809," *Byte Magazine,* **4**(1–3).

Siklossy, L. (1976), *Let's Talk LISP,* Prentice-Hall, Englewood Cliffs, N.J.

Ullman, J. D. (1976), *Fundamental Concepts of Programming Systems,* Addison-Wesley, Reading, Mass., Chapter 3.

Wijngaarden, A. van (1968), *Draft Report ALGOL Language; ALGOL 68* (ALGOL Bulletin 36). Tech Rept TR74-3. University of Alberta, Edmonton, Canada.

Wirth, N. (1970), *Algorithms + Data structures = Programs,* Prentice-Hall, Englewood Cliffs, N.J.

10 AN EXAMPLE OF SYSTEM DESIGN— A REAL-TIME SIGNAL PROCESSOR

10.1 RAISONS D'ÊTRE

The purpose of this chapter is to proceed through the stages of development of a digital instrument so as to illustrate some of the decision making at work. This example cannot, of course, hope to embrace all the concepts and techniques from previous chapters. However, we consider that, starting from a real specification and showing design considerations through the conceptual hardware and software development and trials stages for a project, the *nature* of decision-making can be revealed. Although volume production, volume testing and field maintenance are not covered in detail, it will be clear that decision-making regarding the product at an early stage will have a profound effect on the manufacturability and maintainability of the final design.

The approach detailed in this chapter—the procedure, order of decision-making and design and not least, the final design, are not unique or necessarily optimal. The reasons for designing the product a certain way are based on many circumstances: the components available at the time of design, the development equipment available at the time, product precedents and previous design experience in the relevant fields. To approach the design at a different time and under different circumstances could well cause a markedly different product to evolve.

This chapter is divided into seven sections in roughly chronological order. It will start with the specification of and justification for the product and will then proceed through the "broad-brush" initial considerations, tentative design, hardware architecture, software design and the development procedure. It will close with a design assessment—a debrief of the project. This will allow us to stand back and consider whether the form of the final product achieves the goals set out, at a cost and with the design and operating tolerances desired. Although the chapter layout is chronological, it is accepted that design usually involves repeated "loops" of procedures. A certain commitment to a design is necessary before it is apparent whether it is viable. This is particularly the case with hardware/software interactions. Until some coding has been carried out in key areas, it is difficult, if not impossible, to be sure that the specified performance can be obtained. After some coding in, say, real-time areas, it may transpire that additional peripheral logic is required to "prop up" the system performance. This means reversion to the hardware architecture. Such hardware changes alter the software burden, making recoding necessary.

10.2 PURPOSE AND SPECIFICATION OF EQUIPMENT

The instrument to be considered is a real-time digital processor (Rabiner and Gold, 1975; Taub and Schilling, 1971) which can digitally demodulate frequency-shift keyed (FSK) and on–off keyed (OOK) signals which have been modulated onto a 100 kHz carrier. The carrier corresponds to a common intermediate frequency (IF) encountered in communications equipment. The purpose of the demodulator is to gather statistical information regarding such signals to aid machine reception and translation of manually sent and machine-generated morse messages. Manually sent morse communication is quite distinct from machine morse (e.g. teleprinter) insofar that machine-sent morse is regular and unchanging, correctly formatted at all times and hence easy to read (within the constraints of the reception conditions). However, manually sent morse shows irregularities such as operator fatigue, varying format due to the operator's personal characteristics (his "fist") and the nature of the transmission. Numerical information must be sent with great care because of the lack of redundancy and the inability of the receiver operator to "predict" passages of text. However, plain-language text may often be sent in a "sloppy" manner with some mistakes and poorly formed characters. Operators get very accustomed to sending certain groups of words and certain plain-language tracts, so that inter-character and inter-element pauses tend to be foreshortened and indistinguishable. An instrument which can receive such signals (in real-time) and collect statistical data regarding their element and pause durations, can greatly facilitate algorithmic translation of morse. Information regarding inter-element and inter-character spaces allows the translation algorithm to adapt to variations of the sender's characteristics.

The processing required of such a demodulator may be conveniently partitioned into the following sections:

1. IF to baseband or similar demodulation of the original signal;
2. imposition of signal delay (of possibly several seconds) to the signal, in order that the instrument can wait for spectral analysis of the signal to take place in another instrument;
3. frequency shifting (transposition) of the demodulated signal by up to a few hundred hertz to compensate for the receiver being "off-tune" or to select upper or lower sidebands in a single-sideband transmission;
4. filtering (Peled and Liu, 1976) of the demodulated signal in order to remove unwanted high-frequency components (cut-off frequency a function of the morse transmission rate);
5. adaptive amplitude slicing of the signal to discriminate marks from spaces (but making allowance for signal strength).

This instrument was required to be initialized from data sent via an IEEE-488 (IEEE, 1975) bus to a read/write (RAM) memory.

The instrument was required to work under laboratory conditions, that is, in a noncondensing atmosphere of from 0°C to 40°C. Such a specification allowed commercial (0°C to 70°C) temperature specified components to be used. (In any case, the specification of an IEEE bus system made other than a benign laboratory environment unlikely.)

The real-time specification for the instrument is self-evident. It needs to process information as it arrives in an operational communications network. In order that the hand-sent morse can be processed as it arrives, the necessary statistical information has to be available for immediate use. Time does not exist in this sort of system for off-line processing.

Certain areas of the design were not rigidly defined and were left to the designer's discretion. Foremost of these areas were the technology, processing method, algorithm details, etc. So long as the specification, as written, was met (and at a suitable cost), then implementation flexibility existed.

Specification

(a) *From the communications viewpoint*

Data input: analog ± 5 V, 100 kHz carrier, ± 600 Hz(bandwidth)

Parameters input
Software input $\left.\right\}$ via IEEE 488 bus.

Signal delay: approx. 6 s in steps of 25 ms.
Frequency shift: approx. $\pm$ 500 Hz

Low-pass filter: cut-off frequencies: 20,40,80,160 and 320 Hz at −3 dB: not
less than −30 dB at 2×cut-off frequency or the Nyquist limit (whichever is
less)

Slicer algorithm: algorithm not relevant to this chapter—merely the
arithmetic burden, which was: six eight-bit unsigned multiplications plus
five unsigned eight-bit additions (per iteration)

Output information: to be passed to the IEEE 488 bus, giving durations of
the last 32 marks and spaces (in blocks of 32).

A simplified block diagram of signal flow (in equivalent analog form) is
shown in Fig. 10.1.

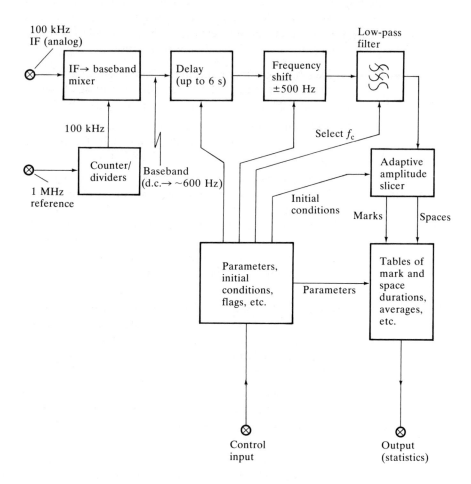

Fig. 10.1 Analog of FSK/OOK demodulator.

(b) *From a digital processing viewpoint*

Although, at this point, it could be argued that no decision exists as to whether analog or digital processing is to be used, the implications of digital processing will be explored, in terms of the specification. This will serve two purposes:

1. It will act as a summary of digital implications to aid the decision process.

2. It will help readers who are not familiar with communications engineering or signal processing to appreciate the demands being made in terms of a digital implementation. By so doing, the specification under (a) can be ignored and the implications outlined here taken as a surrogate specification. The rest of the chapter can then be read and largely appreciated without reference to the relationship between the signal-processing aims and the digital blocks used.

Input signal: Analog, having components in the frequency range 90–110 kHz and an amplitude of several volts. Sampling of signal: twice per 800 μs, pairs of samples to be spaced by $2\frac{1}{2}$ μs.

Delay: Sample pairs to be delayed by up to 8192 sample intervals. The same delay for both members of a pair. Delay to be programmable in delay units of 32 ($\times$ 800 μs).

Frequency shifting: Effectively consists of multiplying each member of a pair by both the sine and cosine of a digitally generated sine wave whose frequency can be varied in steps of about 5 Hz from -500 Hz to about $+500$ Hz. The sampling interval for the sine wave and the frequency with which this (cross-multiplication) operation is to be carried out to be 1.25 kHz (corresponding to the incoming signal sampling interval of 800 μs).

Digital filtering: In effect, the frequency-shifted signal sample pairs are each to be multiplied 15 times by constant coefficients (obtained from a digital memory). Each block of (30) multiplications to be carried out within 800 μs to correspond to the input-signal sampling rate.

Modulus generation: The two signals from the two digital filters to be combined into a single one by treating them as a quadrature pair. That is, they are to be combined by forming the square root of the sum of their squares.

Adaptive amplitude slicer: This is an algorithm which, each 800 μs, requires 6 multiplications and 5 additions to be carried out.

Tables generation:	Results to be formed as tables of up to 32 entries. Each table will need up to 256 bytes as each entry consists of 4 items each of 2 bytes.

10.3 EARLY CONSIDERATIONS

It is conceivable that the processing to be carried out in this demodulator could be wholly analog. Even the IEEE originating commands could be used to drive analog-style circuitry through analog switches (Millman and Halkias, 1972) using field-effect transistors (FET), etc. However, there are several advantages to a wholly digital approach, of which the following are considered most important:

1. Amplitude precision will only be limited by the quality of the ADC(s) (Schmid, 1970) used in the conversion of the incoming signal, whereas analog circuitry will be prone to nonlinearity errors, errors due to power-supply variations, temperature drift and component ageing.
2. As we are dealing with signalling information rather than, say, speech, the phase response of the system is important. To maintain the "waveshape" integrity of signals processed, a near-constant group delay should be imposed, i.e. the phase shift of signals should be directly proportional to their frequencies. To provide a signal delay of several seconds on signals of this bandwidth and integrity requirement by analog means would be quite out of the question.
3. Generation of tables is quite obviously a digital process.
4. Low-pass filtering with variable cut-off frequency is very conveniently done in digital form, especially if maintenance of waveshape is considered.

The first question therefore is how to maximize the amount of *digital* processing and therefore how to convert the incoming 100 kHz signal at the earliest opportunity? (Typical of modern communications receivers, the ones intended to be connected to this demodulator provide a 1 MHz reference source, which can be used to synchronize the converter to the IF output of the receiver.) It should be noted that, from the point of view of digital processing, the information bandwidth is the relevant parameter and the 100 kHz need only affect the analog-to-digital conversion (ADC) (Matley and Bywater, 1977). For instance, if the 100 kHz signal is sampled at 1.25 kHz, i.e. once per 800 μs, using a sampling system which has an aperture time short compared with 100 kHz, then only the modulation components (± 625 Hz) will be present in the output of the ADC (Fig. 10.2). 100 kHz is a multiple of 1.25 kHz and will therefore produce a zero-output frequency component, i.e. its spectral line will "fold" back to zero frequency, when

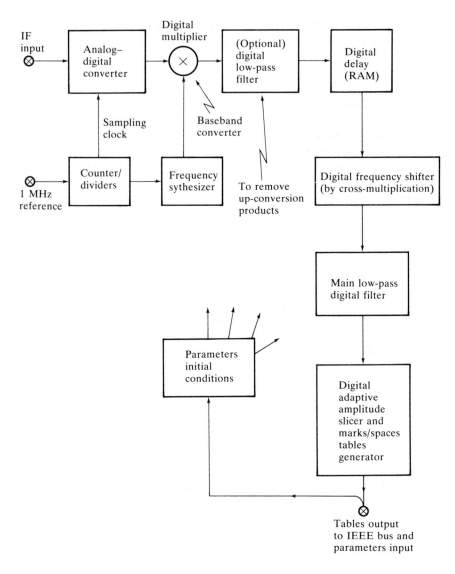

Fig. 10.2 (a) Simplified digital form of a demodulator.

thought of "modulo 1250". This is a phenomenon that arises out of deliberately allowing sampling beyond the Nyquist limit, that is, gross aliasing is taking place. However, the 100 kHz carrier is kept "out of the way" by being reinserted to the baseband (0–625 Hz) frequency slot at zero frequency. However, having been folded back, it will naturally take its sidebands with it. Unfortunately, this gives rise to "negative" frequency

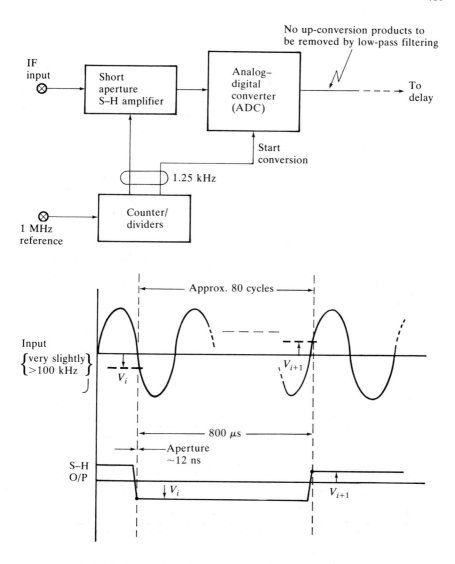

Fig. 10.2 (b) Sub-Nyquist sampling of 100 kHz signal with a very short aperture S–H amplifier.

components, because modulation of 100 kHz gives rise to signals both above and below 100 kHz. This problem can be obviated by quadrature down conversion, i.e. taking samples which are spaced $\pi/2$ in terms of *carrier* phase. The sine and cosine components that arise are then processed separately.

If the original (single-phase) signal were to need reconstituting, then the

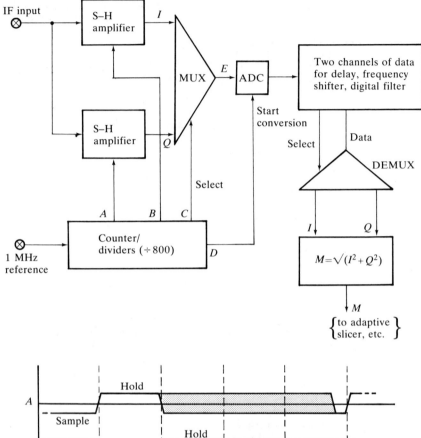

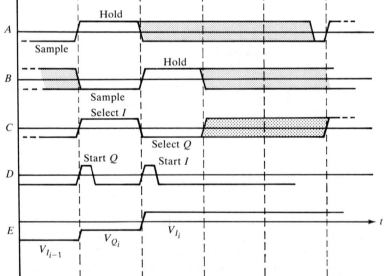

Fig. 10.3 Quadrature (sub-Nyquist) sampling and single-channel reconstitution.

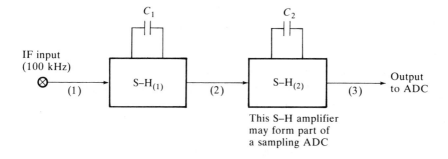

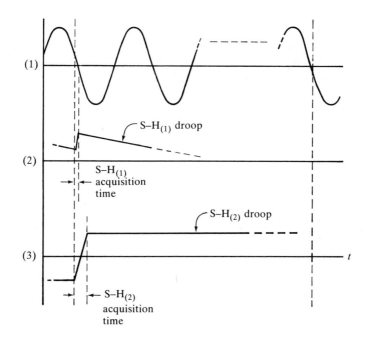

Fig. 10.4 Use of tandem S–H amplifiers to give both fast acquisition and long, droop-free hold.

components could be vectorially added (square root of the sum of squares). Each channel of information now carries 625 Hz of information. The new block diagram appears in Fig. 10.3.

Note: Although it would be out of the question for a conventional ADC, converting analog samples at a kilohertz or so, to be able to capture samples of it within the time that the signal amplitude changes by 1 quantum,* it would be quite easy to precede the ADC with one or more sample–hold (S–H) amplifiers to achieve the required aperture-to-hold ratio. In the implementation of the system suggested, a single ADC can quite easily cope with two conversions per 800 μs, requiring signal holding of 400 μs for each. If two S–H amplifiers are arranged in tandem (Fig. 10.4), the aperture-to-hold time can be "spread", i.e. the first, fast, S–H amplifier need only hold the signal reliably for, say, 1–10 μs. During this hold time, the second one can sample this output and hold it for the ADC for the required 400 μs. (A quality characteristic of S–H amplifiers is the ratio of hold-to-aperture time. This ratio is almost independent of the value of hold capacitor used (Fig. 10.5).)

Turning now to decisions about the digital processing proper, it can be seen that performance is a major factor, as a total of 34 multiplications are needed per iteration of 800 μs. This is based on 4 multiplications for frequency shifting, 2×12 for digital filtering (assuming that a sixth order Butterworth filter (Beauchamp and Yuen, 1979) will achieve the desired

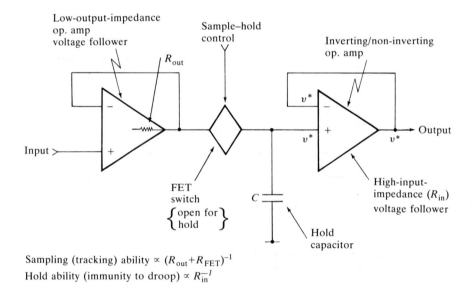

Sampling (tracking) ability $\propto (R_{out} + R_{FET})^{-1}$

Hold ability (immunity to droop) $\propto R_{in}^{-1}$

Fig. 10.5 Simplified schematic of typical S–H amplifier performance.

*A signal(s) of peak-to-peak amplitude 2^k quanta and angular frequency ω is given by $s(t) = 2^{k-1} \sin \omega t$. The maximum slope $\dot{s}_{max} = 2^{k-1}\omega$. For a 100 kHz sinewave being converted to 8 bits, the minimum time to traverse 1 quantum $= \dot{s}_{max}^{-1} \approx 12$ ns.

frequency response without overshoot), and 6 for the adaptive amplitude slicer. Ignoring all other processing, this allows 800/34 i.e. about 24 μs per multiplication. As a rough guide, we might assume that all other processing, additions, etc, will take at least as long as the multiplications alone. From this, we can start to converge on the possible types of processor architecture which can achieve this rate of processing at minimum cost.

In making these decisions, we may discard an approach using a "naked mini on a card" because it would scarcely be able to achieve the processing rate required, and also the cost would be high. At the other extreme, a conventional 8-bit microprocessor would have no chance, if all the functions were committed to software (one multiplication would have taken all the 800 μs available, if not more). Second-generation 16-bit microprocessors can perform multiplications in around 20 μs, but this leaves no margin for the other arithmetic, and no spare time for logical or addressing activities. As 16-bit microcomputers, per se, are quite costly, the possibility of using several in a task-shared multimicroprocessor arrangement need not be given serious consideration. (At this point, it should be noted that many of the

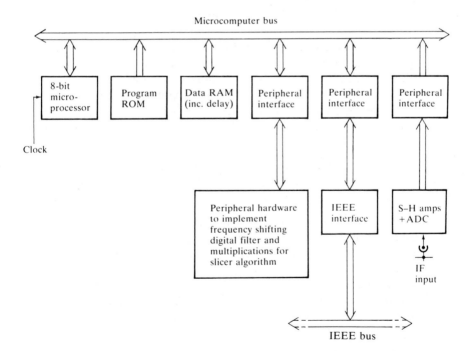

Fig. 10.6 Block diagram of demodulator.

multiplications use 16-bit operands, so that the difference between 8 and 16-bit microprocessor software performance must be based on 16-bit numbers.) The most attractive alternative, and the one finally adopted, was based on a microcomputer, plus peripheral hardware.

Trial software codings show that, provided functions such as multiplication, accumulation (for digital filtering) and trigonometric function generation can be delegated to peripheral hardware, general data and system management can be executed by an eight-bit microcomputer. A suitable unit may be the Intel 8085 or 8748. The peripheral hardware functions can be provided by a combination of a 16-bit monolithic multiplier/accumulator, local RAM for holding filter-delay samples, plus ROM for holding sines and cosines of angles and filter coefficients (Fig. 10.6).

Assuming adherence to an 8-bit micro, plus peripheral hardware, the choice lies between a microcomputer-on-a-card or a "scratch-built" system. The relative advantages and disadvantages are:

1. A scratch-built system should be free from redundant components, supplied as standard by the microcomputer manufacturer. Such redundancies would be excesses of RAM, ROM I/O ports and unused event timers, interrupt processors and bus drivers. However, development time will take longer due to scratch construction of the breadboard, pre-prototypes, etc.

2. If a microcomputer can be procured with a suitable volume of memory and the right mix of other facilities, it is very tempting to specify it. An alternative approach would be to shorten development time by purchasing such a card (even if slightly redundant) and to use it as a development (only), breadboard component. The final production run, depending on production volume, could then be of scratch components.

In order to help the decision making, some feel for memory and I/O volume is necessary. This, in turn, depends on how the peripheral hardware is to be tied into the main microcomputer. Two approaches are possible:

1. Use tri-state components and tie them into the internal data and address buses of the microcomputer, proper. (This is often not feasible if a computer-on-a-card is purchased—as the bus is not always available on the card connectors.) If used, this approach gives fast data communications between the micro and the peripheral hardware. However, it is also likely to mean that the micro must be "frozen" whilst peripheral hardware activities are in progress.

2. Tie the peripheral hardware via the micro's parallel input/output ports. Although data transfer is slower, the micro can proceed with tasks whilst the hardware is doing something else. Furthermore, if

sufficient work is delegated to such hardware, the volume of such communications can be kept down (provided the hardware does not have to keep referring back to the micro for data or instructions).

The peripheral hardware may be clustered together in a bus-orientated system, just as are the micro components. However, the buses would be electrically quite separate. This is the approach adopted (Fig. 10.7).

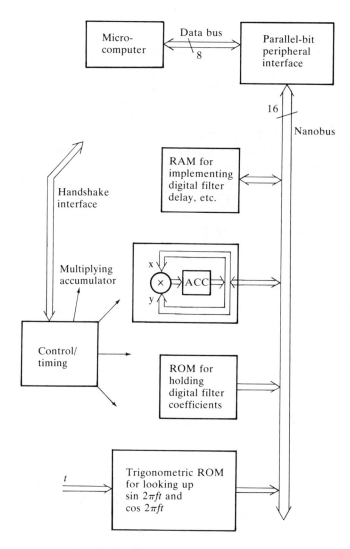

Fig. 10.7 Block diagram of demodulator peripheral hardware shown in bus-connected form.

A final, early, consideration is the one which haunts most real-time processors—namely, the ability to give timely service to all external requesters. In the case of this system, there are only two such requesters—the ADC, which is sending pairs of signal samples every 800 μs, and the IEEE bus. The former is going to have data available in complete disregard of either micro or hardware or IEEE activities and the latter is going to demand a certain minimum service response according to the IEEE hardware specification and the expected IEEE bus traffic. Clearly, it is possible for a "clash" of interests to occur. The response requirements of the IEEE bus (see Section 10.4), with particular reference to interface clear (IFC) and attention (ATN) signals, are clearly laid down. These requirements can be met only with some hardware, in addition to any software. (The IEEE-488 specification demands that participants should relinquish the bus within 200 ns of ATN being asserted by the controller. This requires hardware.) Furthermore, to allocate a fixed fraction of the 800 μs iteration time to IEEE transactions would be unreasonable, as it could interfere with bus-traffic flow for long periods. (The provision of a large number of small time slots in the 800 μs period would waste far too much time in "context" changing and is also discarded.) On the other hand, to allow the IEEE bus to gain (interrupt-based) access to the micro would also be dangerous as it could hog time and leave insufficient for signal processing. Of course, the *chances* of this happening at any time are very small. There are two ways of ameliorating the situation:

1.   It can be arranged that the demodulator becomes a non-listener whilst it is normally processing. This can occupy most of its time. There is no reason why *every* IEEE bus transaction should be intercepted by the demodulator. Most of the them will not be relevant to it, so it is better to use the IEEE bus addressing system to allocate listeners before each transaction, rather than having all participants listening and leaving it to them to discriminate between germane and irrelevant messages.

2.   The rate of receipt of samples from the ADC is low—only two per 800 μs. As the output information from the demodulator is slightly retrospective statistics, it is quite in order to build up a backlog of pairs of samples. These must only be *accepted* by the micro as they become available. They need not be processed immediately. The extent to which the backlog may be allowed to grow can be made parametric. The value designated can be sent as part of the set-up information from the bus-connected host computer. If the backlog limit is reached, the IEEE bus requests can be masked, that is, transactions can be held up by delaying handshaking. ATN and IFC can be held up (in terms of software only) by masking their interrupt signals. Masking of ATN signals in the software does not affect the rapid hardware response for relinquishing the bus: it simply means that talker/listener assignment, which is the normal activity when ATN is asserted, is held up.

10.4 TENTATIVE DESIGN

Referring, once again, to the digital implementation block diagram of Fig. 10.2, we can now ascertain the order in which the various sections of the algorithm have to be processed. This is done bearing in mind that the peripheral hardware and microcomputer can operate concurrently on non-interacting tasks—and where no communication is required. A suitable process flowchart is shown in Fig. 10.8.

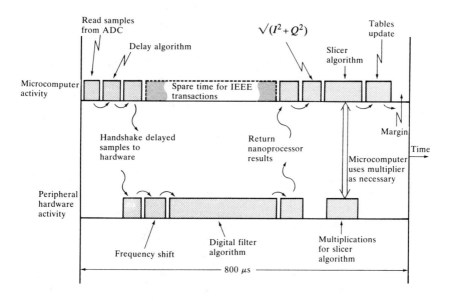

Fig. 10.8 Microcomputer/hardware activity chart.

1. *Sampling and analog–digital conversion* In order to reduce the uncertainty in the sampling to less than 1 bit in the ADC, S–H amplifiers must sample the signal in less than about 12 ns but hold it for the ADC for about 400 μs. In a practical system, this probably means that the same S–H control signal can be used for both amplifiers, as the slower one will acquire the output of the faster one during the latter's hold time. In effect, use is being made of the fact that the fast one will capture its data sample very quickly, responding to the S–H control signal much faster than the other one.

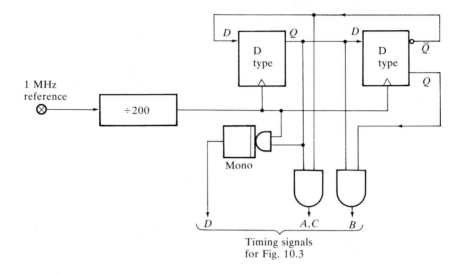

Timing signals
for Fig. 10.3

Fig. 10.9 Timing signals for S–H ampliers and ADC.

The faster S–H amplifier is therefore genuinely in its hold mode before the slower one has even started the transition from sample to hold.

The ADC would, typically, have to convert once per 400 μs to 8 bits, which is easily achieved in a wide variety of commercially available devices. The actual ADC chosen will have a bearing on the S–H configuration, insofar that one which does not hold its sample will certainly make a second S–H amplifier necessary. Otherwise, one with a short-aperture in-built hold circuit might make the slower S–H unnecessary. The sampling logic and hardware is shown in Figs. 10.3, 10.4 and 10.9 and is seen to consist of the two channels of sampling and conversion electronics (for the quadrature channels) plus reference division counters and timing logic.

2. *Delay implementation* Delay is required in units of around 30 ms from 30 ms to about 6 s. Delay can be easily implemented using RAM and a sliding address scheme (Matley and Bywater, 1977) (Fig. 10.10). As samples arrive in pairs at 800 μs intervals, then a 16K byte RAM can be split into two 8K byte sections, giving a pair of delay lines each of $2^{13} \times 800 \times 10^{-6} = 6.5$ s. Addressing consists of establishing start and end of delay addresses before computation and using these to recycle the write and read addresses. As steps of around 30 ms are required, then a 1-byte parameter can be used to define the delay-line length such that 1 quantum corresponds to 32 locations i.e. $32 \times 800 \times 10^{-6} = 25.6$ ms. The maximum parameter value of 256 (2^8) can then represent the full $256 \times 32 = 8$K of RAM.

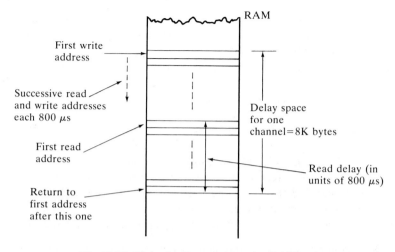

Fig. 10.10 Delay implementation using RAM.

Before computation, the parameter value multiplied by 32 can be subtracted from the initial RAM write address to yield the first read address (Fig. 10.11). As the write and read addresses advance (incremented each

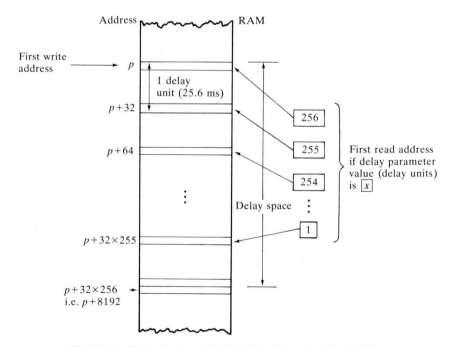

Fig. 10.11 Determination of first READ address for Fig. 10.10.

800 μs), they can simply be checked against the delay-line end address to see when recycling has to take place (Fig. 10.10). No other run-time computation is necessary. The initial read address is computed from the initial write address from the formula (read address)=(write address)+32(256−m), where m is the parameter value. The formula takes account of the modulo nature of the subtraction (mod 8192). (*Note :* The effect of the formula is to disallow a delay value of zero but use a parameter value of m=256 by coding in the parameter as 0. In effect, m=n (mod 256) where 0<n⩽256.)

The whole RAM is used, irrespective of the delay value, the differences in parameter value merely determining the difference between the write and read addresses. The effect of this is to simplify run-time address generation to just incrementing the write and read addresses, once per 800 μs (plus checking when the end of the delay line has been reached). When the end is reached, the address is returned to the beginning of its own 8K byte block.

3. *Frequency shifting* Small changes of frequency are imposed on the base-band signal by cross-multiplication of the two components by the sine and cosine of the frequency shift. If the baseband signals are $A \sin (\omega t+\phi)$ and $A \cos (\omega t+\phi)$ and they are "mixed" with $B \sin \Delta t$ and $B \cos \Delta t$, then products of the form

$$A B \sin [(\omega+\Delta)t+\phi] \quad \text{and} \quad A B \cos [(\omega+\Delta)t+\phi]$$

emerge.

A 1-byte parameter can be used to define the frequency. The parameter f has values in 2s complement notation and therefore has the range $-128\rightarrow+127$. Each quantum can correspond to 4 or 5 Hz, giving frequency shifting of about $\pm\frac{1}{2}$ kHz.

Derivation of sine and cosine frequency-shift components had to be delegated to hardware, to make them available in 800 μs. Putting this computation in the peripheral hardware had two advantages:

1. The sine and cosine of the shift frequency has to be multiplied by the two baseband signals. Placing the trigonometric ROM (TRIGROM) in the vicinity of the multiplier is a way of saving data movements.
2. Rapid calculation of the appropriate angles for the trigonometric (TRIG) device, so that hardware is also needed. Again including this hardware with the peripheral hardware section is advantageous. The TRIG hardware consists simply of a TRIG look-up table connected to the hardware bus.

Although wasteful (in principle), the ROM was programmed to encompass all 2π radians of a sine table. This eased address generation which would have been so much more involved and time consuming if only one quadrant had been burned into the ROM. The extra cost of the larger memory was very marginal.

The address generator simply consists of an accumulator having the same number of bits (c) as the address port of the TRIGROM. The accumulator is incremented each 800 μs with the frequency-shift parameter f. This causes the accumulator to run forwards or backwards (modulo 2^c) at f angle increments per 800 μs. Thus, repeated reading of the TRIGROM synthesizes a sine wave of frequency proportional to f (Fig. 10.12). To read

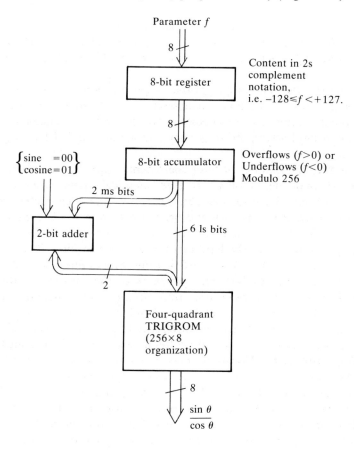

Fig. 10.12 Frequency synthesizer.

cosines, use is made of the fact that cos θ= sin ($\theta+\pi/2$). To implement this, it is simply necessary to add 010----0 to the address needed to read the sine of the same angle. This is because the two most significant (ms) bits of θ define the quadrant currently being read. (Addresses 00xx---x, 01xx---x, 10xx---x and 11xx---x are to be found in quadrants 1,2,3 and 4 respectively.)

To determine the frequency synthesized, it can be seen that if 1000——0 is added to the accumulator each 800 μs, the synthesizer will advance π radians. This corresponds to a real-time frequency of

$$\frac{0.5}{800 \times 10^{-6}} \text{ Hz} = 625 \text{ Hz.}$$

If the value f is treated as a 2s complement quantity, 100——0 actually corresponds to -625 Hz and 011——1 to approximately $+620$ Hz. For an 8-bit parameter f, each quantum would correspond to $620/2^7 \simeq 5$Hz.

4. *Digital filter* The output of the frequency shifter is applied to the digital filter. Thus, so far, data exiting from the (software) delay line in the microcomputer enters the peripheral hardware and does not need to return to the micro until after both frequency shifting and digital filtering have taken place.

To reduce the number of filter coefficients required for a sixth-order Butterworth, implementation was by three identical second-order sections. This also had the advantage that changes to the filter's characteristics by change of coefficients was easy and quick to implement. The equivalent analog block diagrams of a standard second order section, and the complete filter (as programmed in the hardware), are shown in Figs. 10.13(a) and 10.13(b) respectively. It will be noted that this style of filter (second order) defines five coefficients, but that symmetry of the forward coefficients reduces the number of *different* ones to 3. (In the actual instrument, it was found convenient to retain a_0 and $2a_0$ separately because of the coefficient-addressing system used. It made no difference to the size of the coefficients memory as 4 locations per filter cut-off frequency were available, due to the ROM chip employed: 32 locations, making 8 sets of 4 locations available.) The ROM was organized as 32 locations by 16 bits to give sufficient precision to the coefficients (some of them have very small values). Since 8 sets were available, 8 cut-off frequencies could be programmed. The specification called for only 5. Of the 5 address bits, 2 can define the coefficient for a given cut-off frequency; the remaining 3 define the cut-off frequency (Fig. 10.14).

Referring to the complete filter (Fig. 10.13 b), the effect of interleaving the three sections is to reduce the volume of memory to store delayed signal samples. This reduces costs (recall 16-bit operation in this area) and reduces computation by reducing the number of data movements within the delay. The delay is implemented by a RAM (also part of the peripheral hardware). The use of standard 32-location RAM chips left a few locations redundant. However, they are available for holding scratch results from other calculations, such as the amplitude-slicing algorithm).

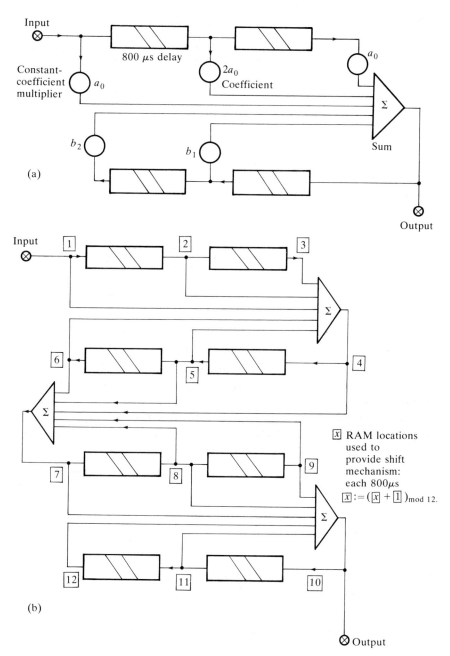

Fig. 10.13 (a) Analog implementation of second-order filter showing symmetry of forward coefficients; (b) three interleaved second-order digital filters provide -3 to -30 dB roll-off in one octave.

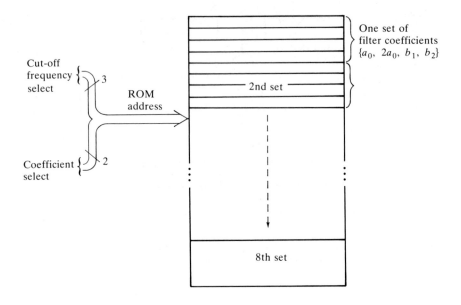

Fig. 10.14   Filter coefficients ROM organization.

5. *Recombination of the two quadrature channels* The two channels form a quadrature (sine plus cosine) pair. To recombine them into a single (amplitude) channel requires vector addition. Strictly, if the two channels are designated I and Q, then M (the magnitude)$= (I^2+Q^2)^{1/2}$. As the amplitude is to be used ultimately in an adaptive-amplitude slicer only, great

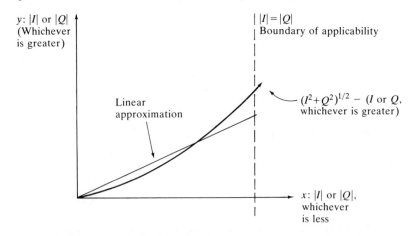

Fig. 10.15   Single-chord linear approximation to $(I^2+Q^2)^{\frac{1}{2}}$ for one octant (0 to $\pi/4$ radians).

precision is not required. As no hardware exists to readily form the square root of a quantity in the demodulator described, and the formation of a square root by micro software would be relatively slow, it was decided to employ a piecewise-linear approximation algorithm. This was simple enough to be executed by micro software (Fig. 10.15). The I and Q channels are constrained to fall in a single octant $(\pi/4)$ by simply forming $|I|$ and $|Q|$. The larger of $|I|$ and $|Q|$ is identified and designated C_{max}, and the other C_{min}. The linear transformation $M = C_{max} + kC_{min}$ is performed, where k is a simple (in terms of binary) fraction. Two easy possibilities for k exist: $\frac{1}{4}$ and $\frac{3}{8}$; these are shown in Table 10.1. The value $\frac{3}{8}$ is easy to implement by shifting and adding and yields a magnitude within 0.6 dB of the true r.m.s. value. If greater accuracy than this is required, a two-section piecewise-linear approximation could be used (preferably using some simple ratio of $C_{max} : C_{min}$, to avoid a proper division).

Q^*	$M=(I^2+Q^2)^*$	$(I+\frac{1}{4}Q)$ (dB)		$(I+\frac{3}{8}Q)$ (dB)	
		Value	Error	Value	Error
0	1.00	1.00	0	1.00	0
$\frac{1}{4}$	1.03	1.06	0.26	1.09	0.52
$\frac{1}{2}$	1.12	1.13	0.05	1.19	0.52
$\frac{3}{4}$	1.25	1.19	-0.42	1.28	0.21
1	1.41	1.25	-0.95	1.38	-0.24

*Based on $I=1$ (i.e normalized to I)

Table 10.1 Comparison of two simple linear approximations to $(I^2+Q^2)^{1/2}$

6. *Amplitude slicer* The details of this algorithm are not really of interest and, in any case, could take many forms. The algorithm merely notes the number of iterations necessary to define a mark or space and at the same time, having decided what constitutes a mark or space, sets the mark/space amplitude-discrimination level to be midway between the two last amplitudes so defined. Computationally, six multiplications, two additions, one shift, one comparison and two incrementations are involved, per 800 μs, in the algorithm used. Clearly, the multiplications are the most time consuming and must be executed in the peripheral hardware (from data supplied by the microcomputer). The other arithmetic operations, add, shift, etc., not being in the hardware's repertoire, are carried out by software in the microcomputer.

7. *Peripheral hardware* The use of a hardware multiplier so slackens the time tolerances for 800 μs, that quite a simple hardware scheme is possible. Nonetheless, in this design example, the hardware performs a number of functions and becomes a very minor processor in its own right.

The term "nanoprocessor" is not inappropriate. Such a term also gives a clue as to its organization, for if the hardware consisted of say, only a multiplier, it could have been connected very easily to the microcomputer. However, an element of "sequencing" has crept into this design (*vide* the digital-filter algorithm). It was felt necessary to recognize the processor-like form of the hardware and to organize it as such. Control is excercised by a nanoprogram ROM, which can execute a limited set of "instructions". The ROM is addressed from a simple counter which replaces the fetch logic of a normal processor. Therefore, this nanoprocessor goes through a fixed sequence with no jumps or loops. It executes, at each stage, one of a limited menu of nanoinstructions—each of which requires just one clock cycle (of the peripheral hardware) to execute (Fig. 10.16). This is therefore a processor of very limited capabilities—it is really a sequencer which performs arithmetic and data-movement functions.

Inspection of the possible functions that are required yields:

1. for the frequency shifter: cross multiplications and additions (accumulation);

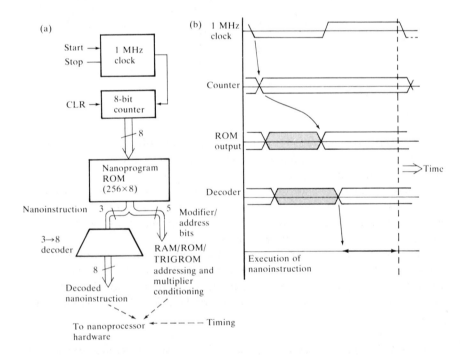

Fig. 10.16 Peripheral hardware timing logic and instruction cycle: (a) logic; (b) timing.

2. the digital filter: multiplications (by ROM-stored coefficients) plus accumulation;
3. the amplitude slicer: straight multiplications and return of products to the microcomputer.

The following list (dependent on components used in the hardware) evolves:

(a) move programmable peripheral interface (PPI) to RAM: (mnemonic PPIRAM);
(b) move multiplier to RAM: (mnemonic MULRAM);
(c) move RAM to PPI: (mnemonic RAMPPI);
(d) move PPI to multiplier: (mnemonic PPIMUL);
(e) move RAM to multiplier: (mnemonic RAMMUL);
(f) move multiplier to PPI: (mnemonic MULPPI);
(g) move ROM to multiplier, multiply using one operand already in multiplier and optionally either add or subtract the previous accumulated products to/from this new product. Result to output register of multiplier: (mnemonic ROMMUL);
(h) As (g), except source of operand is from TRIGROM and not ROM: (mnemonic TRIGMUL).

Instruction mnemonic	Op-code				Modifier/address			
PPIRAM	0	0	0	N	RAM address			
MULRAM	0	0	1	N	RAM address			
RAMPPI	0	1	0	N	RAM address			
PPIMUL	0	1	1	X/Y	←——— N ———→			
RAMMUL*	1	0	0	N	RAM address			
MULPPI	1	0	1	←——— N ———→				
ROMMUL†	1	1	0	N	A/S	ACC	ROM address	
TRIGMUL†	1	1	1	S/C	A/S	ACC	← N →	

Total: 8 bits

ROM address defines a_0, $2a_0$, etc.	X/Y = multiplier input select	A/S = accumulator add or subtract	S/C = sine/cosine select	
N = not defined	* = multiplier X input	† = multiplier Y input	ACC = accumulate product ?	

Table 10.2

All of these functions and options can be programmed into a single-byte instruction format as shown in Table 10.2. There are 8 functions (op-codes), encoded by 3 bits. The remaining 5 bits are used for instruction modification and RAM/ROM/TRIGROM addressing.

Each of these "nanoinstructions" is so simple that it can be computed in a single clock period of 1 μs. This clock step includes advancing the instruction counter, reading the nanoprogram ROM, decoding the function and performing the appropriate data movement or arithmetic. The performance is such that each channel of the digital filter can be processed once per 100 μs, or less. A suitable nanoinstruction flowchart is shown in Fig. 10.17.

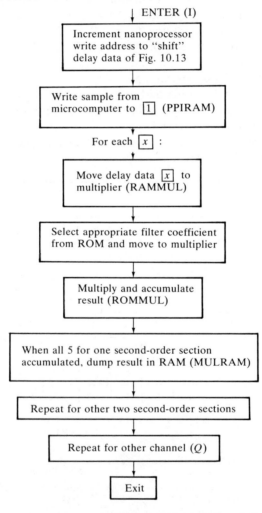

Fig. 10.17 Abbreviated flowchart for implementation of digital filter.

8. *Slicer software* Apart from the use of the peripheral hardware to perform the 6 multiplications, the adaptive slicer algorithm is implemented wholly, in software, in the microcomputer—as is the generation of sets of statistical tables. Sufficient (micro-based) RAM must be provided to hold one complete set of statistical results (32 marks and space durations, etc.) whilst a second, similar, table is currently being generated. This gives the demodulator plenty of time to establish itself as a talker on the IEEE bus and to decant the first table to the appropriate listener.

9. *Non-real-time functions* There are three functions under the aegis of the microcomputer, for which performance is not of great importance. They are:

1. interpretation of the key actuations on the instrument front panel;
2. display of instrument status;
3. self-check routines which can be invoked at power-on.

Because this instrument is connected to a flexible bus system, most instrument status can be issued to the bus controller (the host computer), via the bus. This allows the bus controller to make overall decisions on operating procedure, based on the status of *all* instruments on the bus, rather than allow unilateral actions by the operator on individual instruments.

Self-check facilities take the form of providing the instrument with a sequence of test samples (in pairs) and checking the statistics table generated. The sequence must be such that it exercises the various sections of the system comprehensively with different parameter values. A difficulty is experienced in the length of sequence needed to do this because of the large number of operating options that come about from parametric control.

Note that the ADC is not involved in this self-check because of the problems of tolerancing. The results obtained have to take account of ADC performance variations.

A simpler test of the ADC can be carried out in which the ADC is swept through its dynamic range and the digital outputs checked (with tolerances) against a standard.

An advantage that results from sub-Nyquist sampling is that no analog filters are required. (This does occur with conventional frequency mixing (analog down-conversion): down-conversion using either analog mixers or digital synthesizer–multipliers also generates up-conversion products. Filters need to be added to prevent such frequencies passing through the demodulator.) Sampling at $800\,\mu s$ intervals automatically introduces an $800\,\mu s$ zero-order hold which has frequency components emerging with a $(\sin x)/x$ envelope. (The first null occurs at 1.25 kHz.)

10. *IEEE protocol* The IEEE 488 (1975) standard is quite rigid about the electrical/logical/mechanical definitions of the bus. However, most aspects of the transaction protocol are not defined. For this instrument and bus, certain decisions had to be made about the general format of messages and the handling of anomalous situations, such as invalid messages. The demodulator has both to receive and to transmit large quantities of data of various lengths. It is therefore tempting (as designers frequently find) to define a protocol based on messages of a definable length (packet switching). A fixed-length message precedes all transactions and has a fixed format. In this "header" can be contained the message length, sumcheck (a validity check on the data which, when added to the sum of all other message bytes (modulo 256), creates a pre-agreed value) and other information pertinent to the bus (as a whole). The header is then followed by the message, the format for which can be set parametrically and declared as part of the header.

A slightly more difficult area is that of handling anomalous situations (as they arise). The bus standard allows 15 participants to be connected at any one time. However, parallel polling is restricted to the use of 1 data line per participant. Therefore, the plethora of flags generated by each particip-

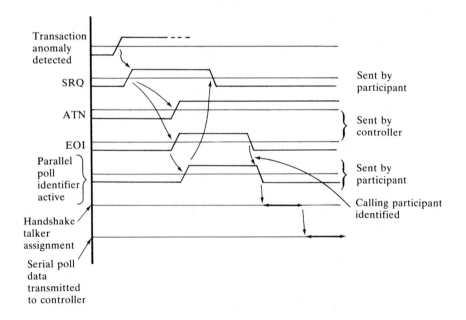

Fig. 10.18 One method for combined parallel/serial polling using the IEEE (488) bus.

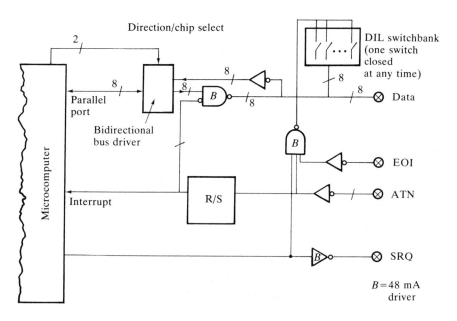

Fig. 10.19   Parallel poll hardware for demodulator.

ant cannot possibly be handled by the 8 data lines, in an unencoded form. One solution is to make use of a part parallel/part serial polling technique using the sevice-request (SRQ) and end-or-identify (EOI) lines. They can form the basis of a handshaking system. The idea is that only participant *identification* is attempted with the parallel-poll facility and that the *nature* of the anomaly is only identified through serial polling. The latter is achieved through the controller by establishing as a talker each participant which answered the parallel poll. When it is a given participant's turn to talk, it indicates the nature of the anomaly by sending a coded message to the contoller, using the normal handshaking protocol (Fig. 10.18). The parallel-poll hardware is shown in Fig. 10.19. However, it should be noted that this is only one of several ways in which this problem can be solved and that different designers have adopted other approaches.

11. *Bootstrap loading* To make the instrument programmable, the specification called upon the controller to send the instrument's software, via the IEEE bus, to its programmable RAM. Of course, a small amount of software must reside in a ROM in the demodulator to make it capable of accepting the main software. This is known as a bootstrap. For this system, the bootstrap must be capable of initializing the instrument (PPIs, stack pointer, etc.), responding to all IEEE protocol including IFC,ATN,

talker/listener set-up and the handshaking in of the software. Because of such capabilities, the various bootstrap functions are written as subroutines and are callable by the main software. This saves duplication of software (for instance, when the demodulator wants to talk to the bus). All of this IEEE software must be agreed and fixed for a given system and adopted by all participants on that bus. Being agreed and fixed, it can, naturally, be committed to ROM.

Having considered how to implement the various individual functions, it is now possible to piece these activities together into iterations of 800 μs, and to see what time is available for each. This has to be done very carefully for this instrument, because of the possibility of concurrent processing in the microcomputer and peripheral hardware. Following the data-flow diagram of Figs. 10.1–10.3, an activity chart can be developed from Fig. 10.8. In order to accommodate IEEE activity, the following procedure can be followed:

1. An outstanding-samples counter (OSC) can be instituted which keeps a record of unprocessed pairs of samples. It is initialized to zero and incremented each time a pair of samples enters from the ADC.
2. OSC is decremented each time a pass (iteration) of the algorithm is completed. As long as OSC is less than the maximum permitted value (set parametrically), the ATN interrupt is left unmasked and IEEE transactions permitted as they occur.
3. If OSC reaches the maximum permitted value, IEEE software activity is suspended and associated interrupt sources masked. This allows the signal-processing software to catch up and thereby decrement OSC.
4. One again, interrupts are permitted.

It should be noted that the system is, in some measure, self-compensating. If signal processing is held up, then, of course, tables of marks and space statistics are not produced. This immediately removes a major source of IEEE bus activity—the transmission of results from the demodulator.

10.5   HARDWARE ARCHITECTURE

As the peripheral hardware is interfaced to the microcomputer via its parallel-bit ports, the hardware does not influence the electrical or logical design of the micro. Therefore, the micro *per se* will be ignored, except to say that it must have sufficent ROM for a bootstrap (say 1K bytes) and sufficient RAM for the main software, delay line and incidental (scratch) data (about

20K bytes). It must also have sufficient parallel-bit ports to support both the peripheral hardware and the IEEE bus interface. Altogether about 6 bytes of ports are needed.

We can now concentrate on the peripheral hardware and bus-interface logic.

Peripheral hardware

The number of data-handling components in this hardware makes bus connection of them very attractive. This gives an orderliness to their inter-connection, ease of printed-circuit (PC) layout and reduction in the number of traces needed on the PC. Many suitable components are available with tristate outputs and low current inputs—both very necessary characteristics of bus-connected components.

The chips for this hardware are:

1. bidirectional bus driver to connect the hardware to the PPI;
2. an accumulating multiplier, i.e. the TRW 1010 series (Fig. 5.26);
3. a 32×16 ROM for the digital filter coefficients;
4. a 32×16 RAM for the digital filter delayed samples;
5. a 256×8 TRIGROM for the frequency synthesizer.

In addition, the instruction counter, nanoprogram memory, function decoder and TRIGROM address generator are needed as control components. A simplified block diagram is shown in Fig. 10.7. The connection to the micro includes not only a data interface but also a sufficiency of control and timing I/O, including handshaking lines, to synchronize the micro and hardware activities and data exchange.

The internal functioning of this hardware is quite easy to validate if it is disconnected from the micro and the instruction counter single-stepped (or made to execute one instruction repeatedly).

Once some confidence in the hardware has been obtained, it can be connected to the micro and elementary sequences of functions and prompts programmed into it. Many microcomputer-testing techniques are applicable to this unit simply because of its very close architectural resemblance to a processor.

IEEE interface

The logic for this unit is very much based on that discussed in Section 7.6. Although shown as discrete logic, a number of manufacturers now market integrated IEEE interfaces (including some compatible with microcomputers). Suitable units, which, with small quantities of discrete logic, will

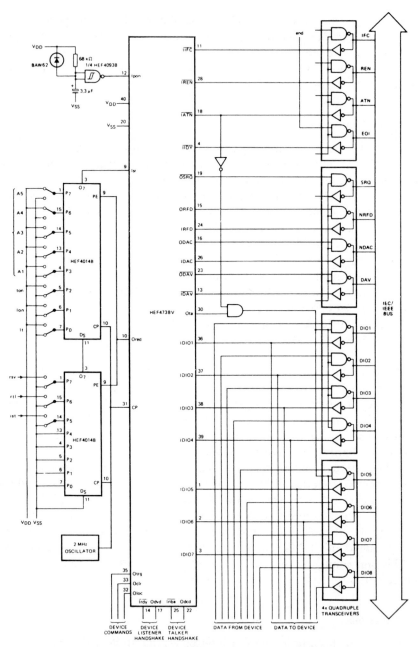

Fig. 10.20 (a) Basic IEC/IEEE bus interface using the Mullard LSI chip type HEF4738V; (b) Application of Mullard HEF4738V showing addressing and transceiver connections. (Drawing reproduced by courtesy of Mullard Ltd., London, UK.)

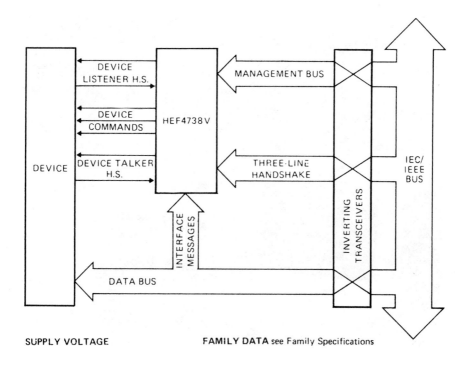

Fig. 10.20 (b)

fulfil the functions required of a talker/listener, are manufactured by Motorola, Philips and others (Fig. 10.20). Note, in particular, the logic to relinquish bus control quickly if ATN is asserted and the use of switchbanks to provide instrument identification, both for talker/listener assignments and for parallel polling.

Several important points must be noted when deciding on components and logic architecture. They include:

1. Testability of logic, either as separate units, exited and monitored by probes, or a logic analyzer (Fig. 10.21), or under software control using already tested sections of the equipment.
2. Maintenance of hardware, including isolation of faulty sections and easy replacement of individual components or PC cards.
3. Components used should, if possible, be available from more than one manufacturer (second sourcing) and have some prospect of a prolonged manufacturing life. Many components are discontinued by

Fig. 10.21   A versatile VDU-based logic state analyzer. (Courtesy Hewlett-Packard Co., Santa Clara, California.)

manufacturers, once improved versions have been established in the market place. The new components are not necessarily electrically, mechanically or logically compatible with earlier types. Furthermore, certain slight differences often exist between ostensibly similar components manufactured by second sources. Care must be exercised in ascertaining that second-source components are *really* suitable.

10.6 SOFTWARE DESIGN

The approach to software development for a system depends as much on the tools available as anything else. The availability of a microprocessor development system or even an emulator can greatly accelerate the process. The advantage of emulation lies in the ability to introduce external parameters and data to the equipment under test. Such signals will include interrupts and panel-key actuations.

This demodulator can be conveniently partitioned according to the functions shown in the data flowchart of Fig. 10.8. Each section of software can be separately tested and then assembled into a single suite. The use of peripheral hardware effectively splits the software burden into two parts. The relationship between the two is not unlike that of a main program (in the micro) to a subroutine (in the hardware). The latter provides specific services for the former—a relationship easily seen from either the hardware or software viewpoints.

Regardless of development method, the software design should be broken down into subroutines, in a multilevel hierarchy, as much as possible. Such partitioning reduces each software section into manageable proportions, and gives a "shape" to it. It also makes amendments and troubleshooting much easier and avoids unnecessary replication of standard routines. Each subroutine should be clearly defined in terms of its function, where it expects to obtain its data (defined registers or memory locations), which register or memory locations it also uses, (and possibly corrupts), and what range of operand values it can handle. Many subroutines may use data (assumed available before subroutine entry) from one or more registers, and corrupt some others. It is therefore often good practice to save the contents of the registers that will be corrupted by putting them on the stack as soon as the routine is entered. They can have their original contents re-established, before returning to the calling routine. Most microcomputers offer a range of "push" (save) and "pop" (re-establish) instructions to do this task. Such instructions automatically update the stack pointer as they are executed. However, unless the micro offers single instruction pushes and pops, which operate on all the registers in one go, it is upon the programmer to make sure that the pop instructions are so ordered that they correctly re-establish the registers. So, if the registers are saved in the order $A,B,C,...$, they must be re-established in the order $...,C,B,A$. Most microcomputers offer almost unlimited subroutine and stacking facilities (single-chip micros, providing RAM on-chip, often impose a severe limit to stacking depth) and thus as much use should be made of them as possible.

It is sometimes also a good plan for a routine to keep a copy of the data input to it (in a register or memory location). This needs to be done only if execution of the routine destroys the original copy of the data.

Lastly, many microprocessors automatically save all registers when an interrupt routine is entered and re-establish them when return to the interrupted routine takes place. The saving of registers is prompted by the hardware-interrupt signal and the re-establishment of the registers is effected by the mandatory RETURN instruction, which must terminate all subroutines (including those initiated by an interrupt). This is a good practice to emulate if the microprocessor used does not do this automatically: it requires only a few bytes to code.

Examples   The Motorola saves the A, B, X, and CC registers automatically when interrupted and provides re-establishment of them all (in the correct order) in the return instruction. The Intel 8080/5 provides a complete set of push and pop instructions so that it can be done under program control. The Motorola method saves code and execution time; the Intel scheme gives freedom of action to the programmer and allows him to choose which registers he saves.

The broad outline of software decision-making has already been laid out. Detailed codings for the demodulator will not be given here as they will be too specific to be of any great utility. Suffice it to say that the software design and coding cannot be carried out for this, and most other, systems as a single exercise. Some trial codings will have been written, simulated and evaluated very early on to help ascertain what, if any, peripheral hardware is needed to prop up system performance. Even after some hardware has been added, fresh codings are necessary to see if performance targets can now be met. If they cannot, it indicates either improper choice of hardware, poor hardware utilization, poor interfacing methods (both from the hardware and software viewpoints) or improper use of interrupt facilities. Until trial codings achieve the desired goals, preferably with a healthy margin, hardware architecture cannot be frozen, and final software design and coding is impossible.

The obvious performance shortcomings of microcomputers make hardware/software interactions very tight, so that changes of design to the one reflect strongly on the other. By the time detailed software is being produced and made into a coherent whole, most individual software routines will have been written and known in detail—even simulated and run on an emulator. Thus, software writing may consist of just putting a number of routines together (linking), prefixing them with initialization procedures and coupling them with routines whose performance is not critical. For the demodulator, the critical routines were those for implementing the delay line, frequency shifting, filtering and amplitude slicing. The initialization routines were those which set up CPU registers, initialized interrupt controllers, interface (I/O) chips and programmable timers. Routines whose performance was not of great importance included those concerned with IEEE transactions and data handshaking. The speed of the latter functions is more likely to be governed by the reaction time of other participants on the IEEE bus and the volume of traffic on it.

10.7   DEVELOPMENT PROCEDURE

Whatever the level of sophistication of the available development tools, the development technique is basically one of growing an edifice of working hardware and software sections. In the case of hardware, the identifiable sections are as follows:

1.   The front-end S–H amplifiers, counters and ADC. They can be tested with an analog sine-wave generator and a DAC at the output, to reconstruct the analog signal. As sub-Nyquist sampling is employed, the output sinewave should be at a frequency which is the difference between the incoming signal and 100 kHz (in the vicinity of 100 kHz). At 100 kHz exactly, the output should be just "residual" d.c. This will also happen at frequencies which are displaced from 100 kHz in steps of 1.25 kHz, i.e. at 101.25, 102.5, 98.75 and 97.5 kHz. (1.25 kHz is the sampling rate).

2.   The IEEE interface. This can be reasonably tested by using a switch bank to emulate incoming signals to the bus (or from the microcomputer's parallel-bit output port). Basic operation is tested quickly, as is any tendency for the interface logic to interfere with either the bus or output port. In particular, inadvertent connection of the output of a logic gate to an I/O interface port, programmed as an output, is to be avoided. When the interface is clearly reasonably "healthy", detailed testing for all possible combinations of operating conditions can be postponed until system software testing can be instituted. Hopefully, exercising of the system through software can be more quickly carried out than by signal probing.

3.   Peripheral hardware testing has already been mentioned in Section 10.5. As with the IEEE interface logic, it will be tested initially by probing (or logic analyzer) for basic healthiness. It will also be checked for such defects as outputs clashing on the IEEE bus. Alternatively it might, in view of the complexity of the peripheral hardware, be considered desirable to design a more comprehensive test jig. As the hardware takes pairs of samples and performs most functions before releasing them to the vector adder, one way of testing the peripheral hardware would be to couple it directly (almost) to the ADC, and to connect a DAC to the hardware's output. The test jig would have to emulate some of the control and timing signals normally supplied to the hardware from the microcomputer. However, there are not many of them and they are not very complex to generate. Such a jig would allow signals (maybe one channel at a time) to be entered to the hardware from a sine-wave source, frequency shifted and filtered and then returned to sine-wave form. Defects in the hardware could be pinpointed quickly by inspection of the analog output. Identification of the defective section would be by use of one nanoprocessor facility at a time. As confidence grew, facilities would be used in groups. By sweeping the input frequency either side of 100 kHz, changing the frequency shift f and the filter cut-off frequency, comprehensive testing is quite easy. As such testing uses almost all of the hardware facilities, it engenders confidence for its use in the

slicer algorithm—without actually emulating the algorithm. The tests also go some way to establish whether the hardware's contribution to the hardware/software interface is satisfactory. The adding of tested sections to the system edifice (although admittedly the testing is incomplete) makes fault finding much easier and quicker than tackling the whole system in one go. (Most faults can be attributed to ill-timing and poor interface methods.)

Much software testing can be carried out by temporarily connecting a DAC to a parallel-bit output port in the microcomputer. This gives a form of signal-trace facility which helps follow the progress of signals through the delay software, vector adder and selected sections of the amplitude slicer. Some software testing (at the end) has to wait until the instrument is connected to the IEEE bus. Under these circumstances, system response to commands sent by the bus controller can be checked. Other such tests would include the instrument's ability to handle the presence of dense traffic on the bus, when it is trying to decant statistics.

Approaches to building the software edifice include:

1. Direct loading of the program material to the micro RAM under a monitor ROM (temporarily occupying the top of memory). The program might be entered via a TTY or VDU.

2. As (1), but loaded from a paper tape or cassette tape, etc., prepared on another computer. The other (host) computer might be programmed in a high-level language or an assembly language (Barron, 1969). It would compile/assemble (Aho, 1978) the code to form machine-readable (binary) code for the microcomputer. This is called cross compilation/assembly;

3. As (2), but with the host computer electrically connected to the target (micro) so that direct (downline) loading is possible;

4. Use of a development system which can hold (partially) developed programs on, say, floppy disk, and which may also be able to compile/assemble programs. The development system, whilst connected to the target, may also be able to run the software and interact with the hardware (emulation). If a development system is available, it could also be employed to emulate a bus controller, when the bus interface commands and transactions are to be checked out (Fig. 10.22).

For this instrument, the software falls into two main areas:

(a) bootstrap;
(b) main software.

If the bootstrap software is developed first using one the methods outlined in the previous paragraph, then a development system or another computer

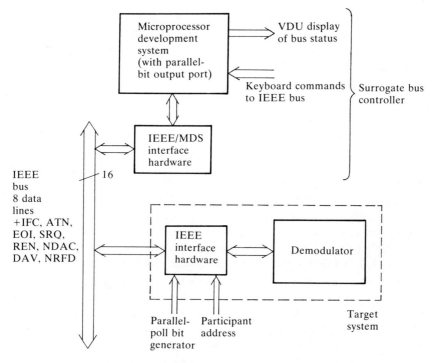

Fig. 10.22 A microprocessor development system can act as a temporary bus controller during demodulator development.

can be used to emulate a bus-connected controller. It would then be a repository for the main software, which would downline load the main software, via the bus, to the micro.

10.8 DESIGN ASSESSMENT AND TOLERANCING

There are several major areas of system evalation to be carried out before even a limited production run release can be made. Some involve just looking at the design—in particular the software; some involve run time and environmental tests.

1. *Software* Once detailed codings have been carried out and exercised on an emulator or in real system, timing margins can be estimated or measured. For this design, it is of particular interest to know what percentage of the 800 μs iteration cycle is needed for one software pass through the algorithm. An initial figure would be based on processing in no way interrupted by IEEE transactions.

Clearly if the figure is close to 100%, it must be inferred that even a small amount of IEEE traffic, involving the demodulator, would tend to make it fall behind with its real-time processing. Note, in this context, that some *outgoing* traffic is generated by the demodulator simply through the need to decant its statistical tables.

If the processing figure exceeds, say, 80%, there is a very good case for looking carefully at the system design to establish which routine(s) is both taking too much time *and* is most amenable to improvement. By this stage, it would be hoped that the performance target was already known to have been met, but, occasionally, margins are gradually eroded through software corrections (debugging) to real-time algorithms.

If processing time has to be saved, it is quite likely that improvements to and rationalization of algorithms will make all the improvement necessary. Often, this can take the form of committing some task to ROM look-up tables rather than algorithmic evaluation. (In this demodulator, the use of a TRIGROM avoided lengthy sine and cosine routines.)

When the raw processing speed is satisfactory, tests must be performed to see to what extent external events, such as IEEE traffic, affect performance. This is probably best carried out under contrived conditions in the first instance so that a quantitave assessment of interference can be made. However, unless traffic/time relationships are known with any precision, only in-system testing can be finally used as an indicator.

2. *Hardware tolerances* Assuming the hardware performs *functionally* as intended, timing margins remain to be checked, particularly in areas of scratch-built logic. Such tests have to be performed over the worst-case extremes of temperature, supply voltage and regulator tolerances. Provided manufacturer's instructions are adhered to in terms of clock speed, bus loading, system configuration and operating temperature, little trouble should be experienced in the microcomputer, *per se*. More likely, difficulties may be experienced with the peripheral hardware, which is fabricated from components by different manufacturers. Of particular importance in this respect are the following:

1. Peripheral hardware clock speed—can all instructions be fetched, decoded and executed in the time allowed?

2. Do RAM write pulses, in particular, conform to those specified by the manufacturer? Over the temperature range, it is quite possible that address and data set-up and hold times, chip enable and other signals will not maintain their correct values. Most of these timings are related to the back (trailing) edge of "write enable". However, the front-edge timings are also important. Troubles will certainly occur if the RAM

address is not stable some time before the "write-enable" pulse arrives. Data may well be written to several RAM locations if timing rules are not observed.

Temperature testing must include both high and low extremes. Some MOS devices (such as microprocessors) can operate faster at high temperatures, although many MOS and bipolar devices do not. (Bipolar devices often are slower because they go deeper into saturation at higher temperatures, and it therefore takes longer to sweep excess base charge from the transistors.) Therefore, the use of a mixture of technologies (as in this instrument) can cause failure because devices do not "track" each other in terms of performance/temperature. Furthermore, some devices, e.g. crystal controlled microprocessors, are intended to work at very rigidly defined speeds, so that no tracking may take place at all.

Some systems can suffer from "switch-on"problems, that is , they work when power is first applied, and fail when warm (or vice versa). In a ventilated machine, be it convection or force cooled, some components operate at ambient (room) temperature and others, further down the "funnel" from the inlet, operate at higher temperature, because the air is warmed as it passes components further forward. However, at power-on, all components are at room temperature. It follows that some devices are subject to small temperature swings whereas others are subject to large temperature swings, as everything stabilizes. If timings are "marginal", there may well be temperature distributions through the machine which can cause failure.

3. *Mains failure* For many systems, mains failure, either intermittent or long term, can have disastrous consequences. Ignoring such issues as which types of alternative supplies can be used and how they may be switched in at time of failure, the efficacy of the mains-failure detector is of paramount importance (Intersil, 1979). Again, there are traps awaiting the unwary if mixed technologies are used. The worst situation is where the devices which demand the tightest supply tolerance are considered. As an example, 74 series TTL can be guaranteed to operate satisfactorily only with a supply of $+5$ V$\pm 5\%$, i.e. $\pm\frac{1}{4}$V. On the other hand, most MOS devices can tolerate $\pm 10\%$—and CMOS even more.

A mains failure detector must "trip" when the supply rail is still well within the tolerance specified, so that sufficient data transfers to nonvolatile memory can take place before shutdown. The testing of a mains-failure detector must take these considerations into account, plus the worst possible time for failure to occur (both in the mains cycle and from the processing viewpoint). Again, temperature tolerances, component tolerances and supply load current must be considered when carrying out such tests.

4. *System reliability* (Clough, 1979) In a system of this type, having no moving parts, i.e. rotating electromechanical memory, complex keypads etc., reliability is inherently high. High amongst components whose reliability is questionable must be friction connectors and semiconductors which dissipate high power. The large number of integrated circuits make their cumulative failure rate comparable with the worst of the individual components.

Integrated circuits fail in service due to several causes, including:

1. chip-to-header bonding failures which, of course, rise with leadout count;
2. high ambient operating temperatures, for which failure rate rises exponentially with temperature;
3. those triggered externally, such as power-rail surges and failure of components to which the one in question is connected.

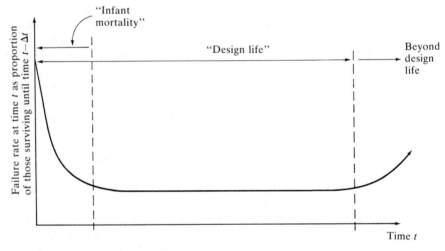

Fig. 10.23 "Bathtub" reliablility curve which is characteristic of most electric components (scales deliberately omitted).

Most components follow the classic "bath-tub" reliability curve (Fig. 10.23) which shows a relatively high "infant mortality rate" (due to manufacturing shortcomings). This is followed by a fairly flat section covering the normal in-service life expectation of the components. During this time, the rate of failure over any time section, of those which *survived* the previous time section, is roughly constant. Stated alternatively, the number of survivors decreases exponentially with time. The rate of failure then tends to rise again, as wear-out failures occur in addition to those subject to the constant "service-life" failure rate.

In addition to the "hard" failures mentioned above, whereby components, at some time, become permanently out of specification, either functionally or parametrically (i.e., unable to fulfil all electrical and tolerancing specifications rather than just logical ones), there are also "soft" errors. These are most common, at present, amongst the very high-density memory chips. Such memories use very little chip area per "cell" and hold very little charge per bit. The charge is typically 5 V on 0.05 pF, i.e. 0.25 pC. This is equivalent to little more than 1 million electrons! Most materials used in device packaging exhibit some degree of radioactivity (one of the epoxy materials used in early ICs was zirconium). The emitted alpha particles sometimes pass through a memory cell and produce electron/hole pairs in the vicinity of the storage capacitor. This can (partially) discharge the cell. The cell is not destroyed as can be subsequently proved by testing. However, a data error occurs at the time of discharge. This is known as a "soft error" and although it occurs very infrequently to any *given* cell, the increased capacity of memories, coupled with smaller charges per cell, is gradually increasing the incidence of such errors. Of course, even if totally nonradioactive materials could be found, cosmic radiation would still cause a small background incidence.

In assessing a system's suitability from a reliability viewpoint, two main issues arise:

1. Is the basic design sound so that the mean time between failures (MTBF) is acceptable?

2. When failure occurs, will the mean time to repair (MTTR) be suitably short because of the testability of the system and the ease with which failed components can be identified and replaced? Clearly, self-check facilities can play an important role in the latter case. However, policies such as spares holdings and construction methods can be an important factor in customer service. A balance must be sought between, on the one hand, customer engineers walking around with small fortunes in terms of subsystem spares for every situation, and on the other, spending excessive time identifying single, low-value, component failures.

5. *System enhancement and future products* Once a system has been evaluated, it is often found that the various (but very necessary) enhancements to the basic design to make it meet the specification leave quite wide performance margins. It is ironic that, for instance, the inclusion of a hardware multiplier may have enhanced the real-time processing performance by a factor of two instead of only by the required 50%! The unintended improvements occur not only because of peripheral hardware additions but also when software routines are "re-jigged". The notion that a "tight" system design should only be amenable to marginal improvements often doesn't apply in these circumstances. Such considerations lead to

several possibilities, ranging from specification revision (to capture a wider product market) through to manufacture of a range or "family" of related products. Each member has different performance and facilities. Discussion of all the strategies is very involved and beyond the scope of this text.

10.9   DESIGN OVERVIEW—IN RETROSPECT

The design of most digital systems follows a fairly well-defined pattern and this project was no exception. At this point, it is worth recapping on the procedures followed and attempting to put them into some sort of order. The design of a complex system involves a large number of decisions which interact. It also involves making a number of (hopefully educated) guesses as to the likely form of the design. Some of these guesses will be wrong and therefore some of the design procedure will have to be repeated. The existence of interactions also means that some parallel design work has to be done so that, to some extent, the tabulation of what appears a sequential approach is both naïve and misleading. However, if the caveats of repeated procedures and parallel design are accepted, a set of design steps can be listed which apply not only to this project but also to most others.

Design listing and decisions checklist

1.   Specification defined and related to possible procedures and algorithms.
2.   Overall approach decided—discrete logic, microcomputer, minicomputer, etc. Answer depends on process to be computed, speed of processing, system flexibility, number of design options to be incorporated, ease of manufacture, testing, ergonomics.
3.   Basic strategy—purely hardware or software approach, possible use of peripheral hardware to achieve performance goals, use of more than one processor.
4.   Identification of "difficult" or "key" areas—maybe where real-time or fast processing is required or the volume of input/output, self-check and ergonomic features dictates. Aportionment of hardware and software burdens in these areas.
5.   Use of simulators to ascertain viability of solutions to "difficult" areas.
6.   Software partitioning into algorithms and procedures. Coding of these procedures.
7.   Assessment of memory and I/O requirements, special transducers, interfaces and ICs needed. Power supplies—if any.
8.   Hardware design (and simulation, if possible).
9.   Elementary hardware tests; simple program checks on hardware; emulation of hardware.

10. Software development including linkage of software routines, sub-routines, etc.

11. Generation of test routines, for self-check facilities and for card check-ing during volume production.

12. Software checking through "dry runs", emulation, in-circuit emula-tion.

13. Performance checks, particularly for real-time processes.

14. Checking of ability of system to recover if anomalous variable values, program counter values and keypad operations are encountered.

15. Testing of test routines for cards by inducing of "mock" fault condi-tions, e.g. stuck-at-logic-1 and stuck-at-logic-0 faults on all logic nodes.

16. Documentation, test procedures, handbook.

EXERCISES

10.1 A microcomputer receives 8-bit unsigned samples of OOK morse signals. The signals are such that each "element" spans at least 5 samples. However, the sample amplitudes corresponding to marks and spaces tend to vary slowly with time (nonetheless, marks are always of greater amplitude than spaces). Pre-pare a flowchart for an adaptive amplitude slicer which will indicate when marks and spaces are being transmitted and write detailed code. What are the limitations of your system in terms of ability to discriminate between marks and spaces and to react to changes of signal levels?

10.2 Design a microcomputer-based emulator (hardware and software) that can be used to check that the coefficients $a_0, 2a_0, b_1$ and b_2 chosen for any filter design are appropriate. It should have an ADC for accepting analog sine waves of varying frequency, a DAC to allow display of filter response on an oscillo-scope and a TTY to input coefficients in decimal.

10.3 Write a computer program which will assemble the 256×8-bit sines of angles between 0 and 2π in contiguous memory locations. The values should be expressed in 2s complement notation, rounded to the nearest 1s bit.

10.4 Using manufacturer's components of your choice, design a suitable 16-bit nanoprocessor for the demodulator described in this chapter. Take care to incorporate handshaking facilities between the microcomputer and nano-processor and to design timing logic.

10.5 Write nanocode for the digital filter described in this chapter. How long does it take to process 1 channel based on $1 \mu s$ per nanostep?

10.6 Using manufacturer's discrete (SSI) components, design a suitable IEEE hardware interface for the demodulator described in this chapter. (ATN and IFC should raise interrupts at the microprocessor when they occur and cause the data bus to be relinquished as soon as possible. Furthermore, ATN and EOI should initiate a parallel poll as described.)

10.7 Repeat Exercise 10.6 but using MSI/LSI components of your choice, includ-ing integrated IEEE (488) chips.

10.8 Write a flowchart suitable for a bootstrap loader for this system which performs the following functions:

(a) initializes the microcomputer and nanoprocessor at power-on;
(b) uses IFC as an interrupt routine to initialize the demodulator and IEEE interface hardware and software;
(c) can be set up as a talker or listener through the use of ATN;
(d) contains (callable) subroutines for the following standard procedures:

   (i)   write a byte to the IEEE bus (talk), and
   (ii) read a byte from the IEEE bus (listen).

Choose whatever IEEE message format you think suitable. However, it must be able to work with messages of differing lengths (bytes) and provide a sumcheck facility.

REFERENCES

Aho, A. V. (1978), *Principles of Compiler Design,* Prentice-Hall, Englewood Cliffs, N.J.

Antonio, A. (1979), *Digital Filters; Analysis and Design,* McGraw-Hill, London.

Barron, D. W. (1969), *Assemblers and Loaders,* Computer Monographs, Macdonald (London)/Elsevier (New York).

Beauchamp, K. G. and Yuen, C. K. (1979), *Digital Methods for Signal Analysis,* Allen & Unwin, London.

Bywater, R. E. H. (1975), "A binary multiplier for signal processing applications," *Digital Processes,* **1,** 261–5.

Bywater, R. E. H. and Mansi, L. S. A. (1980), "Low-cost reciprocals generator" *Digital Processes,* **6,** 97–104.

Bywater, R. E. H., Matley, W. and Brock, D. J. (1976), "Design of a phase reversals modulation correlator," *Radio and Electronic Engr.,* **46**(3), 129–35.

Bywater, R. E. H., Williamson, S. E. and Matley, W. (1978), "A real-time digital filter, " *Int. J. Electronics,* **45**(3), 265–71.

Clough, I. D. (1979), "Reliability assessment for communications equipment," *Electronic Eng.,* April, 48–63.

IEEE (1975), *Standard interface specification (488).*

Intersil, (1979), "How to design non-volatile CMOS memory systems," *Insight,* No. 2, 4–5.

Matley, W. and Bywater, R. E. H. (1977), "A digital high-frequency multi-path propagation simulator," *Radio and Electronic Engr.,* **47**(7), 305–14.

Millman, J. and Halkias, C. C. (1972), *Integrated Electronics,* McGraw-Hill Kogakusha, Tokyo, Section 10.

Peled, A. and Liu, D. (1976), *Digital Signal Processing: Theory, Design and Implementation,* Wiley, New York.

Rabiner, L. R. and Gold, B. (1975), *Theory and Applications of Digital Signal Processing,* Prentice-Hall, Englewood Cliffs, N.J., Chapter 3.

Schmid, H. (1970), *Electronic Analog to Digital Conversions,* Van Nostrand Reinhold, Scarborough, Canada.

Taub, H. and Schilling, D. L. (1971), *Principles of Communications Systems,* McGraw-Hill, New York.

GLOSSARY

Although an index is given at the end of this book, it was felt desirable to provide a handy reference of technical terms and their meanings. In some cases, the terms are self-explanatory. On the other hand, some can be misleading or have several meanings. Abbreviations and acronyms are treated as though they were words. For more complete explanations of terms, the index should be referenced.

Absolute address	Actual memory address used to access instructions or data (*see* relocation, indexed).
Access time	Delay between supplying address to memory and obtaining data.
Accumulator	Register in processor in which arithmetic results are deposited. (Often also supplies one of the operands to the ALU.)
ADC	Analog–digital converter.
Addend	Operand to which some quantity is added in addition operations.
Addressing mode	Method by which the processor calculates an operand address in an instruction (*see* indexed address, indirect address).
Algorithm	Mathematical procedure (sequence) for performing some task.
Aliasing	Sampling error due to abrogation of Nyquist limit. Caused by use of too low a sampling rate in relation to the incoming signal.
ALU	Arithmetic–logic unit.
Analog	A model. In computing, refers to the use of continuous electrical voltages and currents to represent problem variables.

Analog–digital converter	Converts (usually) continuous analog voltages into a series of digital samples.
Annunciator	Indicator or audible alarm often to draw attention to a malfunction.
Arbitrate/ arbiter	A system which differentiates between which of several units first requested attention or service from a common resource.
Arithmetic–logic unit	A programmable unit capable of performing add, subtract, complement and sometimes other logic functions.
ASCII	American Standard Code for Information Interchange.
Assembly language	A language whose mnemonic statements can be assembled into machine instructions on a one-for-one basis.
Augend	Operand which is added to the addend in addition.
Backplane	A digital system may be partitioned into a number of printed circuit cards. These are plugged into edge connector sockets which are interconnected by (back) wiring. This wiring can be replaced by a (large) printed circuit board into which the card sockets are inserted. Back wiring is then replaced with copper print. Such a printed circuit is variously known as a backplane, mother board or platter. The term mother board implies the position of such a printed circuit in the interconnection hierarchy.
Base	Radix to which numbers are represented, e.g. binary or decimal.
Base address	A value, usually held in a register, from which a block of contiguous data or instruction addresses starts (*see* relocation).
BCD	Binary-coded decimal.
Bidirectional	Property of a wire or bus whereby data can flow in either direction.
Binary	Representation of quantities to base 2. Only digits 0 and 1 used.
Binary-coded decimal	Coded method for decimal numbers in a binary computer in which each *digit* is given as a binary number.
Biphase	Method of recording data on tape in which 0s and 1s are recorded as pulses on separate channels.

Bipolar	Both positive and negative versions may occur (in a variable). For transistor: both positive and negative carriers involved.
Bit slice	Logic which is partitioned into identical slices, each operating on one bit in a multibit word, e.g. "bit-slice microcomputer".
Block carry	Logic used in fast adders which computes carries, for several stages, in one level of logic.
Bootstrap	Program, in read-only memory, which is available at power-up to read in software to a computer.
Branch	*See* jump.
Break point	Special instruction in a program to halt processing.
Buffer memory	A small, fast, memory placed between a processor and main memory.
Bus	A group of wires forming a connecting link between subsystems.
Bypassing	Capacitors used to absorb the effects of fast changes of supply-current demand when gates switch. Often erroneously known as decoupling capacitors.
Byte	Small group of bits—usually 8—treated as a single entity.
Caché	Small, fast, memory similar to buffer memory (q.v.).
CAM	Content-addressable memory.
Card	*Also* Printed card or PCB (q.v.). Glass fiber or phenolic paper board on which components are mounted.
Carry (block)	*See* block carry.
Carry-save	Addition method which saves time by saving carries rather than permitting them to be assimilated in full adders
Cathode-ray tube	TV type tube used in visual display and graphics applications.
Cellular	A form of logic fabricated from repeated use of identical units.
Central processing unit	Often just referred to as "the processor". Contains registers and logic for fetching and executing instructions.
Channel	Any system (wires, radio, etc.) which can carry data between points.
Characteristic	Exponent of number expressed in floating point (scientific notation).

Clock	Regular source of pulses for controlling timing of operations.
CMOS	Complementary metal-oxide semiconductor.
Code	Method used for representing digital data.
Collation	*See* masking.
Combinational	Time-invariant (logic) operations. Output only a function of *current* inputs, not of previous inputs.
Compare	Arithmetic operation to determine greater of two operands.
Compiler	Converts high-level language statements into (usually) machine-coded or assembly-language form.
Complement	Opposite form. For binary, 0s & 1s interchanged.
Complementary metal-oxide semi-conductor	Form of MOS which uses both p- and n-channel transistors (in pairs) to form logic gates.
Content-addressable memory	Form of memory which uses the nature of the data, rather than an address, to access information.
Contiguous	In a series with no gaps; n, $n+1$, $n+2$, etc.
CPU	Central processing unit.
(Cross) assembler	Assembler run on one computer to produce machine code suitable for running on another machine.
CRT	Cathode-ray (TV) tube.
Cycle stealing	Irregular access to memory (by a peripheral device) by using memory time slots normally used by the processor.
DAC	Digital–analog converter.
Data selector	Logic for determining which of several data sources shall pass along a single channel.
DDA	Digital differential analyzer.
Decoding	Breaking down encoded information into constituent parts.
Decoupling	*See* bypassing.
Decrement	Reduce a value by some amount (usually one).
Denormalize	Alter the format of a floating-point number from its ideal representation to another one, without changing its value.
Destination	Memory address of the next instruction to be executed when it is not located immediately after the last one executed.
Digital–analog converter	Device for changing digitally coded values into (usually) analog voltages (*see also* analog–digital converter).

Digital differential analyzer	Digital form of analog computer for solving simulation problems and differential equations.
Diode–transistor logic	Form of logic using diodes to perform logic function and transistors to make up signal losses in the diodes.
Direct memory access	Method for transferring large quantities of data between computer subsystems, without involving the processor.
Discrete	Representation of variables to only a limited number of amplitude levels. A property of digital encoding.
Distributed computing	Computing spread over several machines.
Distribution	A statistical plot of the incidence of events against a property being measured.
DMA	Direct memory access.
Down-line load	Transfer of programs from one machine to another through a channel rather than by paper tape or other indirect means.
DTL	Diode–transistor logic.
Dynamic memory	Memory that requires regular refreshing (topping-up) of information contained in it, before it "leaks" away.
EAROM	Electrically alterable read-only memory.
ECL	Emitter-coupled logic.
Edge-triggered	Property of a flip-flop whereby a logic level change (0 to 1 or 1 to 0), rather than a pulse, is sufficient to cause information to pass from its input to its output.
Elastic store	Also known as a "Silo" (as in grain) or FIFO (q.v.).
Electrically alterable ROM	ROM (q.v.) whose contents can be erased or replaced by current pulses rather than by ultra-violet light or other non-electrical means (see ROM and UVROM).
Emitter-coupled logic	A bipolar logic form in which transistors do not saturate and which uses small logic swings. Characterized by high speed.
Emulation	Technique whereby one piece of hardware can appear to operate like another by being suitably programmed.
End-around carry	Little-used technique for complement addition. Carry from the ms (q.v.) adder is fed back to the carry-in of the first one.
Error resilience	Property of a system whereby failures of individual components do not cause catastrophic failure of the whole system.

Executable	Able to be executed in a computer. Specifically "machine-executable" means suitably coded for running on a computer with no further translation or modification.
Execution time	Time for a task to be completed. Sometimes refers to the non-fetch portion of the instruction time—sometimes to the total time (including fetching).
Exponent	Power to which a base is raised before multiplication by the fraction, to determine the total value of a floating-point quantity (*see* characteristic).
Exponent overflow/ underflow	Exponent attempting to achieve a value either more positive/negative than it is able.
Ferrite-core memory	Type of memory using beads of ferrite to hold each bit of information (according to two possible directions of magnetization). Seldom specified for new designs.
FET	Field-effect transistor.
Fetch	That part of an instruction cycle in which the instruction is brought down from memory to the processor.
Fetch time	Time to fetch instructions from memory. For simple instructions, this can dominate the instruction time.
Field	Space to hold information. May be an area of memory or a group of flip-flops in a register.
Field-effect transistor	Transistor whose conduction properties are controlled by an electrostatic field set up by a third (gate) electrode.
Field-programmable ROM	Type of ROM which can have its pattern of bits programmed by the user, rather than at manufacture.
FIFO	First-in–first-out memory.
Firmware	Information which defines the characteristics of a computer, being midway between hardware and software. Firmware *can* be altered but this is only done infrequently. Firmware is often the level at which emulation is introduced.
First-in–first-out memory	A non-addressed memory form which lies in a channel between two communicators and "irons out" the irregularities in their sending and receiving rates (*see* elastic memory).
Flag	A hardware or software "marker" to indicate some sort of status in a machine. In hardware form, it is a flip-flop.
Flip-flop	A two-state memory device capable of being set or reset under software or hardware control.

Floating point	Similar to "scientific notation", but usually reserved to describe binary operations internal to the computer. Sometimes known as exponential form. A quantity is expressed in two parts, a fraction and exponent—rather like logarithms.
Floppy disk	Rotating electromagnetic memory form that is cheaper but slower and less capacious than conventional disk. The disk is made from mylar and rotates in a sleeve from which it is never taken. Typically it is 20 cm (8 in) in diameter and can hold about 4×10^6 bits.
Format	Manner in which bits are arranged to represent some variable or other information in a computer.
Framing error	Can occur in asynchronous transmission systems when the sender and receiver of information lose synchronization.
Full adder	An adder capable of accepting two operands plus a carry from a less significant adder stage and producing a sum and carry.
Function generator	An analog or digital device which can accept one or more inputs and produce one or more outputs which are related to the input(s), according to some schedule defined by the user.
Functional testing	Applies to integrated and discrete circuits. It is that part of testing which determines if the correct logic operations are being carried out by the device (*see* parametric testing).
Garbage	Information taking up space either in the hardware or software of a computer and which is no longer required. Also refers to random power-on values assumed by memory devices before being fed with their first information.
Glitch	Transient disturbance to a signal or logic level which is unplanned and undesirable. May cause malfunction of a system if it occurs at a critical time.
Guard bit(s)	Extra bit(s) added to the end of digital values to increase precision of, e.g., floating-point fractions. Usually only introduced during calculations and then discarded later on.
Half adder	As per full adder (q.v.) but only two inputs—no carry in.

Handshake	A signal(s) for synchronizing the transfer of data from a sender to a receiver. Single handshake—only sender indicates availability of data: double handshake—receiver also acknowledges receipt.
Hardware	The palpable *equipment* and components of a computer. Generally unchanged in form, once installed.
Hard-wired	Logic defined by gates which are wired together and therefore fixed for all time. Compare with logic formed by ROMs in which a change of ROM can change the logic function.
Hazards	Malfunctions of logic causing either glitches (q.v.) to be generated, due to "static hazards" or incorrect sequences to be followed, due to "dynamic" and "essential hazards" (in sequential logic).
Hex/hexadecimal	Base 16 number system. Convenient variation of binary in which bits are grouped into 4s (nibbles) and given single character names $0, 1, \ldots, 9, A, \ldots, F$, for 0000–1111.
Highway	A group of wires connecting several subsystems together. The arrangement differs from a bus in that one subsystem is always the talker and the other(s) always the listener(s).
Hold	Condition of a microprocessor whereby it stops processing and relinquishes control of the address and data buses. This allows a DMA controller control of the bus.
Hybrid computer	Variation of the analog computer having logic or a digital computer in addition to analog elements.
Idle	A loop of instructions executed by a computer in which time is deliberately wasted, whilst it is waiting for the completion of some outside activity. Escape from the loop is usually by the outside device interrupting the processor.
I^2L	Integrated-injection logic.
Increment	Opposite of decrement (q.v.).
Index register	Address register in a processor which can be used instead of, or in conjunction with, the address portion of an instruction, to define an operand location.
Indexed address	Address derived from the use of an index register (q.v.).

Indirect address	An address given which does not refer to the location of some information but to a location which contains the *address* of the information.
Infix notation	A mathematical notation in which the operator appears *between* the operands on which it is to operate. Example $A + B$.
Input/output	The various channels, interfaces and devices which are involved with the entry and retrieval of information from a computer system.
Instruction	A group of bits defining the activity of a processor at a given time. The bits will define the type of operation AND, JUMP, etc., add the addresses of operands to be used.
Instruction register	Register for holding an instruction when it has been fetched from memory. It is located in the processor and has the instruction decoder connected to its outputs.
Integrated injection logic	A form of bipolar logic which uses very little chip area per gate and operates by manipulating the current flow from current "pumps".
Interrupt	A method for informing the processor of events outside the processor, without the processor having to waste time polling (q.v.) status lines for such information.
Interpreter	A form of translator for computer programs in which each statement is changed into machine code and then immediately executed during run time. Compare with compilation in which the translation takes place on the whole program before any execution is attempted.
I/O	Input/output
Iterative	Refers to any procedure which is repeated many times to achieve some goal. May be implemented in hardware or software.
JUMP	Also known as BRANCH. A type of instruction which allows the normal sequence of execution of instructions from contiguous locations to be broken and a new sequence to be started from a completely fresh location.

Keypad
A set or matrix of key contacts which allow data and conditions to be entered to a computer. The contacts are often interconnected to save wires.

Large-scale integration
Integrated-circuit form sufficiently complex that complete subsystems, such as microprocessors, can be formed on a single chip.

Last-in–first-out memory
Otherwise known as a "stack". A non-addressed memory used for chained arithmetic calculations and for "de-nesting" statements using multiple parentheses (in high-level languages).

Latch
A form of flip-flop having a clock input to control when data can be entered. Level rather than edge-triggered (q.v.) and therefore not suitable for situations where the flip-flop output is only isolated from its input by combinational logic.

Latency
The access delay experienced in electromechanical memories (in particular) when the information required is not directly under the read/write heads.

Least-significant
Bit of least weight in a computer field or word. Usually drawn as the rightmost bit in a logic diagram.

LED
Light-emitting diode.

Lexical analysis
Analysis of the form and validity of a statement in a computer program. In effect "reading" of the statement to decompose it into manageable parts.

LIFO
Last-in–first-out memory.

Light-emitting-diode
A diode which, when forward biased, emits light from the diode junction. Some LEDS emit in the visible region, some in the infra-red band. Can be used for displays, opto-couplers etc.

Linkage editor
A program which couples the many sections of a program together to form a whole. Often used to link a user's program and routines made available in the computer's library.

Loader
A program for preparing a user's program for running on the computer. The loader sets absolute addresses according to where in memory the user's program is finally to be loaded.

Look-ahead
Any process carried out in a computer and producing results before they are actually needed. The idea is to save time or better utilize facilities. In adder systems, carry look-ahead is used to speed up carry propagation.

Loop	A hardware or software process which keeps repeating itself, either because the process is iterative (q.v.) or to "idle" (q.v.).
ls(b)	Least significant (bit).
LSI	Large-scale integration.
Lukasiewicz	Notation named after a Polish mathematician which defines the order of processing for arithmetic expressions without the need for parentheses.
Machine-independent	Applied to computer languages which can be run on any computer (having a suitable compiler).
Macro	A user-defined instruction or statement used in a computer program; it is defined in terms of the instructions and statements in the standard menu. A *name* for a group of instructions which can be called whenever wanted in a program.
Magnitude	*See* modulus.
Mainframe computer	Large central computer having a wide range of facilities and forming the focus of processing in an establishment.
Mantissa	Fraction portion of a floating-point number (q.v.).
Mask/masking	To prevent information passing a certain point in a process, i.e. to mask an interrupt. A mask bit, if set, closes an AND gate to which the interrupt is input and therefore inhibits it. The inverse of masking is collation (effectively logical AND).
Mask-programmed	Refers to the pattern of bits in a memory or microprocessor chip—whether it was defined at manufacture by a mask (aluminum pattern) or by the user (*see* field-programmable).
Master–slave	A type of flip-flop, fabricated from a cascade of two latches. Has the property of being edge-triggered.
Medium-scale integration	A level of IC integration which permits complete logic functions to be formed on a single chip, e.g. memory.
Metal-oxide semiconductor	A semiconductor made by forming field-effect transistors on the silicon surface.
Microinstruction	The actions, etc., for one microstep in a microprogram.
Microprocessor	A complete processor formed on a single silicon die.
Microprogram	A set of instructions, normally implanted in a ROM, which define the actions for realizing all the instructions in a computer's menu.

Microprogrammable	Refers to a processor's timer/controller which allows it to be modified (by the user) so as to change the instruction set offered (*see* emulation and microprogram).
Microstep	Usually the period defined by one clock cycle of the processor.
Minicomputer	A computer of intermediate complexity, performance and cost—somewhere between micro and mainframe. Typical wordlength 16–32 bits.
Minuend	Operand from which the subtrahend is subtracted in subtraction.
Mnemonic	Easy-to-remember letter grouping for some piece of information. Example: ADC might mean add with carry.
Modulo	Cycle length for a counting system. Most car odometers work modulo 100 000, i.e. they return to zero after 100 000 miles.
Modulus	The magnitude or value of a quantity (regardless of sign).
Monolithic	From the Greek "single-stone". Formed in a single piece.
Mono/monostable	A type of flip-flop with one stable state. Often used for delaying signals.
MOS	Metal-oxide semiconductor.
Most significant	Opposite of least-significant (q.v.).
Mother board	*See* backplane.
ms(b)	Most significant (bit).
M–S	Master–slave.
MSI	Medium-scale integration.
MTBF	Mean time between failures.
MTTR	Mean time to repair.
Multiplex	To funnel several channels of data onto a single channel. Time-multiplexing is very common in computers, where each source channel is given a slice of the total time in the output channel.
Multiplicand	The operand multiplied by a multiplier operand.
Multiprogramming	Using the same processor to process several tasks—all of which may wait in memory for their turn.
Mutually exclusive	Only one of several entities may be allowed at any one time.
Negabinary	A notation for signed binary numbers. The weight of each bit is $(-2)^k$ where $k=0,1,2,3....$

Nibble	A group of 4 bits, i.e. $\frac{1}{2}$ byte. Sufficient for 1 BCD (q.v.) digit.
Noise margin	The amount which the output of a gate exceeds the minimum input voltage requirements of similar gates, so as to provide a safety factor.
Nonsignificant	The property of a bit or digit that its existence or non-existence does not affect the overall value of a number.
Nonvolatile	Property of memory devices in which no power supplies are needed to retain information, having once been written.
Normalize	Adjust the fraction (mantissa) and exponent of a floating-point number so that the fraction is in some standard form. This is usually with the fraction magnitude lying between $\frac{1}{2}$ and 1. The exponent is also adjusted to keep the overall value of the number the same as when it started.
Object code	The coding of a program *after* it has passed through a compiler or assembler.
Octal	A variation of binary in which bits are treated in groups of 3 and given values 0–7. Effectively base 8.
Offset	A value added to a quantity or address to temporarily increase or decrease its value.
Offset code	Also known as unipolar. A method for signing numbers in which unsigned arithmetic can be used. Frequently found in ADCs, DACs and in the representation of exponents (q.v.).
1s complement	The version of a number in which 0s are changed to 1s and vice versa. A way of representing negative numbers.
Operand	A number or quantity to be operated on arithmetically.
Operation code	Also known as "op-code". The part of an instruction which defines the action to be taken, e.g. ADD or JUMP, etc.
Operator	A symbol indicating an arithmetic or other operation, e.g. $+$, $-$, etc. Also refers to computer personnel who man installations.
Overflow	Condition whereby the correct result of an arithmetic operation is above the highest value that can be represented.

Page/page zero	Memories are often segmented in *blocks* of contiguous words. These are pages and are frequently of 256 bytes. Page zero is the first page, starting at memory address 0.
Paging	Organization and retrieval of information from backing memories in page-size units.
Parametric test	A test performed on circuits to check for adherence to the electrical specification and margins (*see also* functional test).
Parentheses	Brackets or braces used to define precedence.
Partial decoding	A low-cost way of fitting small memories to large memory spaces. Wasteful of available memory space.
PCB	Printed-circuit board (*see* card).
Peripherals	Devices, logic and subsystems outside the main computer.
Physically coexisting	Refers to use of a separate piece of hardware for each task rather than one which is timeshared or multiplexed.
Pipeline	A style of processing in which each part of a task is allocated some hardware and a time slot. The hardware is joined in a line.
PLA	Programmable-logic array.
Polish notation	In memory of the Polish mathematician, Lukasiewicz. A notation in which the operator appears *after* the operands to which it refers. Compare with infix notation.
Polling	Interrogation of many subsystems to determine their status.
Pop	Type of instruction in which data are removed from a stack or LIFO and put back into the processor.
Port	An entry or exit point for data from a computer.
Postfix notation	Same as Polish notation (q.v.).
Post-indexed	Automatic changing of the address value contained in an index (address) register *after* it is used in an instruction.
Post-normalize	Normalize (q.v.) a quantity at the *end* of an instruction.
Pre-fetch	To access an instruction before the processor has finished executing the last one. Saves instruction time by overlapping fetching and execution.
Pre-indexed	Opposite of post-indexed (q.v.).
Priority	Order in which tasks are to be executed or requestors serviced.

Process(ing)/(or)	To carry out computing tasks/hardware or software that processes.
Program counter	Address register which holds the address from which the current instruction was obtained.
Programmable-logic array	IC which contains a NOT/AND/OR/NOT tree whose inputs and outputs can be defined at manufacture.
Programmable ROM	A ROM whose contents can be altered by the user either by electrical programming and erasure or by blowing (rupturing) fuses in the chip.
Programmable timer	An IC (or part of a microprocessor) which can be used to indicate time-lapse, time of day or to count events. Usually sends an interrupt to the processor when finished.
Programmed transfers	Method for transferring information into and out of a computer using instructions (one instruction per byte).
Quadratic convergence	Property of a process or algorithm whereby the error per iteration (q.v.) decreases on a square-law basis. In effect, the number of useful decimal places doubles at each iteration.
Radix	See base.
RAM	Random-access memory (more commonly read/write memory).
Random-access memory	Each access takes a fixed time irrespective of the location of the previous information accessed.
Read-only memory	Memory in which the pattern of 1s and 0s is fixed—either at manufacture or by the user, before the computer is used.
Read/write memory	Memory whose contents can be written under software control as well as read. Normally read and write times are similar.
Real time	A form of computing in which either: (1) the computer response time is sufficiently short it can interact with the user, or (2) the computer can react to events as they occur at their natural pace, i.e. in control systems.
Record	A (usually large) group of bytes joined together to form an entity, e.g. for writing to tape in one operation.

Recursive	Describes a process or procedure capable of calling itself as part of its execution. This causes reversion to the beginning of the process each time the call occurs. An escape must be built into all recursive processes.
Redundancy	Extra components or processes added to a system either intentionally or unintentionally and which *could* be omitted.
Refresh	Process whereby a dynamic (q.v.) memory has its contents rewritten after they may have decayed with time.
Register	A group of flip-flops treated as an entity and having a common clock or strobe line to make them operate concurrently.
Register file	A group of registers, possibly in one IC. Such a file can often be written to and read at the same time.
Relative address	Address used in an instruction which is based on the PC value.
Relocate	Move a program from one part of memory to another.
Return	An instruction which terminates a subroutine and causes control to revert to the calling program (where it left off).
ROM	Read-only memory.
Rotate	*See* shift.
Round-off error	Error in representation caused by the use of a finite number of bits in a computer.
RTL	Resistor–transistor logic.
Sampled system	Recording of continuous information by a series of (digital) samples. Example is analog–digital conversion.
Sample–hold amplifier	Analog device which can hold a sample of an analog signal for future use.
Saturation	In transistors, a condition whereby the collector current drawn reaches a maximum (because of circuit conditions).
Scaling	A floating-point operation which changes the format of one operand so that its exponent is the same as that of the other operand.
Schottky clamp	A low forward voltage diode used to reduce saturation effects in transistors.
Scratch-pad	A fast RAM used in a processor instead of individual registers.

Semantics	Pertaining to language, its use and meaning of terms.
Semi-random	A memory whose access time is *partially* determined by previous accesses, e.g. a disk file having many tracks.
Sequential	Taking place in a sequence. Magnetic tape is sequentially accessed, as the information is held in a long line (ribbon).
Serial	Similar to sequential, although usually refers to the handling of digits in an ALU (q.v.).
S–H AMP	Sample–hold amplifier.
Shift	To move bits sideways in a register to alter significances.
Significance	The weight of a bit, as defined by its position in a word.
Significance error	In floating point, a zero result arising from the subtraction of two quantities because of lack of precision in their representation.
Silicon-on-sapphire	An IC technology in which sapphire is used as a nonconducting substrate, to reduce stray circuit capacitances.
Simulation	Formation of a model of a process for running on a computer.
Slice	*See* bit slice.
Small-scale integration	An IC technology in which a small number of gates (maybe less than 20) are formed on a single chip.
SOS	Silicon-on-sapphire IC technology.
SSI	Small-scale-integration IC technology.
Stack	An area of memory or a group of registers used in the manner of a LIFO (q.v.).
Stack pointer	A register used to indicate the location of the last entry in a stack.
Static	A type of RAM which does not need periodic refreshing (q.v.) in order to hold its information for long periods.
Status	The condition of a subsystem or its readiness for operation.
String	A group of bits or bytes forming a message. Also a track on a printed-circuit card.
Strobe	*See* clock.
Subroutine	A separate program from the main program which can be entered at any time to carry out some frequently occurring task. Saves having to write the task many times in the main program.

Substrate	Supporting frame or material on which something is mounted.
Subtrahend	Quantity which is subtracted from a minuend in subtraction.
Supervisor	A program for controlling the execution and general management of programs in a computer. Such a program must normally be permanently resident in primary memory to prevent it losing control of computer activities.
Syntax	Pertaining to the grammar and punctuation of a language.
Tag register	Register holding the address from which some information has been obtained.
Teletype	Proprietary name for an electric typewriter which can be connected to a computer. Often also fitted with a paper-tape reader and punch.
Termination(or)	Component network for placement at the end of a transmission line to prevent reflections.
Three-state	A type of logic capable of being set to logic 0, logic 1 or rendered inactive, so that many such devices can be connected together on a single bus.
Tie-OR	Connection of a number of gate outputs together. Has the effect of creating an OR function without the use of additional gates.
Totem-pole	Use of two active devices in the output circuit of a gate so as to make both the logic 0 to 1 and 1 to 0 transitions fast.
Transaction	Any message sent between two subsystems.
Transducer	A device for converting information in one form to another, e.g. a strain gauge to convert strain to a voltage.
Transistor–transistor logic	A popular logic form in which both the logic decision and current amplification are provided by transistors.
Transmission line	An interconnecting link sufficiently long that it cannot be considered simply as a lumped electrical circuit.
Tree	A cascaded set of logic devices, software entities, etc.
Tri-state	*See* three-state. (Tri-state is a registered trade mark of National Semiconductors, Inc.)
TTL	Transistor–transistor logic.
TTY	Teletype–software-controlled electric typewriter.

ULA	Uncommitted-logic array.
Ultra-violet erasable ROM	A form of ROM using MOS transistors of such a form that a charge representing a logic state can be erased by exposure of the chip to UV light. Such chips have a quartz window to admit the UV light.
Uncommitted-logic array	An LSI chip, partitioned into cells, each of which may contain one of a menu of simple logic devices. The customer specifies to the IC manufacturer what should be in each cell and how the cells should be interconnected.
Underflow	A condition whereby the quantity to be represented is more negative than the ALU can handle.
UVROM	Ultra-violet erasable ROM.
Valve	(Thermionic) vacuum tube.
VDU	Visual-display unit.
Vector	A value or location in a computer which points to some address.
VLSI	Very large-scale integration.
Volatile	*See* nonvolatile.
Voting	Decision-making according to a majority decision. Unlike the human counterpart, computer voting usually entails each voter being given a weight, i.e. number of votes, according to past performance, etc.
Weight	Value of a binary bit or digit.
Wired-OR	Same as tie-OR (q.v.).
Word	A group of binary bits—often corresponds to the number of bits per location in the main memory.
Word processor	Computer used to manipulate words, language, plain text and editing. Used in office systems.
Workspace	An area of memory set aside to have the status of a register bank. Saves using flip-flop registers in the processor.

INDEX